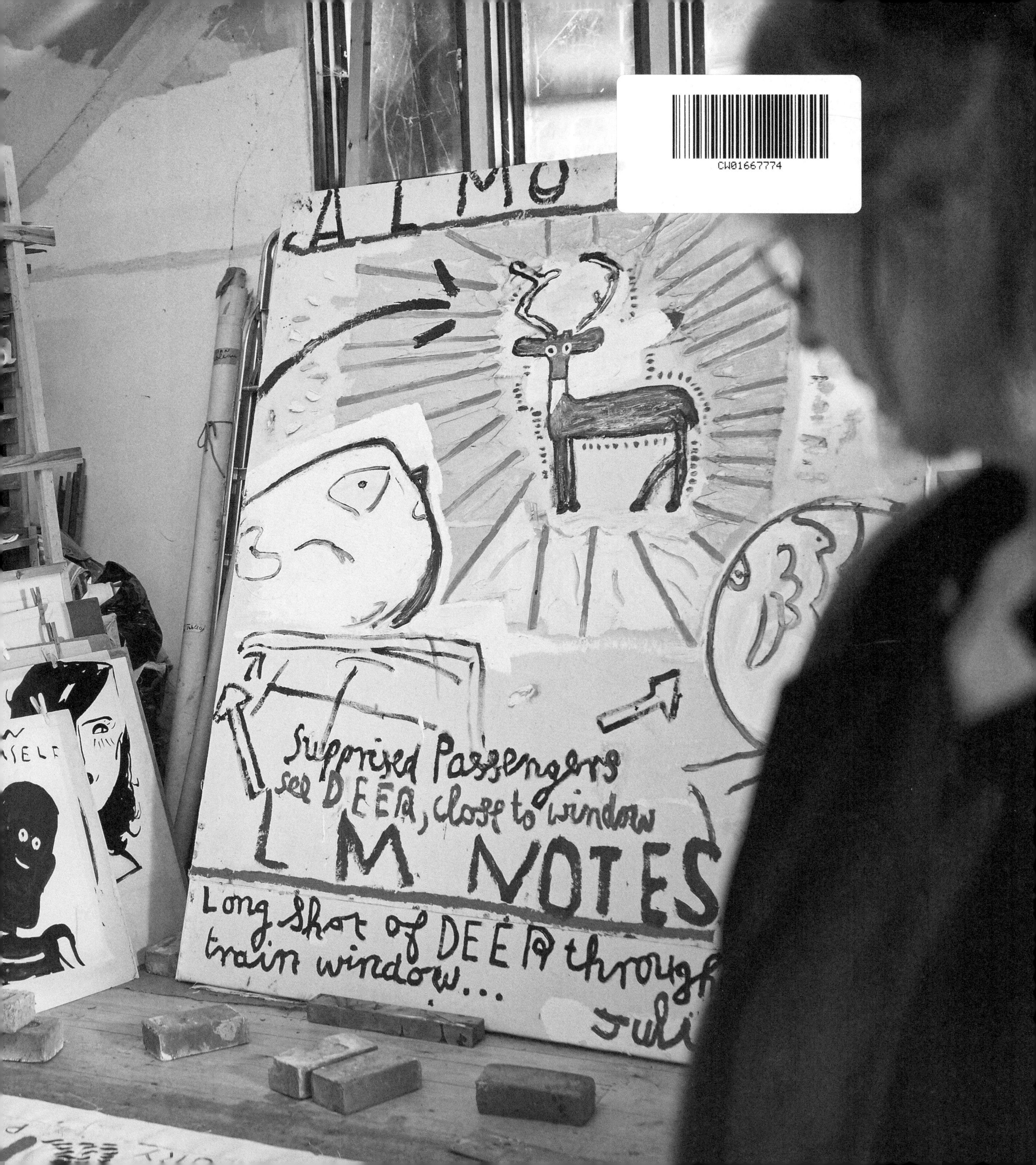

Supprised Passengers
see DEER, close to window
M NOTES
Long Shot of DEER
train window...

CW01667774

Rose Wylie

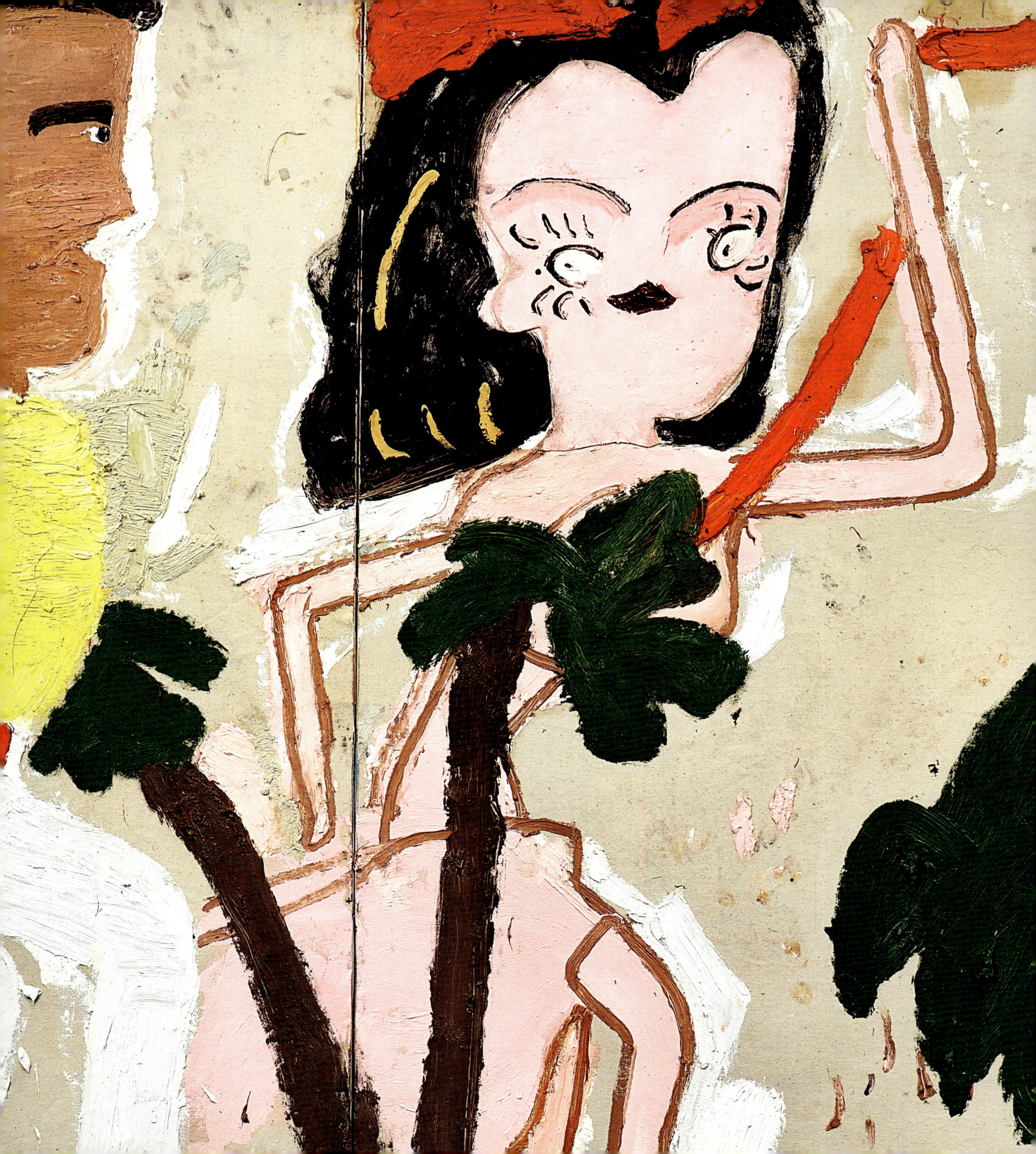

Rose Wylie

Clarrie Wallis

LUND
HUMPHRIES

Contents

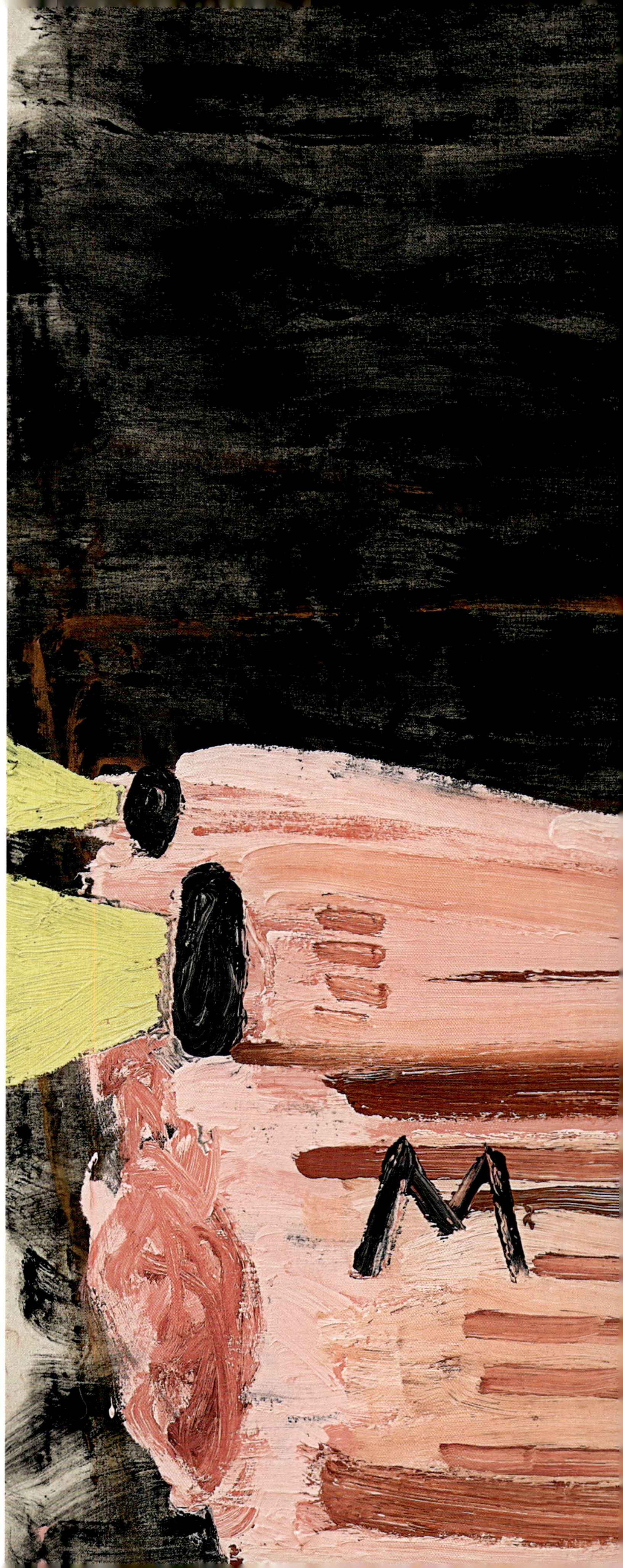

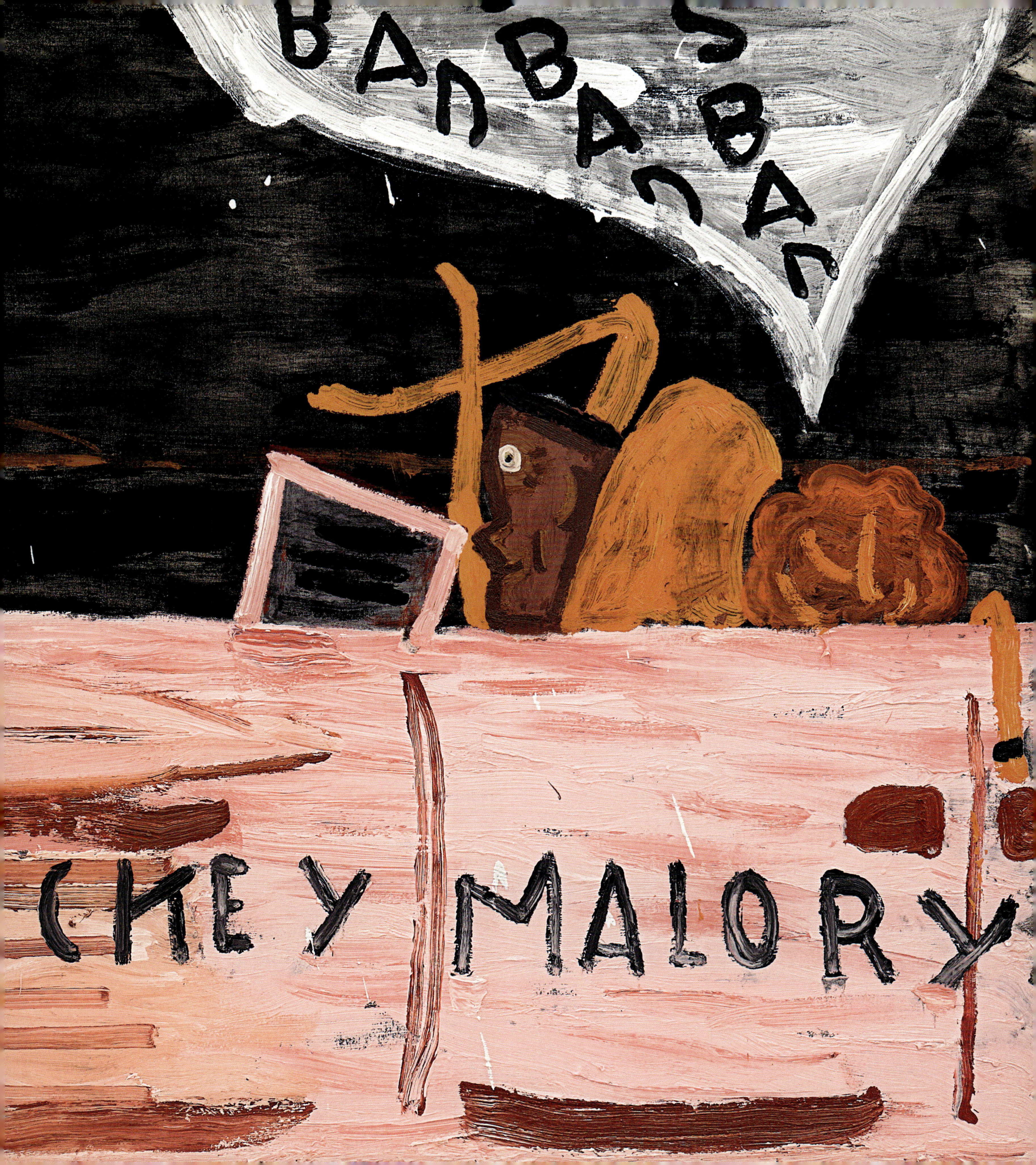
CHEY MALORY

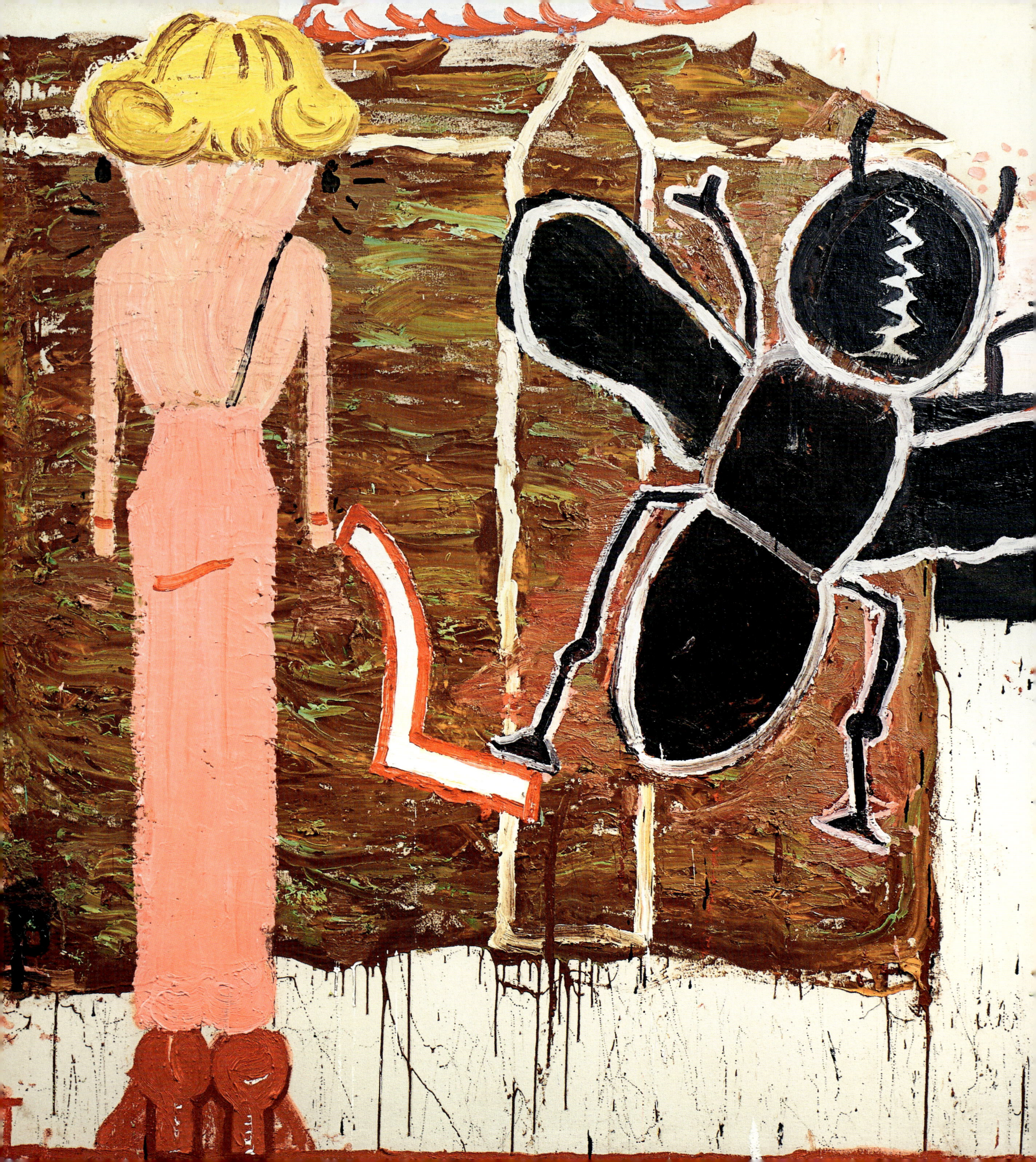

Paint like it looks

ONLY THE FAINT EARTH-GREEN outlines remain of the fifteenth-century wall painting, *The Legend of St Eustace*, which covers an entire alcove off the north aisle of Canterbury Cathedral. Dating from around 1480, it tells the story of a Roman hunter named Eustace who had a vision of Christ crucified between the horns of a white stag (visible at the bottom right-hand corner). He is converted on the spot and eventually goes on to become a Christian martyr. Set in woodland with a variety of wild creatures, the story unfolds in a series of scenes which includes his wife being taken off by pirates in a ship and a son carried off by a wolf. It ends with his family reunited and being roasted to death inside a brazen bull for refusing to worship pagan gods. Their faith rewarded, at the top of the painting, all four souls ascend to heaven and the spirit of God in the form of a dove waits to receive them. This wall painting was the inspiration for Russell Hoban's extraordinary novel *Riddley Walker*, written in strange, phonetic Estuary English.[1] Set in Kent in a remote future long after a nuclear holocaust, humanity has regressed to an iron-age, semi-literate state, where nomadic groups attempt to survive. Cultural artefacts (including a fragment of the account of *The Legend of St Eustace*), along with important texts, are passed down from generation to generation but there is no clear understanding of the significance of the stories from which these symbols originated. Characters known as 'connection men' – acting as a sort of shaman or tribal priest – have the job of trying to piece things together in order to make sense of the chaotic and often brutal world around them, and to reinforce the codes that bind their small communities together. This involves both seeing connections between things and 'unriddling' the puzzles of life. The story is about the acquisition of knowledge in a world full of ritual and superstition. Full of dreams, omens and coincidences, it explores how all of these things are understood through feeling or intuition and how individuals react and reason about them.

Detail of **Black Strap (Red Fly)** 2014, fig.49, p.58

1
Wearing a Check Skirt 2002
Oil on canvas, 183 × 336 cm (72⅛ × 132⅜ in)
Private collection

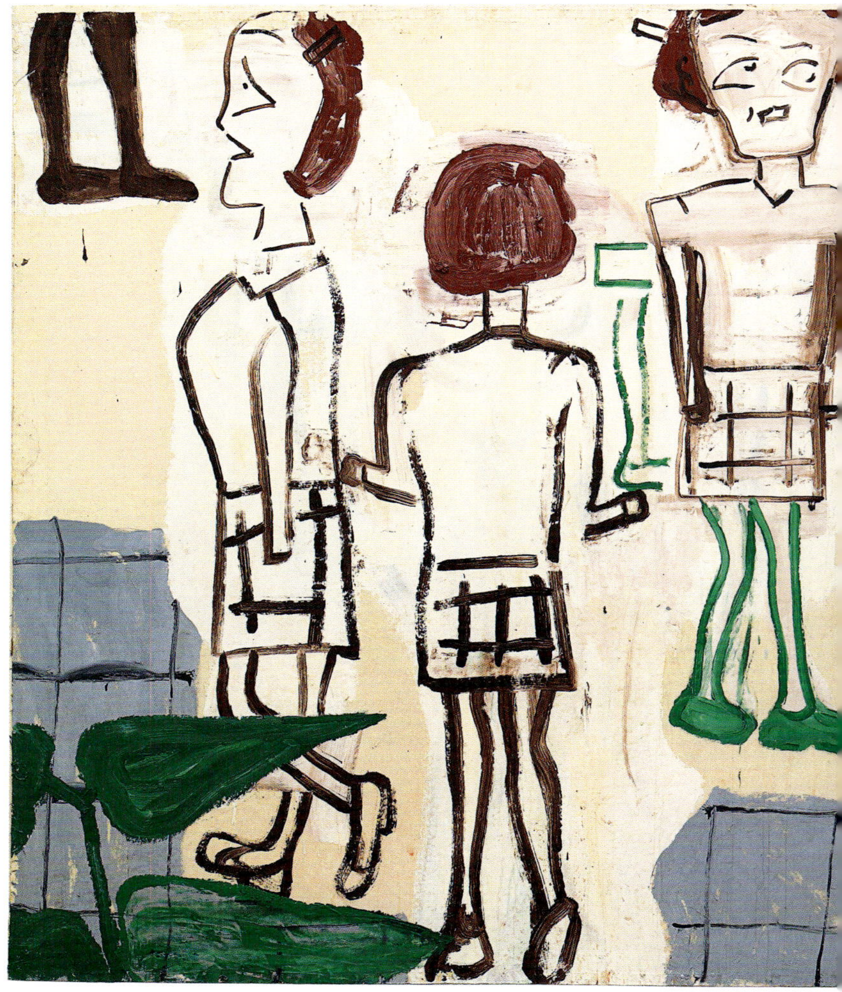

Like one of Hoban's 'connection men', Rose Wylie, one of the most innovative British painters working today, weaves together imagery from different sources. Coincidently, like Hoban, Wylie has lived in Kent for over sixty years and her work reflects her situation as she interjects elements of the personal into her paintings. Wylie makes large-scale paintings on unstretched and unprimed canvas inspired by a wide range of visual culture. Her subject matter ranges from contemporary Egyptian Hajj wall paintings and Persian miniatures to films, news stories, celebrity gossip, quotidian objects and observations on daily life. Wylie purposely chooses subjects which are accessible to all. Alongside images of footballer John Terry (fig.55), the Queen of Sheba (fig.57) and Marilyn Monroe (figs 43 and 109), Wylie paints everyday events such as a girl munching a chocolate biscuit (fig.69), her cat (figs 11 and 20) or attending an art world private view (fig.62). Other works pay homage to a personal pantheon of film directors the artist admires. Wylie's painting is instinctive. The imagery comes to her through the filter of her memory and, while the paintings can be understood as a diary of her life, they also succeed in presenting us with subjects that are at once familiar and universal.

The paintings have a raw immediacy that the critic Mel Gooding has described as 'at once visual, tactile, mental and emotional'.[2] Her large pictures are painted in a kind of visual shorthand that is direct and legible. The ability to elicit a range of responses is made possible precisely because of her reduction of form to an essential vibrancy that incorporates, via the very physicality of her medium, not just what the artist sees but an accompanying multitude of thoughts, feelings and memories. Wylie's work is a sophisticated transmutation, or sifting of perceptual experience, carrying as it does a wealth of affective and allusive resonances, into the painted form.

Wylie's non-linear way of thinking or approaching subject matter has parallels with the thought of the French philosopher Gilles Deleuze. Deleuze contrasted the tree – as a traditional metaphor for thought – with the rhizome. The tree has a single root and promotes thinking in terms of hierarchies, linear growth and dualist oppositions. Rhizomes, in comparison, are complex root networks, and figure thought as an open structure in which

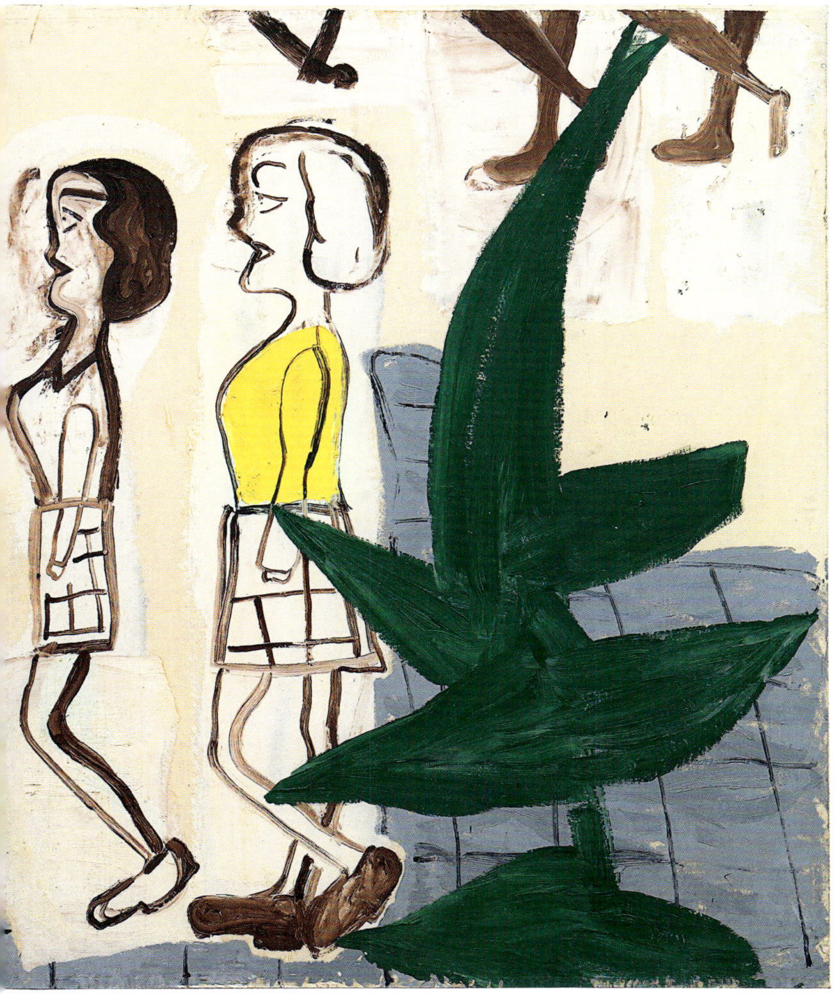

any point can connect to any other point. This rhizomatic approach encompasses both process and finished work, method and subject matter. Wylie's approach is holistic; her paintings have a radical openness, a democratic equality of the different elements of imagery that coexist and suggest a multiplicity of interconnections.

Rosemount (Coloured) 1999 (fig.2), for example, is a highly personal history painting of her childhood home (fig.3) during the Second World War. In the centre of two large canvases butted together, stands the silhouette of her house, blacked out against Luftwaffe bombing raids. Captioned arrows point out to an allotment and chicken run, and other details including Elm Park (the name of the street) and the names of her mother's favourite flowers. On the right-hand side, the artist's disembodied eye gazes up at an ominous-looking doodlebug in the sky above, as missiles, with jagged explosions coming from their tails, fall – one directly on to the property next door. In contrast, Wylie's painting *Celebrity* 2006 (fig.4) depicts an elfin female figure in a white dress which is surrounded by a penumbra of white that follows closely the outline of the body: the white is suggestive of innocence and purity. The woman is thin and has very long legs – perhaps a comment on the ideal body type represented by the media. There is a minimal suggestion of a theatrical setting, with yellow drapes or curtains at the top of the picture; but otherwise the figure floats, divorced from any real context, a fairy-like vision in pink and white. There is also a small fan, which may be an allusion to the famous scene in *The Seven Year Itch* 1955 where Marilyn Monroe's dress, also white, is lifted by a blast of air through a grating, but this is a diminished and less iconic version. At the bottom of the picture is the text 'Celebrity' and beneath it, very faintly, are the words 'Chocolate Cake': celebrity is as alluring and ephemeral as a piece of cake.

Although Rose Wylie has become familiar to the general public in the last few decades, she has spent much of her life in relative obscurity. She was born in Hythe, Kent in 1934. Her father Alexander Forrest Wylie OBE (1888–1964) was a civil engineer and Director of Ordnance for India. Wylie's portrait of him, *AFW* 1997, started out as a self-portrait. As the artist began to paint her eyes

2
Rosemount (Coloured) 1999
Oil on canvas, 186 × 183 cm (73¼ × 72⅛ in)
REGINA Gallery, Moscow

3
Rosemount, 1942
Collection of the artist

she was overtaken by a powerful memory of her father looking at her, and decided to paint his piercing blue eyes instead of her own. A civilian in an army position, he worked primarily in India with army personnel on the supply and maintenance of weaponry, munitions and other military equipment for the British war effort. It was while he was working there that he met and married her mother, Barbara Hewat Gillmon (1894–1964) who, Wylie recalls, was very musical. Her paternal grandfather was James Hamilton Wylie (1844–1914), Oxford historian and author of *The Reign of Henry the Fifth*, who together with Matthew Arnold campaigned for free education for all children, and it is therefore no coincidence that the portrait of Henry V occurs in a number of paintings, including *Yellow Henry* 1996 (fig.5), where he is depicted in profile with a 'pudding bowl' haircut, shaved clear above both ears and at the back of his skull.

Wylie was the youngest of seven children. Often left to her own devices, she had a happy childhood and describes her upbringing as 'traditional' with 'the usual slightly Victorian moral standards'.[3] There was no expectation of her making a career, except, she says, 'as a get-out clause'.[4] Wylie spent the first few years of her childhood in India. From an early age she wanted to draw, and she remembers having a green Winsor & Newton paint box which she used to colour in the illustrations in books on Greek mythology that she had been given, but had 'little sense of any wider artistic context'.[5]

At the beginning of the Second World War the family moved back to England. They initially lived in a house in Talbot Road in Bayswater, West London which belonged to a great aunt, before moving to a home in Farnborough Park, near Bromley (depicted in the painting *Rosemount (Coloured)* 1999 described above). She attended Bramble Wood Primary School which had only seven pupils, run by a Mrs Prynne, the mother of the poet Jeremy Halvard Prynne (b.1936), a direct contemporary of hers. Wylie has spoken of how she used to spell phonetically at school – words written how they sound, not according to the rules of spelling – and believes this helps account for how she likes to draw.[6] As she explains, 'You spell like it sounds and paint like it looks. It's the same thing. It is phonetic.'[7]

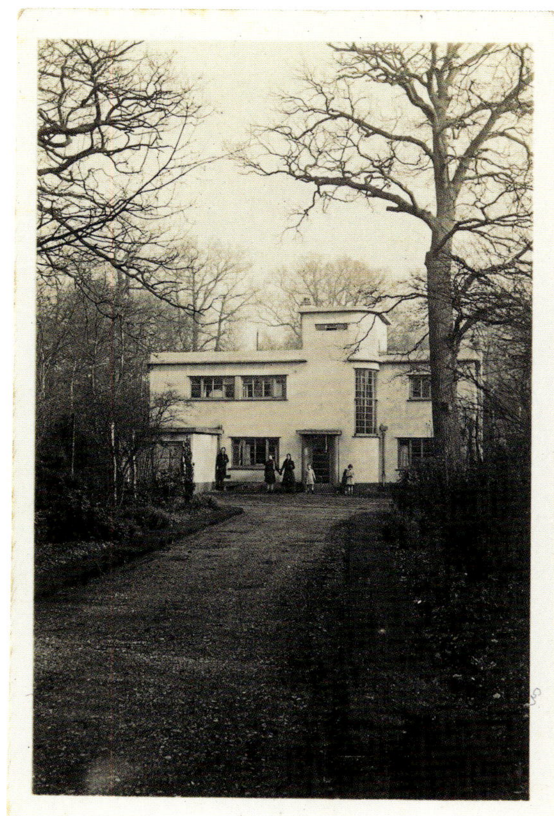

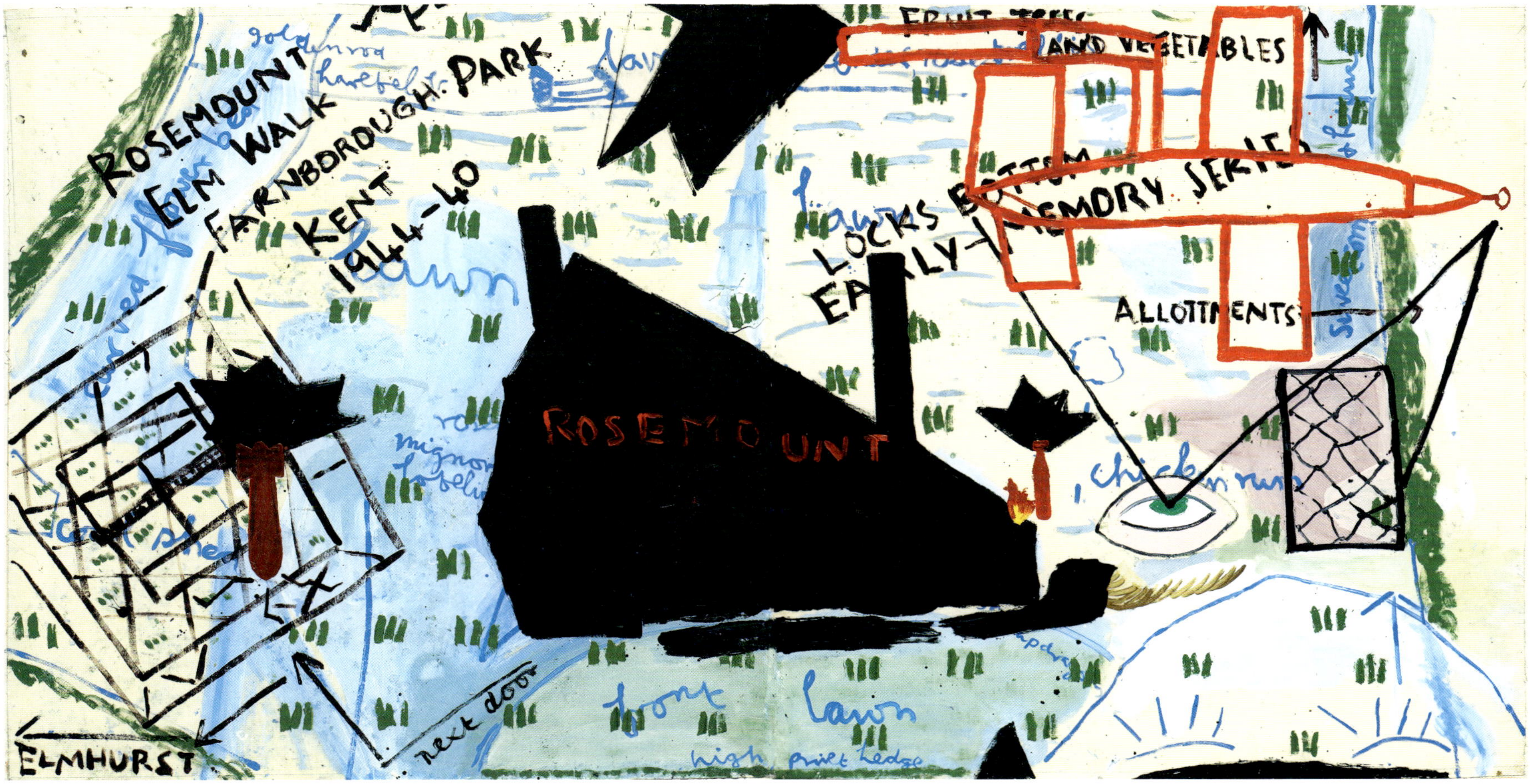

At the end of the war the family moved back to their holiday home in Hythe, a small coastal market town in Kent on the edge of Romney Marsh. Like its neighbour Folkestone, Hythe was a popular, smart seaside resort. Located next to the golf course and the Victorian promenade, Wylie's house looked directly across the English Channel to France some 21 miles away. During the Second World War, Britain's southern coastline had been vulnerable to enemy invasion. As soon as war was declared, the beaches were planted with mines, barbed wire and other obstacles, and access to front-line coastal towns such as Dover and Folkestone was heavily restricted. Unsurprisingly, due to its front-line coastal position, Hythe suffered at the hands of the Luftwaffe. By the end of 1944 it was a battle-scarred husk of its former self. Wylie recalls that

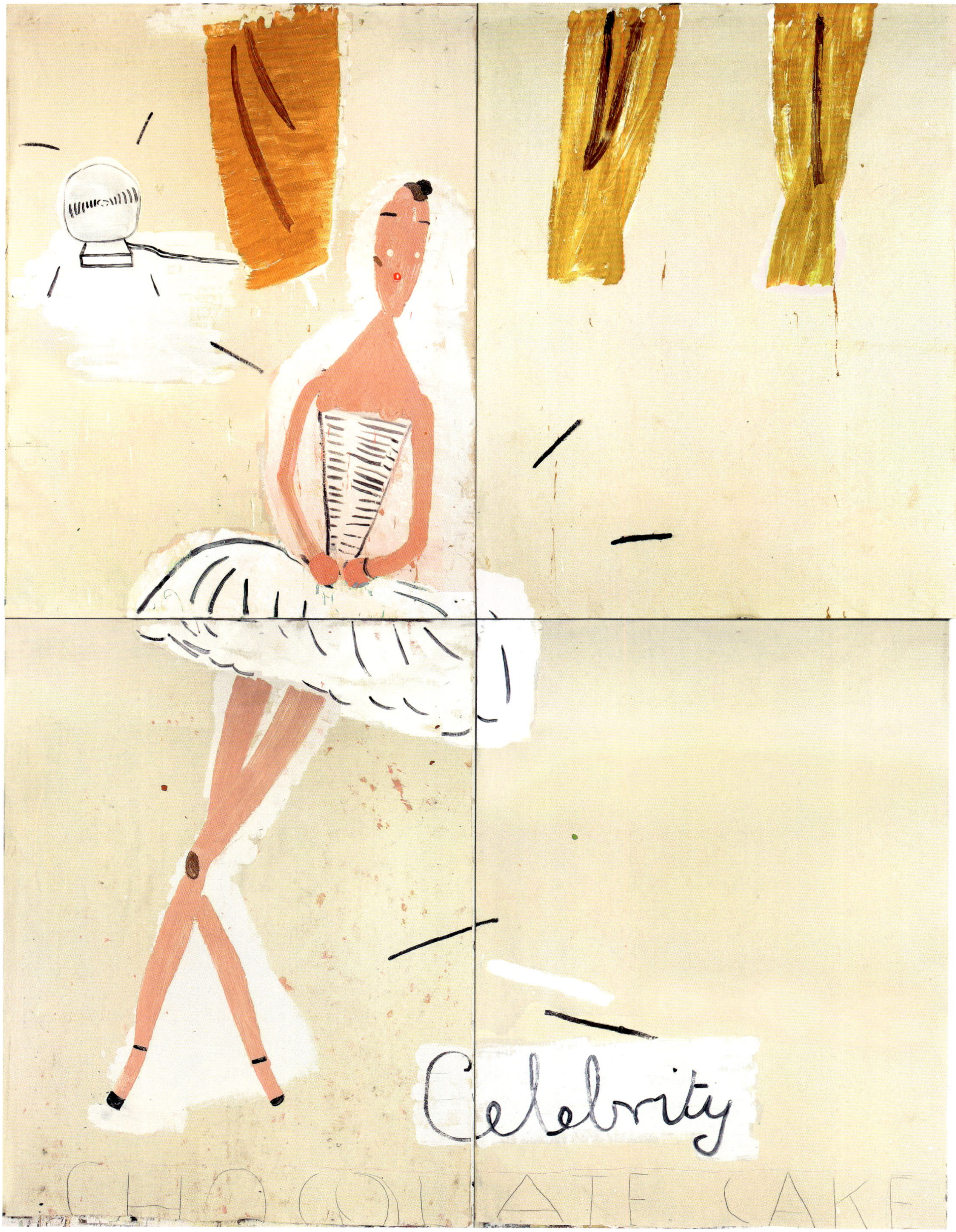
Celebrity
CHOCOLATE CAKE

4
Celebrity 2006
Oil on canvas, 305 × 366 cm (120⅛ × 144⅛ in)
The Bjørnholt Collection, Norway

5
Yellow Henry 1996
Oil on canvas, 183 × 168 cm (72⅛ × 66¼ in)
Private collection

despite being allowed back on the beach there were still many dangers present in going there. Unexploded ordnance, debris such as rusty barbed wire and lots of firebombs were common sights.[8]

While the memories of the beach are not present in any of Wylie's paintings, it is clear that the war had a strong impact on her which has repeatedly found its way into her work. For example, she clearly remembers how in June 1944 the Germans launched thousands of V-1 flying bombs at London. 'The doodlebugs used to go over our garden . . . You could see them and hear them, very low and they had a tiny propeller at the front, but were driven by some sort of rocket device that meant they went a certain distance, then divided and exploded. If you saw them and they were still going, you knew that you were going to be alright.'[9] As she describes it, they were 'just part of the war: Air raids, shrapnel, barrage balloons, rationing, all of that'.[10] Recurring images of doodlebugs crop up in paintings such as *Artist's Early Memory Series II, Doodle-Bug* 1998 and *Artist's Early Memory Series Flying Bomb* 1998 where a simple but sinister black flying bomb is depicted gliding past white, puffy clouds against a cobalt-blue background. The doodlebugs are always painted moving from left to right, heading in the direction of London.[11] Wylie recalls how as a child during the war she was given a chart for aircraft recognition to help her spot enemy planes.[12] She has also described how she was fascinated by the aeroplanes' different shapes, and they have consistently appeared in works over the years, including *Fairy and Aeroplane* 1989 where a fairy, like a guardian angel, looms over a plane, the solid pure black mass of *Stealth Bomber* 2016 (fig.6) and *Iraq* 2014 (fig.7). She has also painted a portrait of *Herman Goering* 1989, ace pilot and one of the most senior politicians in Nazi Germany and close confidant of Hitler. Goering is depicted in profile with raw, gestural brushstrokes, that we tend to associate more with abstract than figurative painting, bringing a sense of immediacy and urgency to the work. His large head, wearing a fighter pilot hat and goggles, dominates the otherwise empty canvas and somehow gives the impression that he is flying into battle. More recently for her show at the Serpentine Sackler Gallery in November 2017, Wylie revisited childhood memories of Kensington Gardens during the Blitz. Recollections of visits to the park as a

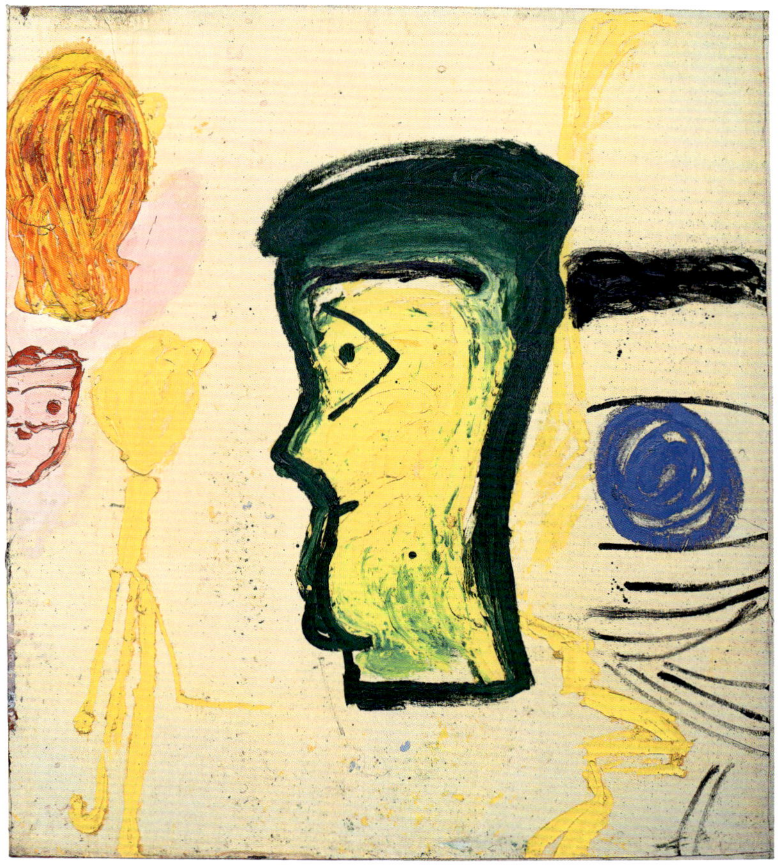

6
Stealth Bomber 2016
Oil on canvas, 238 × 336 cm (93¾ × 132⅜ in)
Collection of the Institute of
Reconciliation, La Paila, Colombia

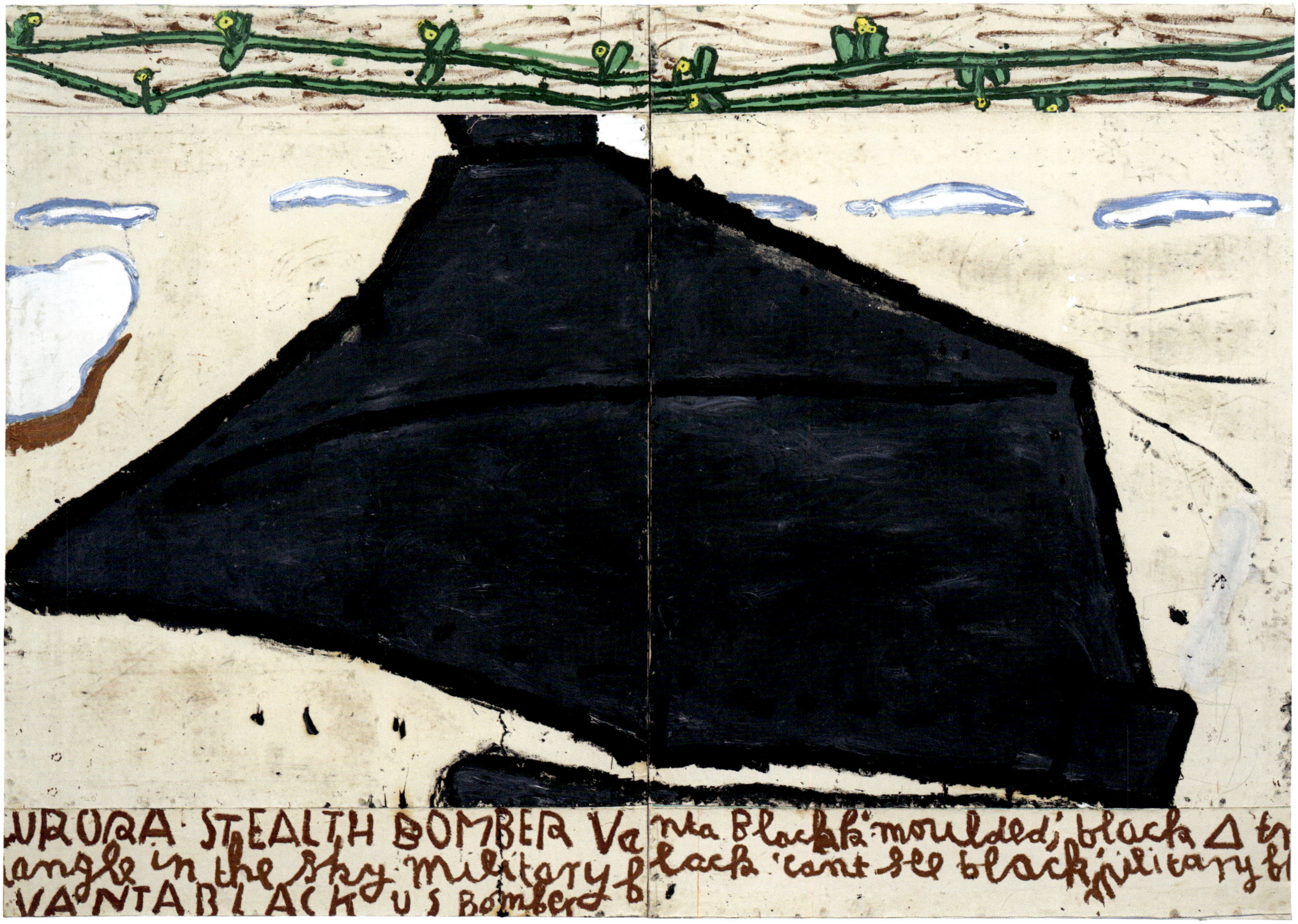

7
Iraq 2014
Oil on canvas, 186 × 170 cm (73¼ × 67 in)
Private collection

8
Airbus 2014
Watercolour, ink and collage on paper
62 × 89 cm (24½ × 35⅛ in)
Cassina Projects, New York

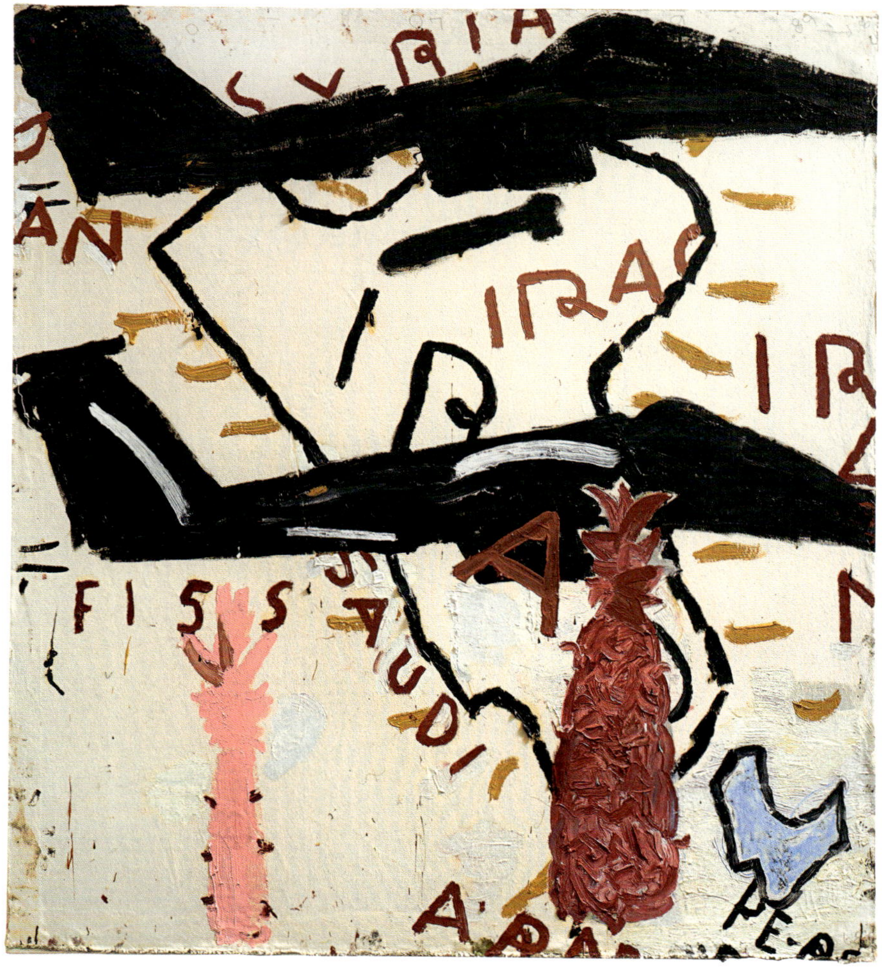

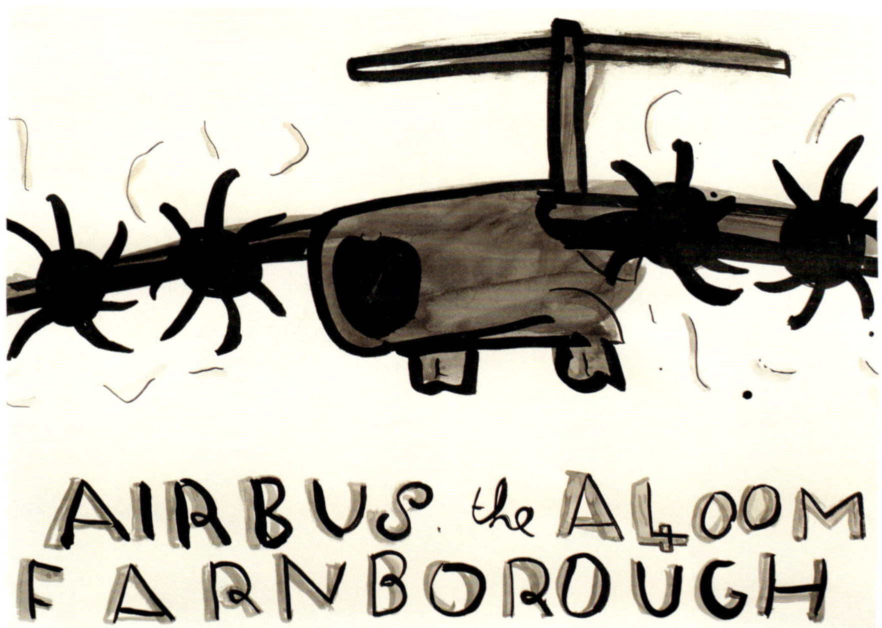

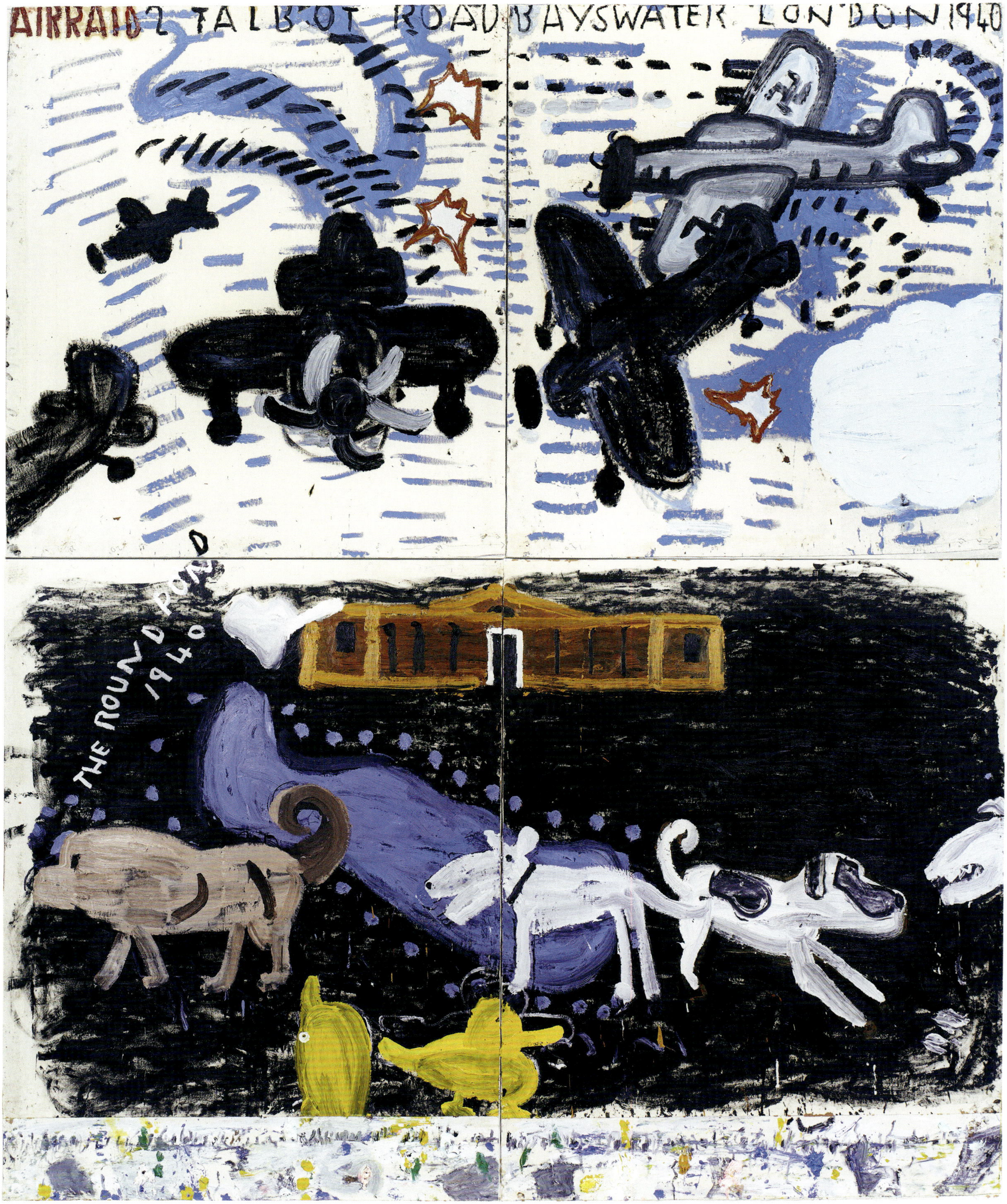
AIRRAID 2 TALBOT ROAD BAYSWATER LONDON 1940
THE ROUND POND 1940

9
Park Dogs & Air Raid 2017
Oil on canvas
393 × 331 cm (154¾ × 130⅜)
Private collection

10
Giovanni di Paolo, *St John the Baptist Retiring to the Desert* 1454
Egg tempera on wood
30.5 × 49 cm (12⅛ × 19⅜ in)
National Gallery, London

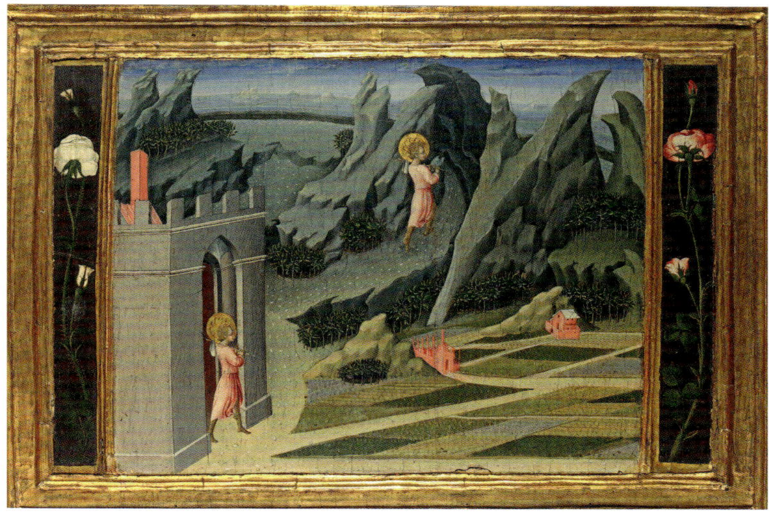

child are merged with the sounds and smells of wartime London. The title of the painting *Ack Ack* 2003 refers to Wylie's memories of the word for the anti-aircraft ('Ack Ack') guns in operation, London's last line of defence against German bombers. In *Park Dogs & Air Raid* 2017, dogs and bright-yellow ducks run about by the Round Pond, while Spitfires and Messerschmitt planes fight overhead.

Wylie's first encounter with art was on a trip to Europe in 1948, where her mother took her to the Prado and the Louvre. At 17 she visited the National Gallery in London to look at the painting of Giovanni di Paolo (1398–1482), one of the greatest Sienese painters of the Renaissance. Di Paolo's intense, fertile imagination, and his highly individual way of using line and colour, have proved to be a long-term inspiration. Wylie has always appreciated his carefully articulated compositions, as seen in works such as *St John the Baptist Retiring to the Desert* 1454 (fig.10) where the young saint is depicted twice: leaving the home of his parents and walking into the wilderness. The narrative is framed by depictions of roses seen from below.

Parallels can be drawn between di Paolo's individual depiction of narrative subjects and Wylie's approach to composition, subject matter and use of detail. She has always been attracted to di Paolo's shifts in scale, and these have found their way into her paintings: for example, *Ascension Picture* 1992 where a tiny figure on a bare background is floating up to heaven surrounded by a small dense blue cloud. In an imaginary interview between them she states: 'Your people are always much too big, and I like that. I find I can draw a person with the right sized head and its junk – make it bigger and everything gets better. I suppose it's to do with my attraction to that out-of-scale, or jumps of scale aspect of your work, which is why I like to separate things out and re-present them . . . the reality of Rembrandt does not get me like that *other* reality in your work.'[13] Wylie also sees a connection between her approach to composition and the artist Fernand Léger's (1881–1955) aesthetic of the isolated object. During the late 1920s and 1930s Léger painted single objects isolated in space and sometimes amplified to gigantic size.[14]

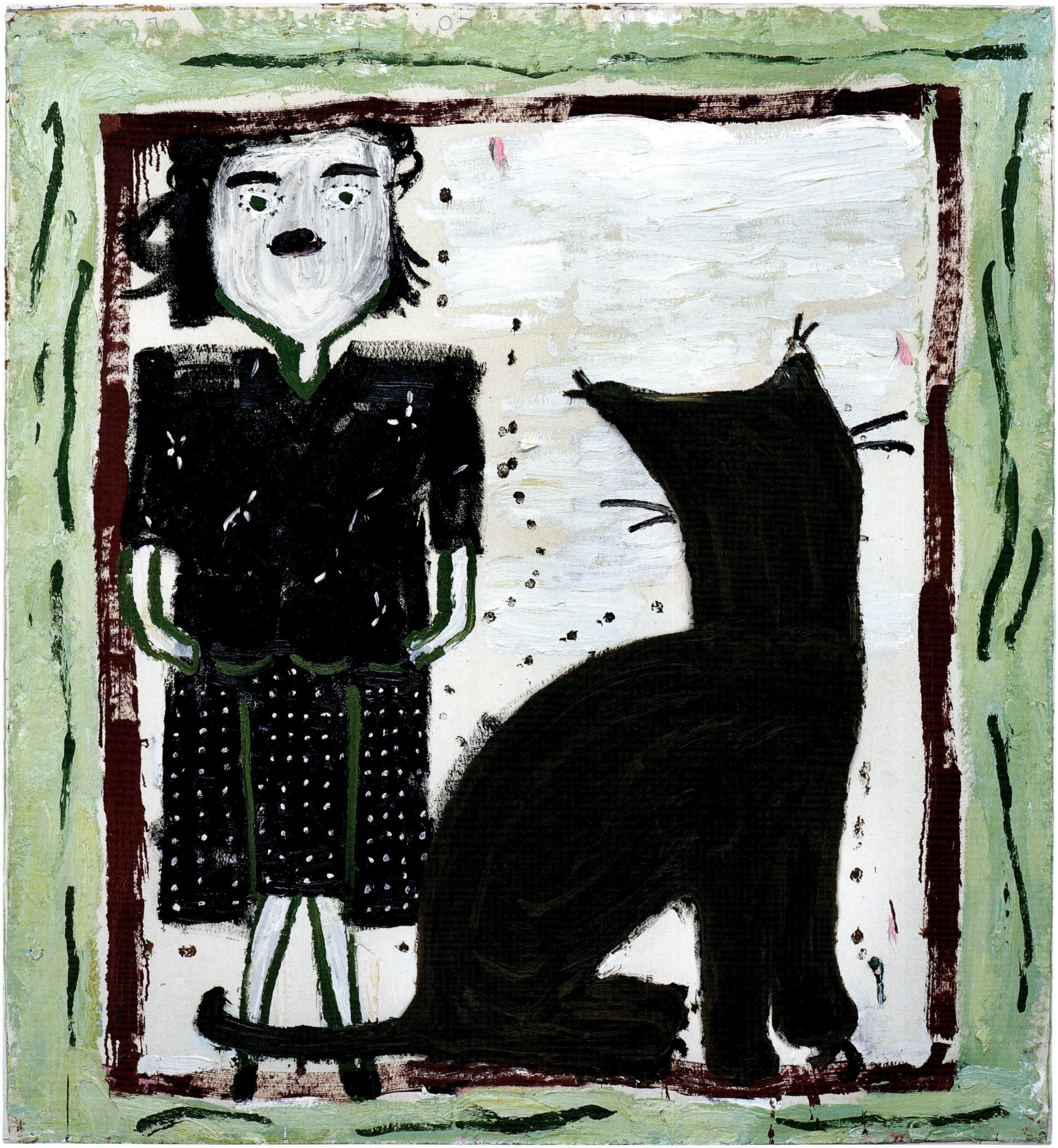

11
Party Clothes (RW & Cat) 2016
Oil on canvas, 183 × 169 cm (72⅛ × 66⅝ in)
Private collection

12
RW & Bird 1996
Oil on canvas, 183 × 168 cm (72⅛ × 66¼ in)
Private collection

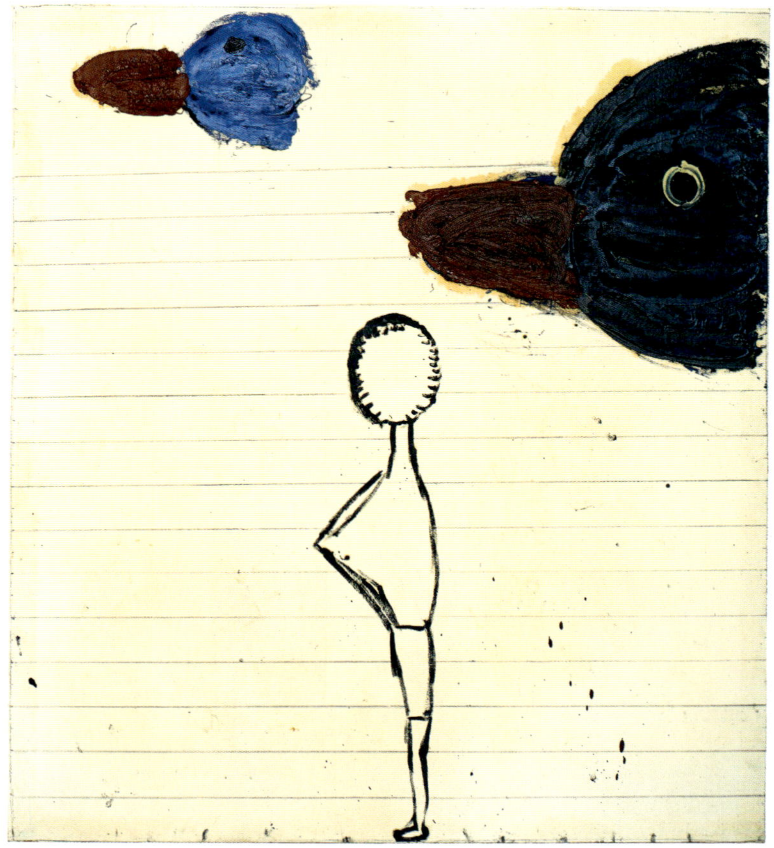

Looking and seeing are of profound, perhaps central, importance to Wylie's work, informing the process she brings to bear in making it. For Wylie, looking is always an extraordinary act. It is not simply a matter of observation in which the viewer passively receives perceptions, but a process that not only produces the world, but alters and disrupts it. The raw perceptual input from our surroundings is transformed by the intentional act of looking, and Wylie's work reminds us of this, showing us how the seen is always in dialogue with the unseen – feelings, thoughts, intuitions and memories – and how both enable us to reach an understanding of the world around us. As advocated by Henri Matisse (1869–1954), it is an approach which is synthetic rather than analytic.

In the early 1950s, Wylie applied to study art at the Folkestone and Dover School of Art. She remembers that her mother always regretted not having pursued music more seriously so as to have had her own career as a concert pianist. While she hoped her daughter would become a barrister, she was sympathetic to the visual arts and keen for her daughter to have an 'escape route' from the traditional route of marriage, and so supported her application. Wylie's portfolio included watercolour paintings of the interiors of St Leonard's Church, which is set high above Hythe's old town. Virtually unchanged since the fourteenth century, it is a large church, reflecting the importance of its position on the pilgrimage route to Canterbury Cathedral. The portfolio also consisted of still lifes of shells found on the local beach, bags of sugar, a lamp and a lamp stand and some life drawing.

She was accepted on to the Fine Art course and studied for a National Diploma in Design (NDD) from 1952 to 1956. The structure of the NDD perpetuated the dominant mode of British education that had been in the academies of art, founded on the ideals of the Italian Renaissance. The development of a student's skill and technique persisted as the dominant process of art education. Candidates for the NDD could choose one or two subjects from two lists which included over fifty options.[15] Wylie completed two years of intermediate study followed by a period of specialisation that lasted two more years where she focused on painting with textiles as a subsidiary subject. Sixty years later, *Irreverant Anatomy*

13
Henri Matisse, *Tea* 1919
Oil on canvas, 140.3 × 211.3 cm (55¼ × 83¼ in)
Los Angeles County Museum of Art, Los Angeles

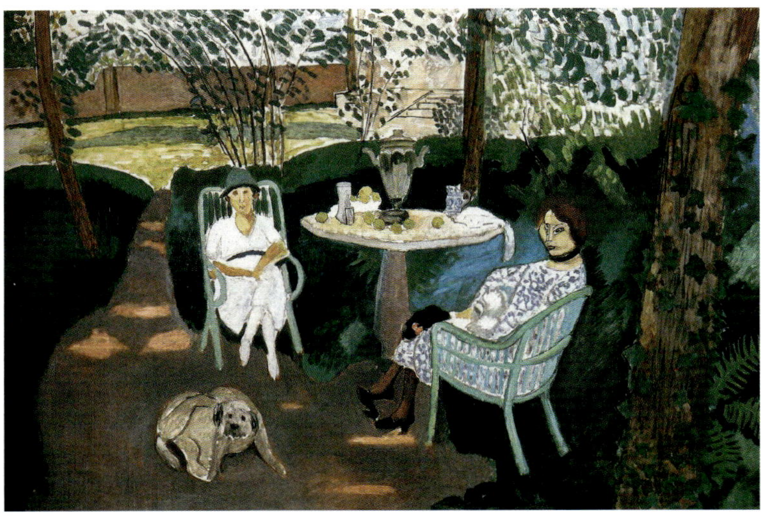

14
Irreverant Anatomy Drawing 2017
Oil on canvas, 182 × 165 cm (71¾ × 65 in)
Collection of Edwin Oostmeijer

Drawing 2017 (fig.14), a picture of a brown pantomime-like horse, where Wylie attempts to label parts of the horse's skeleton from memory, humorously recalls the anatomy and memory exams which were part of an art student's training in the 1950s.

During her time at art school Wylie and her fellow students made regular trips to the Tate Gallery and were advised by tutors to look at work by artists who were 'mostly English; American came later'.[16] Among these recommended English artists were John Piper (1903–1992), Henry Moore (1898–1986), Paul Nash (1889–1946), Graham Sutherland (1903–1980) and Samuel Palmer (1805–1881).[17] She also went to the Victoria and Albert Museum to look at their textiles collection which includes objects that span a period of more than 5000 years, from Predynastic Egypt to the present day.[18] Wylie remembers how she enjoyed looking at textiles, tapestries and carpets – woven silks from the Near East, European and Chinese tapestries, English medieval embroidery, Safavid carpets, and Indian and Arts and Crafts fabrics.

This interest in the decorative can also be linked to the rich and decorative aspects of paintings by Matisse. At a time when much of British painting was dominated by the 'Kitchen Sink' group – characterised by the work of John Bratby (1928–1992), Derrick Greaves (b.1927) and Edward Middleditch (1923–1987) – Matisse was considered by many to be a source of inspiration, and cuttings of his work were regularly displayed on the life-room walls at Folkestone.[19] Wylie appreciated his 'revolutionary spirit'.[20] In the early 1930s, Matisse created his murals of *The Dance* for the Barnes Foundation in Philadelphia and provided a model for exactly the kind of liberated painting that Jackson Pollock (1912–1956) and others would become famous for. Moreover, debate around the idea of the 'decorative' in relation to painting raged at this time, led by Clement Greenberg, the influential American critic and champion of abstract expressionism, who used the word 'decorative' as a negative term. Preoccupied with the distinction between high and low art, Greenberg was not a fan of mass culture or pop art which he characterised as kitsch, a watering down of modernist innovations, a pilfering of the high by the low. Thus, on one level Wylie's attraction to the decorative and everyday subject matter

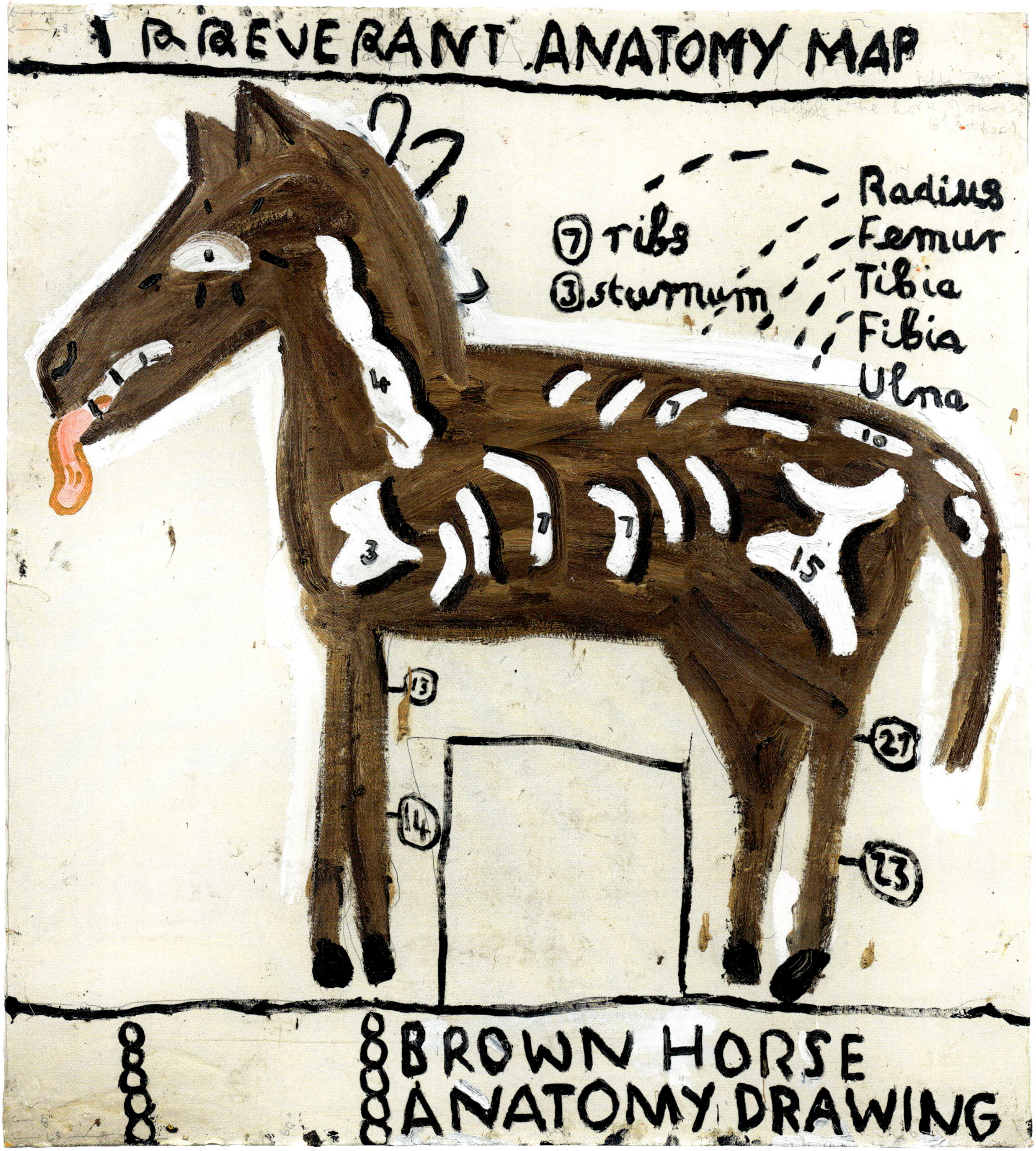

I RREVERANT ANATOMY MAP
7 ribs
3 sturnum
Radius
Femur
Tibia
Fibia
Ulna
4
7
10
3
15
13
14
27
23
BROWN HORSE
ANATOMY DRAWING

can indirectly also be understood as a contrary response to the formalism preached by Greenberg that was so prevalent at the time. Reflecting in 2014 on the influence of Matisse on her practice, Wylie explained:

> I paint figuratively as I think it's more interesting both to do and to look at. I like the specifics of the real world (and the visually relational) which does not mean I go for copying it; I like being specific in a painting. Henri Matisse once said that when you're drawing you should 'bring in everything at your disposal.' He advised 'synthesis' not 'analysis' . . . It's hard to make an image which is wonderful while hanging on to some sort of realism – Henry [sic] Rousseau does it and it's why Matisse's 1919 painting *Tea* [fig.13] is so good; there is no distortion, or even abstraction in it, but its transformative connection to what we know prevents it from becoming in the least bit dull or meaningless. To distort or not, or how much, or in what way are the central questions in figurative painting.[21]

As a young woman, Wylie regularly modelled for the artist John Stanton Ward CBE (1917–2007) who, along with the art historian Kenneth Clark, was a Governor at the Folkestone and Dover School of Art. Ward was an English portrait artist, landscape painter and illustrator for *Vogue* whose subjects included British royalty and celebrities: his friend Anthony Devas (1911–1958), a fellow portrait painter, met and painted Wylie while staying with him in 1955. The painting for which Wylie sat was one of a series of portraits commissioned by Rowntree's for use in an advertising campaign for its Aero chocolate bar. J.W. Thompson ran the campaign, inviting well-respected artists to paint studies of young women's heads in oil. These portraits were used in adverts with the slogan, 'For her, AERO – the milk chocolate that's different!' The campaign ran from 1951 until 1957, consolidating the brand as sweet rationing ended in February 1953 and competing with Cadbury's Dairy Milk. The pictured women – known as the Aero Girls – were not credited but given fictitious names: Devas's portrait of Wylie was labelled 'Alice' (figs 15a and b), and by the time Wylie had started studying at Goldsmiths College in 1956, it had been published in the *Daily Express*, *News of the World* and *People Illustrated*. 'Alice' is portrayed head and shoulders and, in common with the other Aero Girls, she is represented both as beautiful and as a 'girl next door', with none of the trappings of high-society portraiture. Wylie's eyes look directly out, her bold gaze meeting that of the viewer; combined with the slight pout of the full lips there is a hint of sexual frisson, a come-hither look to the implied male viewer. The end of sweet rationing was felt as a victory over austerity, and chocolate was promoted as being a luxury, but there was a paradox in that it was once again freely available. The Aero adverts gender and sexualise the suggestion of extravagance; chocolate is 'for her' and there is an implication of romantic reciprocation for the gift. These multiple connotations of chocolate, and its importance as a symbol of the

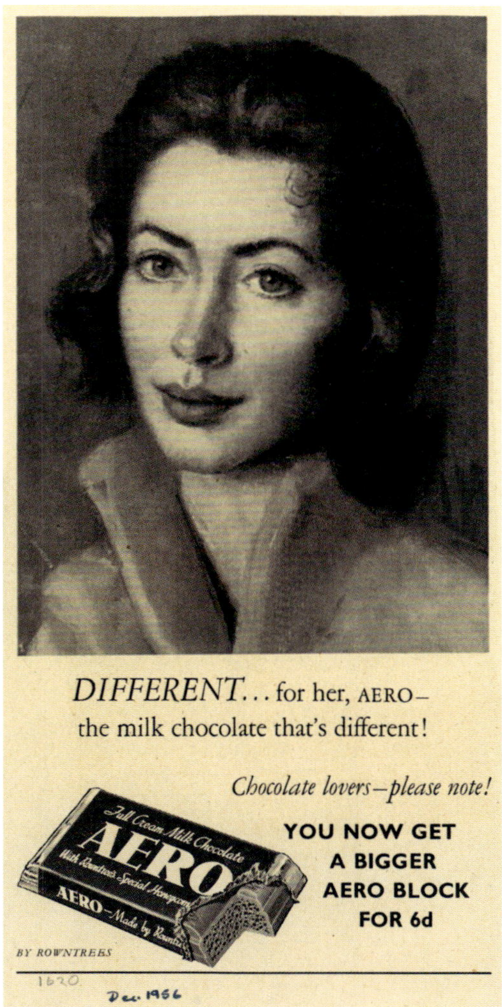

15a
Aero advert, 1956
Borthwick Institute for Archives,
University of York

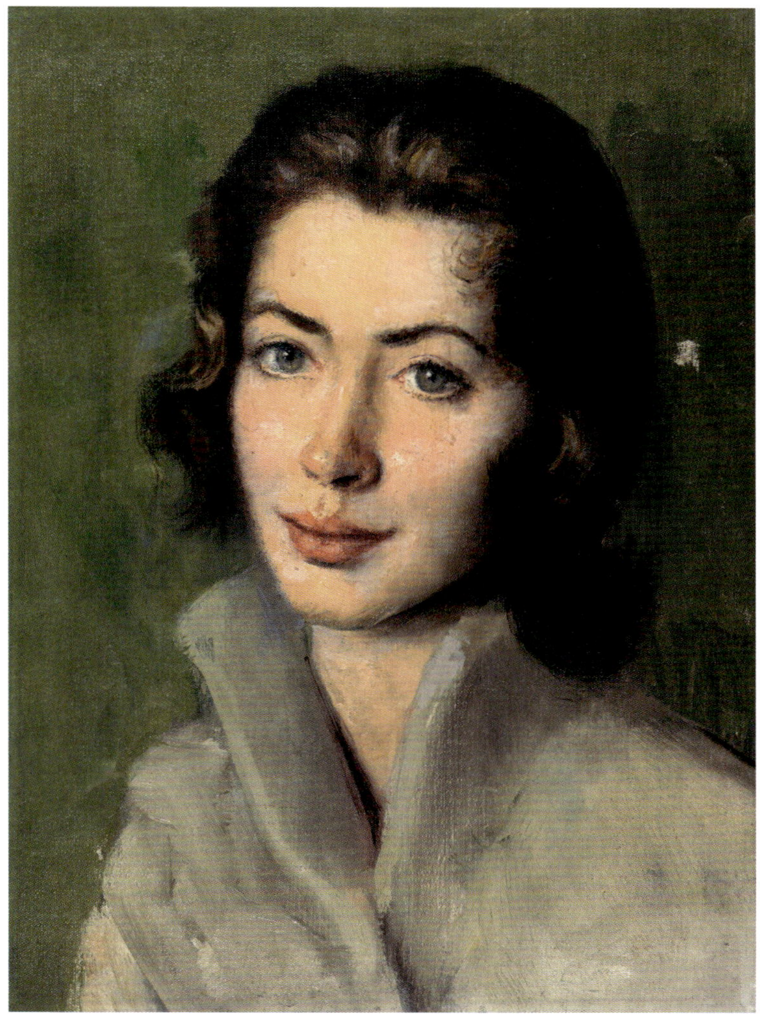

15b
Anthony Devas, *Alice* c.1950
Oil on canvas, 40.6 × 30.5 cm (16 × 12⅛ in)
Borthwick Institute for Archives,
University of York

resumption of normal life in post-war Britain, may well have made an impression on Wylie; for her, quotidian objects are not mute but are part of a history, rich in allusive meaning.

In 1956, having recognised the need to balance making work with a job to provide an income, she enrolled on a teacher training course at Goldsmiths College, London. After a whirlwind romance, she married Roy Oxlade (1929–2014). Oxlade was a fellow painting student, who had studied under David Bomberg (1890–1957) at the Borough Polytechnic (now London South Bank University). A prolific writer and influential figure in arts education, Oxlade contributed regularly to *Modern Painters* and other arts magazines. He gained a reputation as an outstanding teacher, mostly at the Adult Education Centre in Tunbridge Wells and in the College

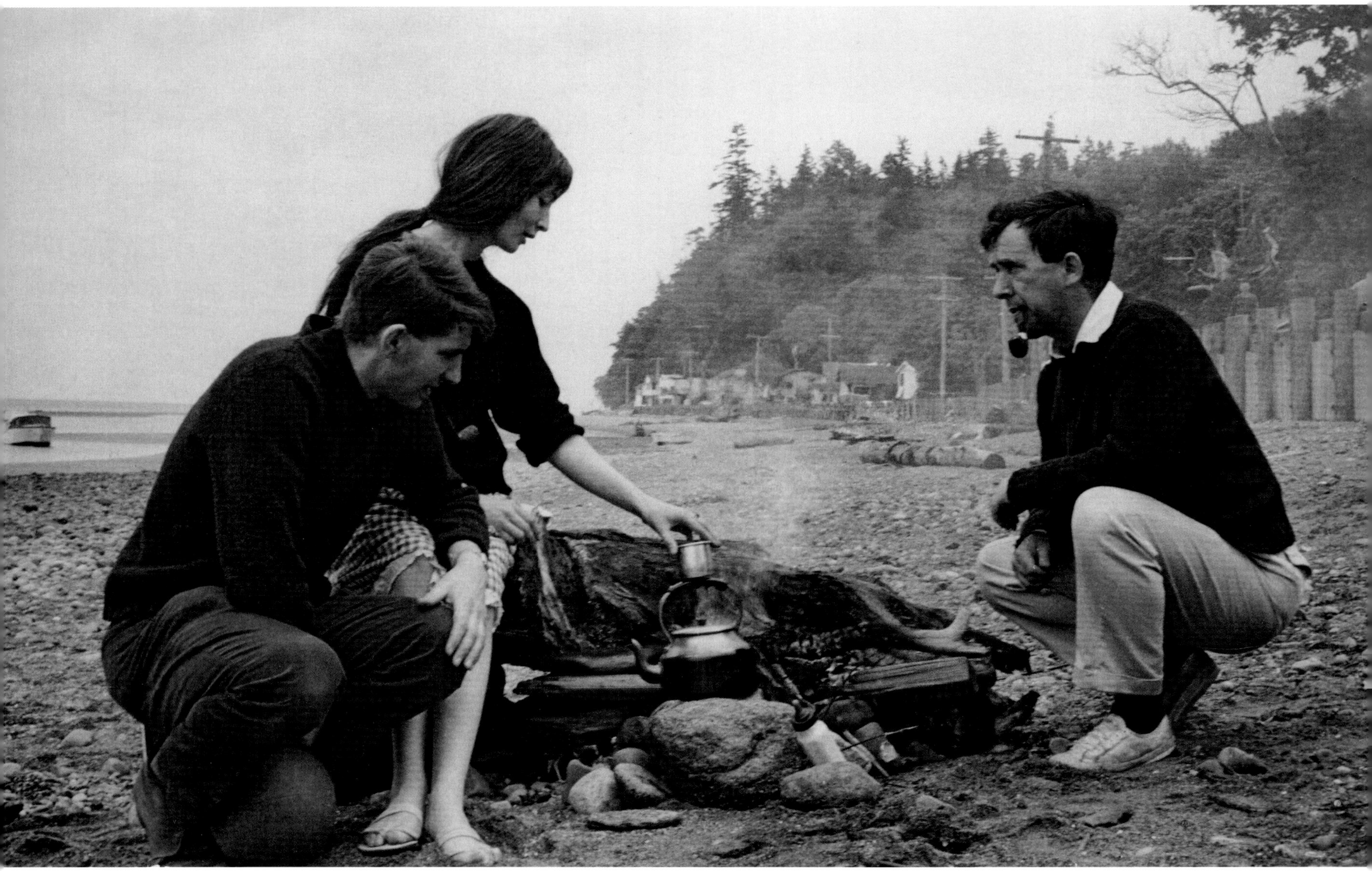

16
Rose Wylie in Vancouver,
with Roy and her brother Richard, 1959
Collection of the artist

17
Rose Wylie teaching the Art Foundation at Denbighshire Technical College, 1967
Collection of the artist

of Further Education at Sittingbourne, where he presided over popular summer schools and moved in circles which included the artists Dennis Creffield (1931–2018) and Anthony Hatwell (1931–2013), the critic Peter Fuller, the poet Peter Redgrove, and Bob Fowler, a national adviser for the arts and principal of the Royal Central School of Speech and Drama.

As newlyweds the couple lived in Watford. In 1958, Luke John, the first of their three children, was born. In the same year, keen to start afresh somewhere new and exciting, they decided to move to Vancouver, where a friend was living in addition to one of Wylie's brothers (fig.16). There, Oxlade worked as a high-school art teacher, and their second child Elizabeth was born in 1960. Wylie soon missed Europe, especially its rich sense of history.

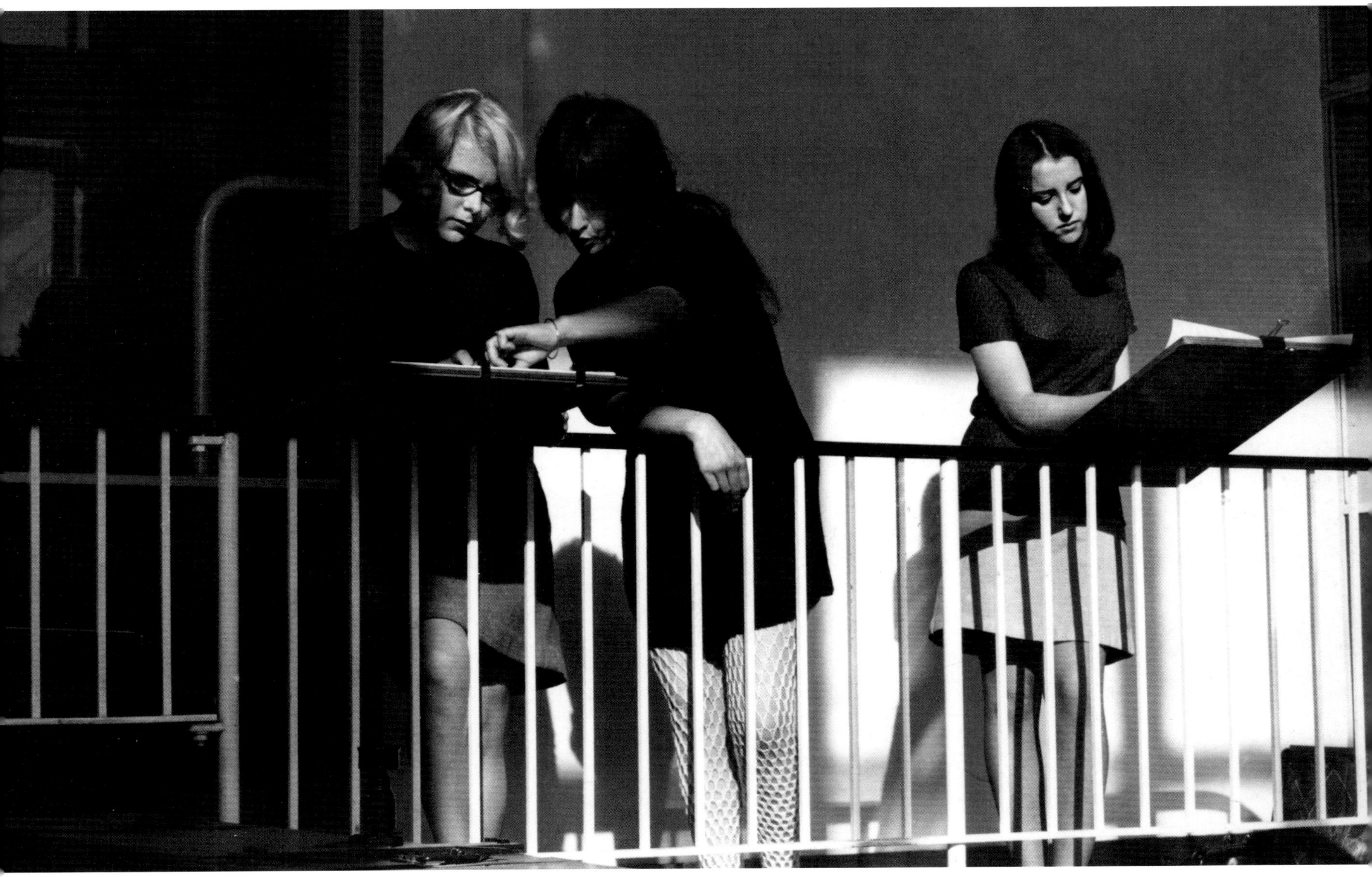

18
Rose Wylie, portrait, 1984
Collection of the artist

She did not find the Canadian art scene particularly exciting: it was dominated by the Group of Seven and Emily Carr (1871–1945), and Wylie felt little affinity with their transformation of the Canadian landscape and its dense forests and endless lakes into a transcendent, spiritual force.[22]

In 1962 they decided to return home to Britain. Oxlade was offered a job as Senior Lecturer in Art at Cartrefle College of Further Education in Wrexham, Wales, and so the family moved to Bryniau Bach in Llangollen, and later to Bank Cottage in Rhostyllen, a mining village, south-west of Wrexham. Life was difficult. Not only were they the only English family in a small, insular community, but they were also artists, and so were subject to suspicion. From 1964 to 1968 Wylie was a full-time Lecturer on the Art Foundation course at Denbighshire Technical College teaching painting, drawing and textiles (fig.17). The couple's third child Henrietta was born in 1966. The family lived in Wales until 1968 when Oxlade was appointed Head of the Art Department at Sittingbourne College of Further Education and they moved to Newnham, in rural Kent, buying Forge Cottage, the late sixteenth-century house where Wylie continues to live today.

With three young children Wylie and Oxlade recognised that it was impossible for them both to pursue careers as artists, and it was clear from an early age that Elizabeth, their second child, would need extra support. As Wylie explains, 'I think bringing up children is important, and locking yourself into the solitary and engrossing activity of painting would interrupt this.'[23] Furthermore in the 1960s women's access to the art world was still heavily circumscribed – the ideology of the painter as a heroic male genius was prevalent and the networks of teaching and support were typically dominated by men. Wylie switched roles from 'artist' to that of 'artist's wife', and focused on raising the family while Oxlade focused on his teaching and studio practice. After twenty years of putting her energies into family life, Wylie resumed her career in the early 1980s. As she makes clear, 'I don't feel there is any time I "stopped" – I just put my energies into making food or curtains or clothes instead of paintings. As the children left home, I had space for a studio.'[24]

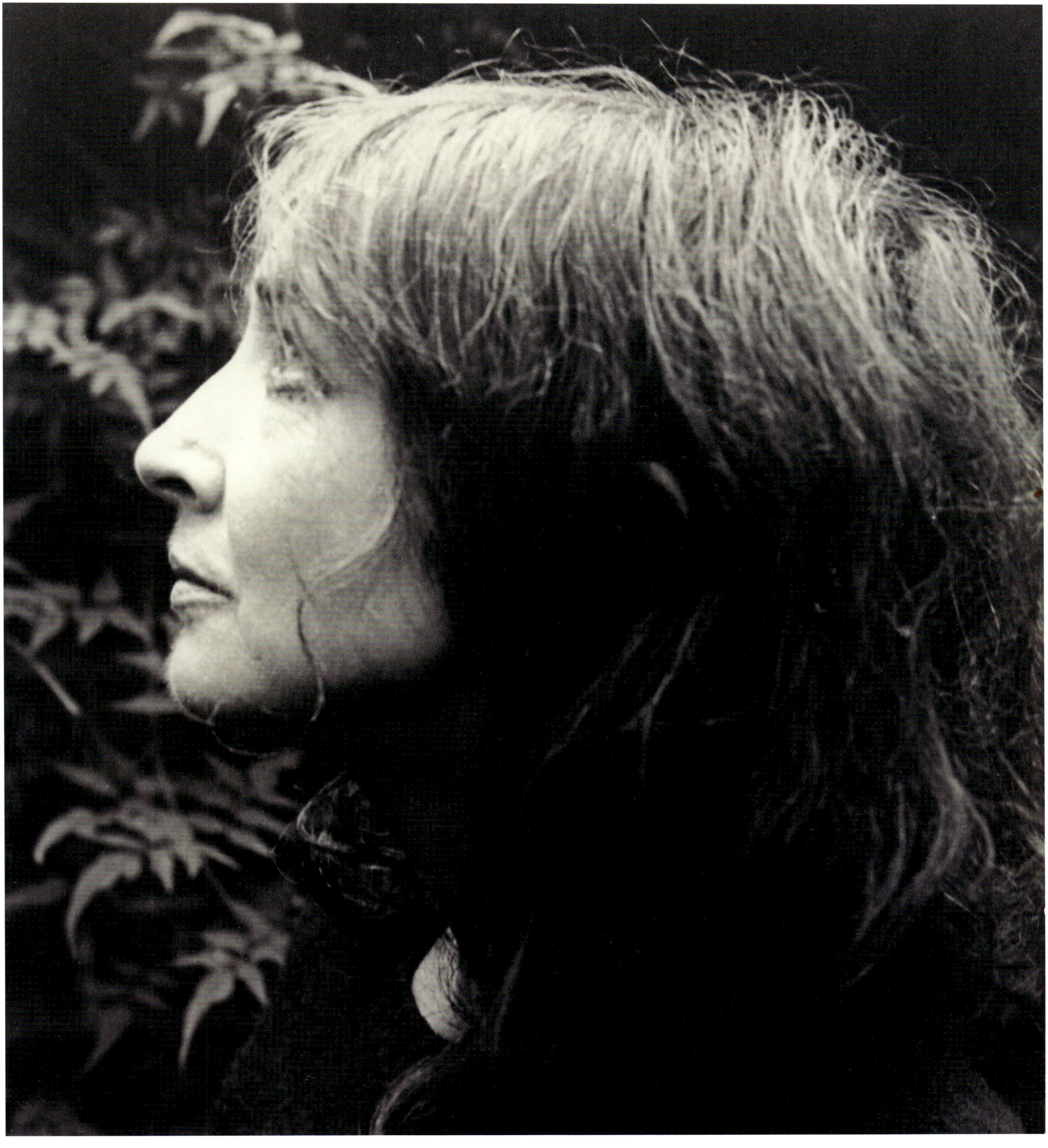

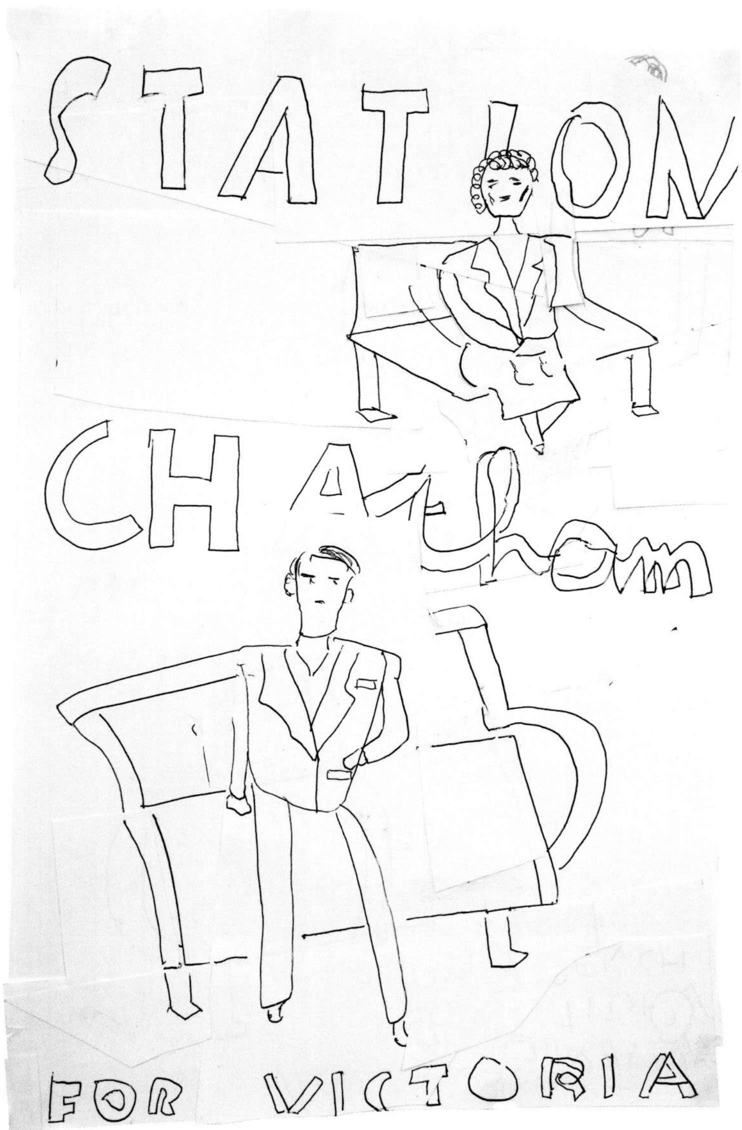

19
Chatham Station, for Victoria 2018
Biro and collage on paper
33.7 × 21.5 cm (13¼ × 8½ in)
Private collection

At 45, Wylie returned to study as a mature student in the Department of Cultural History at the Royal College of Art between 1979 and 1981. Here she wrote an MA dissertation which focused on the language of drawing and how it is taught in English art schools.[25] Her investigations into drawing and the translation required in the act of looking reveals a lot about Wylie's approach to art and her ambition to grasp the how and why of making and visual thinking. In her dissertation, Wylie explored the role and status of drawing and questioned how the teaching of drawing across the centuries has led to complex theories about copying, hierarchies of genres, and an emphasis on representation of the body and responses to nature. She posed the question, 'What do we mean by "objective drawing"? a) Is it a means of conveying or recording an idea or b) is it a way of recording what we see or c) expressing how we feel, opening up the conversation between figuration and abstraction . . . and the slippage between the two?'[26]

The thesis situates drawn works between objective and subjective poles, especially as exemplified in different approaches to teaching drawing. It celebrates Eugène Delacroix (1798–1863), Matisse, Bomberg, Paul Klee (1879–1940) and Wassily Kandinsky (1866–1944) amongst others, but also illustrates, analyses and proposes ways to approach drawing in general and the ideas and theories that inform it. Evolving from the RCA students' discussion of their own influences, the work focuses on Leonardo da Vinci (1452–1519), John Ruskin (1819–1900), Walter Sickert (1860–1942) and Bomberg. For example, it explores Bomberg's account of the frustration of academic training. It also highlights how 'there are attitudes to teaching drawing that support systems of drawing other than those centred on a purely optical concern', in which Wylie references the work of Peter Fuller, who in turn made use of the ideas of the writer and psychoanalyist Marion Milner and the art critic Adrian Stokes.[27] Her enquiry also supports the position that drawing 'may be autonomous, a closed entity, a thing in its own right with a responsibility only to itself'.[28]

While Wylie is primarily known for her paintings, drawing is central to her own practice. This was acknowledged early on by her inclusion in the *Hayward Annual: British Drawing* exhibition in 1982, the year after she finished at the Royal College of Art.

20
Pete 2016
Coloured pencil, pencil and collage on paper
29 × 21 cm (11½ × 8⅜ in)
Private collection

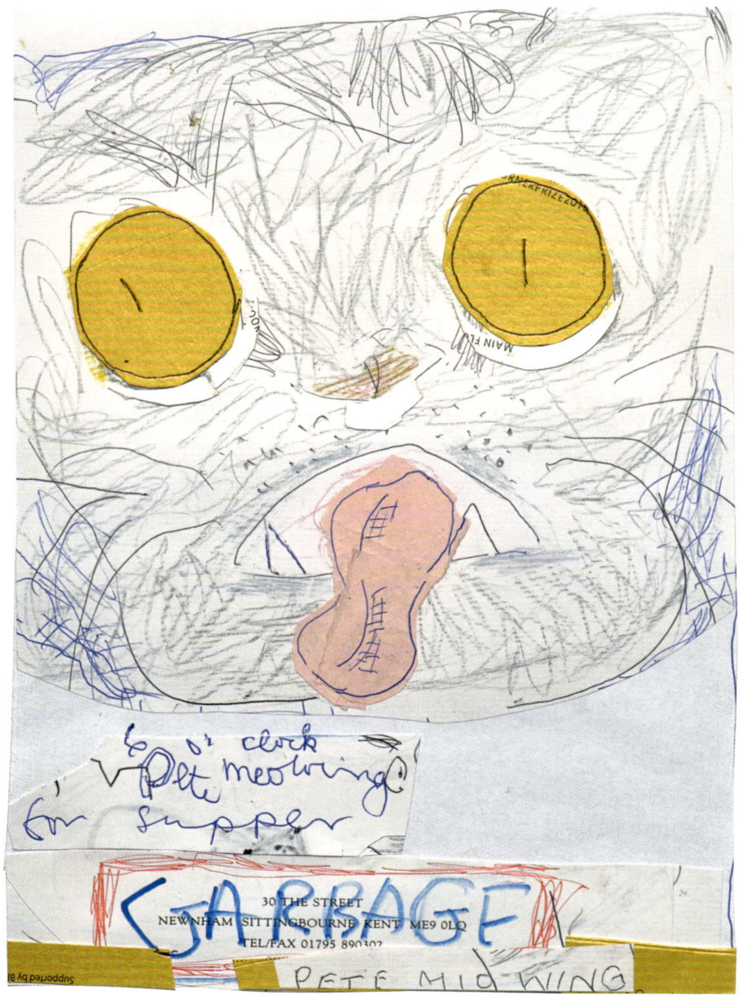

This coincided with her decision to start making work again as a professional artist and teaching with Oxlade at the hugely popular annual painting and drawing summer school at the Adult Education Centre in Tunbridge Wells. As visiting lecturer Peter Fuller said: 'I soon formed the view that Roy and Rose were two of the most original and challenging teachers of art that I had come across.'[29]

In a catalogue introduction for her exhibition *Lined Paper Paintings* at the Stephen Lacey Gallery, London in 1999, Wylie outlines her thoughts on her practice. Titled 'How I would like my paintings to be and what I do', the text is a manifesto of sorts. Wylie sets out her aims, primarily the hope that her works will 'look more like something than look like paintings – look more like paintings than look like art'. She also wishes to perform 'poetic transformations' and to be unrestricted, synthesising influences as disparate as Manuel Ocampo (b.1965) and Nicolas Poussin (1594–1665), colouring books and children's transfers. The resulting painting should be 'more theatre than flow, more active than continuous' and 'placed in a general direction towards [the] metaphysical and emblematic'. She summarises: 'I like image as a memorable, clear representation of something, with opposites, jumps of scale and the isolation of cut-outs . . . also fragments.'[30]

There is a directness in Wylie's approach, and her drawings and paintings retain a kind of truth, with no disguise. Wylie draws what she feels without compromise, or worrying about what others think. Her pictures are rooted in acute observations of the natural world, human behaviour and an appreciation of the small, unremarked incidents of everyday life: *The Well Cooked Omelette* 1989 (fig.21), served on a decorative blue and white plate, her cat (fig.20), a carrot peeler (fig.27), flowers and birds in the garden seen out of her kitchen window as she waits for the potatoes to boil (figs 23–25), people waiting on the platform at Chatham station for the train to Victoria (fig.19) or fruit (fig.28). The watercolour and collage *Gas (3 Times)* 2012 (fig.22) consists of three close-up studies from slightly different angles of a lit gas ring. Reminiscent of a celestial globe adorned with blue flames, it is an object 'familiar to women throughout the ages who have stood over it'.[31] However, the shape of the central gas ring reducer looks like a swastika and introduces an unsettling, sinister element. Its association with Nazi symbolism and mass murder is reinforced by the word 'Gas' written above.

21

The Well Cooked Omelette 1989

Oil on canvas, 122 × 153 cm (48⅛ × 60¼ in)

Private collection

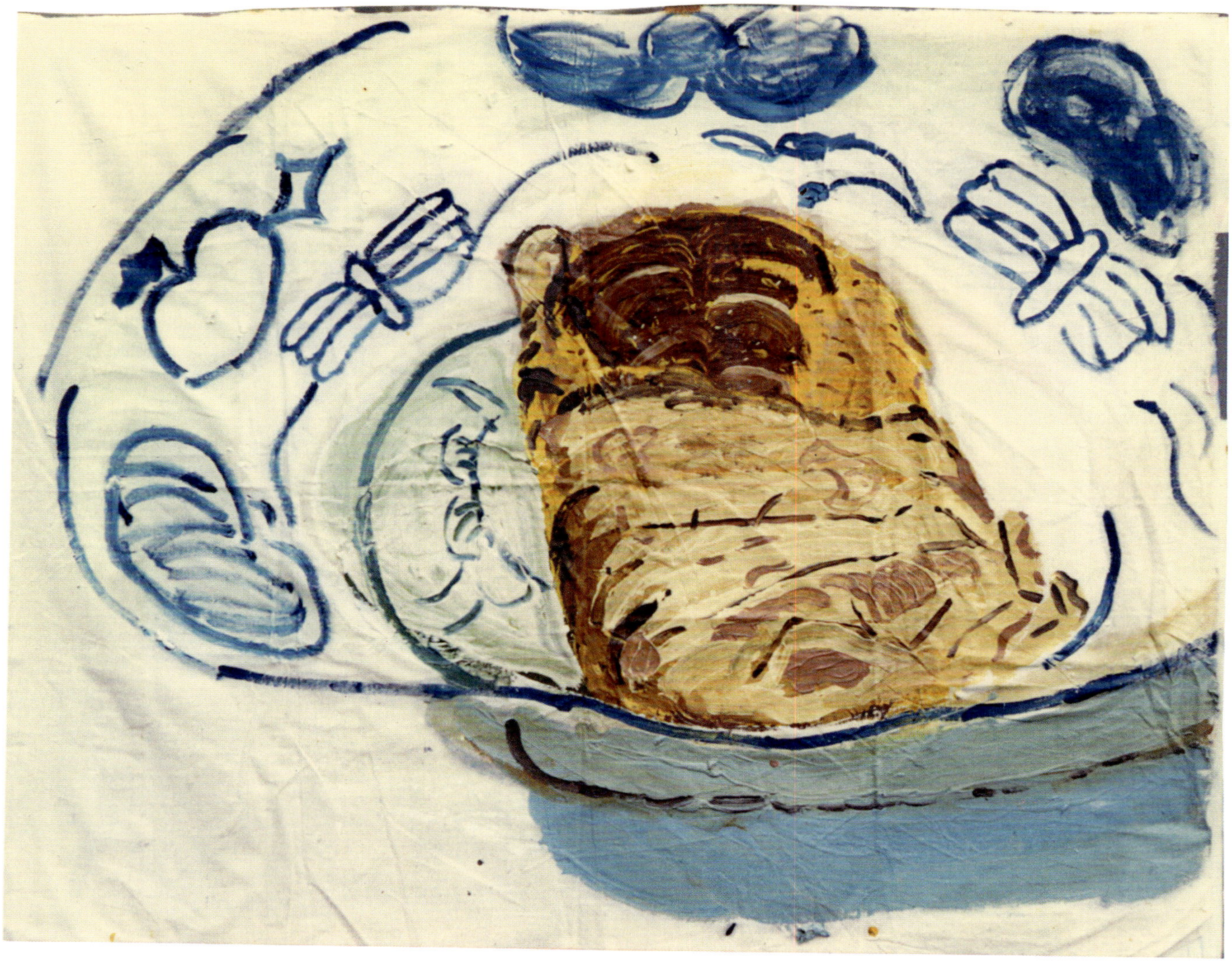

22

Gas (3 Times) 2012

Watercolour and collage on paper
90 × 181 cm (35½ × 71⅜ in)
Private collection

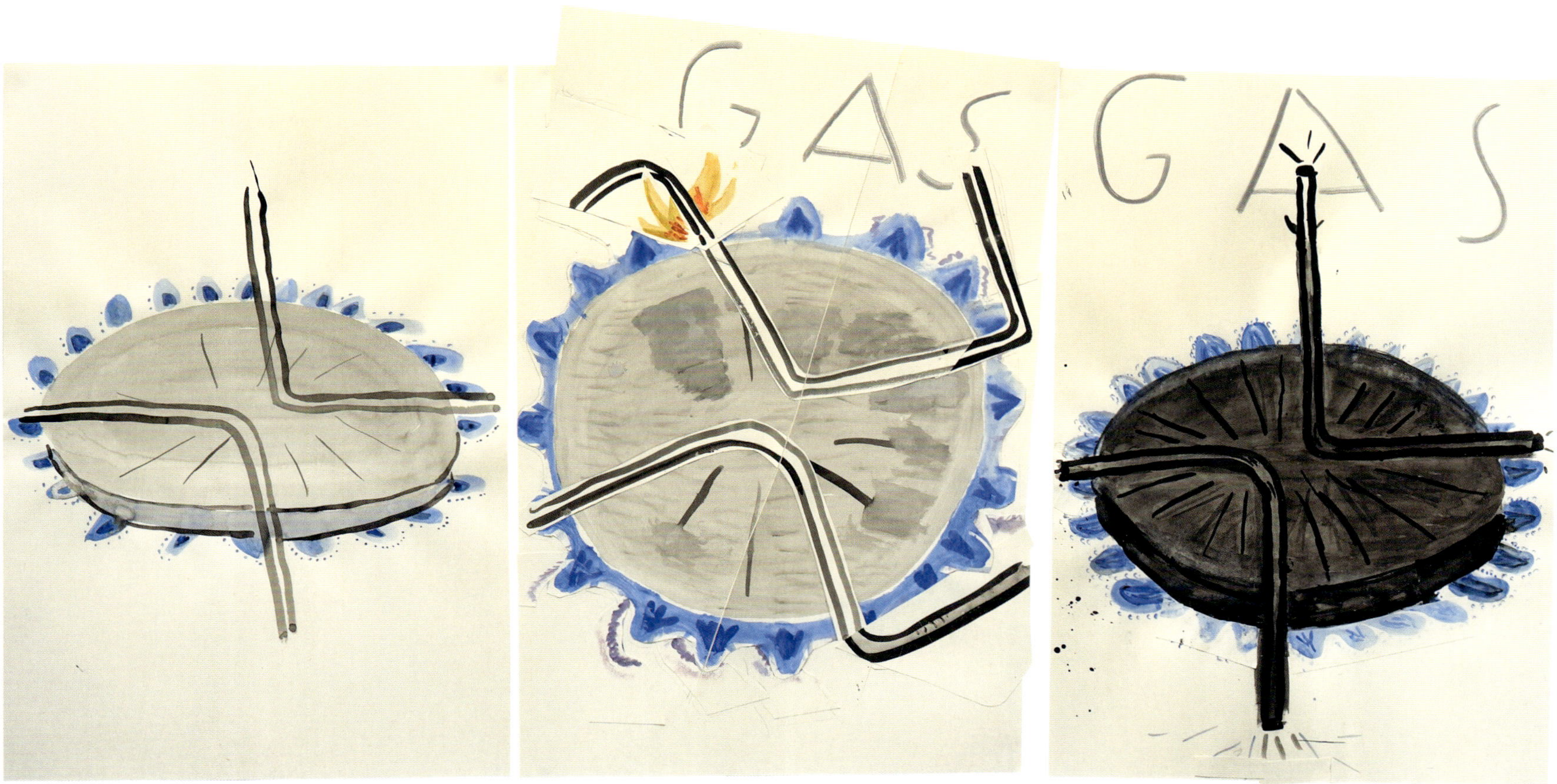

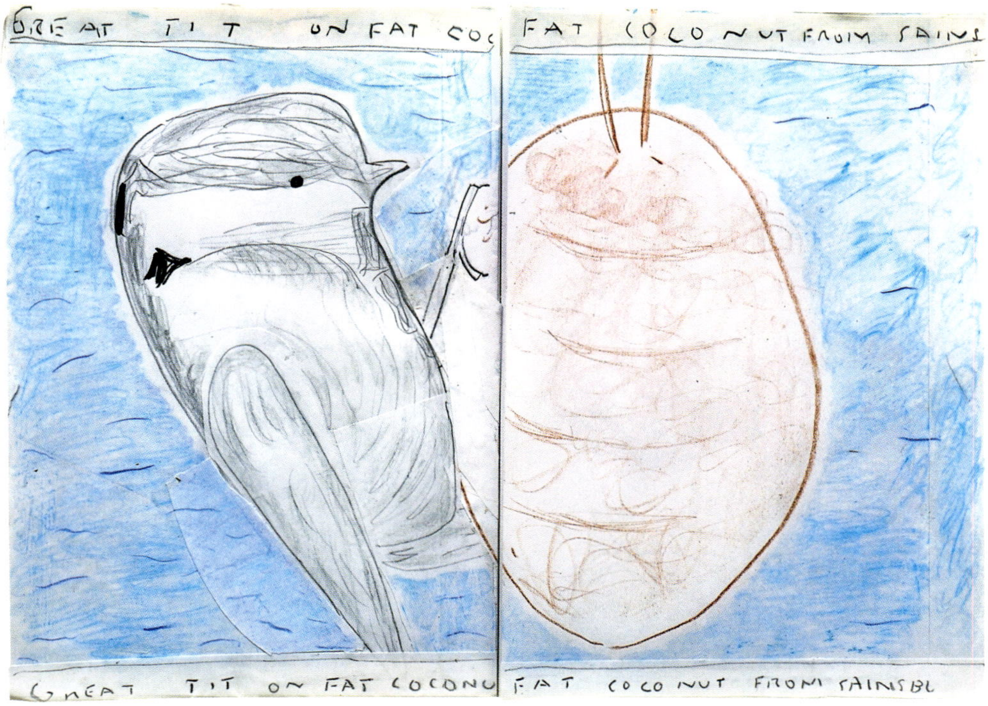

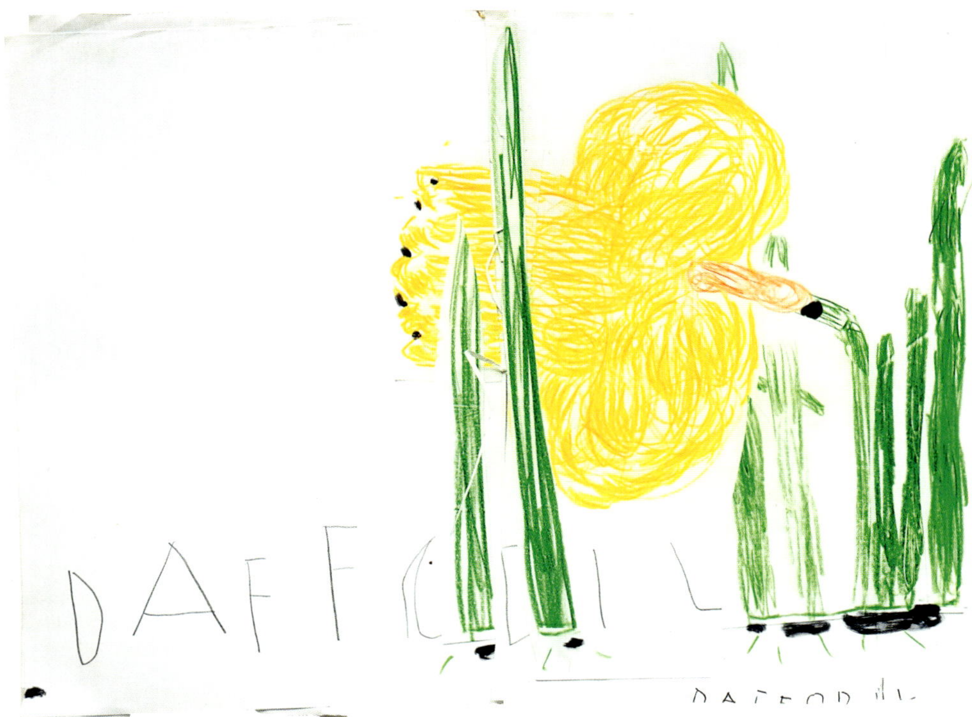

23
Great Tit on Fat Coconut 2008
Coloured pencil and collage on paper
30 × 42 cm (11⅞ × 16⅝ in)
Private collection

24
Daffodil 2009
Coloured pencil and collage on paper
30 × 42 cm (11⅞ × 16⅝ in)
Private collection

25
Little Mauve Flower 2014
Pencil, flower water, ink and collage on paper
92 × 62 cm (36¼ × 24½ in)
Private collection

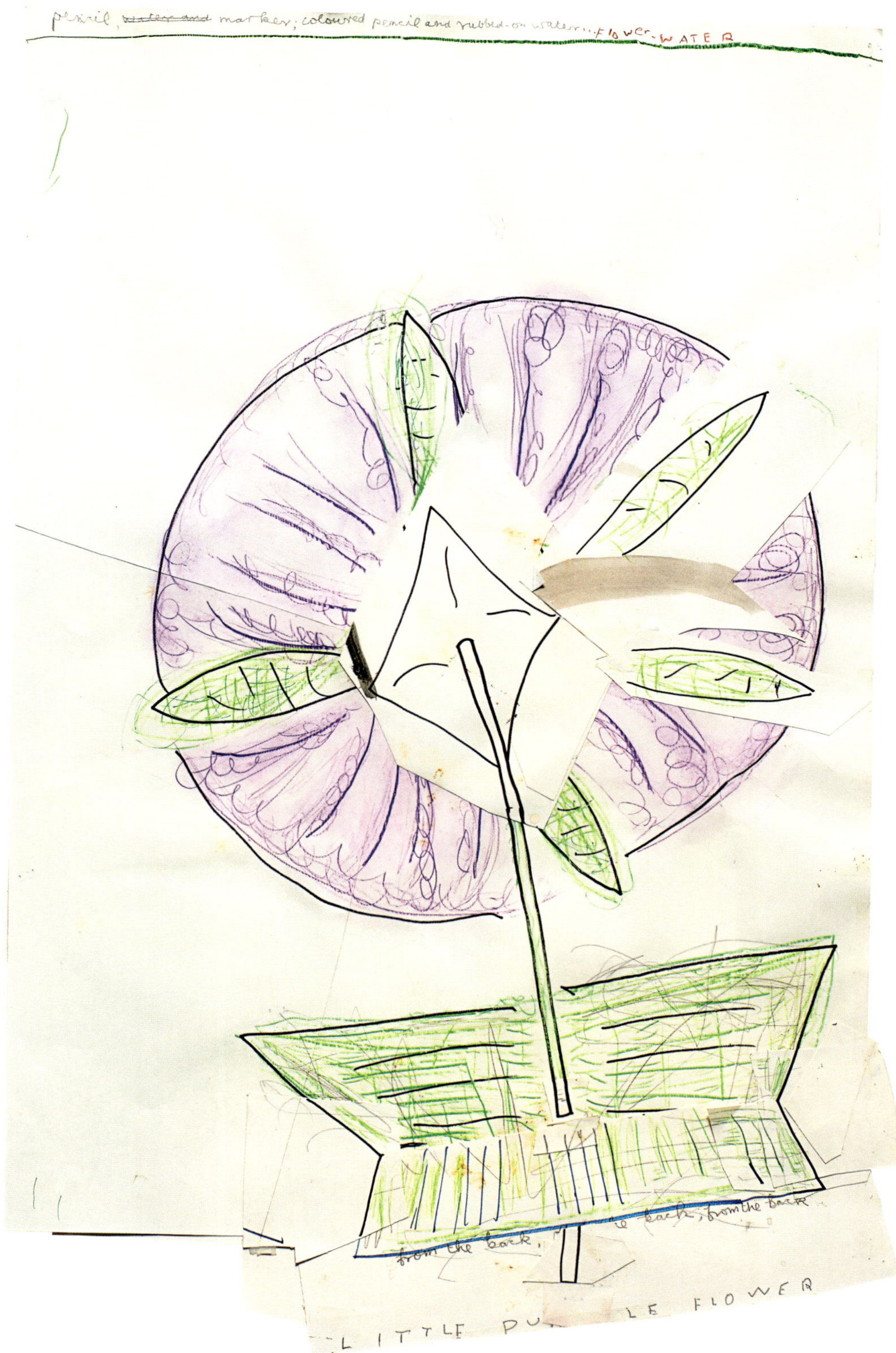

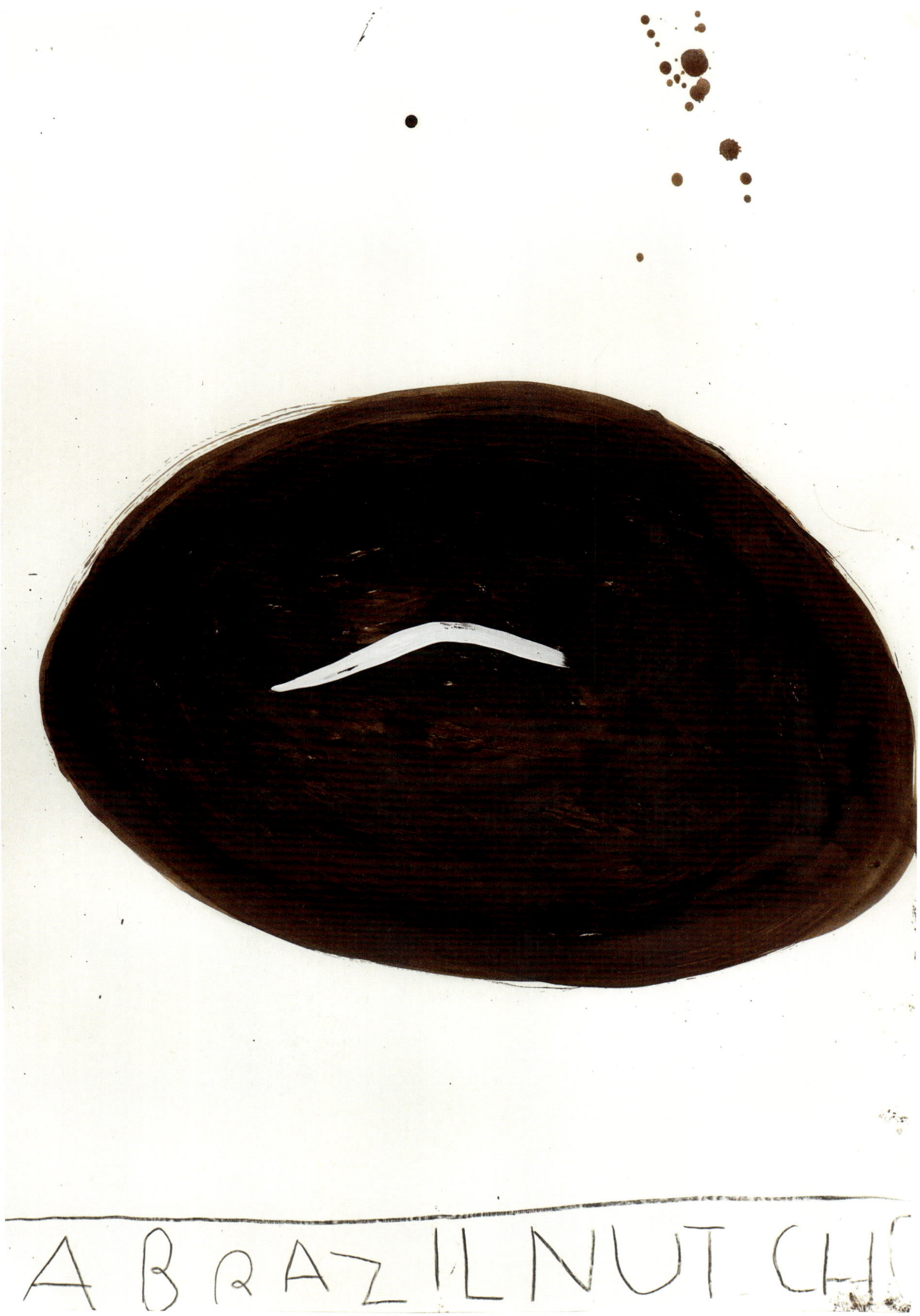
A BRAZIL NUT CH

26
Brazil Nut Choc 2016
Watercolour and pencil on paper
84 × 59 cm (33½ × 23¼ in)
Private collection

27
Carrot Peeler 2011
Watercolour and pencil on paper
84 × 59 cm (33⅛ × 23¼ in)
Private collection

28
Pineapple (Black and Red) 2013
Watercolour and collage on paper
87 × 59 cm (34¼ × 23¼ in)
Private collection

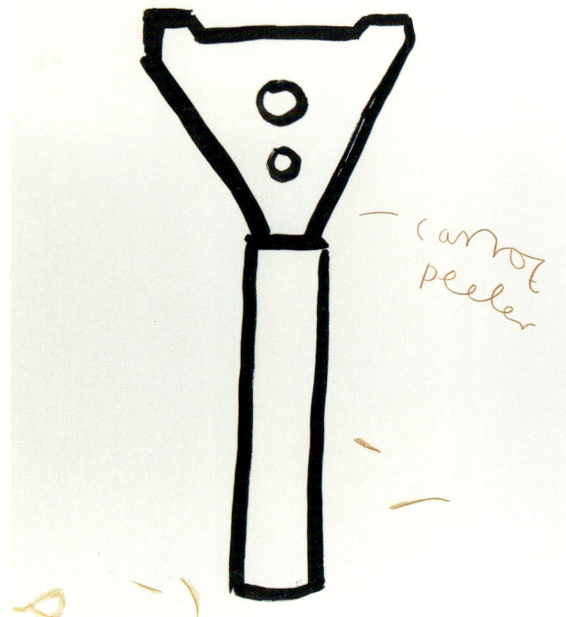

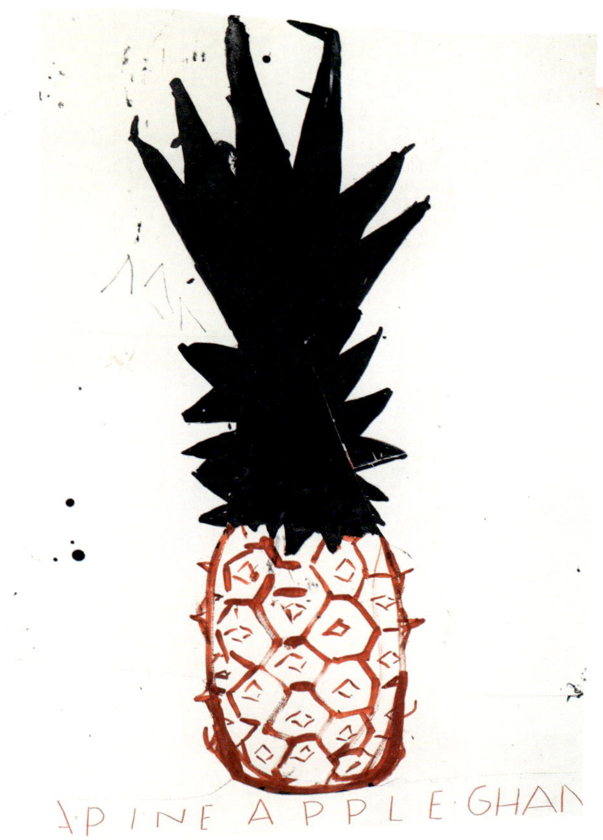

Wylie's work is irrepressibly experimental and draws upon a bewildering jumble of inspirations, including *Faversham Hedge Dog* 2000 (fig.29) – a painting of a privet dog priced at £1,499 which caught Wylie's eye in the local garden centre – or *Belgium Painting – Cloven Shoes* 1996 (fig.30), which shows a pair of shoes she observed on a visit to Antwerp. In the watercolour *Brazil Nut Choc* 2016 (fig.26), Wylie's little chocolate brazil nut is round, shiny and appealing. Inspired by a bag of sweets purchased in Margate by the artist's daughter, this Brazil nut encased in plain chocolate is rich with ordinary, familiar appeal. Elsewhere a series of three chocolate-related paintings, one displaying a bat, another a gravestone, a third a ghost – *Halloween Chocs, Finger (Close Up)* 2015, *Halloween Chocs, Ghost (Close Up)* 2015 and *Halloween Chocs (Line-up)* 2015 – comes from a box of Halloween chocolates the artist was given and demonstrates how her choice of everyday subject matter is direct and unapologetic.[32] Anything and everything captures her attention, and she responds to the particularity of each experience in the hope that she can find a way to describe the character of things as vividly and accurately as possible. *Arsenal & Spurs* 2006 (fig.31), for example, presents a bird's-eye scene of a football match as deadly combat, with the players reduced to numbered shirts under the command of their team's symbols, one of which is a cannon, the other a cockerel.

29

Faversham Hedge Dog 2000

Oil on canvas, 183 × 179 cm (72⅛ × 70½ in)

Collection of Luke-John Oxlade

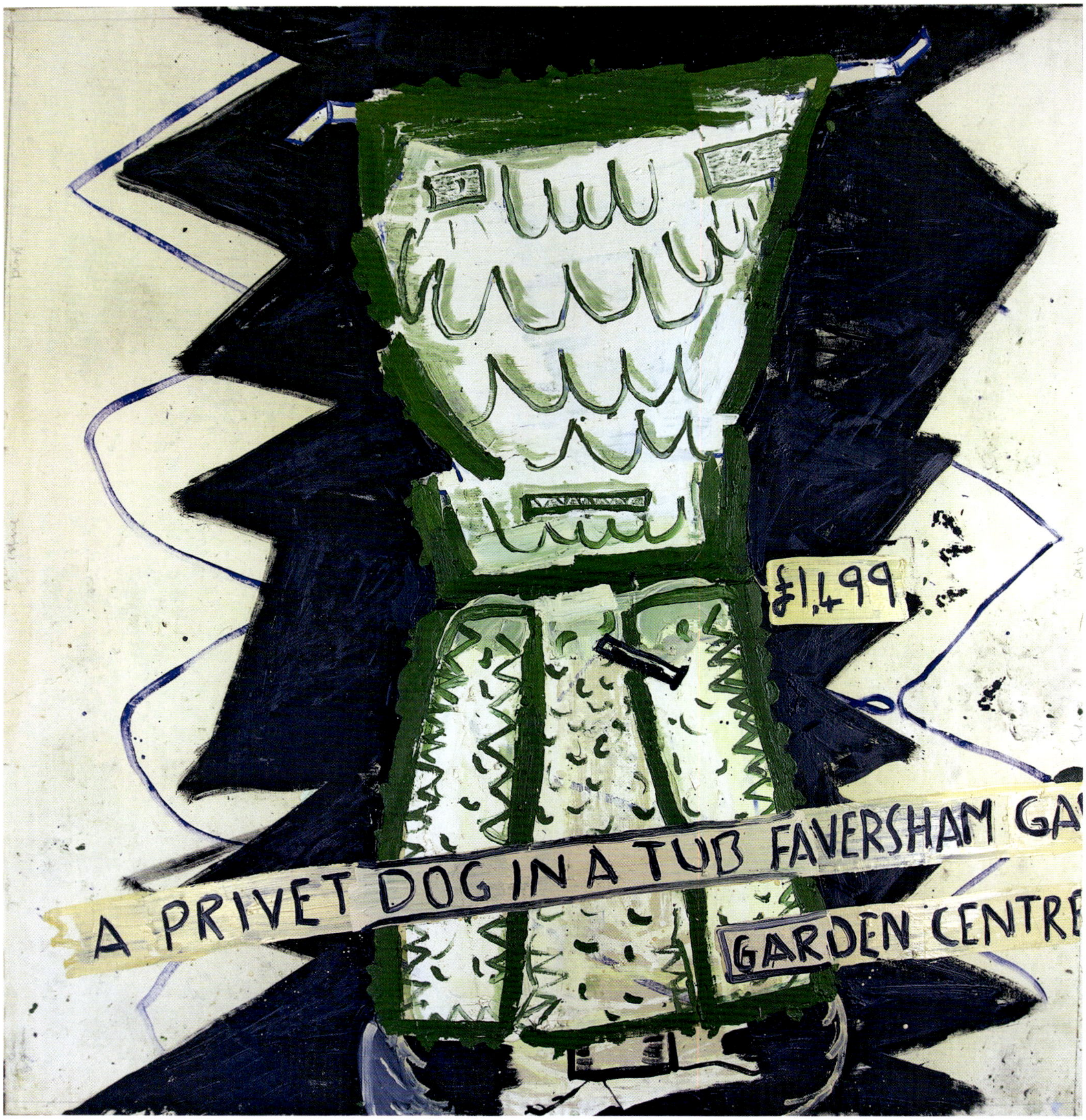

30
Belgium Painting – Cloven Shoes 1996
Oil on canvas, 183 × 165 cm (72⅛ × 65 in)
Private collection

31 (overleaf)
Arsenal & Spurs 2006
Oil on canvas, 165 × 366 cm (65 × 144⅛ in)
Private collection

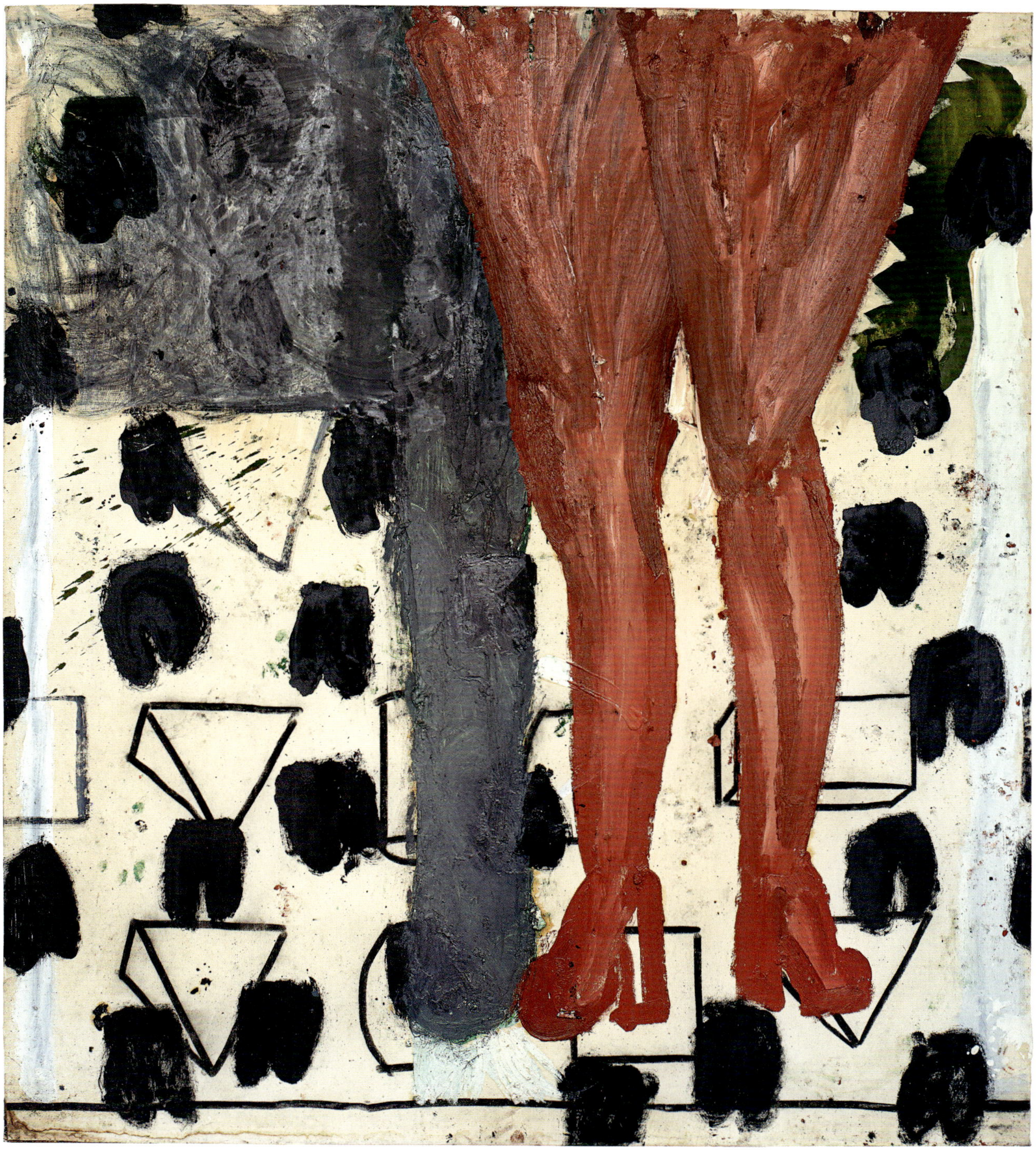

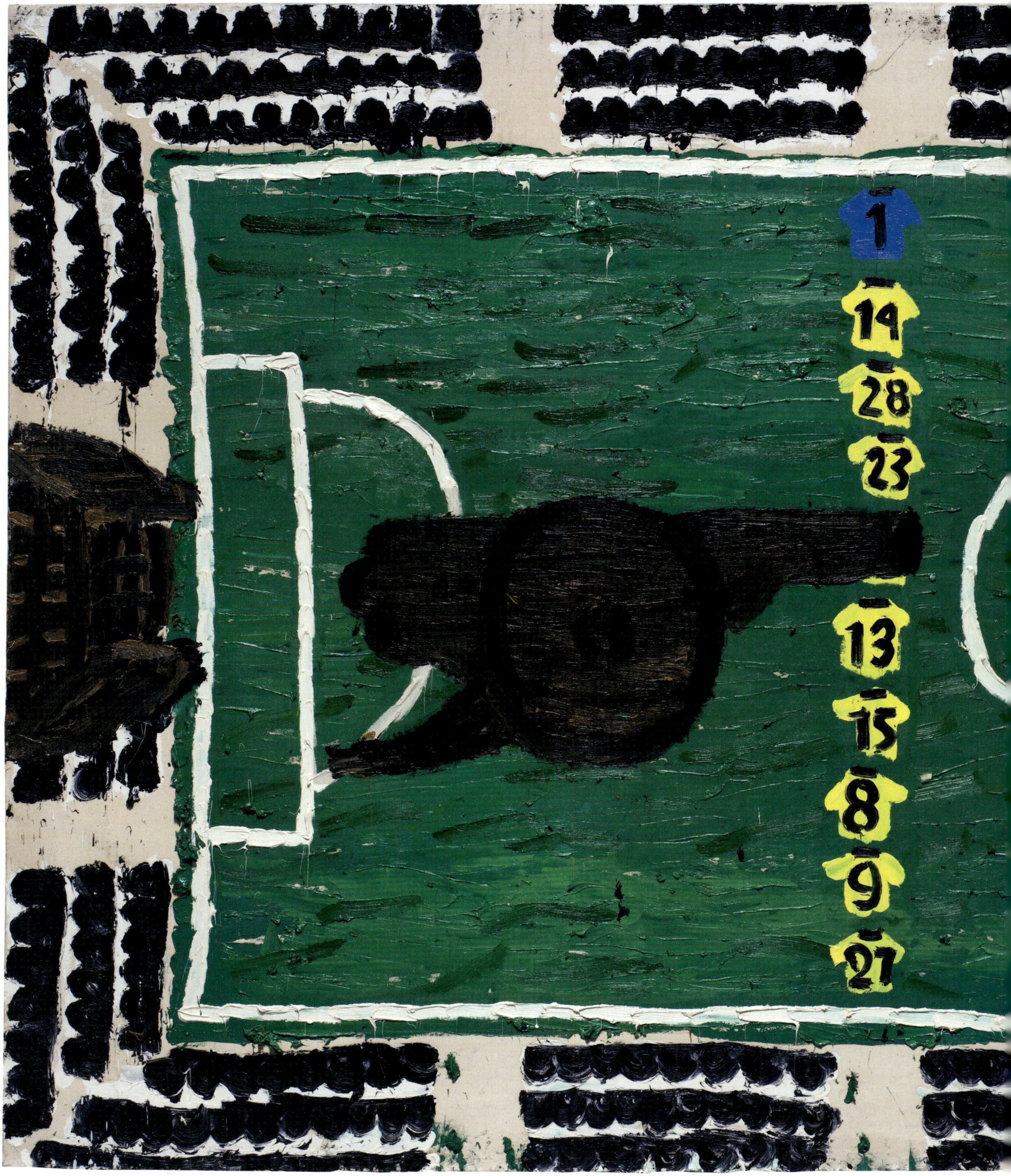
1
14
28
23
13
15
8
9
27

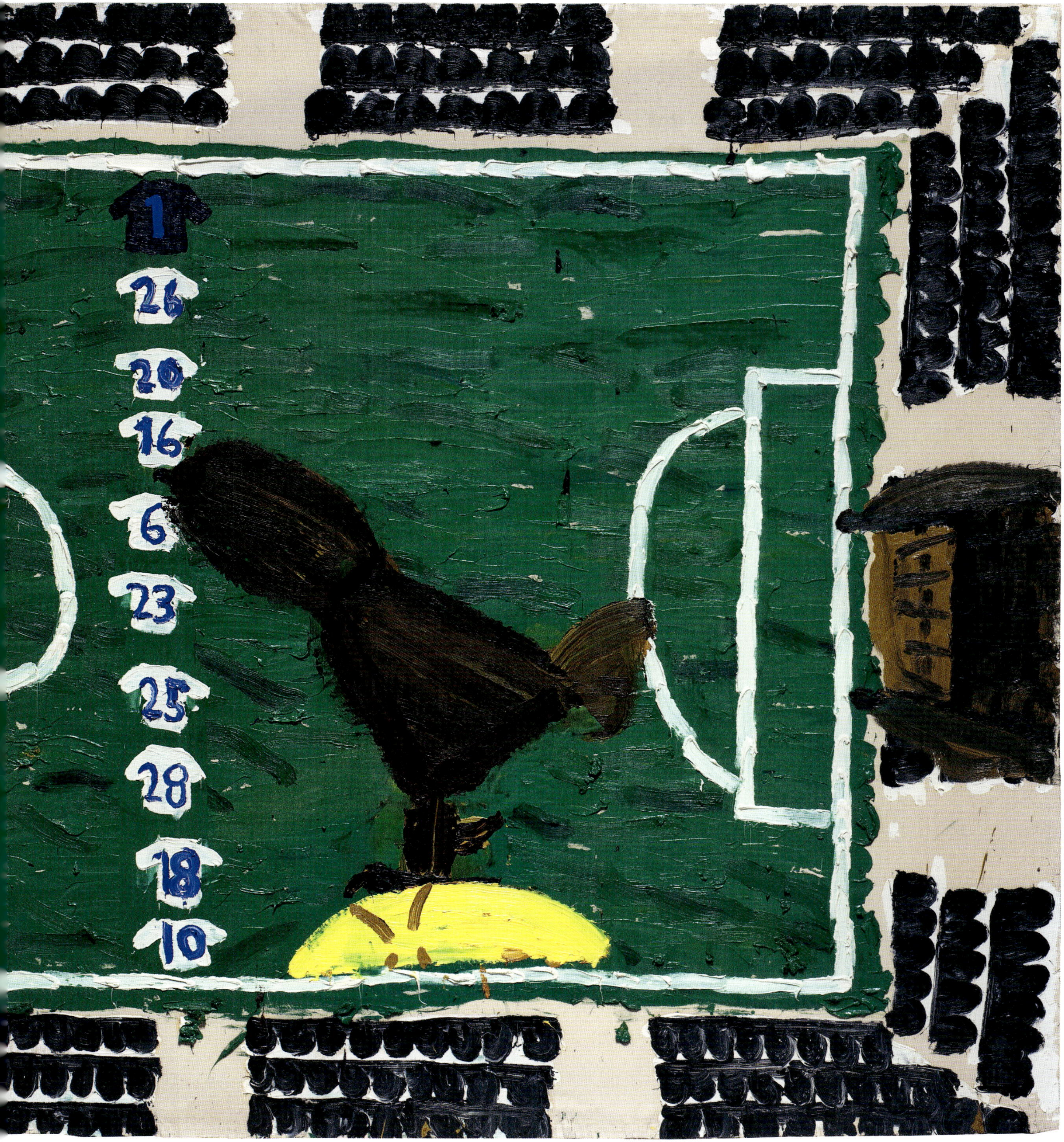
1
26
20
16
6
23
25
28
18
10

Images are gathered from different sources and developed in biro or pencil drawings. Leaves and brambles (figs 32 and 33), for example, hold a particular appeal, as do the dragonflies, black beetles and worms typically found in an English garden in the summer (figs 34 and 35). As Wylie explains, 'The image is arrived at through many drawings, evolving from a process of observation, personality and response: keeping something of the original subject, but hoping for a transformation into a poetic and particular form or whole, free from conventional representation.'[33] She draws to achieve a certain likeness to the subject and then paints to achieve a certain likeness to the drawing. Each painting is planned in great detail, and her particular working methods allow for interpretations and reinterpretations that lend themselves to second thoughts, corrections, re-drawings and re-orderings so that there is a certain nonchalance present in the final work.

32
Pale Primrose Leaf 2015
Watercolour on paper
84 × 60 cm (33⅛ × 23⅝ in)
Collection of Chen Yan Chi

33
Blackberry in August 2015
Watercolour on paper
84 × 60 cm (33⅛ × 23⅝ in)
Collection of Joe Chien

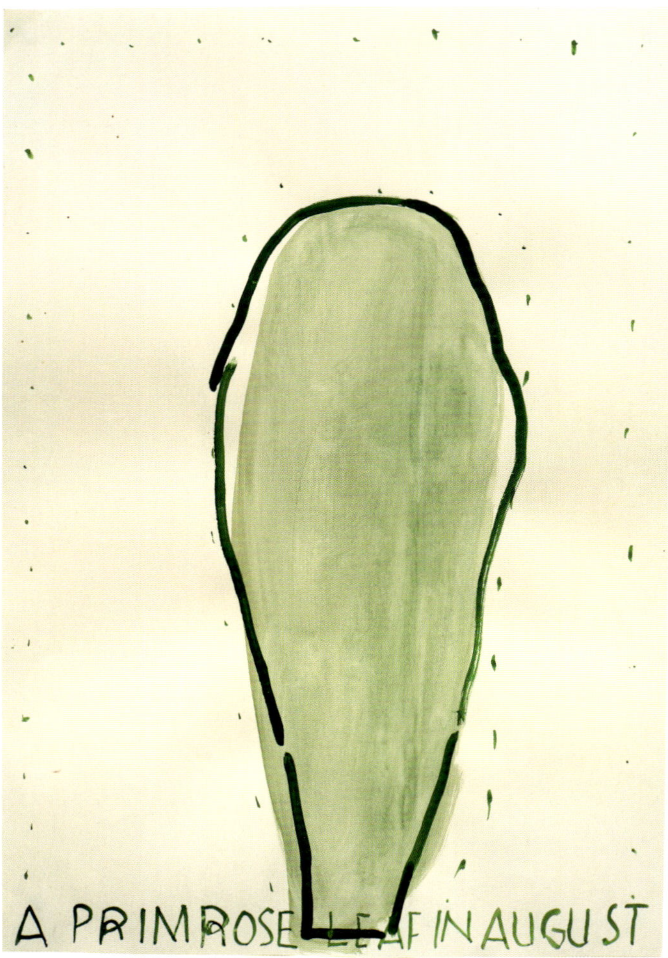

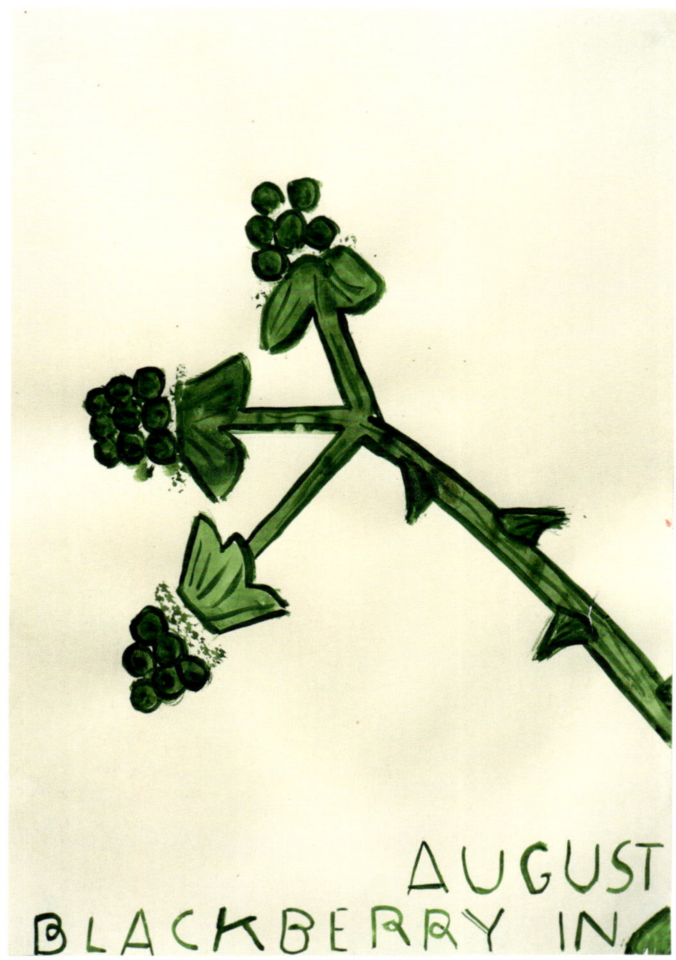

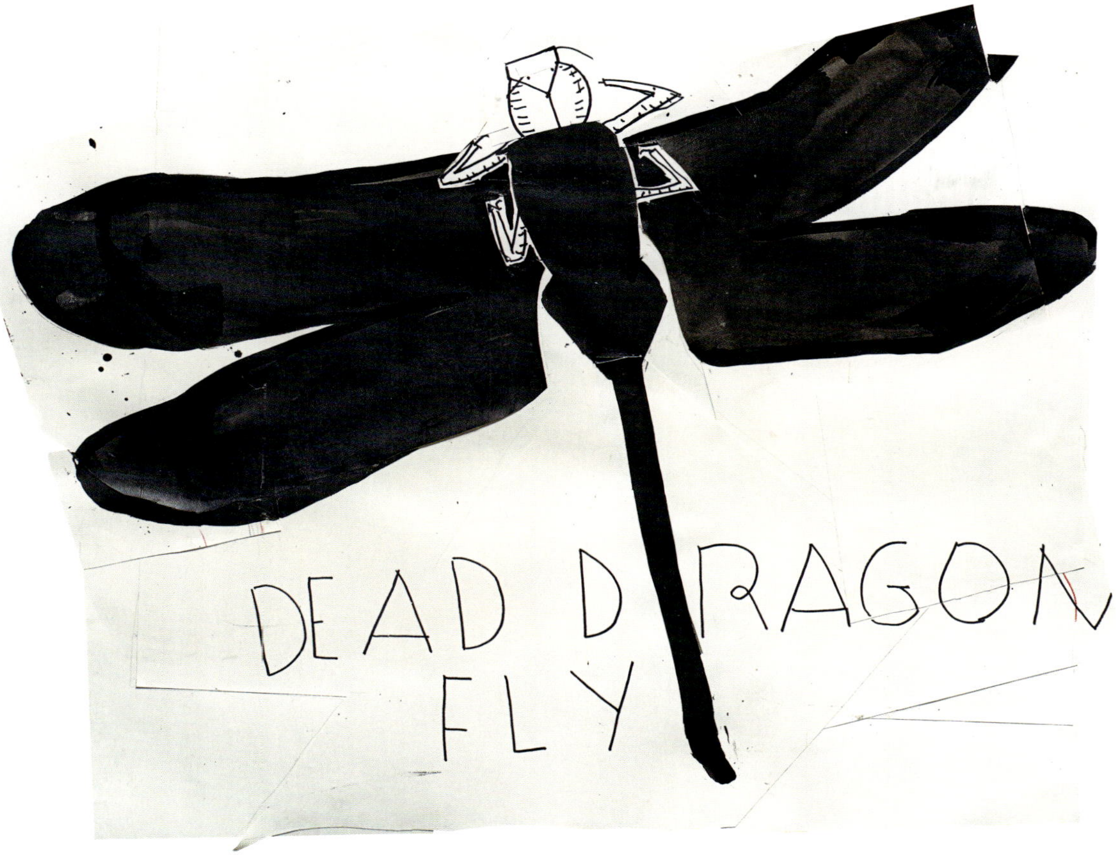

34
Dead Dragonfly 2014
Ink and collage on paper
75 × 109 cm (29⅝ × 43 in)
Private collection

35
A Eunice 2014
Ink, marker pen and collage on paper
79 × 99 cm (31⅛ × 39 in)
Collection of Brad Hajzak

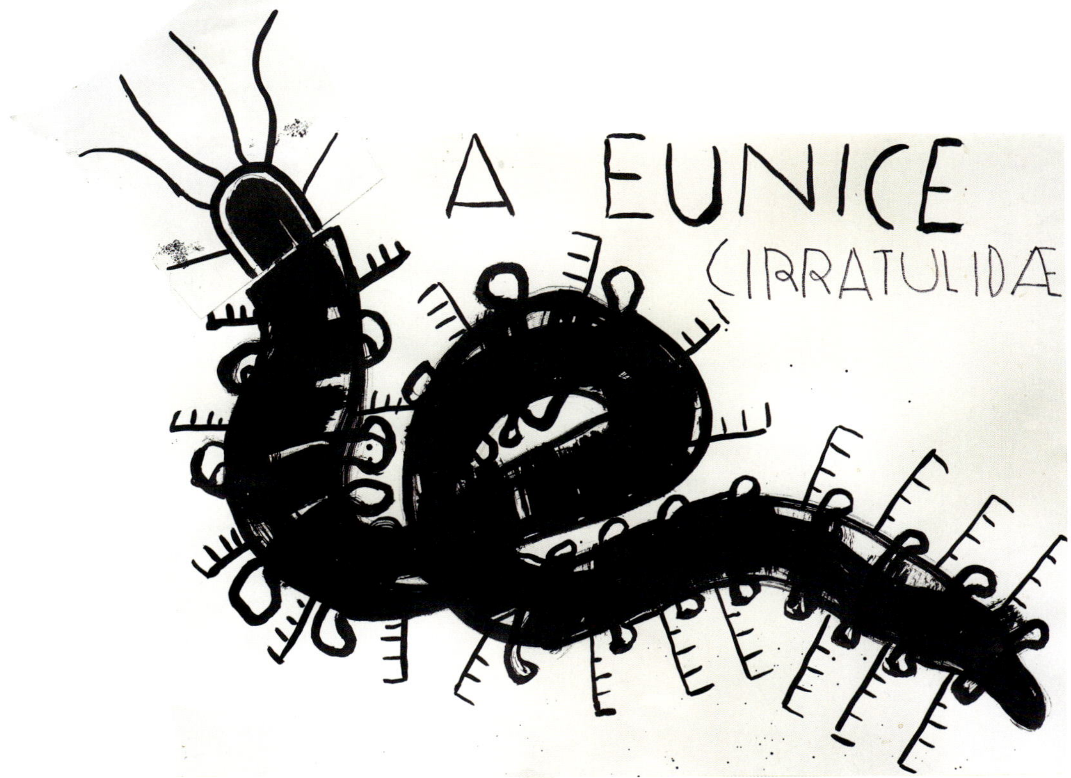

36
H & O Tennis 1999
Oil on canvas, 183 × 335 cm (72⅛ × 132 in)
The Bjørnholt Collection, Norway

Wylie has been influenced by the American writer Gertrude Stein's view of art, understood by Stein in the broadest sense to include writing.[34] Perhaps the clearest exposition of Stein's views is found in her 1936 lecture *What Are Master-pieces and Why Are There So Few of Them*, which sets out what she considers the prerequisites for an art masterpiece.[35] The essential distinction Stein makes is between 'identity' and 'entity': 'the master-piece has nothing to do with human nature or with identity, it has to do with the human mind and the entity that is with a thing in itself and not in relation'. True art is not concerned with identity because an understanding of the identity of something relies on established networks of relations that are 'common knowledge': in contrast the relationship between mind and entity (i.e. the thing in itself) evades our habitual, tacit understanding of things and sees them anew. For Stein a masterpiece, like an entity, 'is an end in itself' and not a representation of something else.

Stein's views resonate with the philosophical movement of phenomenology, first formulated by Edmund Husserl. Phenomenology aims to experience the world without any prior knowledge or preconceptions. This setting aside of knowledge and preconceptions is called the phenomenological reduction; 'it is the experience of astonishment. The "knowing" we have in this experience stands in stark contrast to the "knowing" we have in our everyday lives.'[36] Phenomenological 'knowing' is comparable to Stein's understanding of the entity; everyday 'knowing' to her understanding of identity. In Wylie's work we get a sense of this openness to (phenomenological) astonishment which transcends subjectivism.

Ideas similar to those of Gertrude Stein and to those of phenomenology are also found in the work of art historians and theorists. The painter André Lhote (1885–1962), for example, wrote extensively on art in the context of post-cubism. Lhote emphasised that art does not merely copy reality, but rather creates 'under the pretext of imitation, pure plastic elements: measures, directions, ornaments, lights, values, colors, matter, distributed and organized according to the demands of the laws of nature'.[37] Lhote's emphasis on finding the essential core of phenomena recalls Stein's focus on the entity, the thing in itself or phenomenology's primal vision.

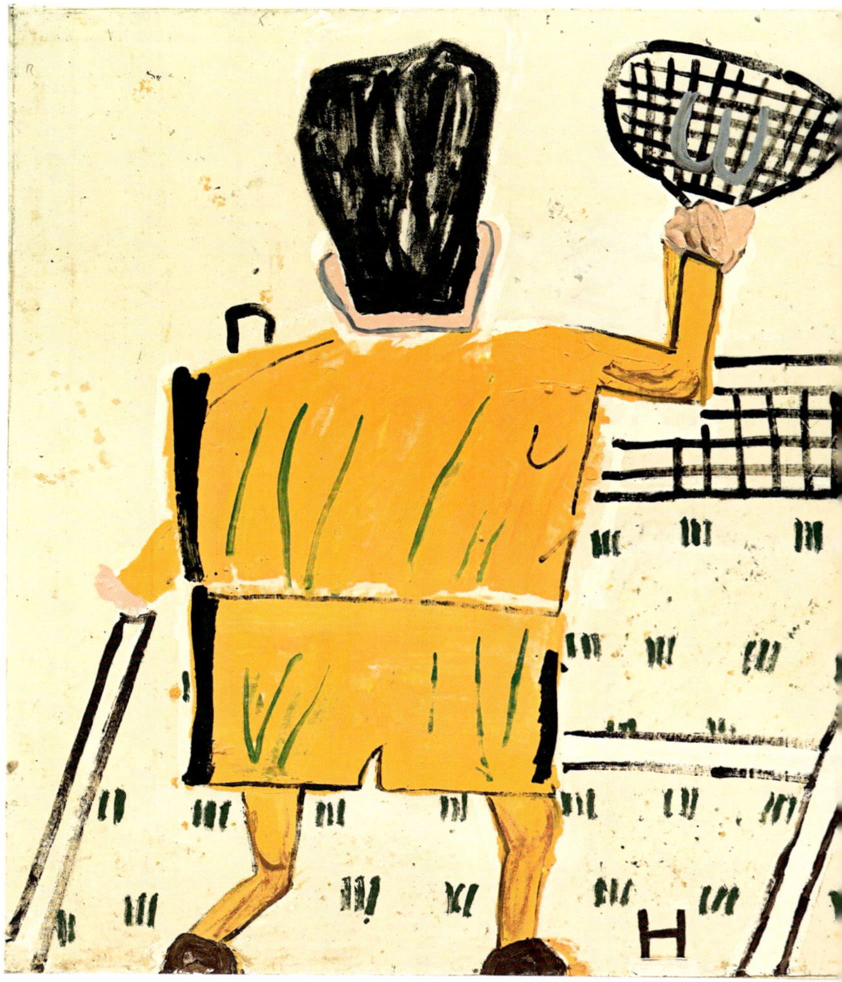

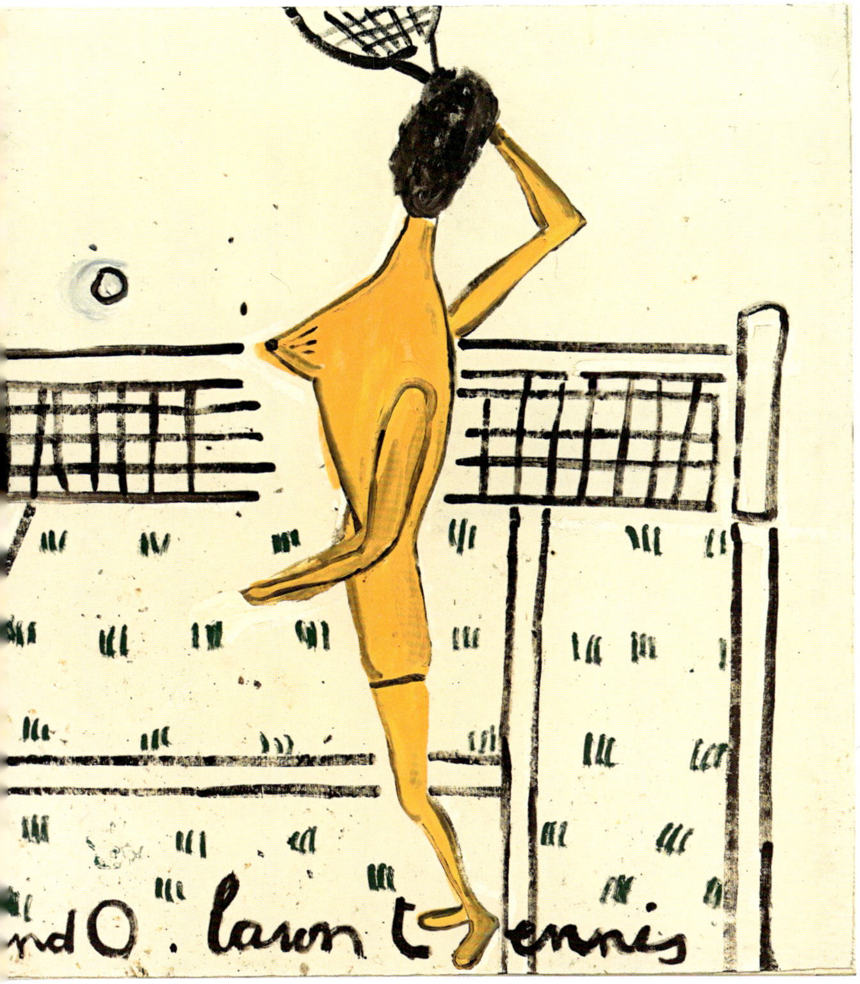

Wylie often uses 'known' subject because, as she explains, 'the viewer can see a connection in the transformation, which will have taken place . . . And with the "known" subjects the painting taps into a shared consciousness rather than the private and closed world of the artist.'[38] This is reflected in her paintings of pin-ups, film stars and sports stars. For example, fascinated by Tim Henman's hair and Venus Williams's athletic stride, the painting *H & O Tennis* 1999 (fig.36) shows them playing tennis side by side with their backs to us, and *Golf Picture* 2006 (fig.37) is painted out of respect for Tiger Woods's achievements as a golfer. The large painting *Yellow Strip* 2006 (fig.41) shows five footballers bouncing balls, while *Footballers' Heads* 2004 (fig.38) brings together Wylie's observations from watching football on the television with her husband, on Wayne Rooney, Peter Crouch ('his shorts just hang off his legs'), the German goalkeeper Jens Lehman, and Ronaldinho who 'twitches his pony-tail and does a lot of back kicks'.[39] For Wylie,

> Painting is not about generalities but particularities, and although whose (or which) particularities they are may not be recognised at once, I hope it is seen that they are there anyway: otherwise the 'look' would not be as it is. I feel a particular 'look' of, say, a leg, which gets you going in the first place, should strongly be there in the painting, otherwise there's no point. It is the moving from legs-in-general to this leg that I would like people to get. There is none of this in abstraction. Another route to particularity is to make a written description of a person (or tree) and then to illustrate that list in the painting. This allows a summing-up of observed particulars, but with another kind of visualisation at work. So, it is about readability, but from a different-yet-linked beginning, with its own process: conceptual projection from a mental image. The result, the image, will be easily 'read', but the 'sideways jump' from direct observation to get there, would be less obvious.[40]

While it may seem odd that work teeming with aspects of contemporary popular culture should also be rich in associations to art history, the contrast highlights Wylie's singularity. Like medieval paintings that garland the actions of saints with scrolled scriptural

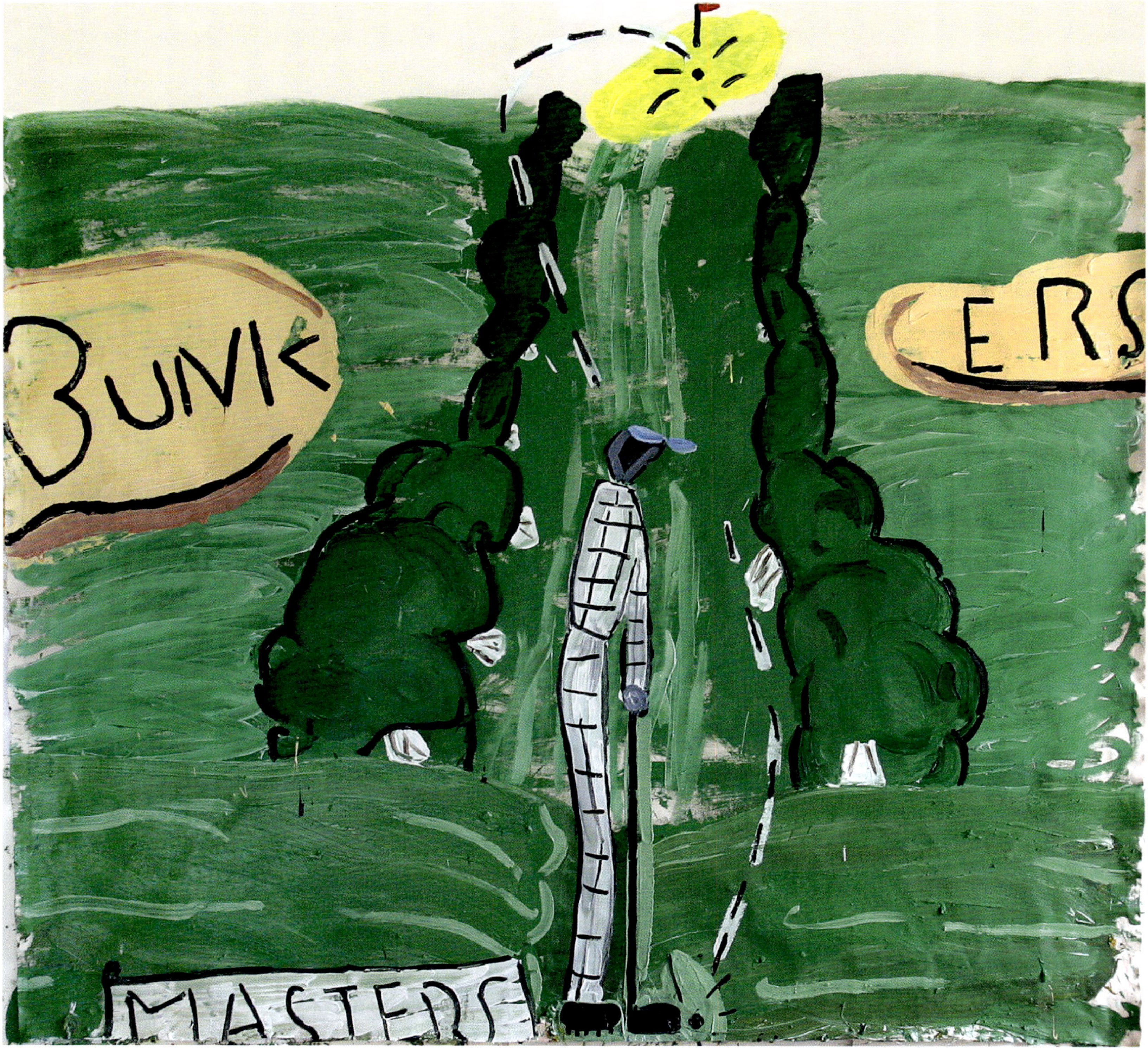
BUNK
ERS
MASTERS

37
Golf Picture 2006
Oil on canvas, 183 × 183 cm (72⅛ × 72⅛ in)
Private collection

passages, bracketing meanings between image and word, Wylie's robust paintings and refined prose do the same. 'I see my paintings continuing an art-historical conversation in every sense, from all of art history but particularly from the ancients. They are always so good.'[41] She is equally enthusiastic about Sigmar Polke (1941–2010), a key figure in a generation of German artists who emerged in the 1960s, as well as about comic books, children's transfers, manga, illuminated manuscripts and Mexican votive paintings, because in all these sources she has identified a tendency to isolate and individualise rather than to knit elements of the picture together to create a seamless illusionistic whole. The illustrations from Jean de Brunhoff's 1931 classic story *Babar the Elephant*, one of Wylie's favourite children's book, also made an impression on her, as seen in the green and yellow colour palette of *Yellow Lily* 2004 (fig.42) and the rendering of the tufts of grass which surround the white flower.

What unites Wylie's output is a kind of anarchic and satirical attitude or world view, a tongue-in-cheek, subversive spirit that has little time for stuffy hierarchies or bourgeois conventions. Her distinctive works have a sense of fluidity that suggests that they have been executed in a short space of time, yet this is not the case. Though they may seem to embody a sense of simplicity, Wylie is actually a careful and meticulous worker. Each painting is planned in great detail, and images are gathered from different sources and developed in drawings.

Her compositions and motifs are informed by cut-and-paste techniques, collaging fragmented images and snippets of information, and framing devices such as cartoon strips and the predella panels found at the base of Renaissance altarpieces. Figures, often culled from newspapers, films, books and photographs, are chosen for the effect the image has had on her – the feelings, memories, ideas and associations it brings about. For Wylie, painting always has a subject, and each is an attempt at comprehension, to catch the reality behind the immediate. As Cherry Smyth describes:

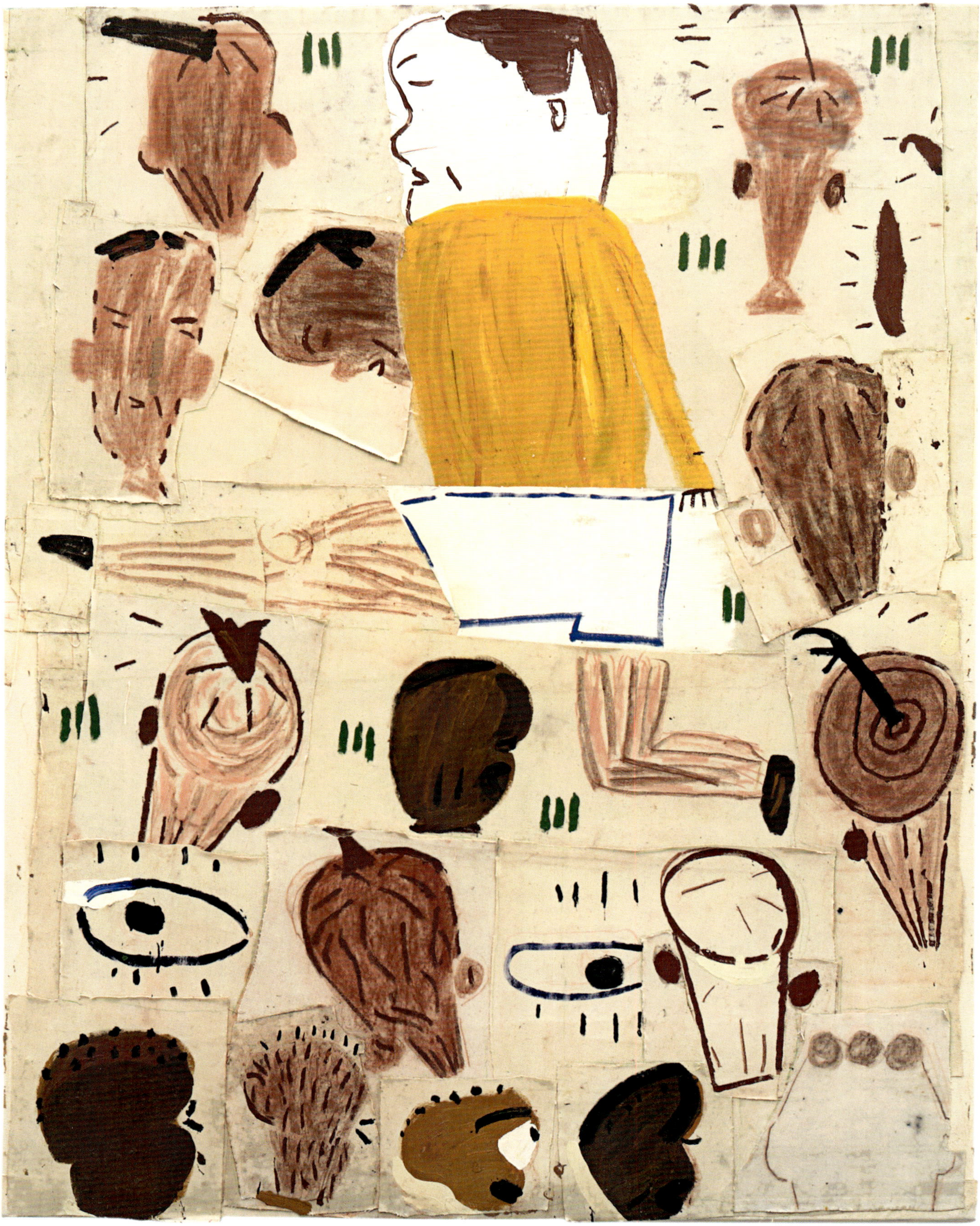

38 (left)
Footballers' Heads 2004
Oil on canvas, 207 × 168 cm (81½ × 66¼ in)
Private collection

39
Rooney & Ronaldinho 2006
Pencil, biro and collage on paper
30 × 42 cm (11⅞ × 16⅝ in)
Private collection

40
Footballer Heads 2006
Chalk, coloured pencil and collage on paper
30 × 43 cm (11⅞ × 17 in)
Private collection

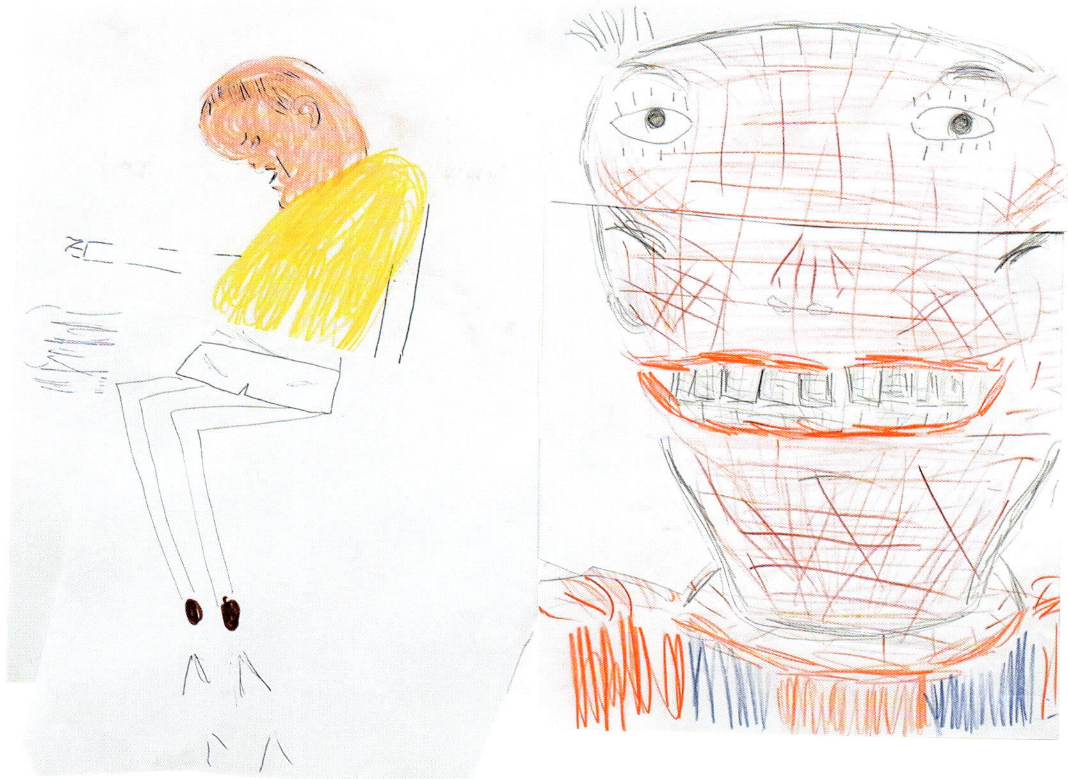

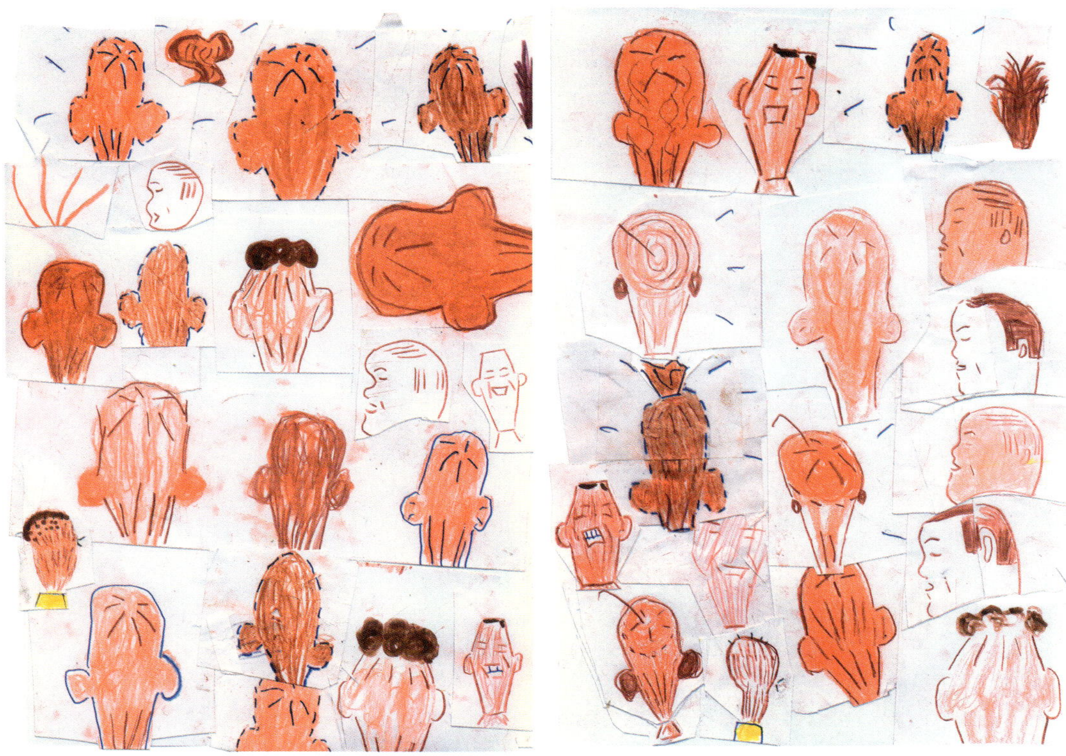

Wylie uses a levelling of perspective, awkward composition and unruly scale, so that no line or gesture is granted more importance than the next, which delivers an enthralling freedom for the viewer. The eye has to relearn where to go. It has to re-navigate the rules of representation by examining how she resurrects subjects to convey her own, very different and idiosyncratic reality.[42]

To return to the painter André Lhote, as Wylie points out, Lhote's exploration of 'direction' notes that contrary to the more realistic linear perspectival convention, 'lines of perspective in drawing can go the opposite way'.[43] For example, with Eastern, rather than Western, conventions of visual representation, the lines of sight 'open out' from the narrow concentration of 'near' to wide inclusion of breath, in the distance of 'far'.[44] This use of reverse perspective has the visual effect that objects farther away

41
Yellow Strip 2006
Oil and chalk on canvas
183 × 777 cm (72⅛ × 306 in)
Private collection

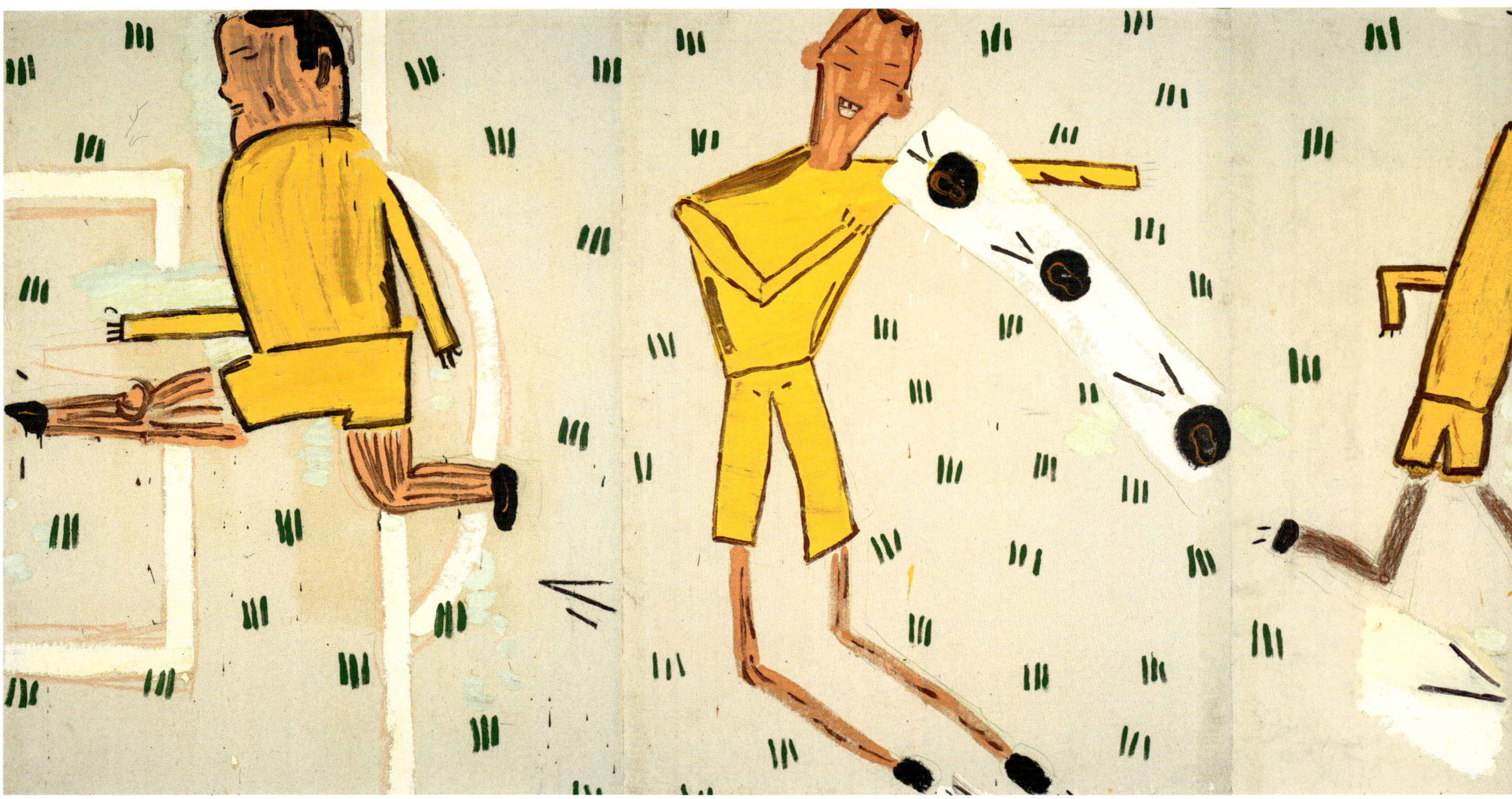

from the viewing plane are drawn as larger, and closer objects are drawn as smaller. This technique is found in Byzantine and Russian Orthodox icons, both admired by Wylie; it is also found in the art of many pre-Renaissance cultures, and was sometimes used in cubism and other movements of modern art, as well as in children's drawings. Elsewhere, as Wylie is keen to note, in order to achieve their careful edition of reality, the artists of Ancient Egypt also avoided a single perspective – for example, a room seen from one corner. Instead, they adopted the most characteristic aspect of each element, building up a composite perspective image. Over five hundred years, from around 3100 to 2600 BCE, they developed a harmonious canon of proportions, controlling the angle of view, and the size of each part in relation to the whole. As Wylie explains, 'I also use perspective . . . and sometimes within the Eastern perspectival theories of André Lhote or the

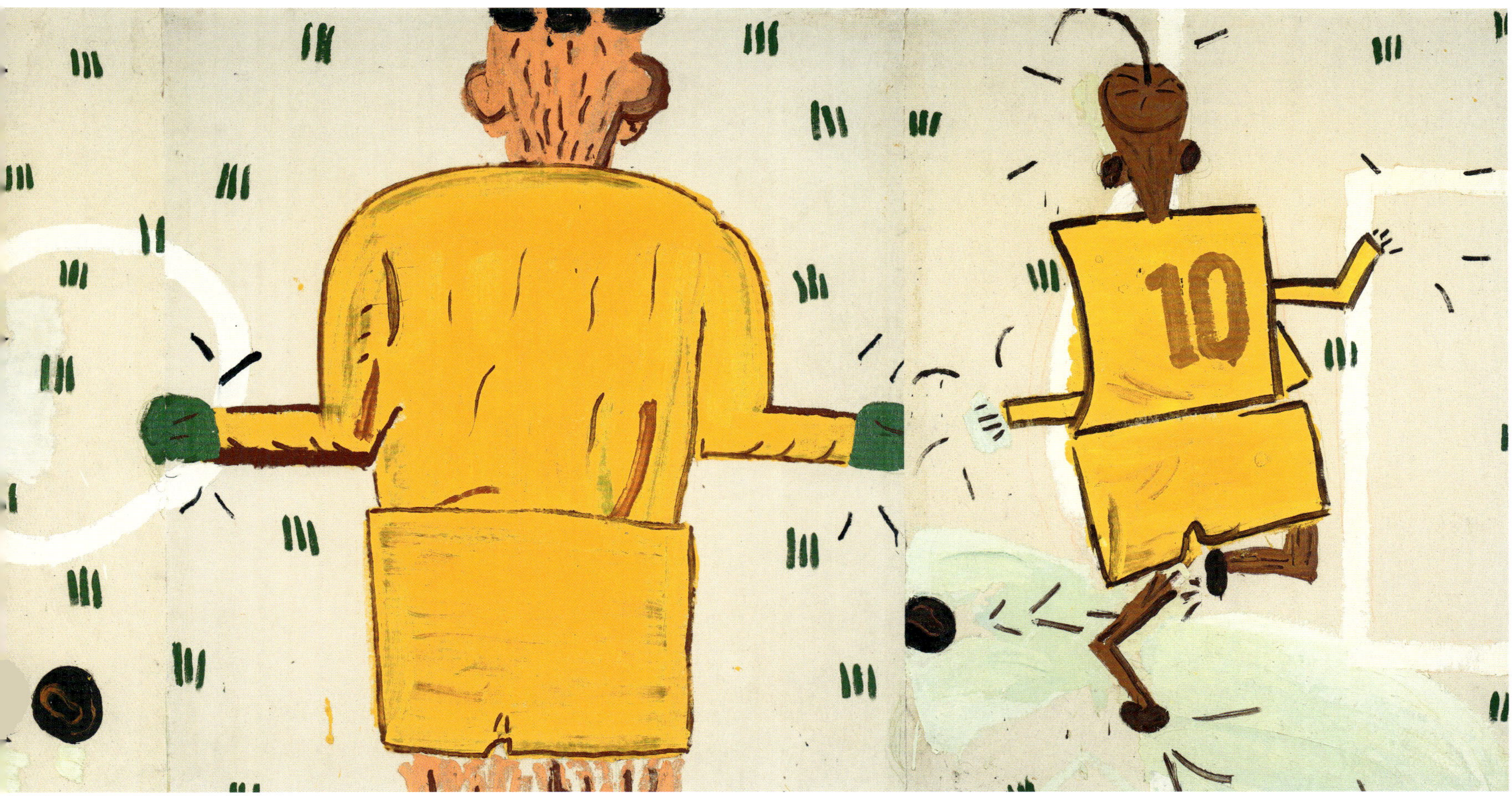

42
Yellow Lily 2004
Oil on canvas, 183 × 183 cm (72⅛ × 72⅛ in)
Private collection

principles of Russian icon painting. Or I may organise space from the ideas of "objects in isolation" of Fernand Léger, or some system or another of the most important form as the biggest (i.e. head or eyes).'[45]

Wylie uses memory as a useful sidestep from the neutrality of direct observation and drawing. The elements of chance (or happenstance) are also something that informs much of the artist's practice. Her works are populated by accessible, shared figures from film, art history and the everyday, magnified. Transformations are easier to spot if you know the subject, and her work brings this to the fore in a montage of remembered images and references. Wylie often makes changes to her drawings and adds to them if necessary, as for example in *Pip Up and Porn Queen Jigsaw* 2005 (fig.43), a painting on four panels. The pin-up head is loosely based on the actress Marilyn Monroe and the flower-printed outfit she wore in the film *The Misfits*, directed by John Huston in 1961. The semi-cross-hatch treatment of her hair echoes the cross-hatching technique in the woodcuts of Albrecht Dürer (1471–1528) whose work the artist admires, especially the simpler work. The porn queen figure, shown in profile on the upper right-hand panel looking at the pin-up, is based on the pornographic film star Annabel Chong. This was drawn from Wylie's memory of watching a TV documentary about her where 'her soft turban style headgear' particularly struck her.[46] The black jigsaw-like pattern of dotted lines and numbers originated from a related drawing where the patterns of numbered collage pieces became an integral part of the work. This method of adding sections to make her working area larger as and when required also extends to her paintings where her linear language is translated onto large unprimed and unstretched canvas, until recently, laid out on the floor, preferring it as an alternative to an easel or wall as it gave her more room to work with. When asked about it she replied: 'I suppose it's the opposite of the rather fancy male painter on his easel. Traditionally men go out to work and women potter around the house cleaning. Painting on the floor linked to a lot about women's lives – or far too much of it, anyway – things about scrubbing and cleaning on your hands and knees.'[47]

Wylie likes to work on a number of paintings simultaneously. The drawn and re-drawn layers and collaged elements give them a

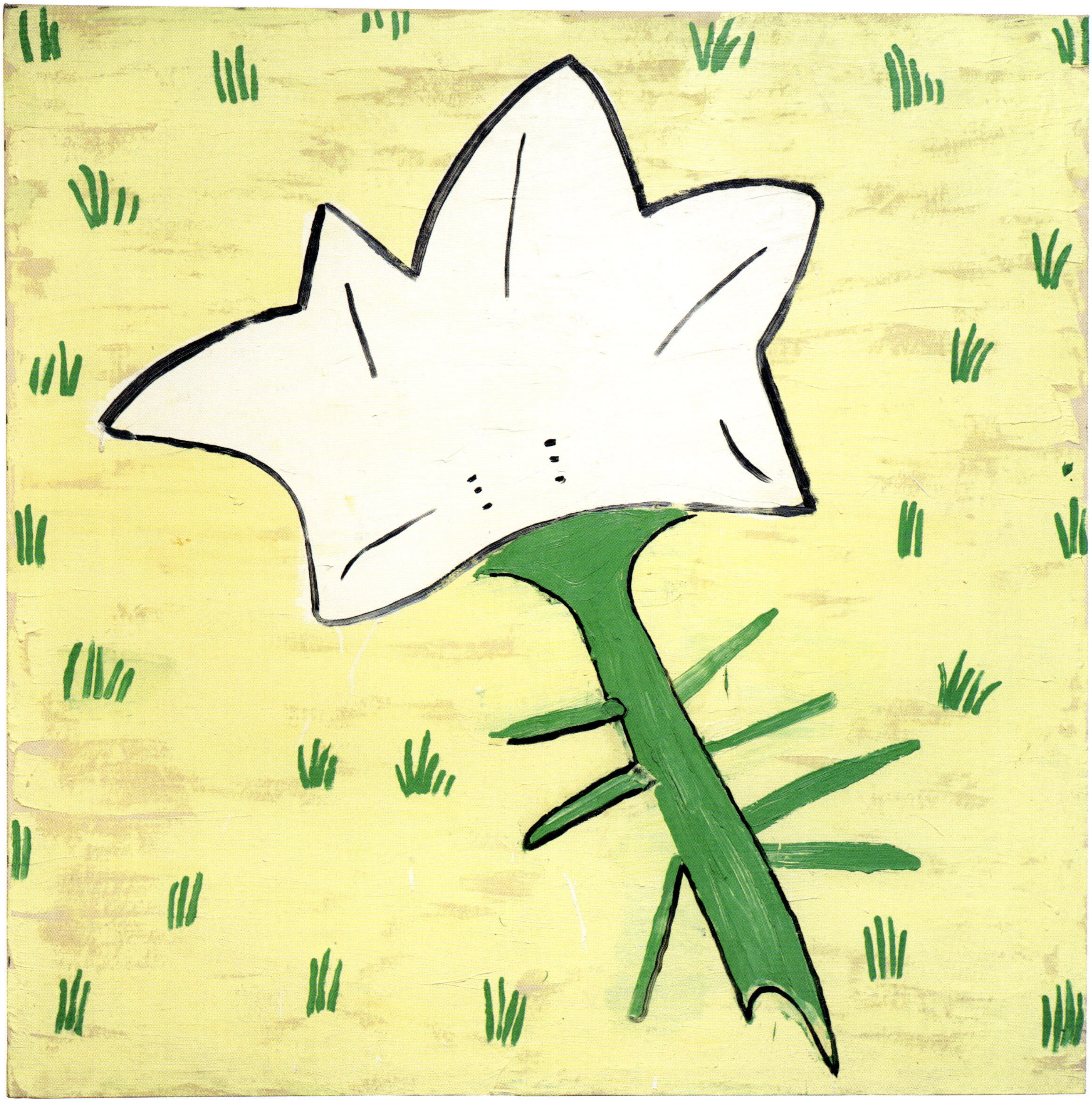

43
Pin Up and Porn Queen Jigsaw 2005
Oil on canvas, 346 × 346 cm (136¼ × 136¼ in)
Tate

relaxed feel. She tends to paint right up to the edges and later glues the canvas onto large strips, which are then attached to a stretcher. The object quality of the painting is important. Her work is associative. Often using 6-by-6 ft square units, discrete paintings can be grouped together in ever-varying combinations. They are frequently arranged like an open book, so that they take on the angles found at the corner of a room and create pictorial spaces reminiscent of antique frescos or friezes, extending around a bend or up the wall. As the artist explains, 'I do like big work. I like billboards. I like very early decorated churches where the paintings go from floor to ceiling and up arches and round the door. I've always thought it's a very convenient way of using spaces in galleries and spaces anywhere. I find it more exciting and it can expand.'[48] And:

> I often make a lot of drawings of one subject, then, the choice of which one to paint from, if any, is the next jump; and as work progresses, or ends, there is sometimes the nagging feeling that another choice could've been better: so I try another drawing . . . it isn't necessarily better, not at all . . . but it's different: it keeps things open, and to the point here, more work gets done. This moves me on through many possibilities, and keeps me 'at it' . . . and would also account for a series of related paintings as in the three *Boy Meets Girl* group [figs 44, 45 and 48]. Or, as in the five *Black Strap* paintings [figs 49–51], some alternatives were reconsidered, or simply built on, or redirected . . . though none of this engages with any qualitative difference between the paintings, but only with exploration. This process means I can try something new, something that without it would not have happened: one new 'try-out' is suggested by an earlier 'leave-it-as-it-is', and the more you have going, if you can face it . . . the better.[49]

Wylie's graduation from the Royal College of Art in 1981 coincided with the exhibition *A New Spirit in Painting*, which opened at the Royal Academy in spring of that year.[50] The exhibition included the first presentation in Britain of work by an international group of artists: representatives of an emerging generation of German painters such as Gerhard Richter (b.1932), Georg Baselitz (b.1938) and Sigmar Polke, artists of the Italian Transavanguardia, together with Philip Guston (1913–1980), late Willem de Kooning (1904–1997)

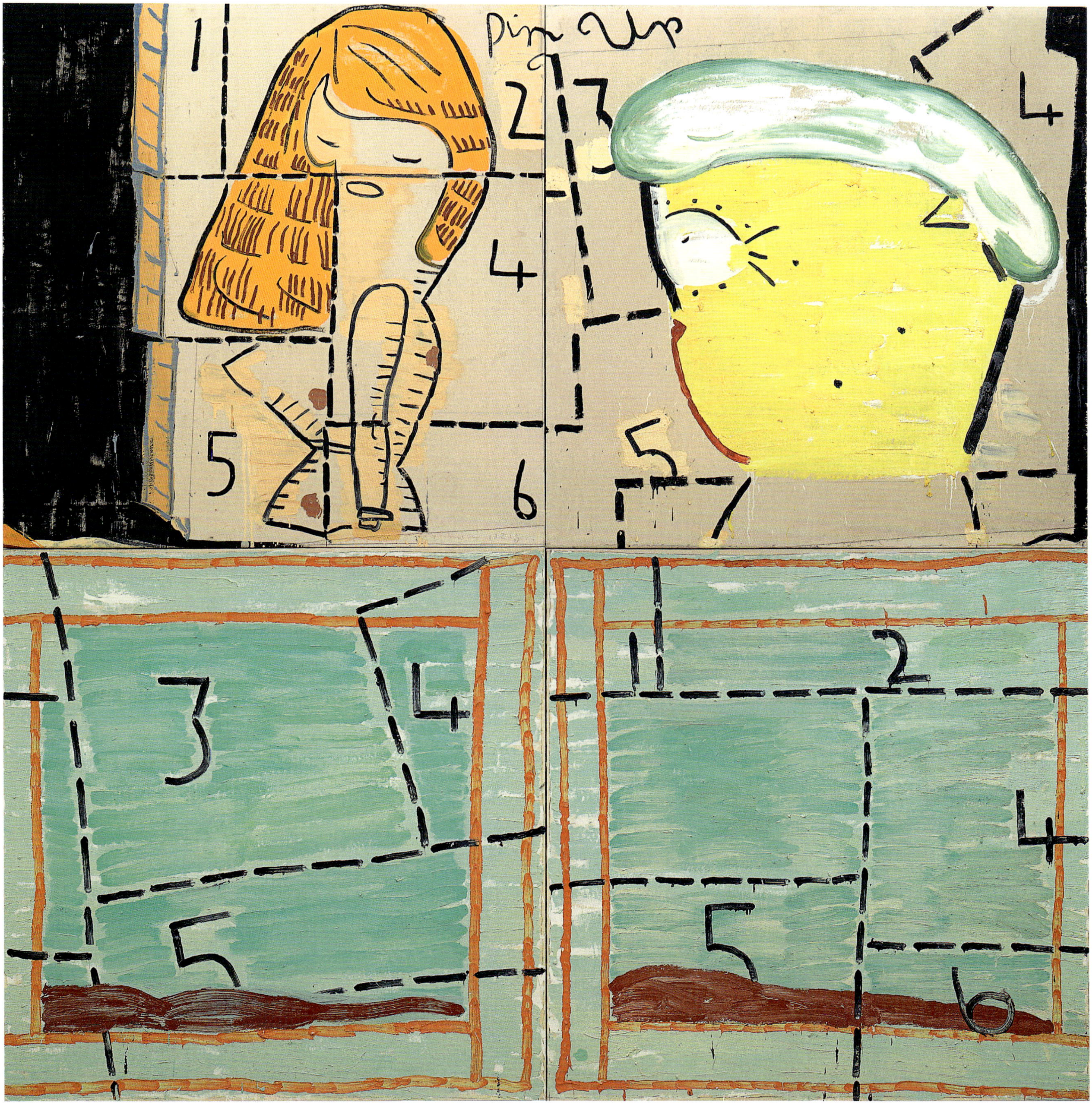
Pin Up

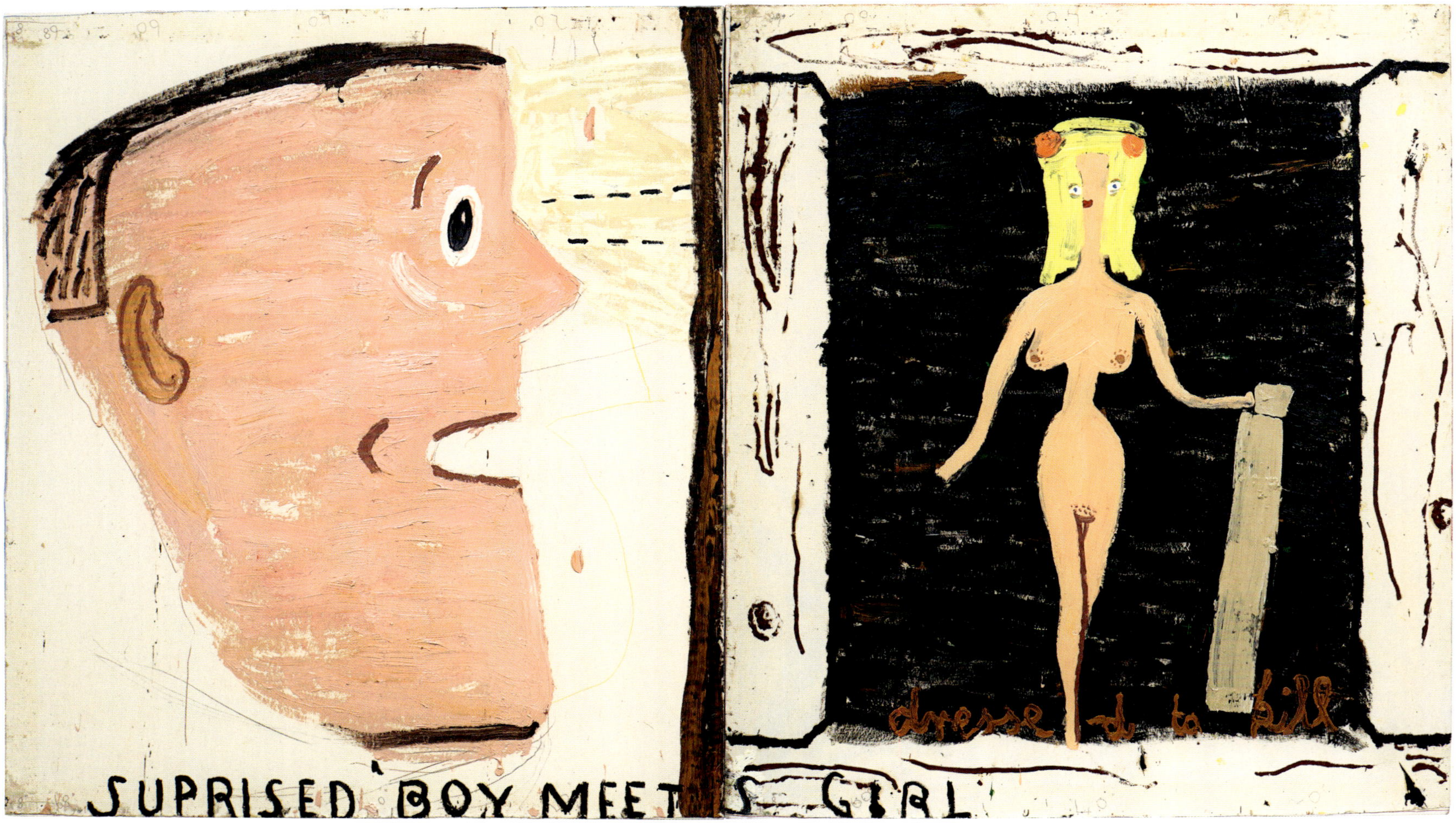

44
Surprised Boy Meets Girl 2015
Oil on canvas, 183 × 328 cm (72⅛ × 129¼ in)
Private collection

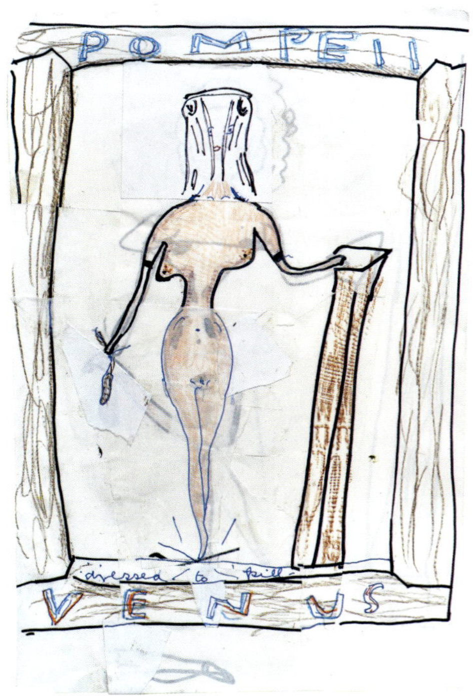

45
Boy Meets Girl from Pompeii
(study for painting) 2015
Coloured pencil, marker, biro and collage on paper
30 × 42 cm (11⅞ × 16⅝ in)
Private collection

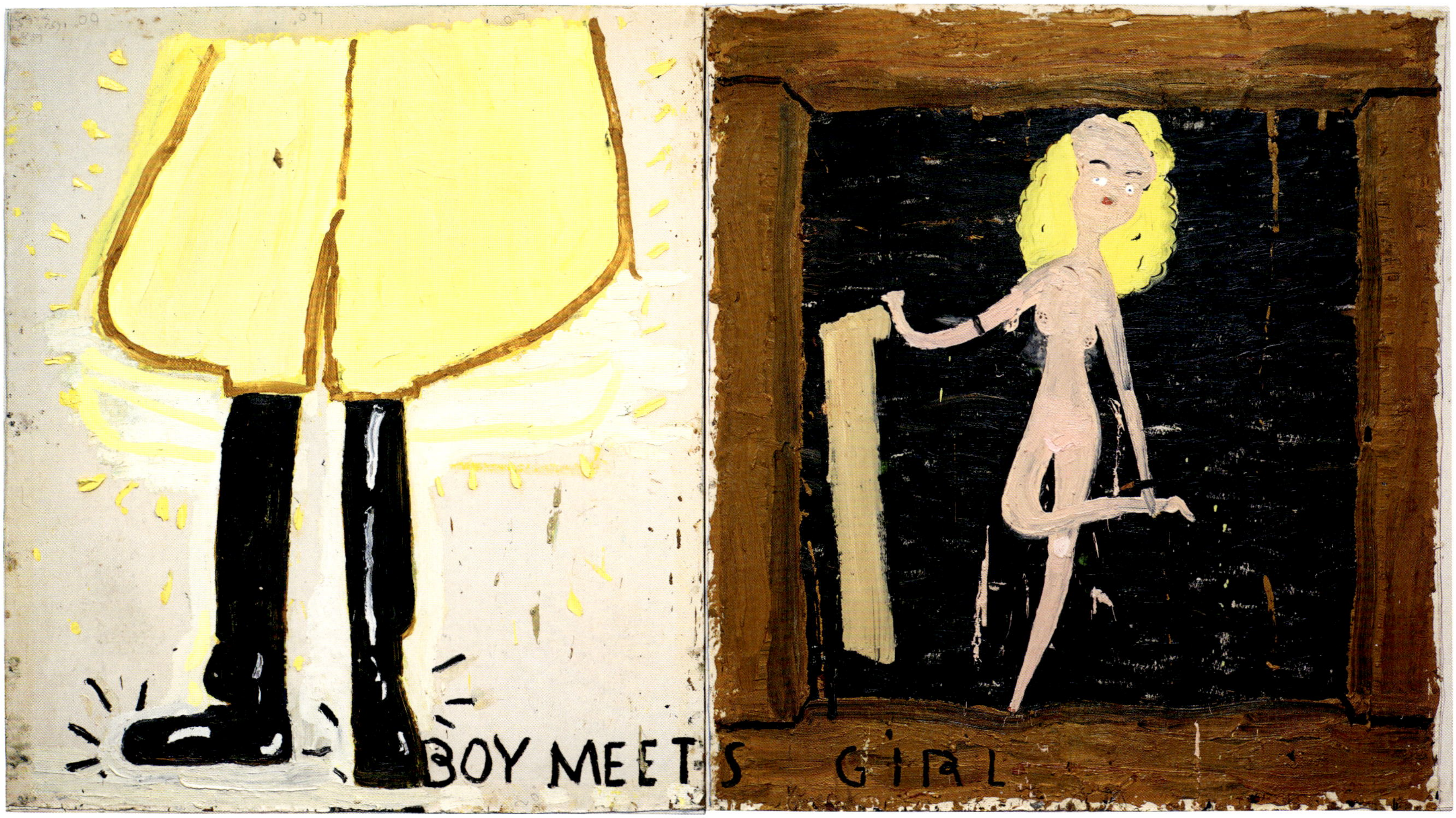

46
Boy Meets Girl (Boots) 2015
Oil on canvas, 183 × 328 cm (72⅛ × 129¼ in)
Private collection

47
Venus (Girl) (Study 6 – Dressed to Kill) 2015
Marker, pen, coloured pencil and collage on paper
30 × 21 cm (11⅞ × 8⅜ in)
Private collection

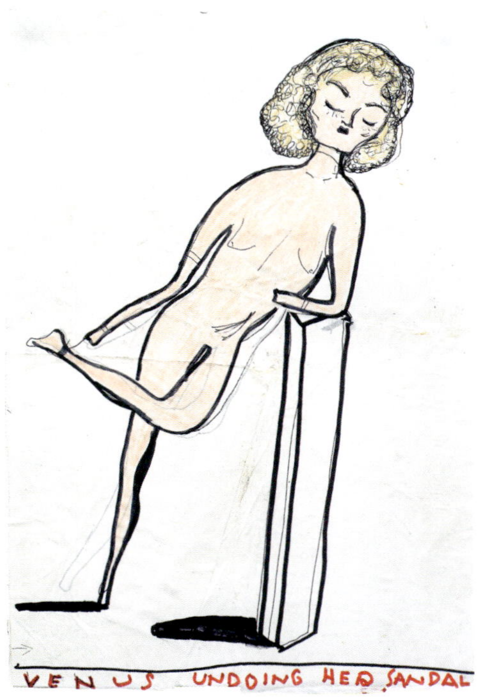

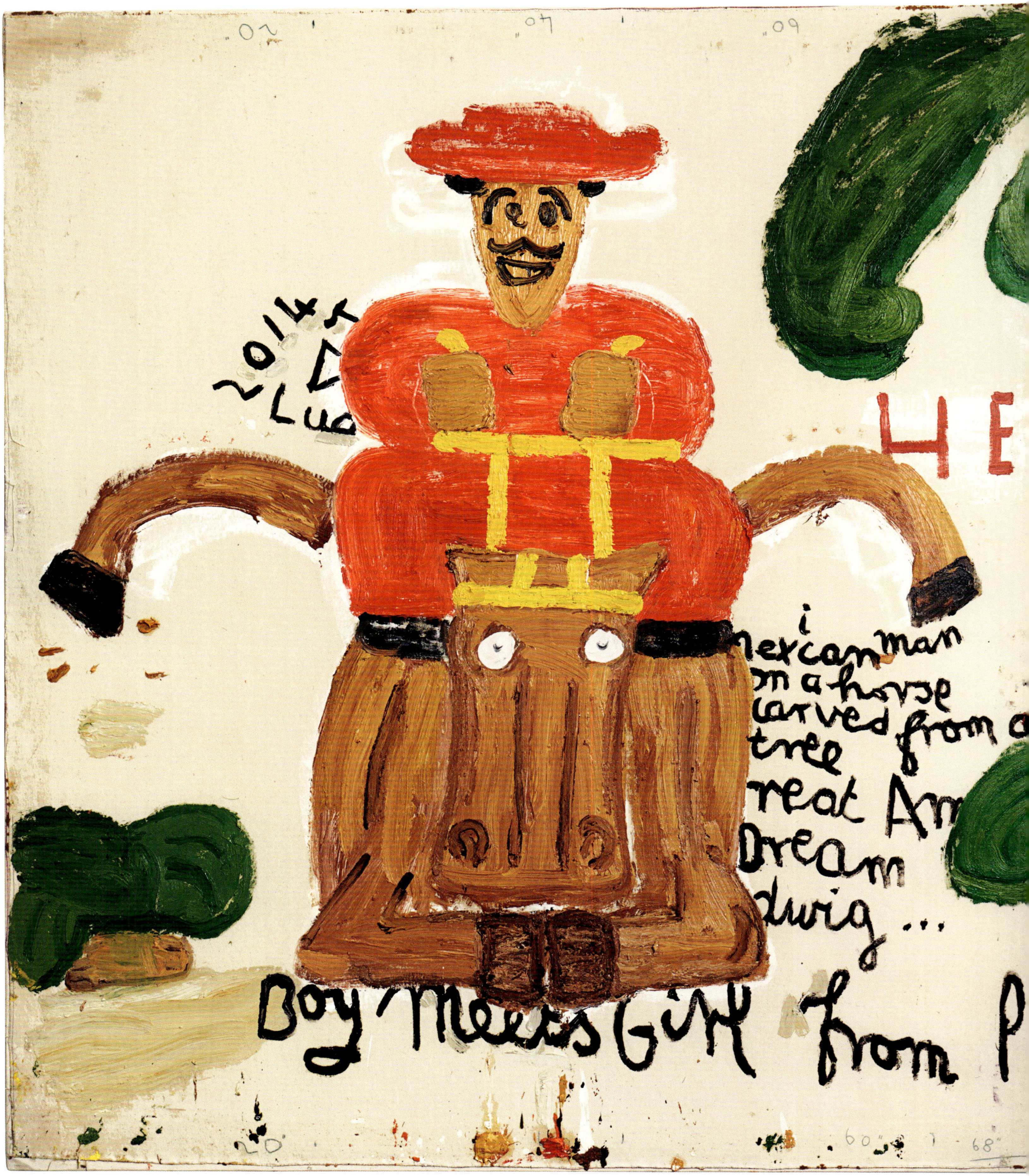
2014
HE
i
excan man
n a horse
carved from a
tree
reat Am
Dream
dwig ...
Boy Meets Girl from

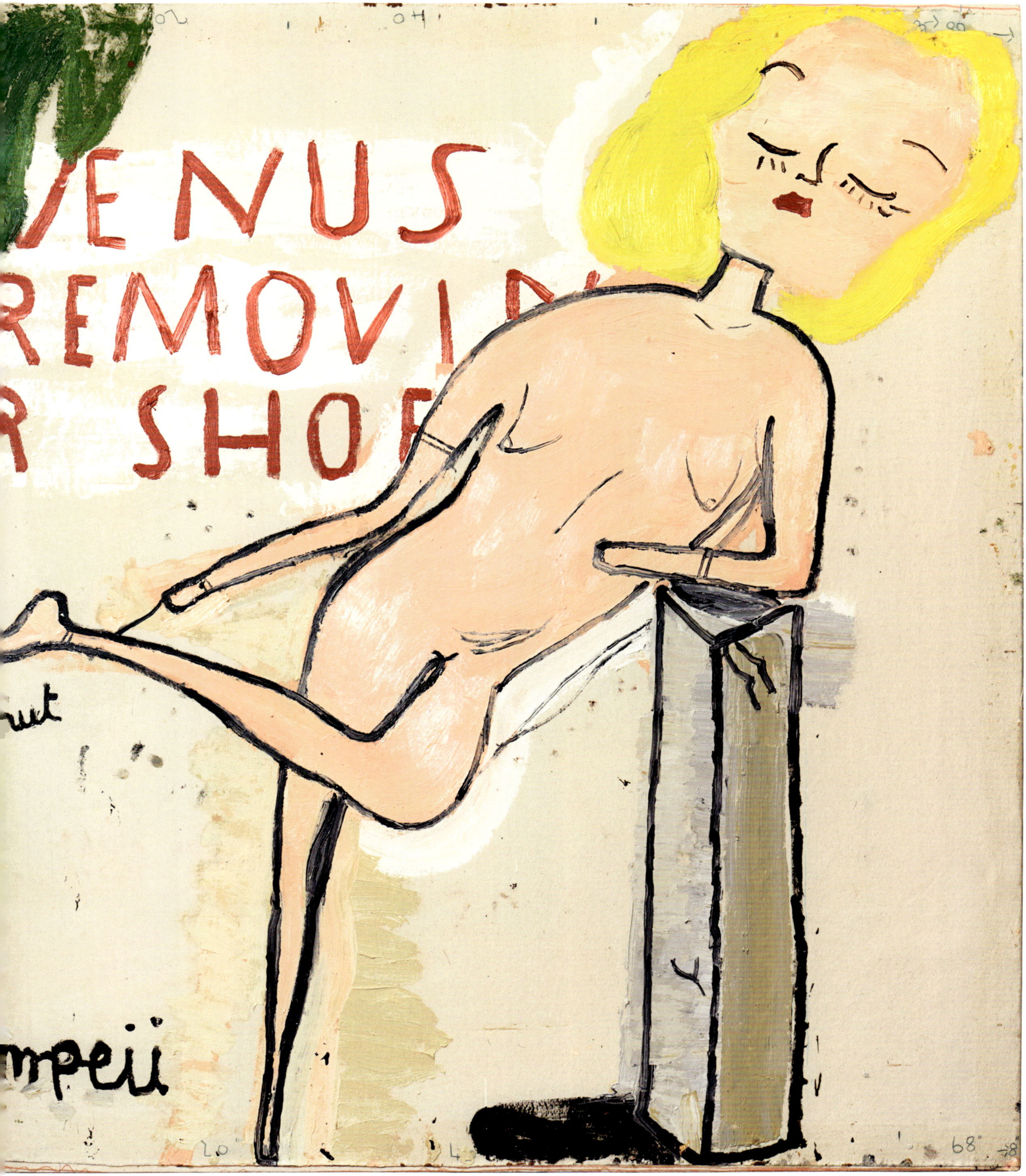
ENUS
REMOVI
R SHO
ut
mpeü

48 (previous page)
Boy Meets Girl from Pompeii 2015
Oil on canvas, 184 × 335 cm (72½ × 132 in)
Collection of the Institute of Reconciliation, La Paila, Colombia

49
Black Strap (Red Fly) 2014
Oil on canvas, 184 × 332 cm (72½ × 130¾ in)
Private collection

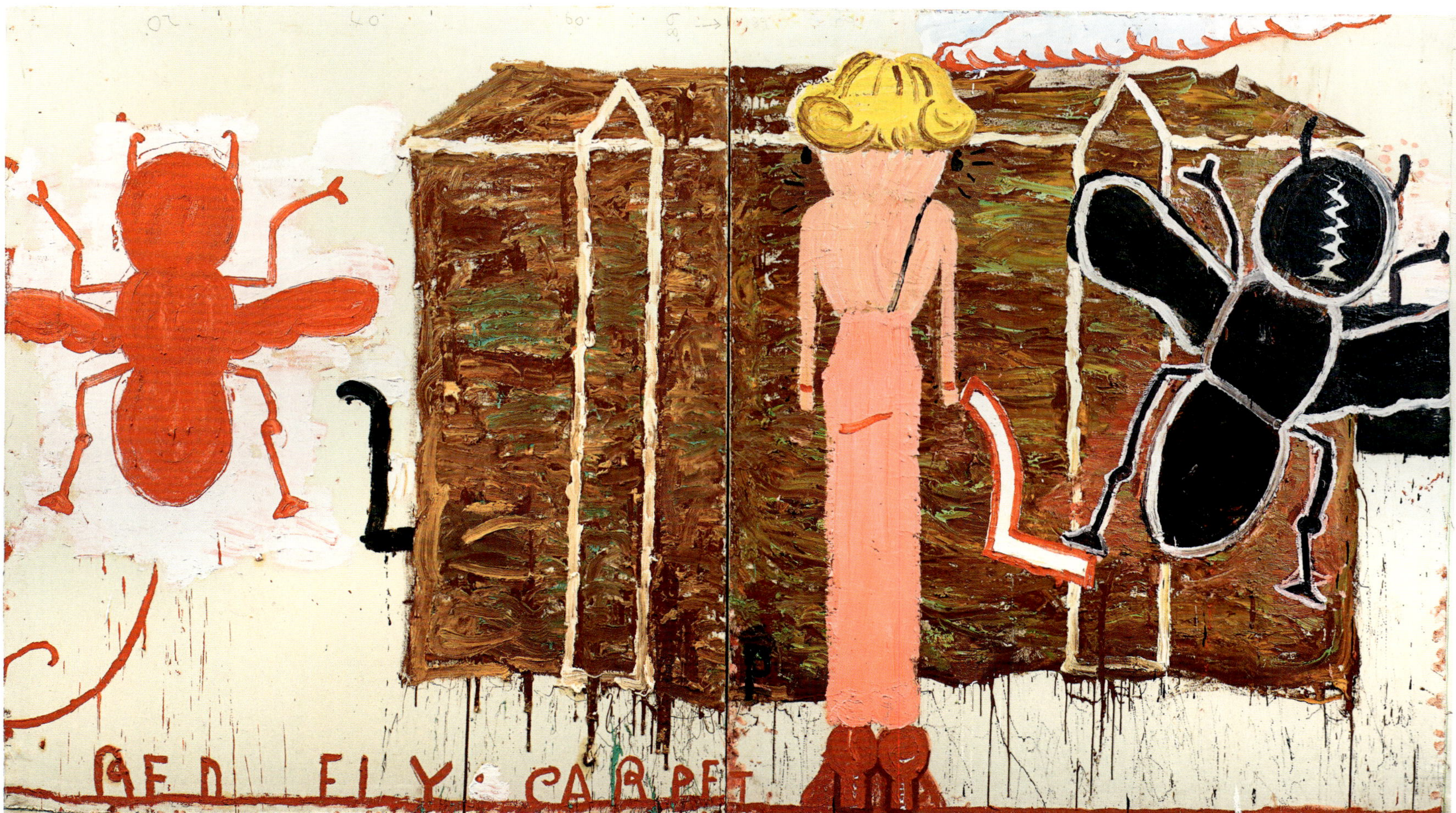

50
Black Strap (Eyelashes) 2014
Oil on canvas, 184 × 331 cm (72½ × 130⅜ in)
Private collection

51 (overleaf)
Black Strap (Eye) 2014
Oil on canvas, 184 × 326 cm (72½ × 128⅜ in)
Private collection

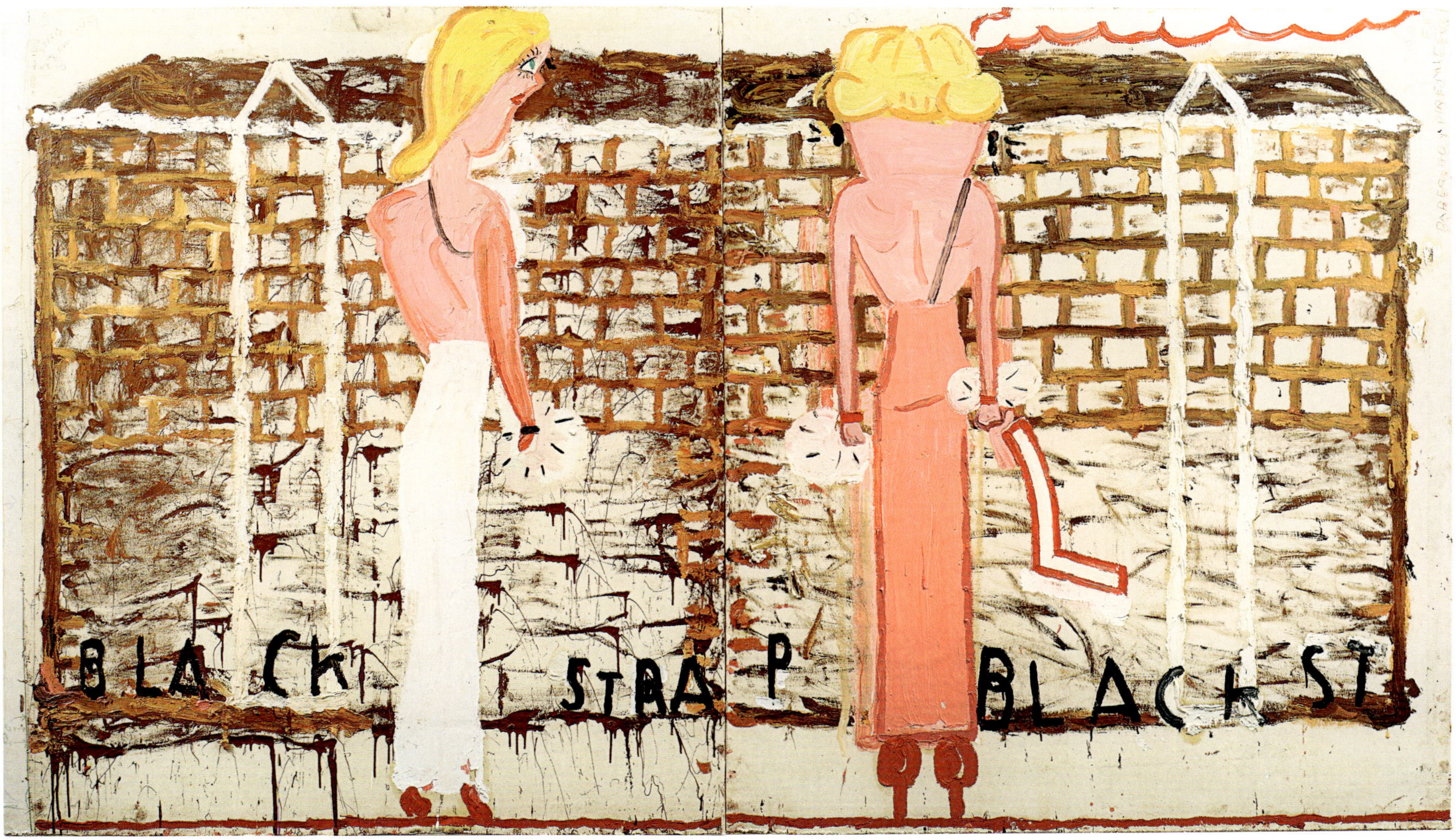

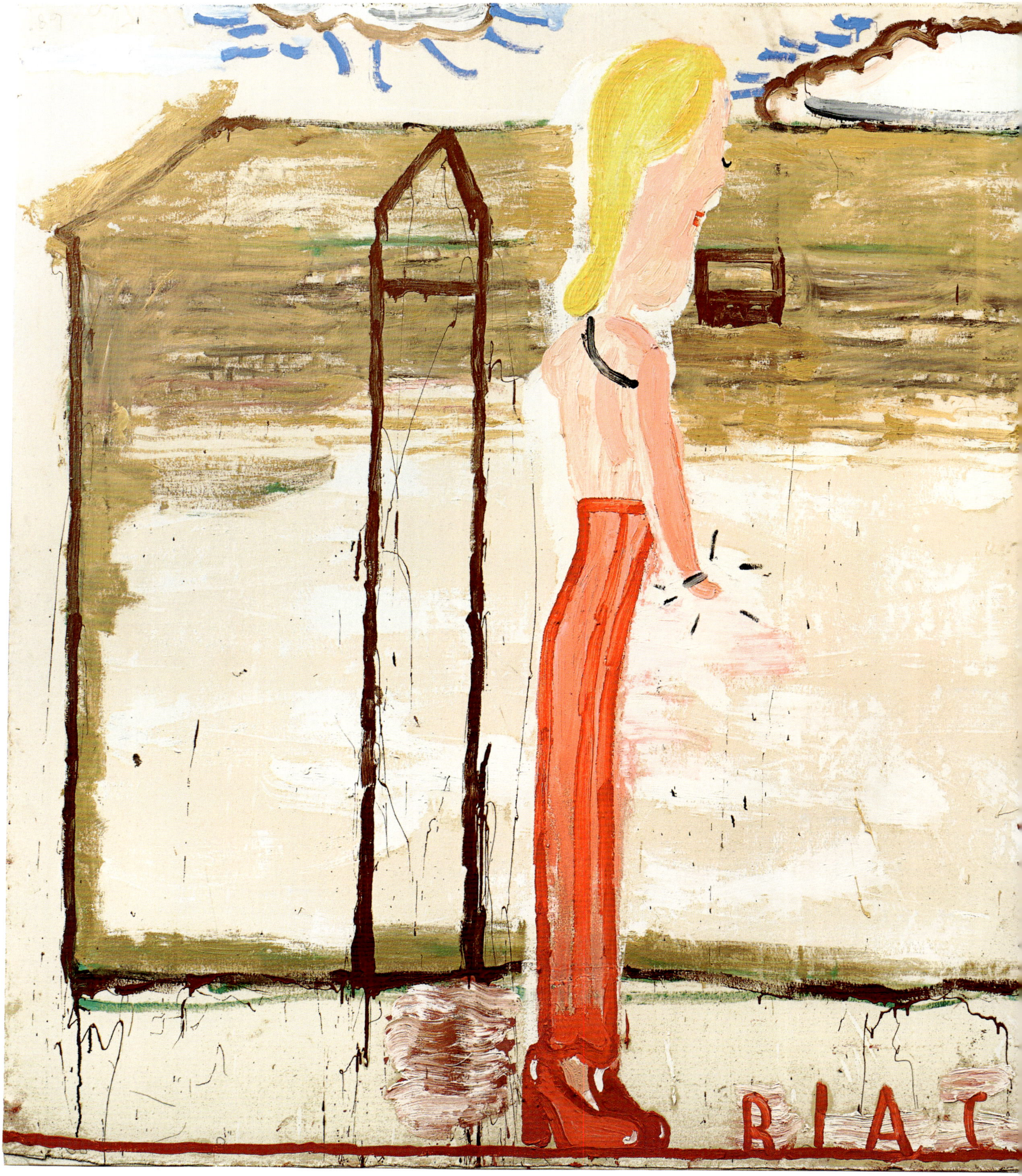
R I A

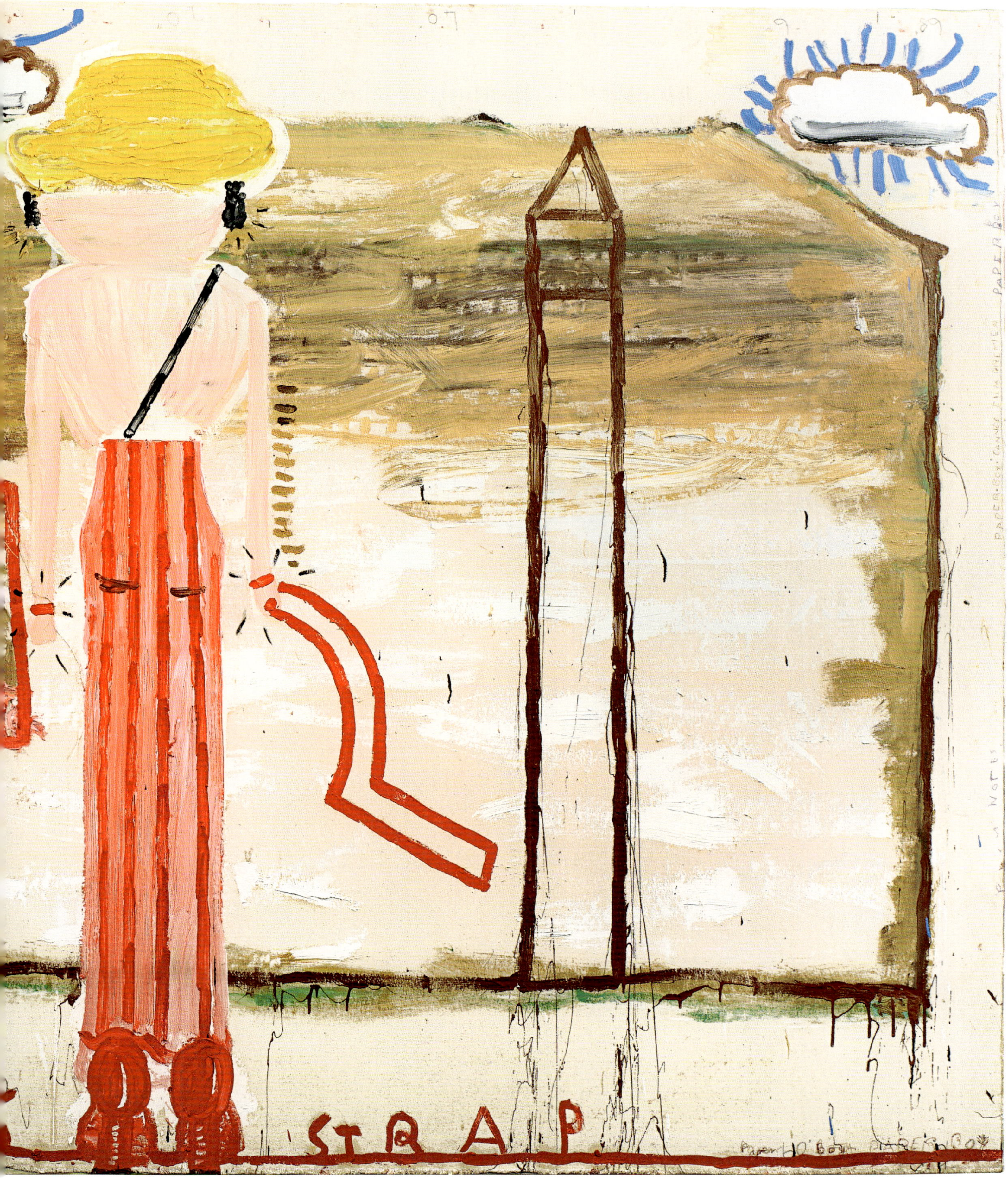
STRAP

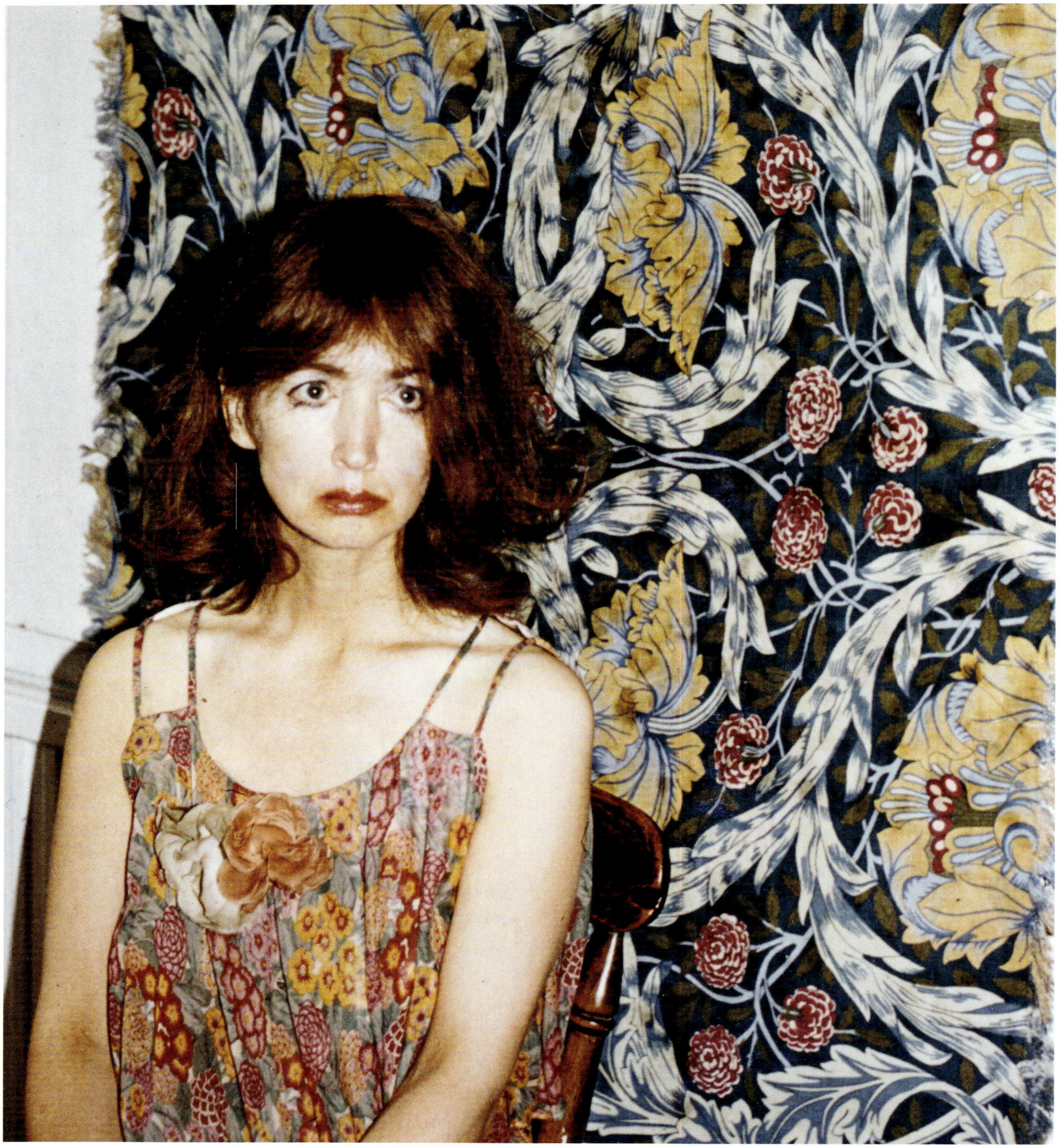

52
Rose Wylie, 1982
Collection of the artist

and a young Julian Schnabel (b.1951). This exhibition captured the zeitgeist and changed the perception of contemporary painting on both sides of the Atlantic, signalling a revival of figuration and self-expression as well as a recovery of myth, history, symbols and eroticism as subject matter. The use of narrative, language, the figure and explicit references to art history and the real world are all found within Wylie's practice too.

Wylie's long hiatus from painting makes it difficult to position her work comfortably into the standard trajectory of British figurative painting in the 1980s which includes the work of Frank Auerbach (b.1931), R.B. Kitaj (1932–2007) and Paula Rego (b.1935) or other 'figurative' and expressionist artists of the time – for example, Peter de Francia (1921–2012), Timothy Hyman (b.1946), Jeffery Camp (b.1923) and Ken Kiff (1935–2001). In this sense it is apparent that she is not part of a 'generation' but rather she forged her own path, drawing on her own influences and only later re-engaging with the art world. Recognition for women artists has not always come quickly or easily. It could also be that her lack of engagement with the art world throughout the 1980s and 1990s and her comparative invisibility was a result of her singularity and a mark of her difference from those more acclaimed painters of her generation. However, Wylie's selection for **EAST***international* in 2004, curated by Neo Rauch and Gerd Harry Lybke, offered a significant opportunity for first exposure and led to her being represented by the gallerist Jari Lager. As Sarah Elson explains, 'I think this context revealed Rose's work to be more knowing than the naiveté of her style suggests. Like a lot of the Leipzig painters, Rose's quirky rawness is dramatically graphic but purposely opaque or even devoid of meaning. It is visceral and direct, and doesn't distinguish between tragic, comic, mundane or violent subject matter.'[51]

It was Elson, along with the curator Sheena Wagstaff, who in 2010 selected Wylie for *Women to Watch*, a biennial exhibition programme held at the National Museum of Women in the Arts, Washington, D.C., designed to promote promising female artists. The Washington exhibition featured Wylie's painting *Lords and Ladies* 2009. This international exposure marked a decisive turning point in her career.[52] It led to her work being championed by the feminist writer Germaine Greer, who visited her studio.[53]

Greer's article in *The Guardian*, titled 'Who is Britain's Hottest Artist? A 76-Year-Old Named Rose Wylie', gave Wylie the push that seemed necessary to increase her visibility.[54] This was shortly followed by the American art critic Roberta Smith's review of her New York show who described her practice as 'one of the few women . . . to enter the Jean-Michel Basquiat/Donald Baechler sweepstakes'.[55] This positive attention at the age of 76 led to a growing recognition of the singularity of Wylie's vision that was consolidated over the following eight years with solo presentations at the Jerwood Gallery, Hastings (2012), Tate Britain, London (2013), Chapter Gallery, Cardiff (2016) and the Serpentine Sackler Gallery, London (2017) amongst others. In retrospect, one can argue that she developed her own distinctive style, largely in isolation from the pressures of the art world and fads and fashions: looking back, Wylie has described how she had 'a long time painting without pressure; and getting the confidence from working without outside encouragement or fashionable demands, relying completely on yourself'.[56]

During the 1980s it was the expressive painting of Julian Schnabel and Philip Guston that captured Wylie's attention.[57] Wylie was drawn to Schnabel's open and unpretentious approach to making work, which seemed refreshing in comparison to the relatively restricted set of resources employed by the majority of American painters in the late 1970s. She was particularly interested in his paintings which drew on Roman Catholic iconography or looked like *milagros*, the votive offerings left on church altars and holy shrines throughout Mexico, given in thanks for an answered prayer or as a plea for a miracle. The use of devotional imagery that runs through Schnabel's work – for example, the severed heart in *The Afflicted Organ* 1987 – finds a parallel in a work such as *Holy Doors Picture (Film Notes)* 2011 (fig.59) by Wylie. Both artists engage with Christian iconography as used in not only the high art tradition, but also popular folk art – as evidenced by Schnabel's painting *Gothic Run Riot or Kathy Painting* 1986 (fig.58). Schnabel has first-hand experience of such folk art: when young his family lived in an area of Texas with a large Catholic Mexican population. Wylie has a more mediated relationship to such imagery, through film for example, and since the late 1980s her subject matter has often referenced characters in biblical stories.

Salome and John the Baptist's Head 1988 (fig.53), for example, depicts traditional subject matter with a well-established iconography. Salome is a New Testament figure, the daughter of Herod II and Herodias, who called for and was given the head of John the Baptist. In medieval Christian art, Salome was depicted as an embodiment of female seductiveness that lures men from the path of salvation. Salome was a subject of both painting and literature in the late nineteenth century; an embodiment of feminine evil. The *fin-de-siècle* portrayal of Salome was heavily sexualised and gendered, dwelling on both Salome's reception of John's head and her eroticised dance, mentioned in the Bible. In contrast, Wylie's *Salome* refuses this tradition: its dynamic and spontaneous neo-expressionist style retains only the basic essentials – Salome and the severed head – and avoids the orientalist trappings and

53
Salome and John the Baptist's Head 1988
Oil on paper, 143 × 178 cm (56⅜ × 70⅛ in)
Private collection

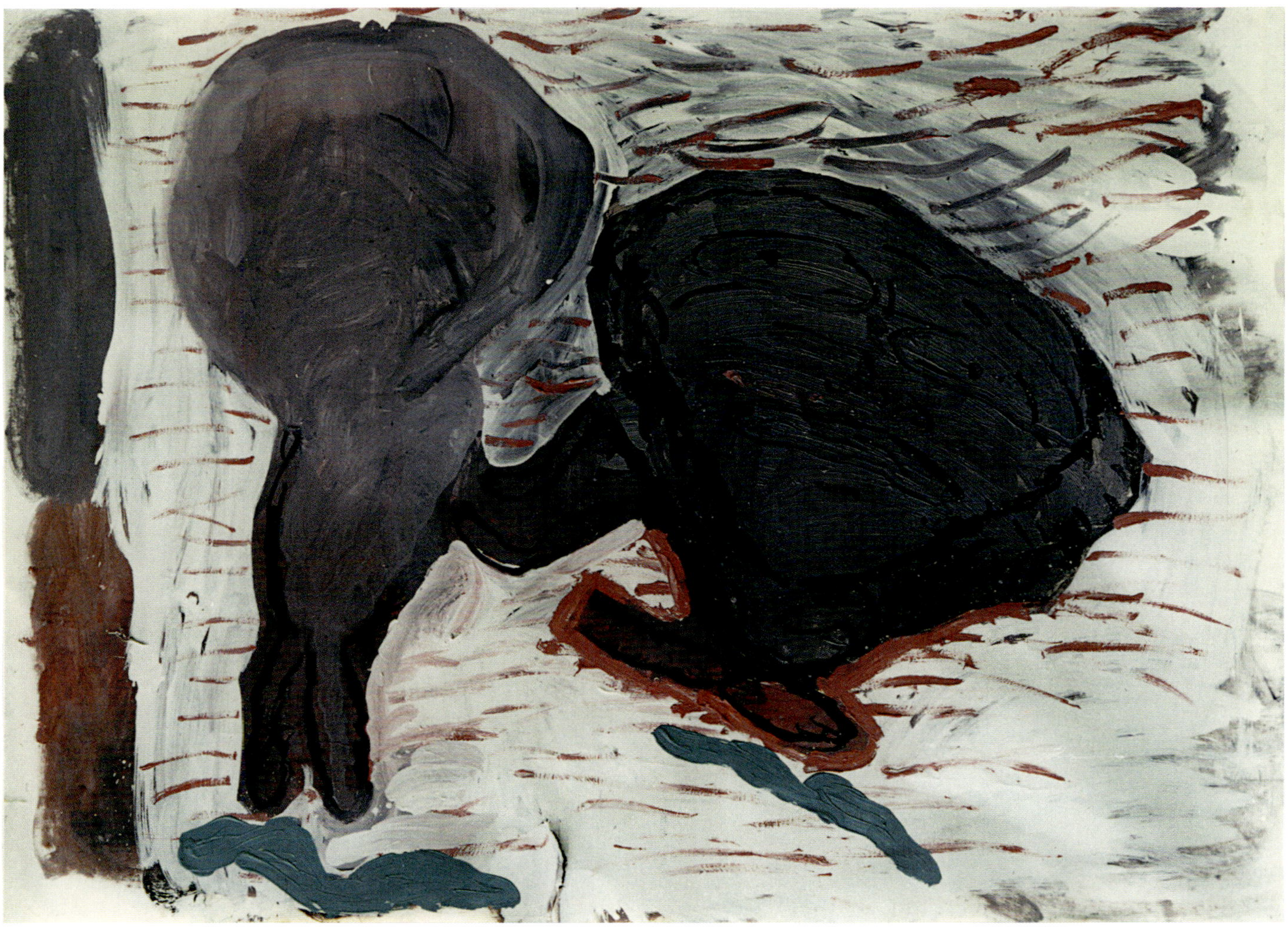

54
St Francis and with Patches 2000
Oil on canvas, 183 × 366 cm (72⅛ × 144⅛ in)
Private collection

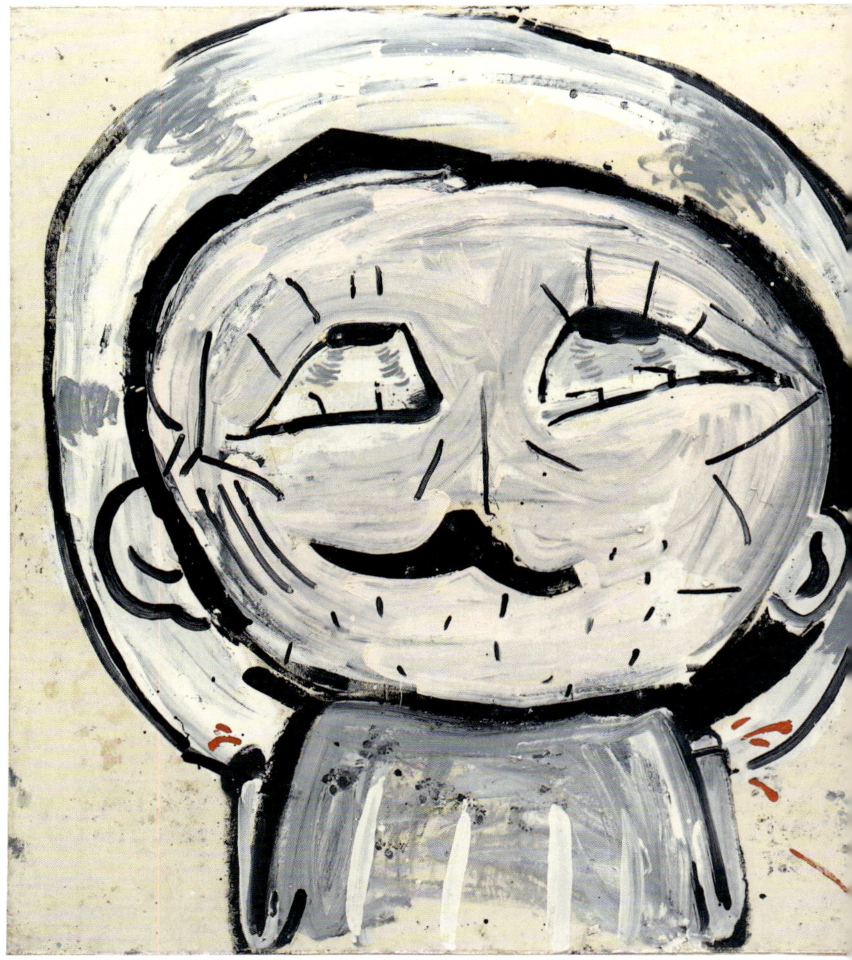

aestheticised sensuality of earlier portrayals. Salome is portrayed in a simplified, non-realist style. The outsized head is tilted back, with the eyes closed and mouth open in an ambiguous expression. John the Baptist's head is disproportionately large and seems to merge with Salome's arms and hands that hold it. The severed head, in contrast with Salome, has open but empty, dead eyes and the neck has a nimbus of scarlet blood. The blood extends from the head, flecking the background with red lines. The atmosphere of the picture is nightmarish, refusing allegorical meaning in favour of a palpable evocation of a violent event.

St Francis and with Patches 2000 (fig.54) draws from a painting by the Sienese artist known as Sassetta (1392–1450). Painted predominantly in monochromatic colours with a hint of pink, Wylie's version shows the saint, splendid with black handlebar moustache and halo, looking up towards heaven. A picture such as *Queen of Sheba and JT* 2012 (fig.55) is based on a traditional story that has been told and retold over centuries and has also been the basis of many painted versions. The original narrative is found in the Bible and tells how the Queen of Sheba visited King Solomon, hoping to test his reputation for wisdom. She arrived in Jerusalem 'with a very great retinue, with camels bearing spices, and very much gold, and precious stones' (I Kings 10:2). In later retellings more and more detail was added. In a common version King Solomon hears that the queen has hairy legs and feet that are cloven like a goat's. The king has a floor of glass built, and the Queen of Sheba, thinking it is water, raises her skirt to cross it. Her hairy legs and cloven hoof exposed, she is reprimanded by Solomon. Wylie's painting on the theme is a contemporary version that was started after seeing a reproduction of a fourteenth-century Persian miniature depicting the story in Marina Warner's 1994 book *From the Beast to the Blonde: On Fairy Tales and Their Tellers*, and in response to the availability of a new tin of emerald-green paint.[58] This dual inspiration, in an art historical source and the materiality of what is at hand (the emerald paint), shows Wylie's engagement with the process of painting itself. The emerald green is used in the dress worn by the three figures of the queen. The

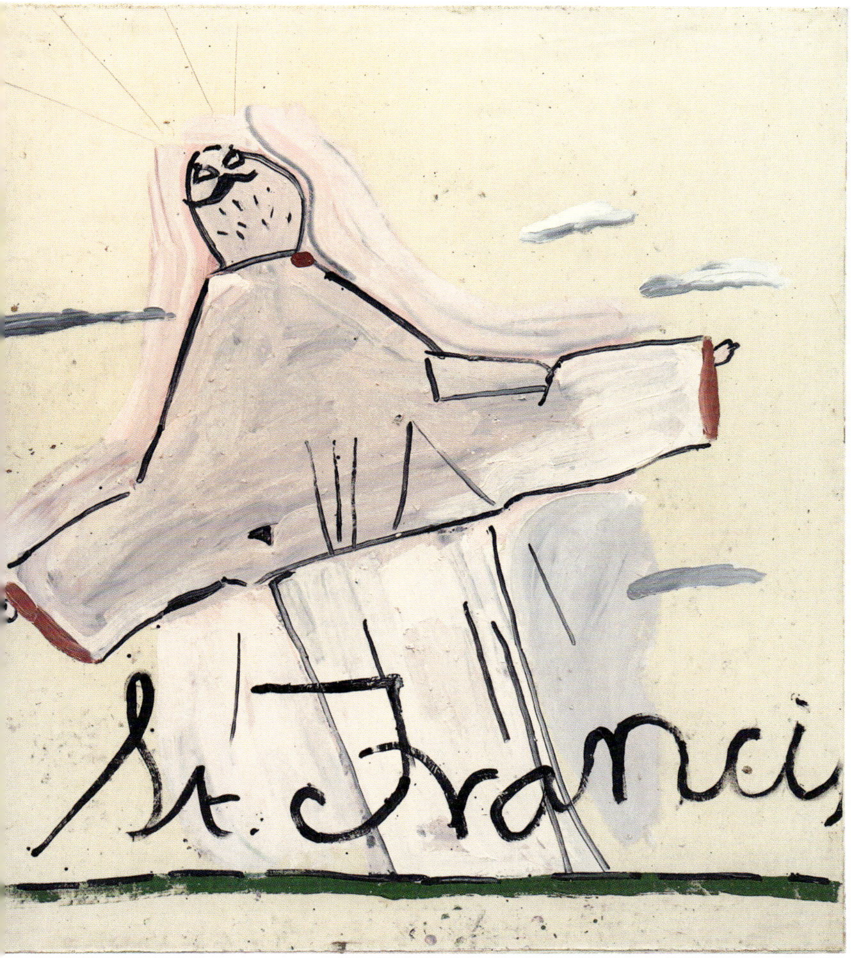

picture is further complicated by the presence of a man's head which is based on the footballer John Terry (the JT of the title) – Wylie says she has always admired his nose. Terry presumably stands for King Solomon. Wylie had also noted that Piero della Francesca (*c.*1415–1492), in his painting of the story, did not make the Queen of Sheba truly Ethiopian but instead depicted her as an Italian beauty; Wylie's queen is emphatically black. Wylie is perhaps obliquely touching on questions of race and representation. She also shows the queen's cloven hoof, which Piero della Francesca does not: the beauty of the queen has an element of real physical animality rather than being merely an ideal. In companion works *Queen of Sheba with Gold Lump* 2012 (fig. 57) and *Palm Tree and Camel* 2012 (fig. 56), Wylie's paintings depict a camel, palm trees and the Nile (in what looks like a schematic map), all of which locate the queen as African, while her jewelled crown and the ruby signify her wealth. Wylie considers these elements to be 'props' which, like film props, serve to set the stage for the narrative. The multiple figures of the queen suggest the unfolding of the narrative, but she is overshadowed by the large man's head that seems to watch over her. The picture suggests the dominating male gaze that defines the propriety, or not, of the queen's body.

In *Holy Doors Picture (Film Notes)* 2011 (fig.59), the word 'Madeinusa' on the picture refers to the 2006 film of that name. The film tells the story of an Andean town during the 'Holy Time' that spans Good Friday and Easter Sunday. 'Holy Time' is not part of the traditional Catholic calendar but the townspeople think that during this time God is truly dead and that therefore they can sin with impunity and without remorse. The young girl Madeinusa, after whom the film is named, has been chosen as the Mater Dolorosa (Mother of Sorrows) by the townspeople. The film is replete with folk Catholic imagery and Wylie has sought to capture this: the central dark triangular shape in the painting represents both the mountain and the costume of Madeinusa. The hands seem to offer blessing, the lines radiating from them suggesting the efficacy of this benediction. The floating figures at the top of the painting, while referencing angels or cherubs, appear to be neither, looking

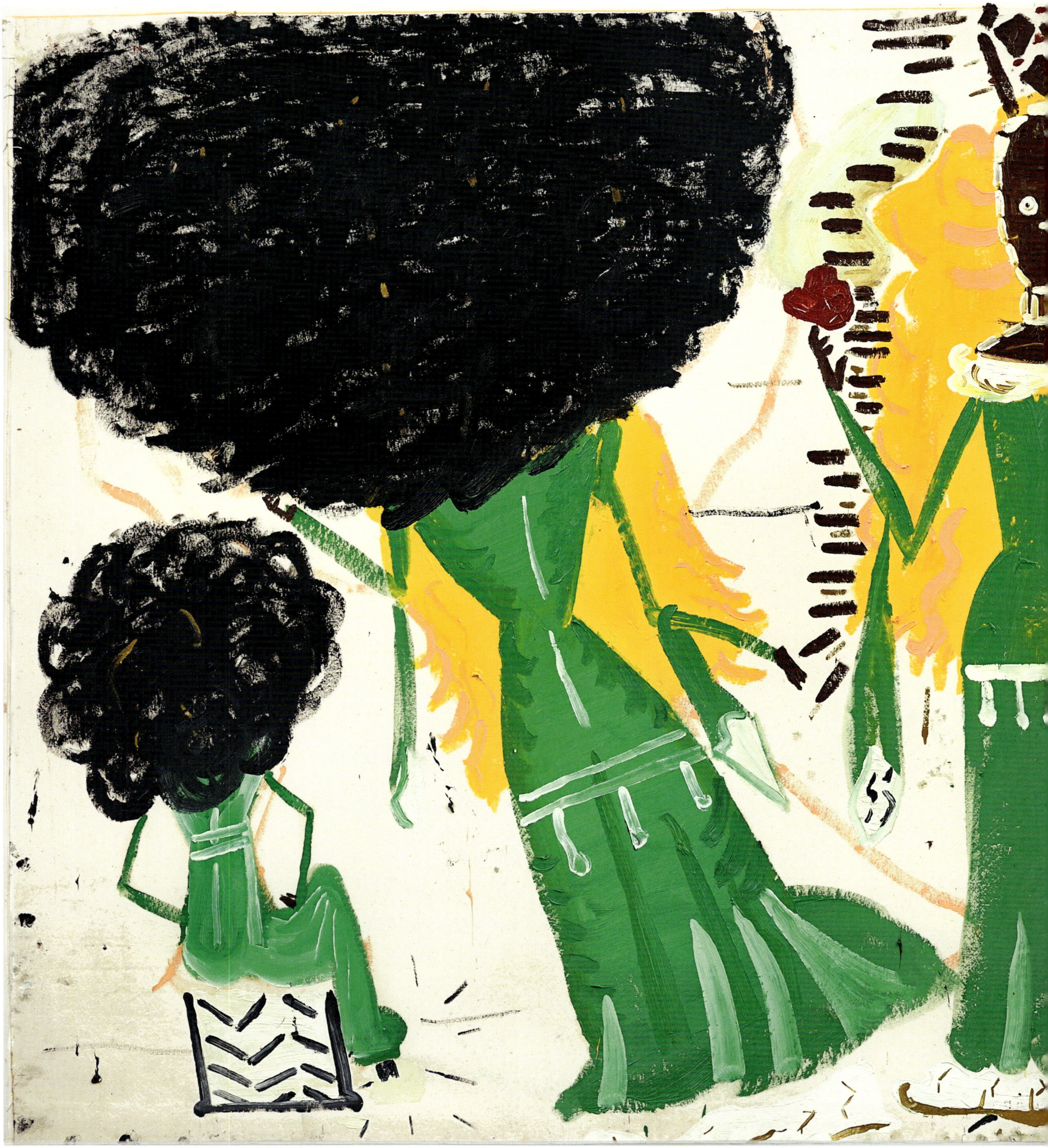

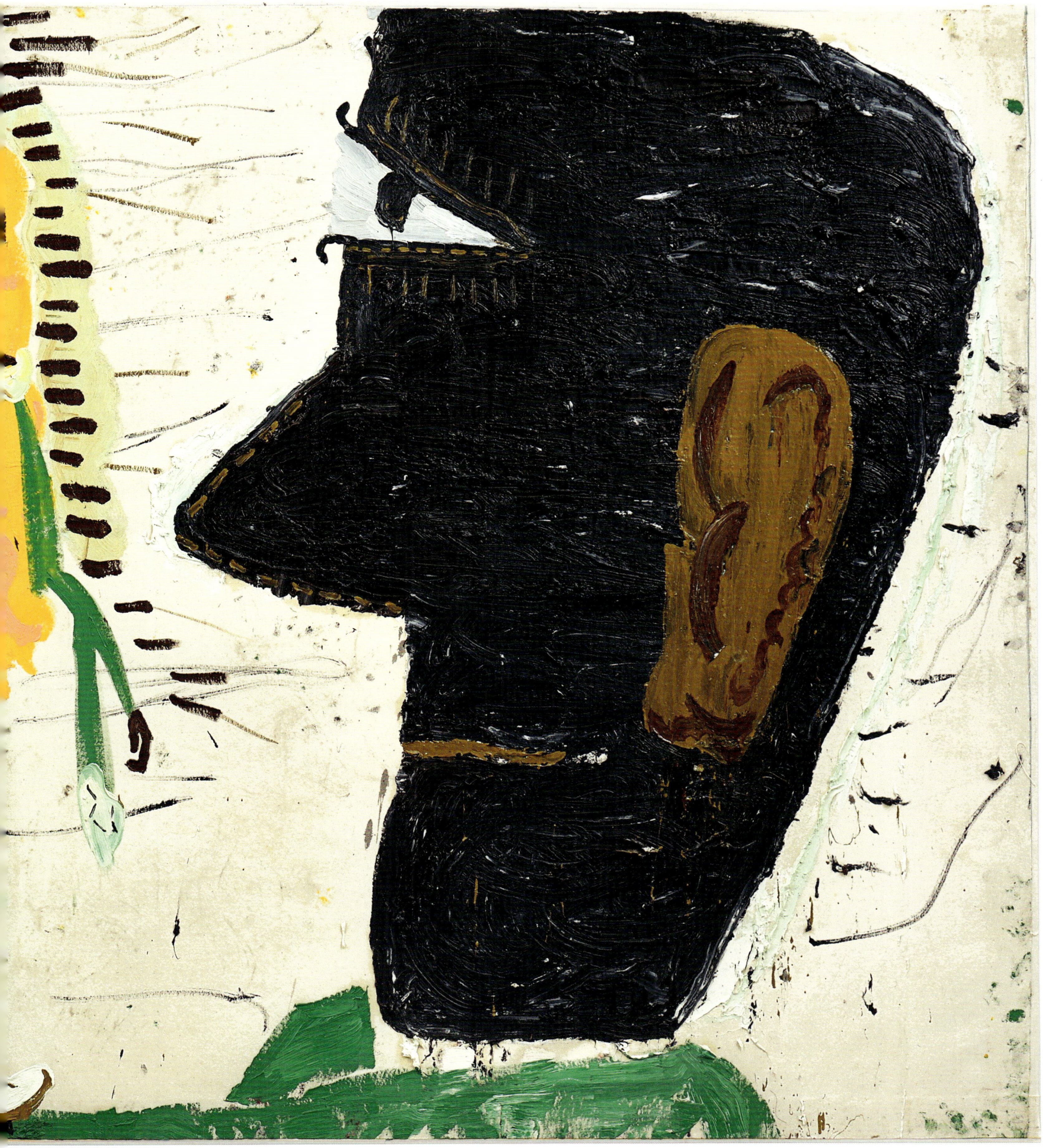

55 (previous page)
Queen of Sheba and JT 2012
Oil on canvas, 182 × 342 cm (71¾ × 134¾ in)
Collection of Christina Chen

56
Palm Tree and Camel 2012
Oil on canvas, 181 × 328 cm (71⅜ × 129¼ in)
Monsoon Collection, London

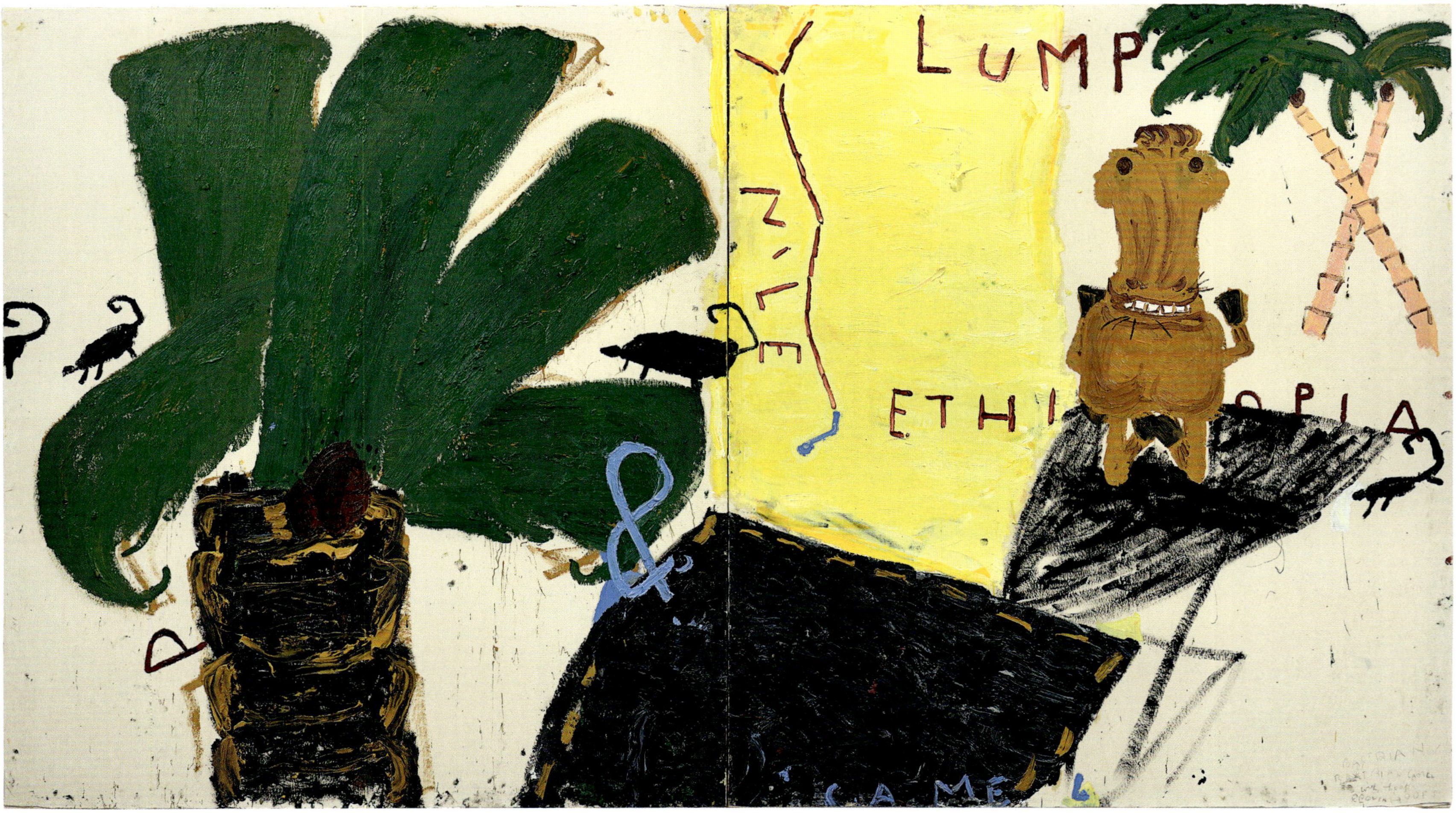

57
Queen of Sheba with Gold Lump 2012
Oil on canvas, 183 × 348 cm (72⅛ × 137⅛ in)
Private collection

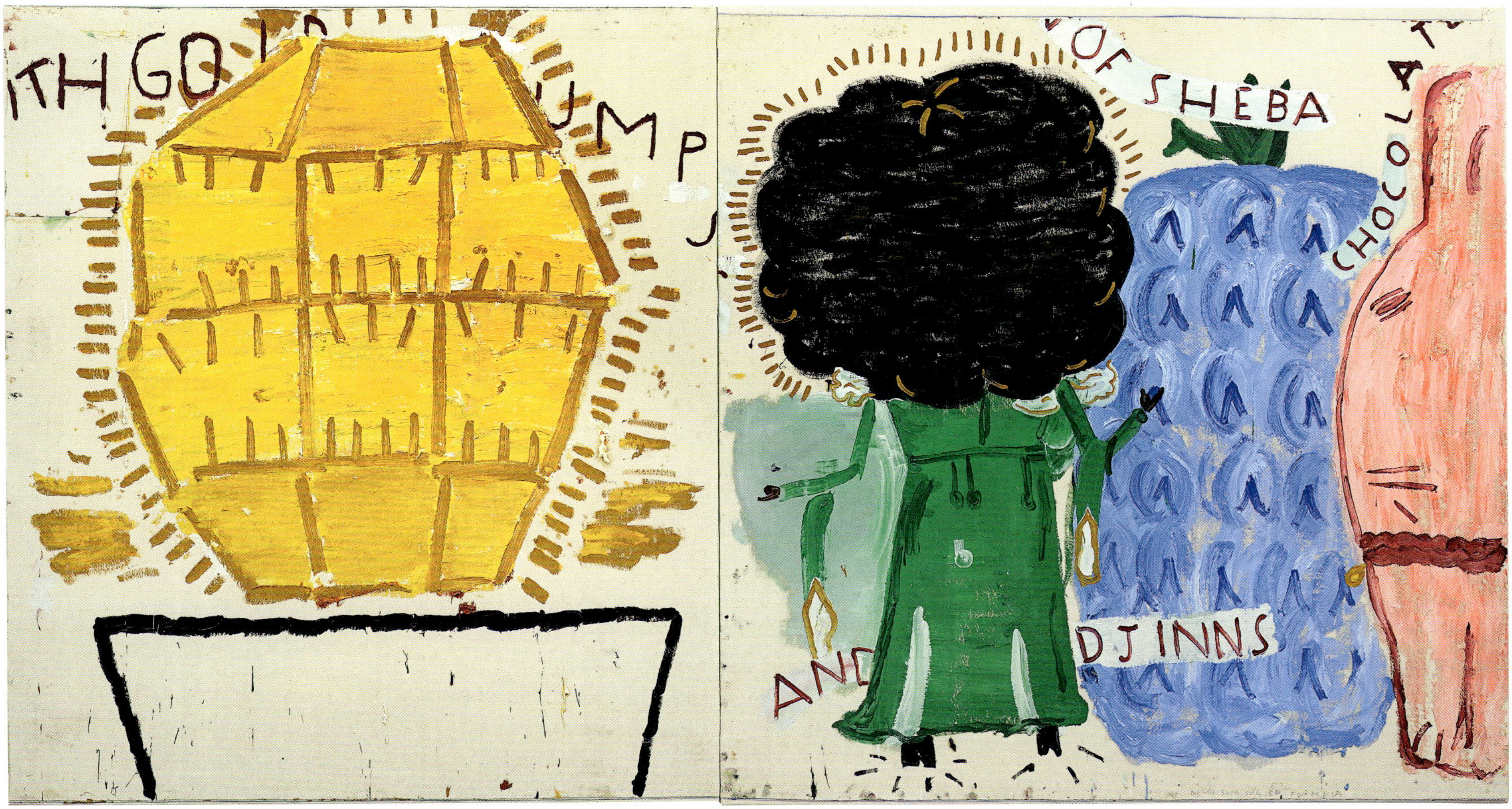

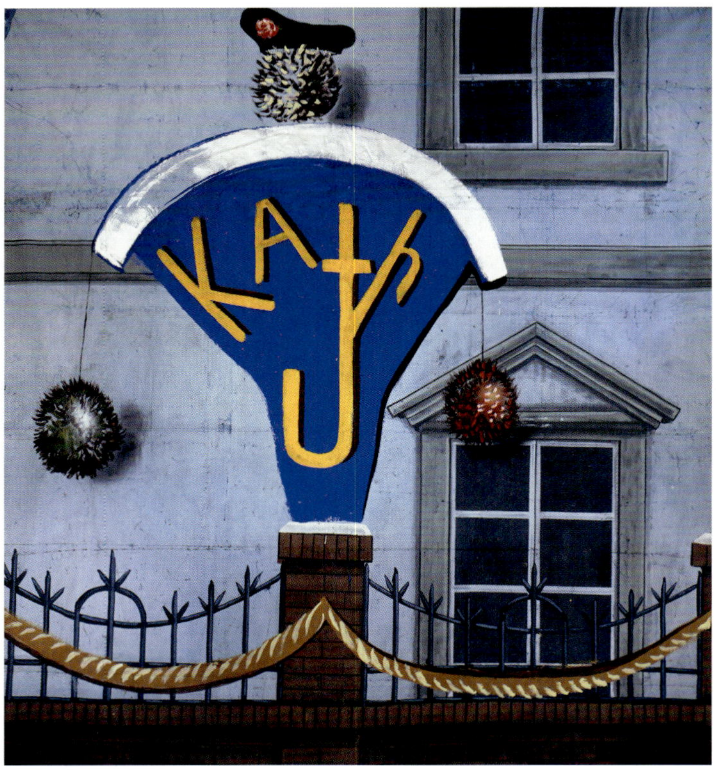

58
Julian Schnabel, *Gothic Run Riot or Kathy Painting*, 1986
Oil, wax, tempera on Kabuki theater backdrop
366 × 351 cm (144 x 138 in)
Private collection

59
Holy Doors Picture (Film Notes) 2011
Oil on canvas, 183 × 166 cm (72⅛ × 65⅜ in)
Private collection

rather disconcerting or even sinister. While Schnabel and Wylie both believe that art has a redemptive power that is similar to that of religion, Wylie, by referencing the peculiar beliefs represented in the film, is perhaps more equivocal about the nature of the religious impulse.

In practice, Wylie often becomes fascinated by a single motif: for example, the pensive Eve figure, resting on a mountain, inspired by a medieval manuscript in the British Museum. In a series of five paintings, Eve is painted in different colour palettes, sensual, pink, floating on a turquoise ground and, in *Eve on a White Mountain* 1998 (fig.61), reclining on a black background while being watched by a big-eyed green elephant taken from the artist's childhood memories of India.

Wylie's own use of such iconography is also reminiscent of the use of the emblematic art which was developed in the sixteenth century. The emblem, a combination of image and text, relies on a set of shared meanings and thus tends to be allegorical, unlike symbols which are metaphorical. As John Manning writes of traditional emblematic art:

> Life was essentially emblematic because, to some degree, many aspects of daily experience were self-consciously presented as part of an emblematic theatre, in which no event could be presented without an accompanying gloss. For this reason human history, legend and myth needed to be taught and remembered, because these fictions and constructions of the past repeated themselves in essence, and could, in turn, throw light on present events and happenings.[59]

Despite this background in history, legend and myth, the emblem did not have a single meaning but through joke, allusion and pun has had a wide range of culturally specific meanings. Wylie similarly deploys image and text but, unlike traditional emblems, her works cannot rely on our knowledge of a core set of allegorical meanings informed by Christianity. Instead she negotiates a network of references that sit between the personal and the public. These exist in unison and are painted with equal significance.

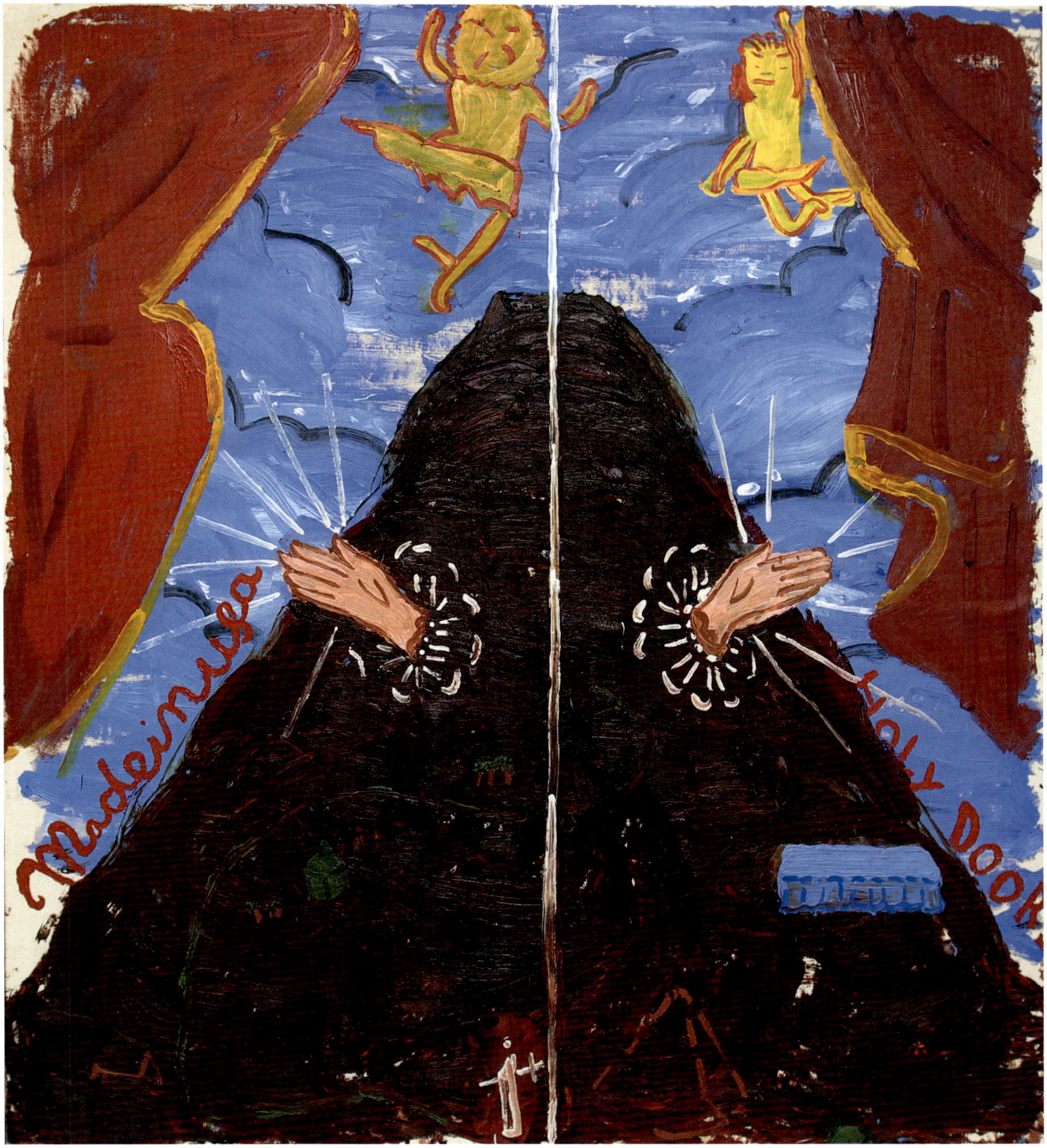
Madeinusa
HOLY DOOR

60
Philip Guston, *Painter at Night* 1979
Oil on canvas, 174 × 204.5 cm
(68⅝ × 80⅝ in)
Private collection

61
Eve on a White Mountain 1998
Oil on canvas, 183 × 168 cm (72⅛ × 66¼ in)
Private collection

Wylie also admires the late work of Philip Guston (fig.60), who in 1966 unexpectedly abandoned abstract painting, developing a representational cartoonish style completely at odds with what went before. Like Pop artists Roy Lichtenstein (1923–1997) and Andy Warhol (1928–1987), he developed a new figurative vocabulary and style indebted to commercial cartoonists such as George Herriman (1880–1944), Al Capp (1909–1979) and Walt Disney (1901–1966). Guston confounded the art world with a new figurative style in which blunt cartoon shapes were used to create a complex and highly personal iconography. Crudely painted, certain images reoccur in these paintings, from the hooded figures of Ku Klux Klan members to everyday objects such as people's heads, shoes, light bulbs and cigarettes, all of which seem to have a life of their own.

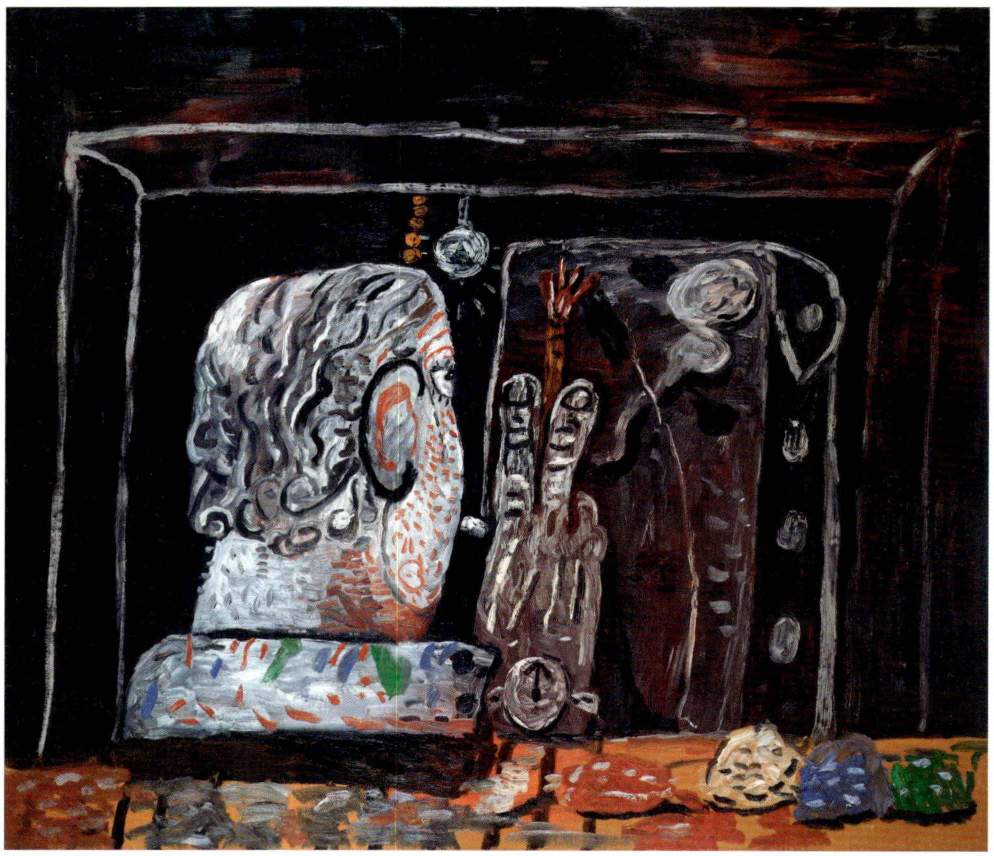

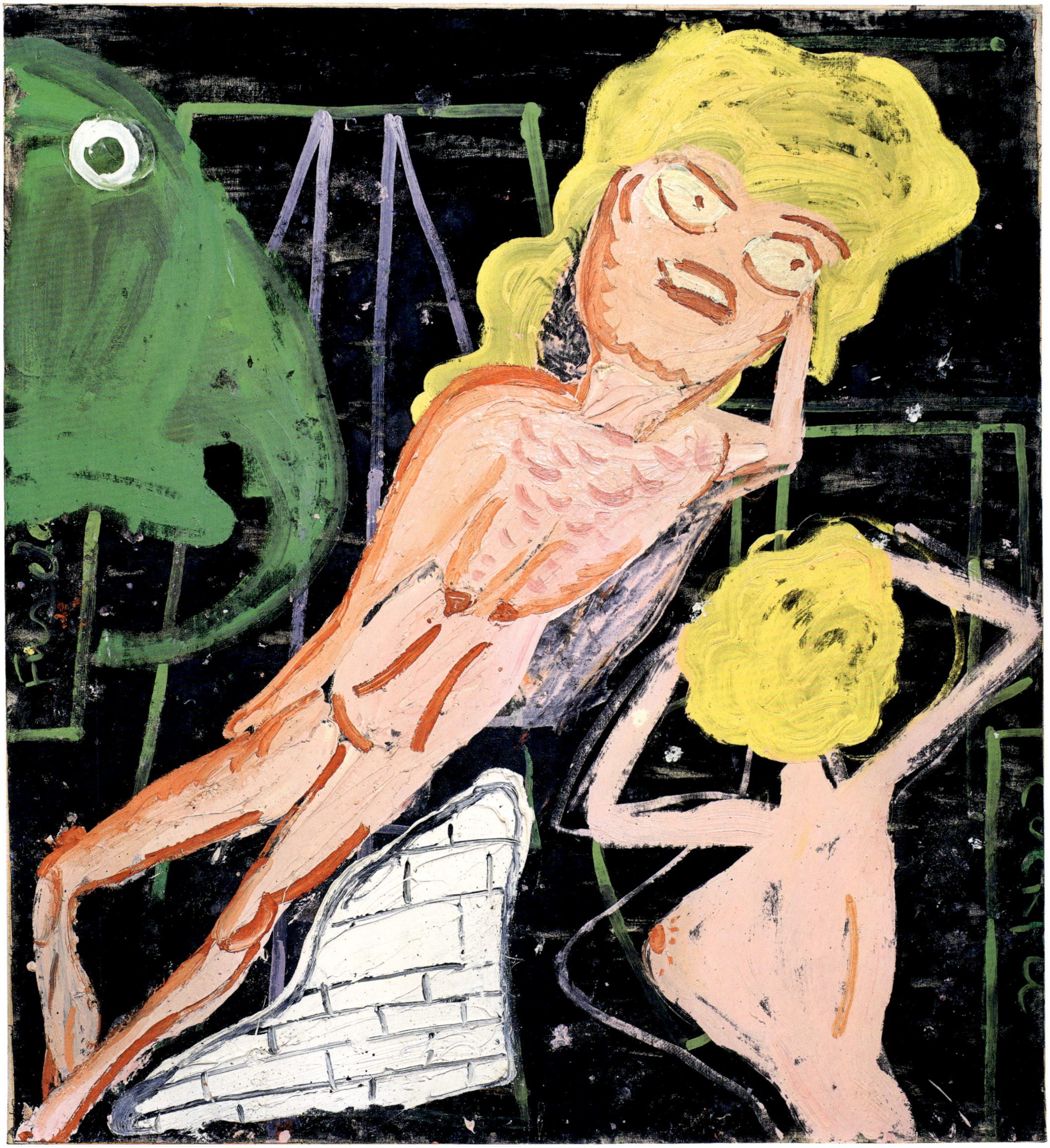

62
PV, Windows and Floorboards 2014
Oil on canvas, 181 × 334 cm (71⅜ × 131½ in)
Walker Art Gallery, Liverpool

These drawings and paintings often have a cartoon-like economy that grasps the essentials of what is to be portrayed. As far as Wylie is concerned, the economy of cartoon is another means to deploy in her picturemaking – although evidently one with which she is very comfortable.

While the cartoon can be a caricature, which exaggerates for comic or satirical purposes, it can also sympathetically portray an ideal type or individual. In its popular forms cartooning can capture something universal in its portrayals. *The Beano*'s Bash Street Kids, for example, presents the very essence of a teacher and his unruly class, a readily identifiable figure that is still particular enough to avoid empty stereotype. Some artists have used cartoons as subject matter, a pretext. Lichtenstein, for example, explores the formal aspects of comic-book cartooning and the materiality of the medium. Other artists, such as Guston, use a cartoon style to their own expressive ends. It is to the latter group that Wylie belongs.

Like Guston, she deliberately employs a direct, child-like drawing style that combines with a frank approach to her subject matter. Her drawings are nearly always based on observation, and she is very keen on the specific and the particular. For example, *Breakfast Table (Dining Room)* 2015 (fig.113) depicts a coffee-stained teaspoon on the same page as a drawing of a 'late flowering small purple flower' found in the garden in early September, while *Favourite Silk Skirt on a Hanger (Bedroom)* 2015 (fig.114) simply shows the item of clothing hanging up. *Mascara Wand* 2012 (fig.64) is a profile portrait of the artist's daughter Henrietta looking into a mirror and adding mascara to her eyelashes. The background is white, and the flesh is flat and somewhat sallow looking. It is the artifice of the make-up that appears vivid and stands out: the red painted nails, the thick black of the thickened eyelashes and the mascara wand itself. The painting's title appears above the head of the applicator, the word 'wand' suggesting magic – but the implicit promise of magical transformation is undercut by the accentuated eye which is held wide open, exposed and seemingly vulnerable.

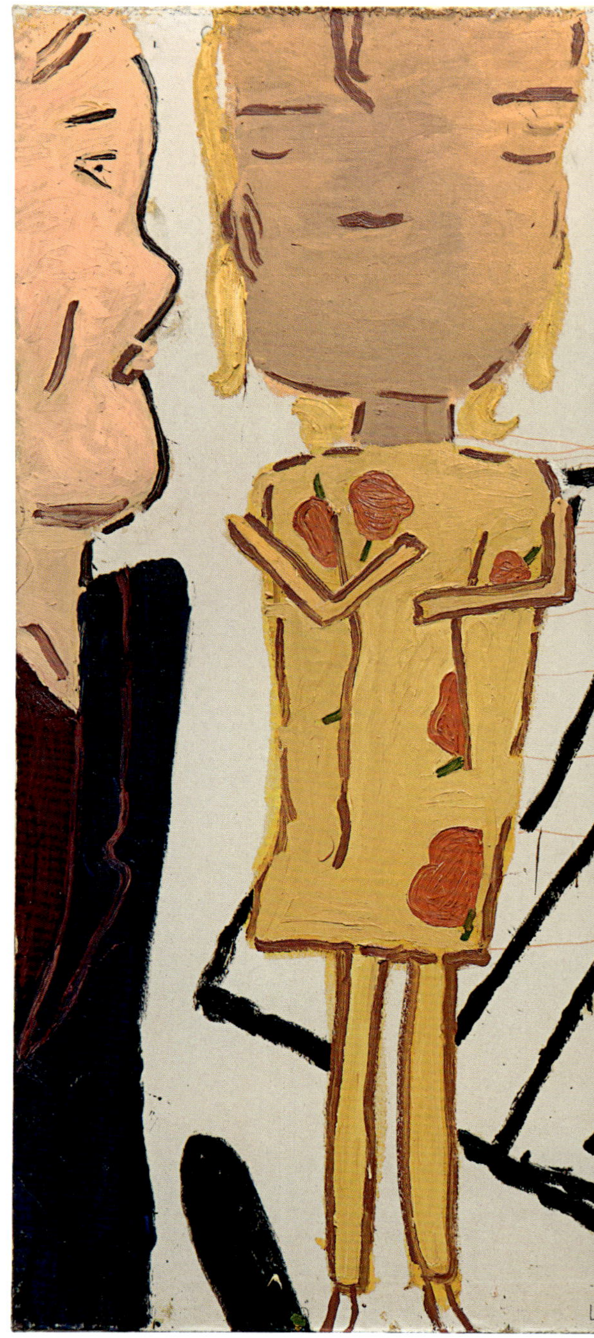

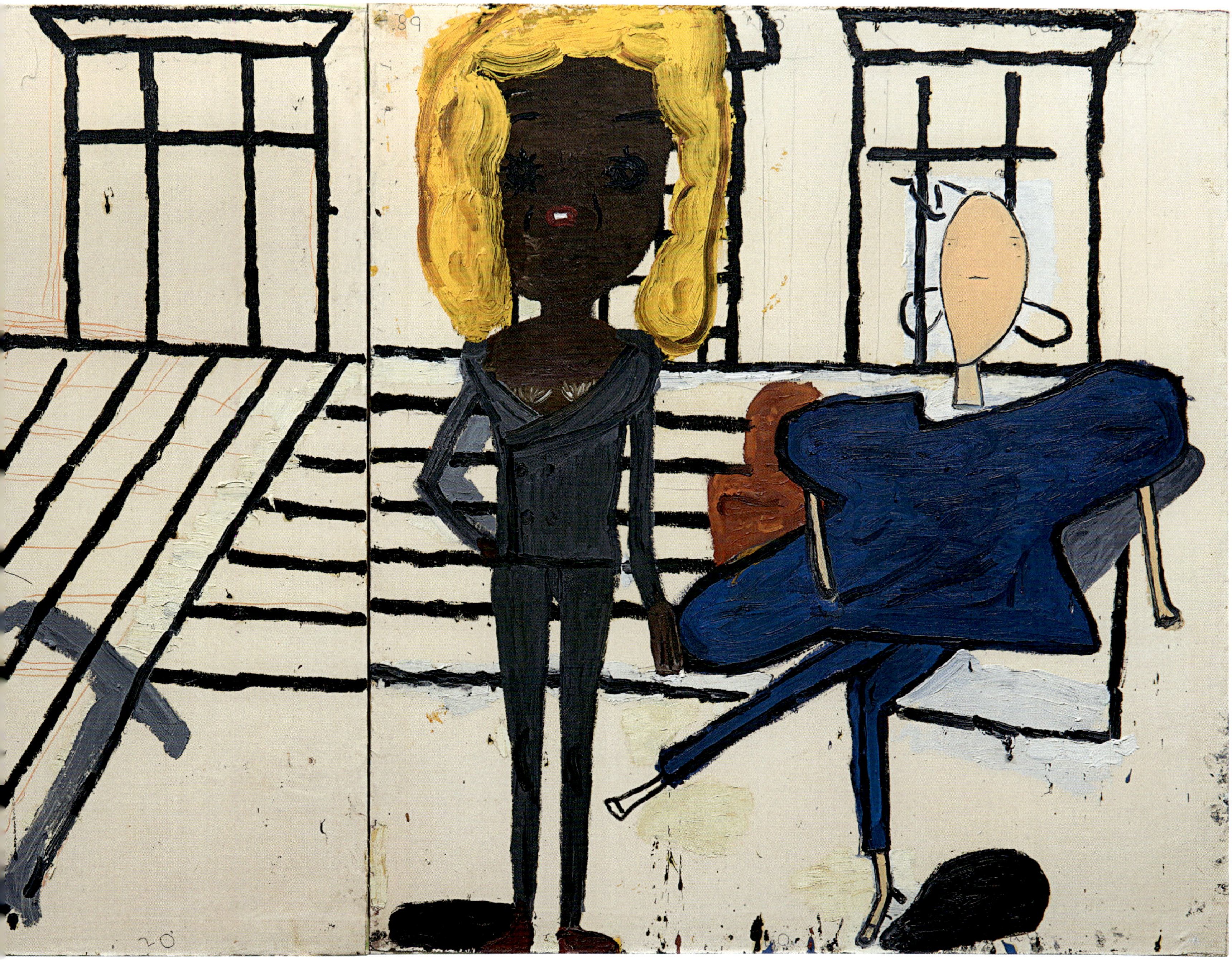

63
Painter R.O. (Roy Oxlade) I 1989
Oil on paper, 84 × 60 cm (33 1/8 × 23 5/8 in)
Private collection

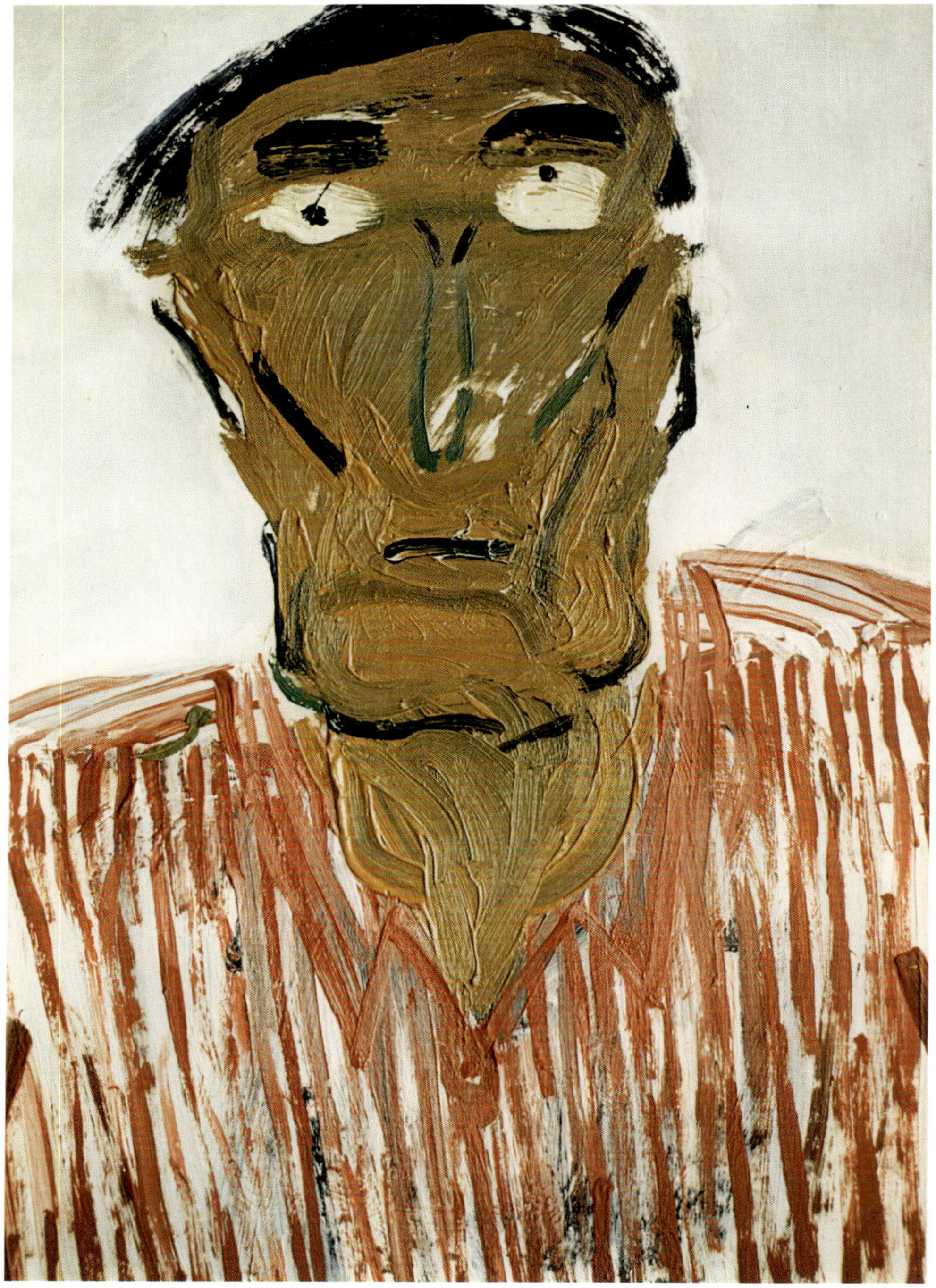

Wylie attempts a portrayal of reality, of objects in themselves, and many of the works pursue this aim with a very cartoon-like simplicity of line. A portrait of her husband *Painter RO (Roy Oxlade) I* 1989 (fig.63) depicts him in a stripy and white shirt, fine-chiselled cheekbones defined with black paint, heavy brows and piercing stare, while a large work on paper *Black Cherry, Close Up* 2013 (fig.68) is cropped in such a way that the form of the fruit exceeds the edges of the picture plane and there is the almost palpable sense of its sweet, juicy flesh.

Her bold style of working in paintings such as *Tree Canterbury* 1997 (fig.66) can also be compared to Henri Rousseau (1844–1910). His goal was to paint in a realist manner, yet his paintings, as well as drawings and prints, were highly personal in their rendering and imagery. Simplified images of humans, animals and nature painted in flat, bright colours are representative of Rousseau's individualised approach to painting that on the face of it shares many affinities with Wylie's. In Rousseau's work, like in Wylie's, reality and imagination fuse into one (fig.65). His jungle scenes were assembled from observations of exotic plants in the Jardin des Plantes' hot houses, caged wild animals in the Paris zoo or stuffed examples found in dioramas in the city's museum of natural history, illustrations in popular publications such as *Bêtes Sauvages* and oversized domestic plants and trees. Yet Wylie's paintings are

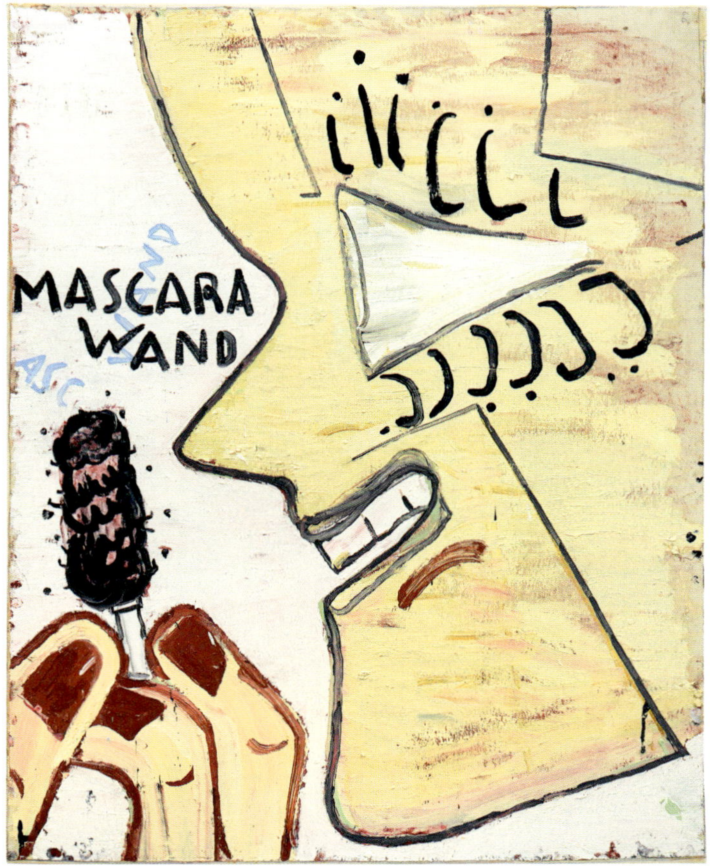

64
Mascara Wand 2012
Oil on canvas, 183 × 149 cm (72⅛ × 58¾ in)
Collection of Luca Santini

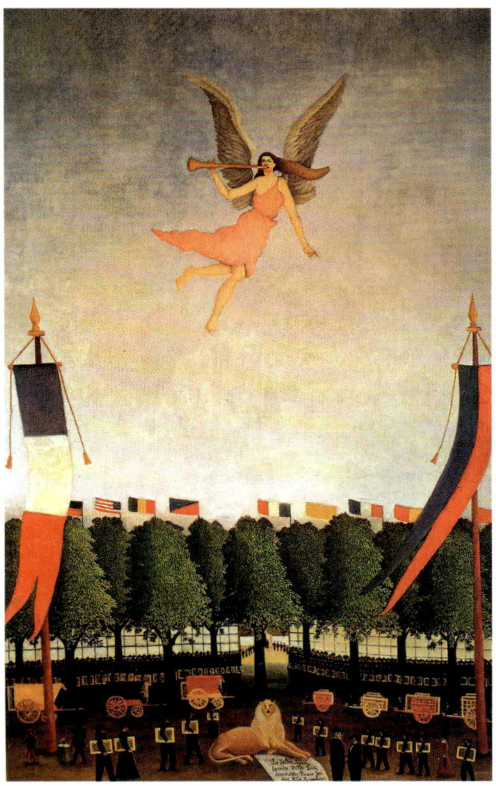

65
Henri Rousseau, *Liberty Inviting Artists to Participate in the 22nd Exhibition of the Independents* 1905–06
Oil on canvas, 175 × 118 cm (69 × 46½ in)
Bridgestone Museum of Art, Tokyo, Japan

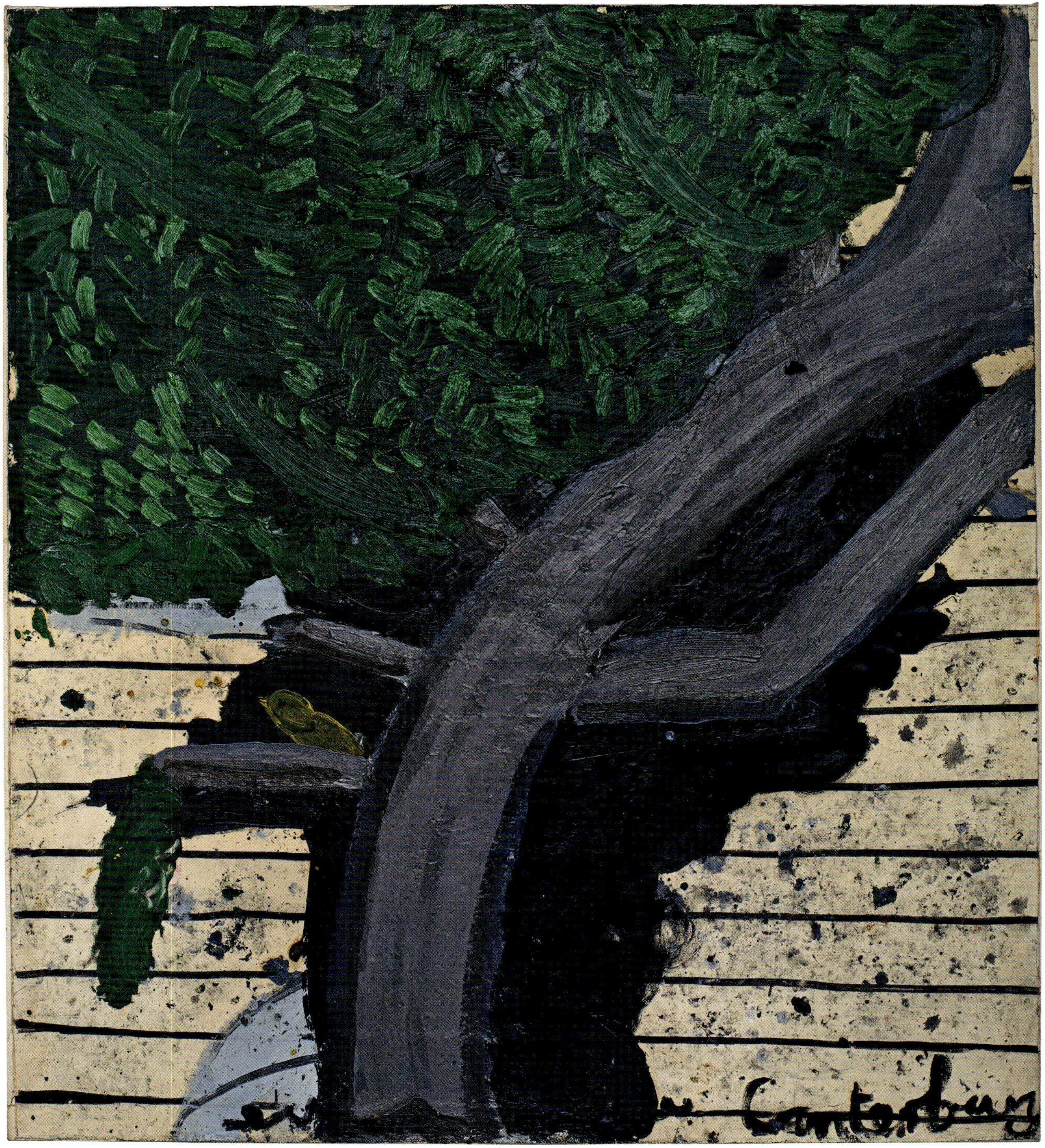
Canterbury

66 (left)
Tree Canterbury 1997
Oil on canvas, 183 × 167 cm (72⅛ × 65¾ in)
Private collection

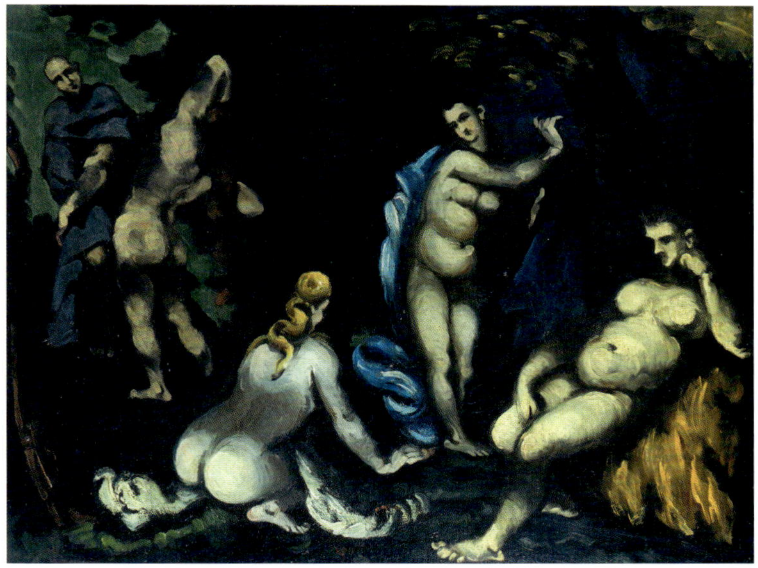

67
Paul Cézanne, *The Temptation of St Anthony* 1870
Oil on canvas, 57 × 76 cm (22½ × 30 in)
Bührle Collection, Zurich

68
Black Cherry, Close Up 2013
Watercolour and collage on paper
87 × 59 cm (34⅜ × 23¼ in)
Private collection

not naïve. Her engagement with the 'real' world is in a style that is direct, humorous, honest and at times even uncomfortable.[60]

Choco Leibnitz 2006 (fig.69) is a witty work that uses a minimum amount of line work to suggest its subject. A red arc and three deft lines above suggest a mouth and nose: the mouth is open to receive a biscuit, the basic shape of which is simply outlined with a few scratched lines to suggest its surface. The biscuit seems to be moving by itself with no visible means of support – it is not held by fingers. The biscuit has 'Choco Leibni' lettered on it, with the remaining letters 'tz' next to the biscuit. These extra letters float ambiguously – they occupy the picture's background and yet complete the biscuit's name. It is as if the name is more important than the thing itself. We eat not just *a* biscuit but rather consume this particular brand. Indeed, the centrality of the biscuit and the cartoon-like speed lines surrounding it make it look as if the product is propelling itself towards the passive, receptive mouth under its own volition.

Although the paintings have diverse subjects and formats, they are united by Wylie's very particular way of using paint and emphasising structure and composition. And in each instance, the way she has done so has grown directly out of her response both to her subject matter and her ongoing engagement with the history of painting; from the works of Paolo Uccello (1397–1475) to Piero

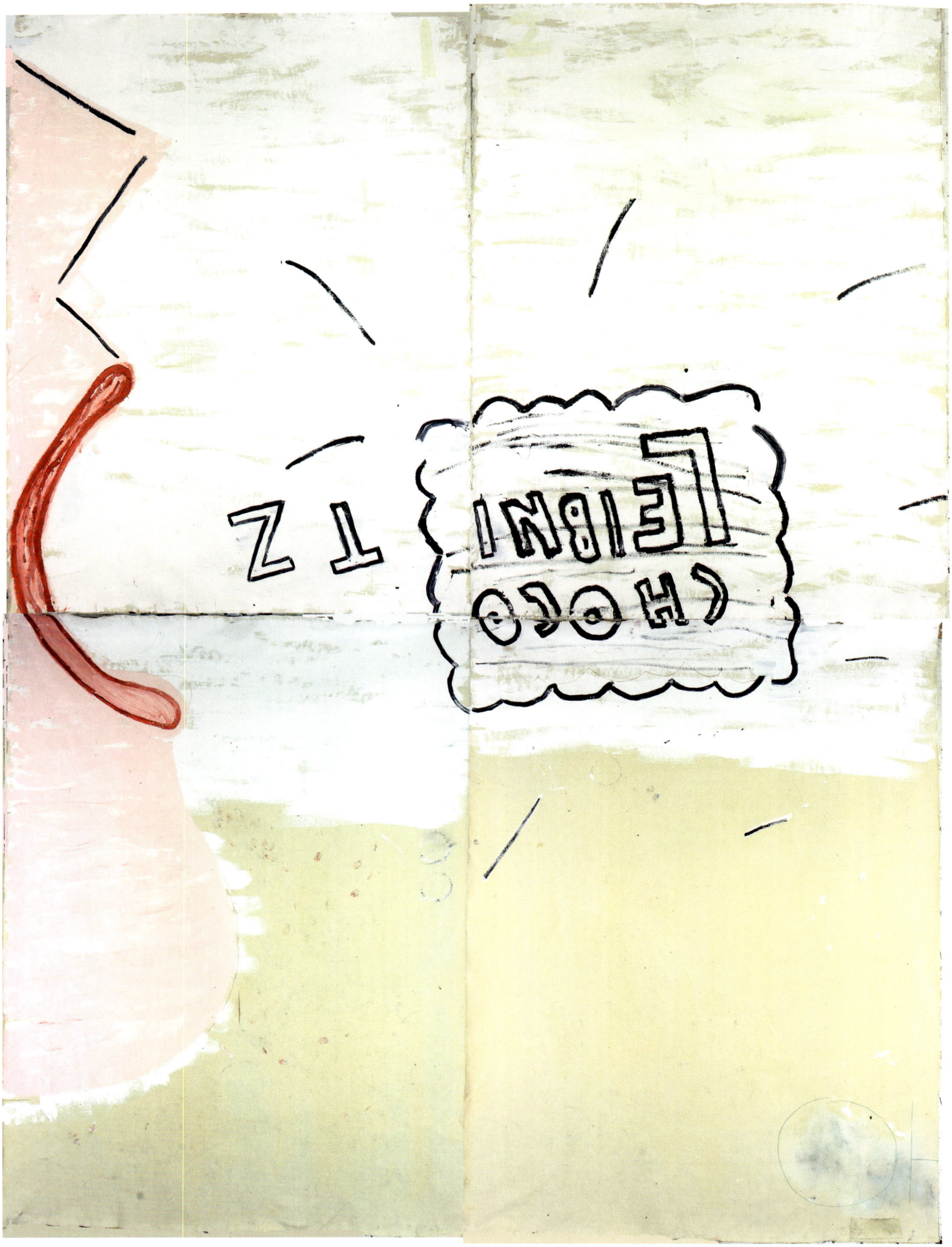
LEIBNITZ
CHOCO

69
Choco Leibnitz 2006
Oil on canvas, 366 × 305 cm (144⅛ × 120⅛ in)
Private collection

70
Eating a Black Biscuit 2007
Marker on paper, 30 × 21 cm (11⅞ × 8⅜ in)
Private collection

della Francesca, Francisco Goya (1746–1828) and Paul Cézanne (1839–1906). Wylie has particular affection for Cézanne's early work which she describes as 'lumpy'.[61] It is often concerned with the figure or groups of figures in the landscape, and includes many imaginatively painted examples such as *Girl with Parrot* 1859–1860, the highly decorative *The Four Seasons* 1861 painted for his father's mansion the Jas de Bouffan, *The Temptation of St Anthony* 1870 (fig.67) – a subject Wylie has also explored (fig.106) – and *Reapers* 1875–8, a work Wylie considers 'fantastic . . . looks just like a Tarantino'.[62] Throughout his life Cézanne struggled to develop an authentic observation of the seen world by the most accurate method of representing it in paint that he could find. Wylie has also cited the English painter Robert Peake the Elder (*c*.1551–1619) as an inspiration. Appointed as royal picture maker, Peake made several portraits of the English monarchy during the seventeenth century. In Wylie's *Henry P.O.W.* 2013, she makes reference to Peake's painting of Henry Frederick Stuart, Prince of Wales, from about 1608. In her painting he appears, outdoors, baby faced and posturing in an oversized, jaunty, green hat and breeches. Likewise her four-part monumental painting *Elizabeth & Henry with Birds* 2013 (fig.71) references his portraits of King James I's children, Elizabeth and Henry, seen standing outside a grey fortress with birds flying above. Wylie has emphasised that it is not the royal content of Peake's work that interests her, but something in the way that he paints, in his 'magic' as an artist.[63] The motif of a castle also appears in the painting *Black Tower* 2000 (fig.72). A visit to Museum Island

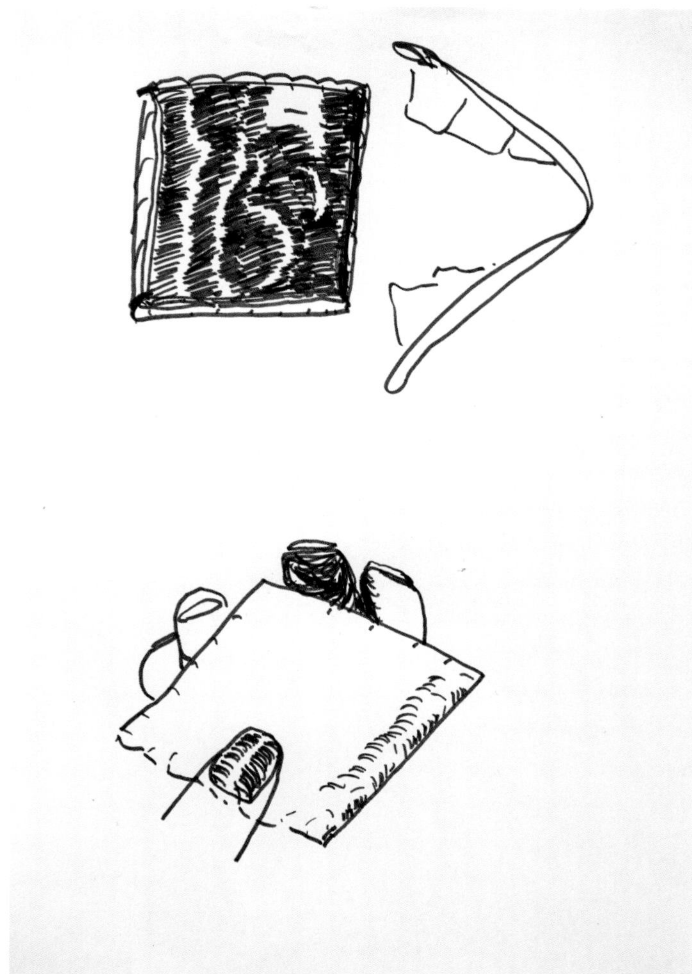

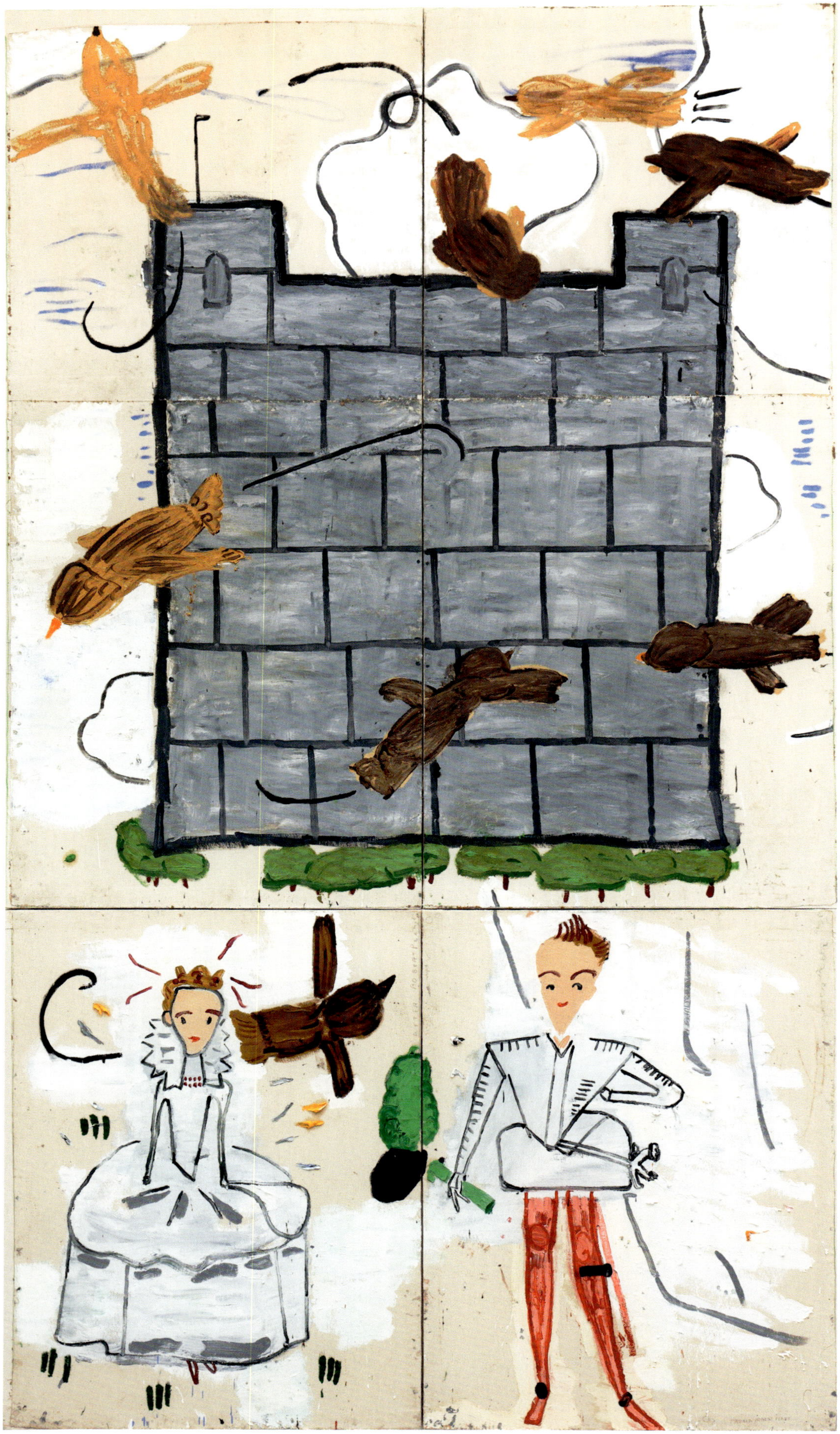

71
Elizabeth & Henry with Birds 2013
Oil on canvas
503 × 296 cm (198⅛ × 116⅝ in)
Private collection

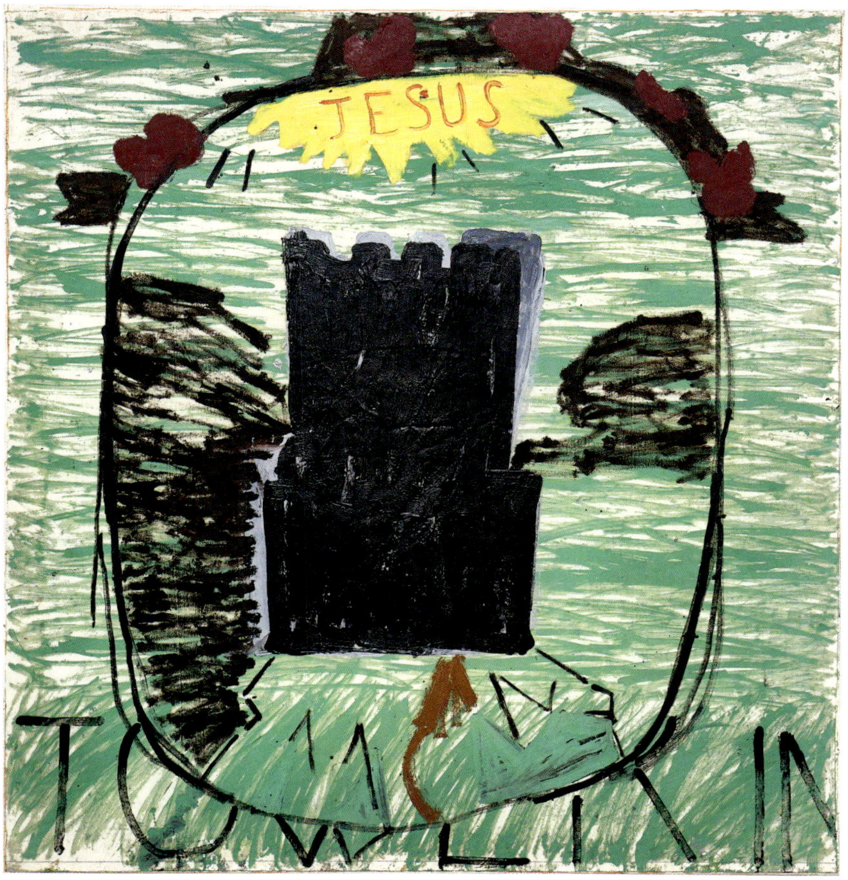

72
Black Tower 2000
Oil on canvas, 183 × 173 cm (72⅛ × 68⅛ in)
Private collection

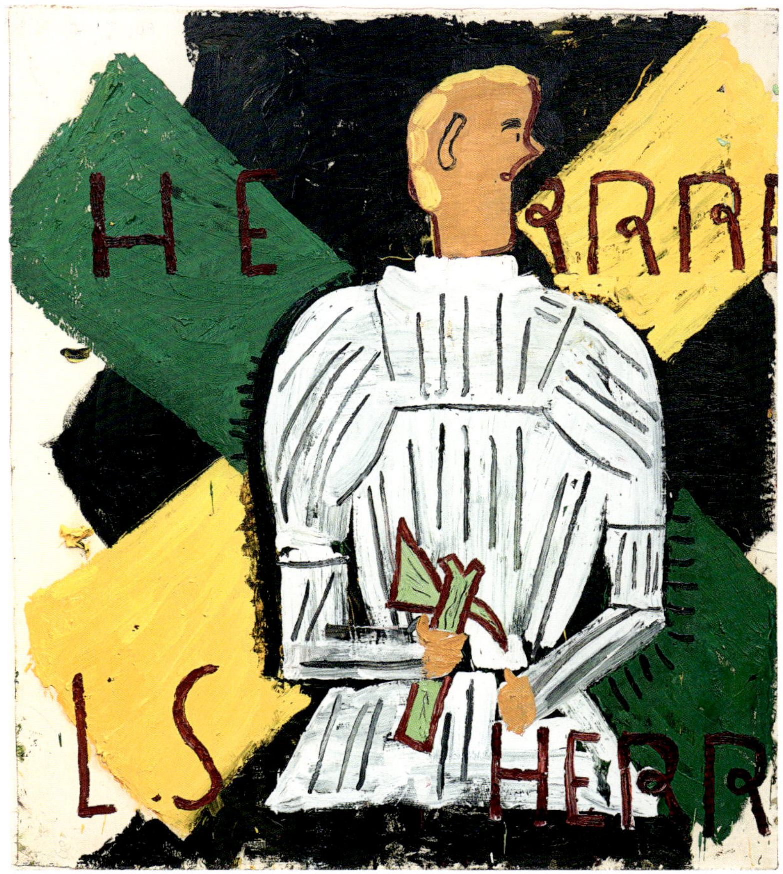

73
Herr Rehlinger in White Armour 2014
Oil on canvas, 186 × 169 cm (73¼ × 66⅝ in)
Kolon Collection, South Korea

74 (overleaf)
The Young & Old Herr Rehlinger 2014
Oil on canvas, 185 × 336 cm (72⅞ × 132⅜ in)
Collection of Bernhard Martin

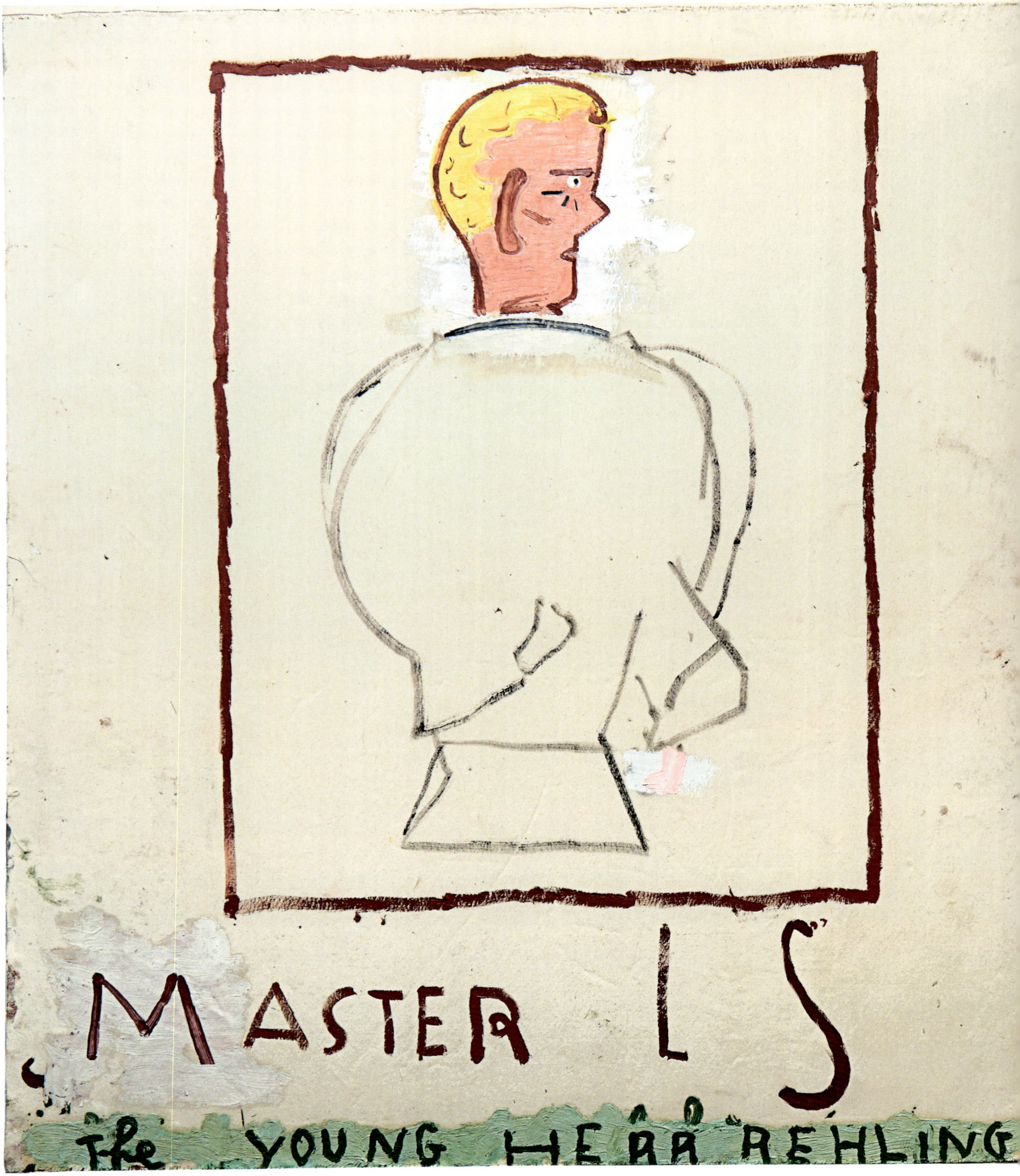
MASTER LS
The YOUNG HERR REHLING

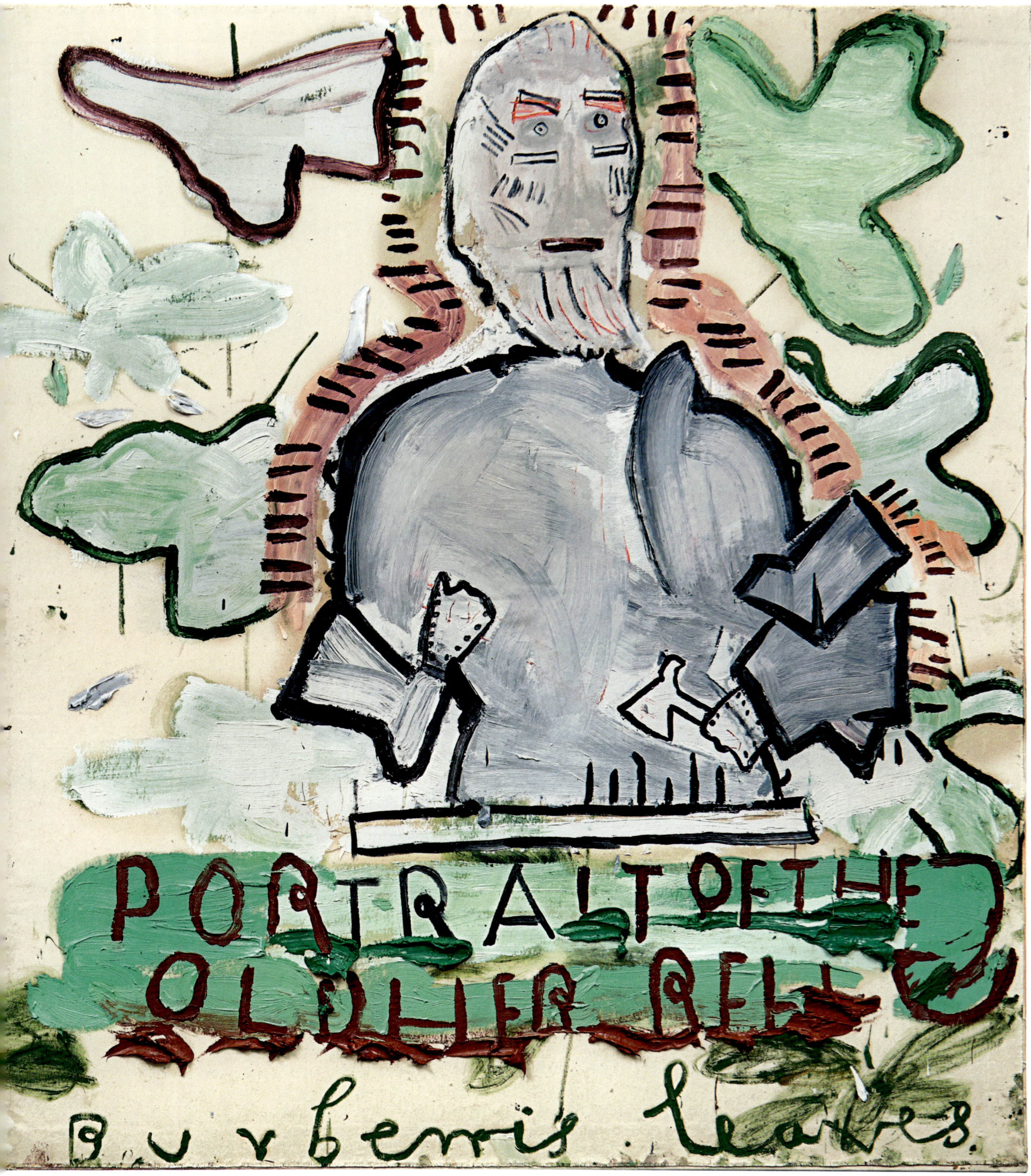
PORTRAIT OF THE
B u v berris leaves.

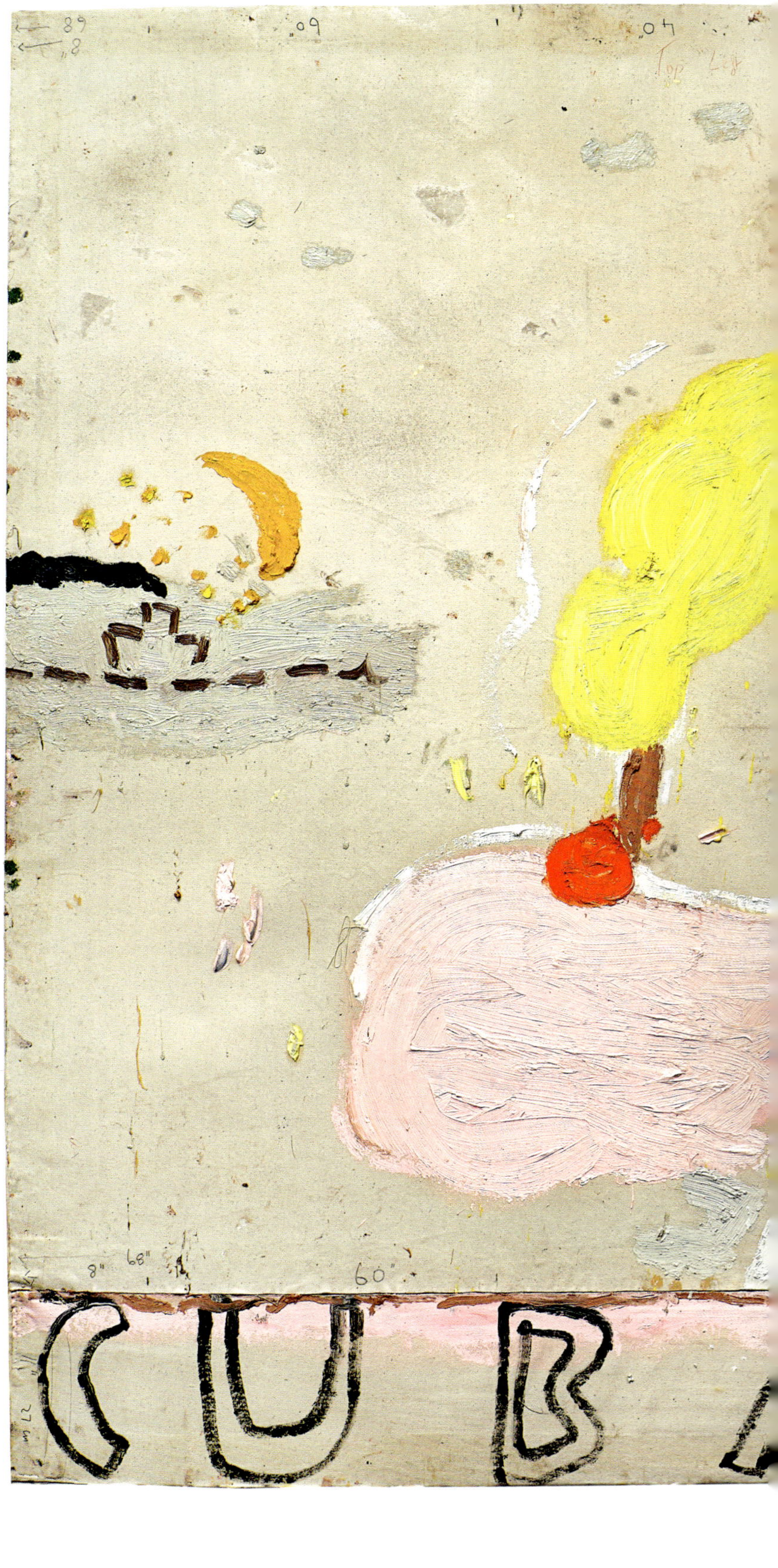

75
Cuban Scene, Smoke 2016
Oil on canvas, 208 × 340 cm (82 × 133⅞ in)
Private collection

was the inspiration behind the painting *Herr Rehlinger in White Armour* 2014 (fig.73), which won the Charles Wollaston Award, given to the 'most distinguished work' in the Royal Academy's Summer Exhibition.[64] In its companion painting, *The Young and Old Herr Rehlinger* 2014 (fig.74), two portraits are placed together. One shows a young boy while the other depicts the whitened, ghoulish face of either his father or perhaps himself in old age.

Although Wylie has a wide-ranging knowledge of art history, she is equally inspired by the energy, variety and idiosyncrasy of the art of the everyday, including folk and street art. Steeped in tradition and often created by anonymous, self-taught artists and artisans, folk art is a recognised subject in many countries; however, in Britain the vitality and influence of the genre remains elusive. Rarely considered in the context of art history, it is marginalised as part of social history or folklore studies. Wylie's interests and influences span this divide between high and low culture, art and artefacts. Likewise, even though the term 'street art' has been used since the late 1970s, the work, by its very nature, is in constant flux and hard to categorise: broadly speaking it has come to define the more visual and engaging urban art as opposed to text-based graffiti. Over the years Wylie has taken inspiration from the directness of the ancient wall paintings of Pompeii (fig.45), the moving murals of African lorry art (fig.76), a poster advertising salsa dancing (fig.75) and Mexico's strong graphic tradition. This Mexican tradition offers social and political commentary while its businesses and restaurants employ colourful, hand-painted creations to advertise their wares. *Mexican Barber* 1991 and *Mexican Floosie* 2002 draw on both of these sources.

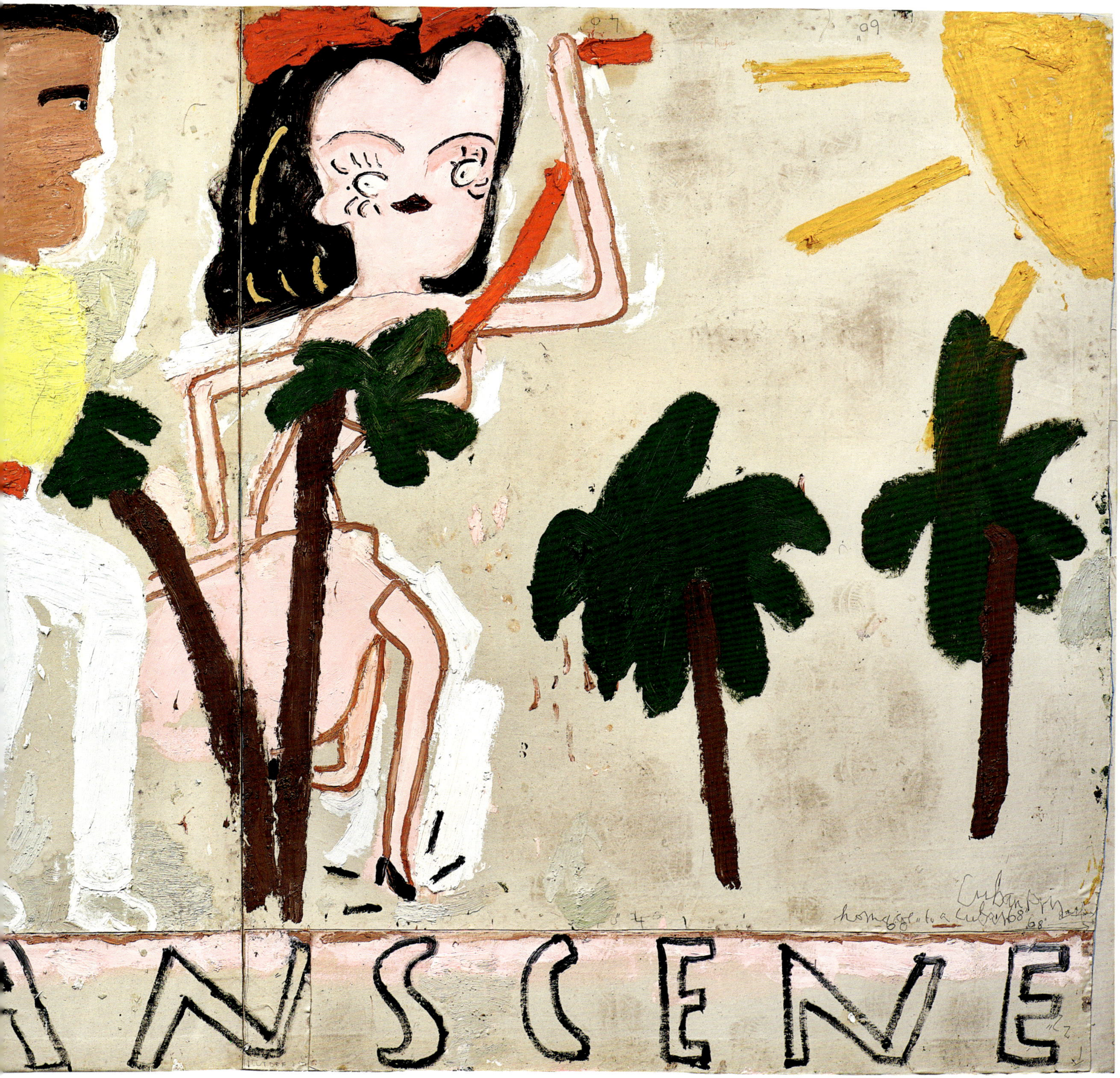
NSCENE

The large two-panel painting, *Lorry Art* 2010 (fig.76) is a brightly coloured work in which two lions are seen to be chasing a zebra through grassy terrain. Scrawled across the image are the words 'Zebra', 'Lorry' and 'Art' in red capital letters. Wylie's painting is deliberately direct and economical. It celebrates the decorative qualities of African cargo trucks, which are a common sight on the highways, while the image of the zebra in the painting came from a picture of a zebra woven into a doormat that the artist saw in the high street in Faversham (fig.77). Like mini travelling exhibitions, these trucks are painted with a wide range of themes, including landscapes, celebrities, beautiful women, mythical creatures, religious imagery and national heroes, and are often coupled with lines of poetry, religious calligraphy or common phrases, which represent the driver's identity and regional background.

Other artists including Manuel Ocampo, Jean-Michel Basquiat (1960–1988) and Raymond Pettibon (b.1957) have used writing within their work – emblems match images with a short gloss of text. With Wylie this matching of image and text is used in a number of ways: as a kind of surrogate gesture, as an economical method of making allusions, as a way of introducing an independent or even contradictory sign system into painting, or for purely aesthetic reasons. Wylie's litany of names, initials and phrases has elements of all of these approaches but is equally influenced, as the artist explains, by 'unknown artists from the 15th century in my alchemy book . . . enjoyment of book covers, early manuscripts where lettering is superimposed on the picture, or under it'.[65] As Wylie says:

> I like painting letters – they have all the options of other stuff you paint, but in a way are easier . . . They can be used to unify a painting, like Léger's use of black outline . . . and used to oppose presuppositions. I paint in names and titles, as doing this settles them in the total framework of the painting and in my visual experience. Also I like to write backwards or upside down, as that breaks the familiarity of knowing exactly how something goes and allows for 'awkward' potential.[66]

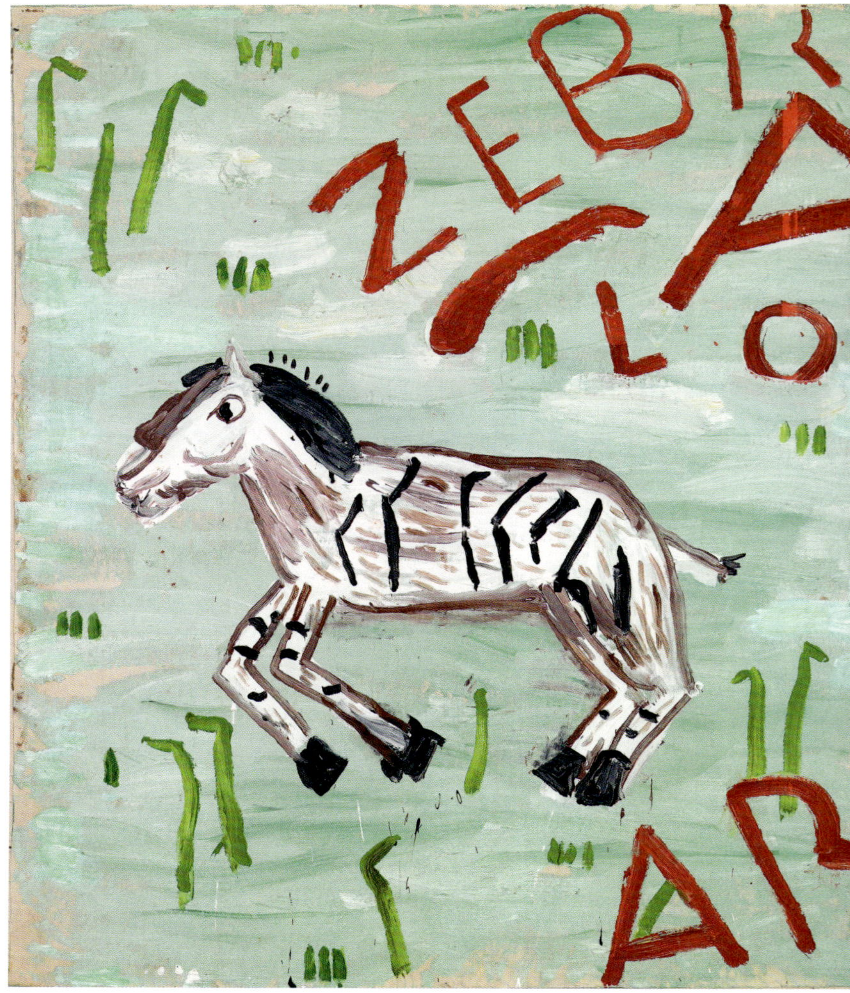

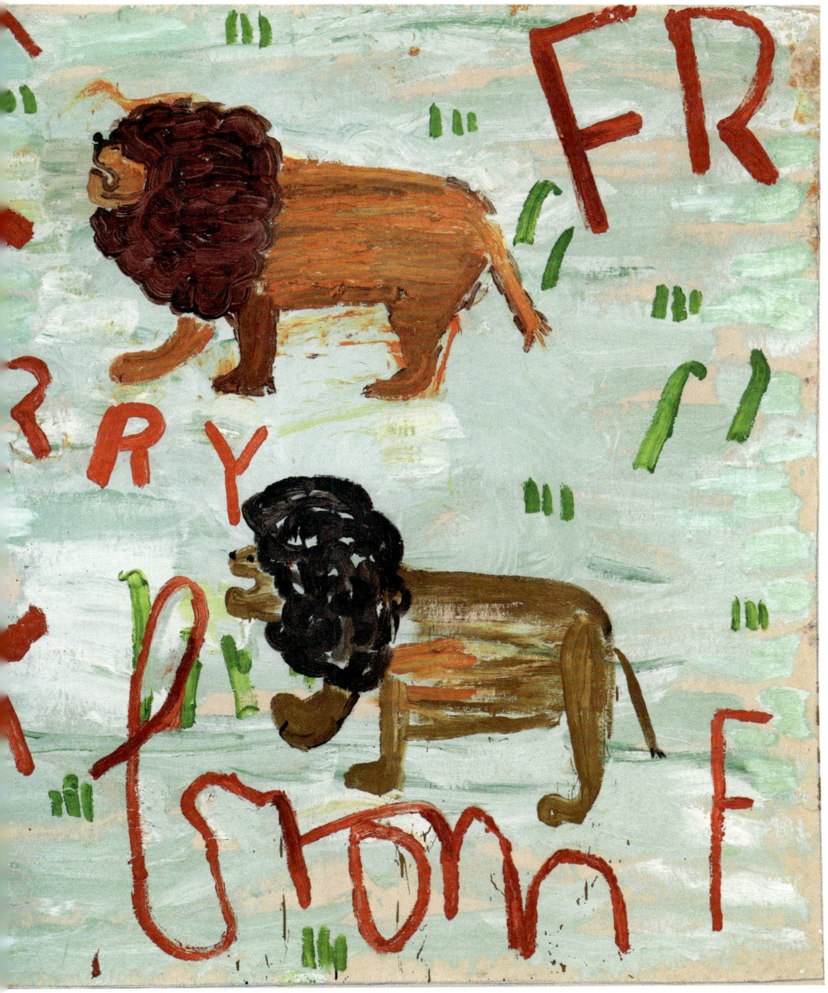

The large triptych *Arab and Dancing Girl* 2006 (fig.78) is heavily indebted to Wylie's interest in the richness and variety of Hajj paintings. Since the seventh century, the Hajj, or Great Pilgrimage to Mecca, has been a lifelong goal of devout Muslims throughout the world. Pilgrims traditionally celebrate their sacred journey by commissioning a local artist to depict their religious odyssey on the walls of their homes. The murals are often a reflection of their adventures, for example, showing a lion to represent dangerous travel to Mecca. The Hajj is a living tradition, influenced by new conveniences and obstacles which is reflected in its artistic representation. Graffiti and consumerism now play a role in this time-honoured practice, but nevertheless the paintings remain an expression of faith. Wylie's painting is dominated by two large side views of a man's head depicted against a background of palm trees. One of the heads is bare, while the other, bearded one is wearing a plain white keffiyeh. On the right-hand side the dancing girl has arms outstretched, as if to steady herself in mid spin. The outline of a simple, small aeroplane in the foreground and hint of Arabic writing offer a link back to the original impulse for the subject matter; the trompe-l'oeil bricks at the bottom of the work are a direct reference to the outdoor wall paintings of Hajj artists. Its companion picture, *Peter Pan and Wendy* 2011 (fig.79), depicts two gigantic heads of a property developer and his partner, portrayed again with reference to Egyptian Hajj paintings.

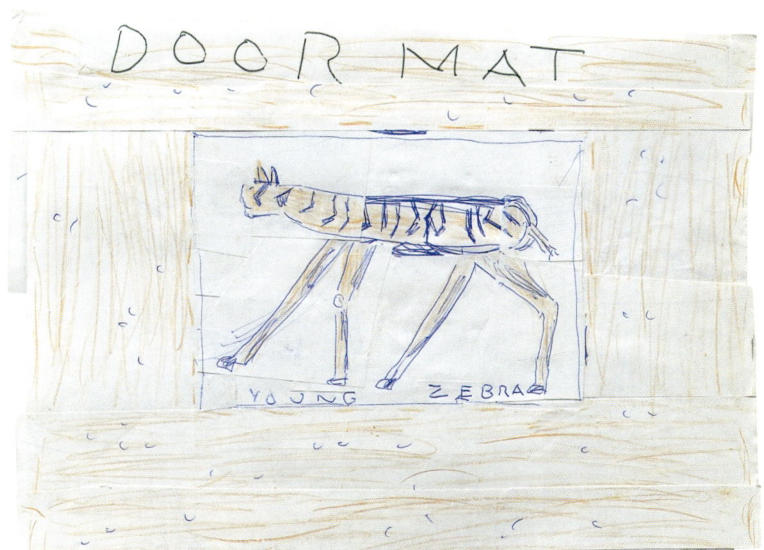

76
Lorry Art 2010
Oil on canvas, 185 × 334 cm (72⅞ × 131½ in)
Tate

77
Young Zebra (Door Mat) 2007
Coloured pencil and collage on paper
22 × 30 cm (8¾ × 11⅞ in)
Private collection

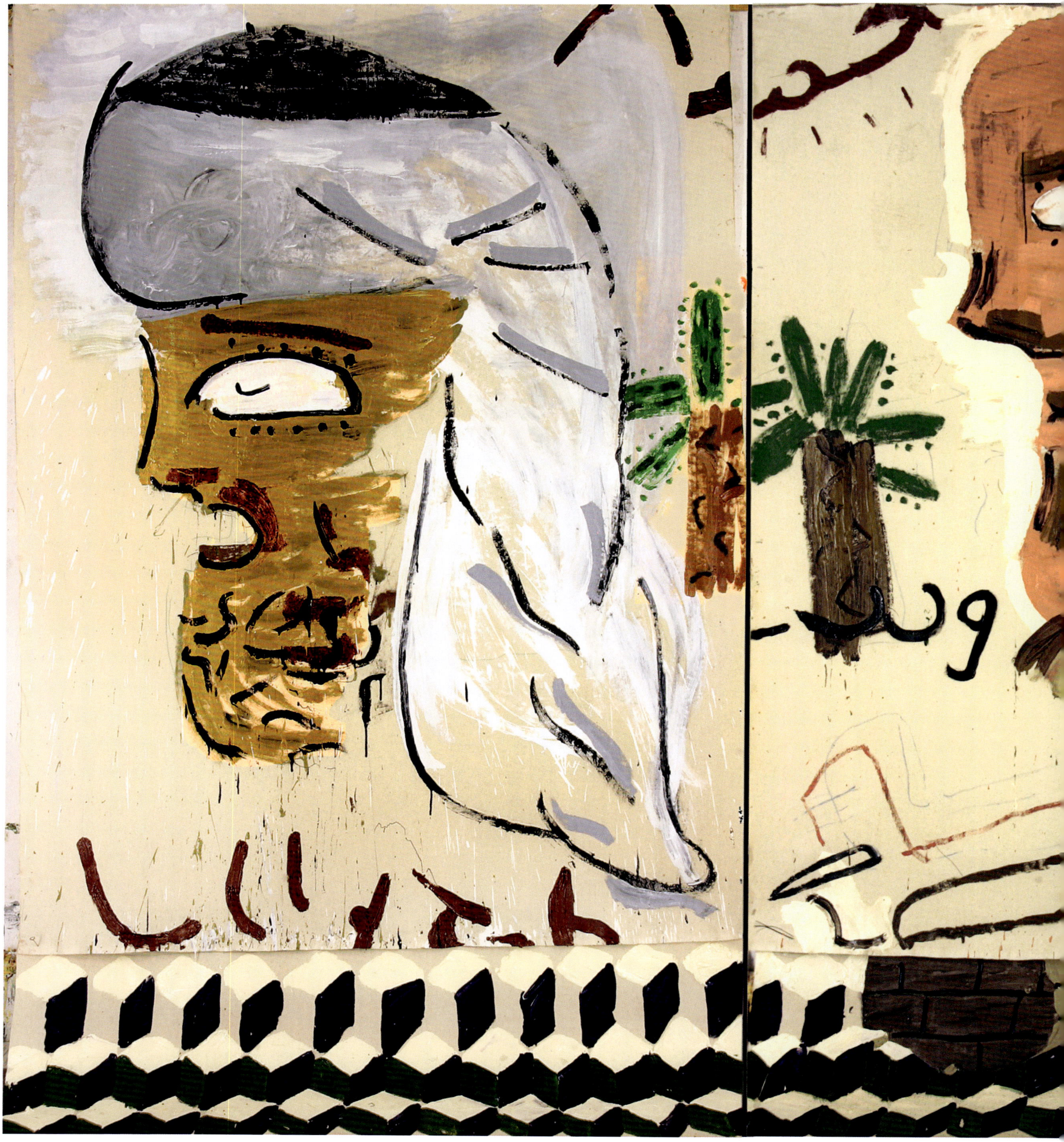

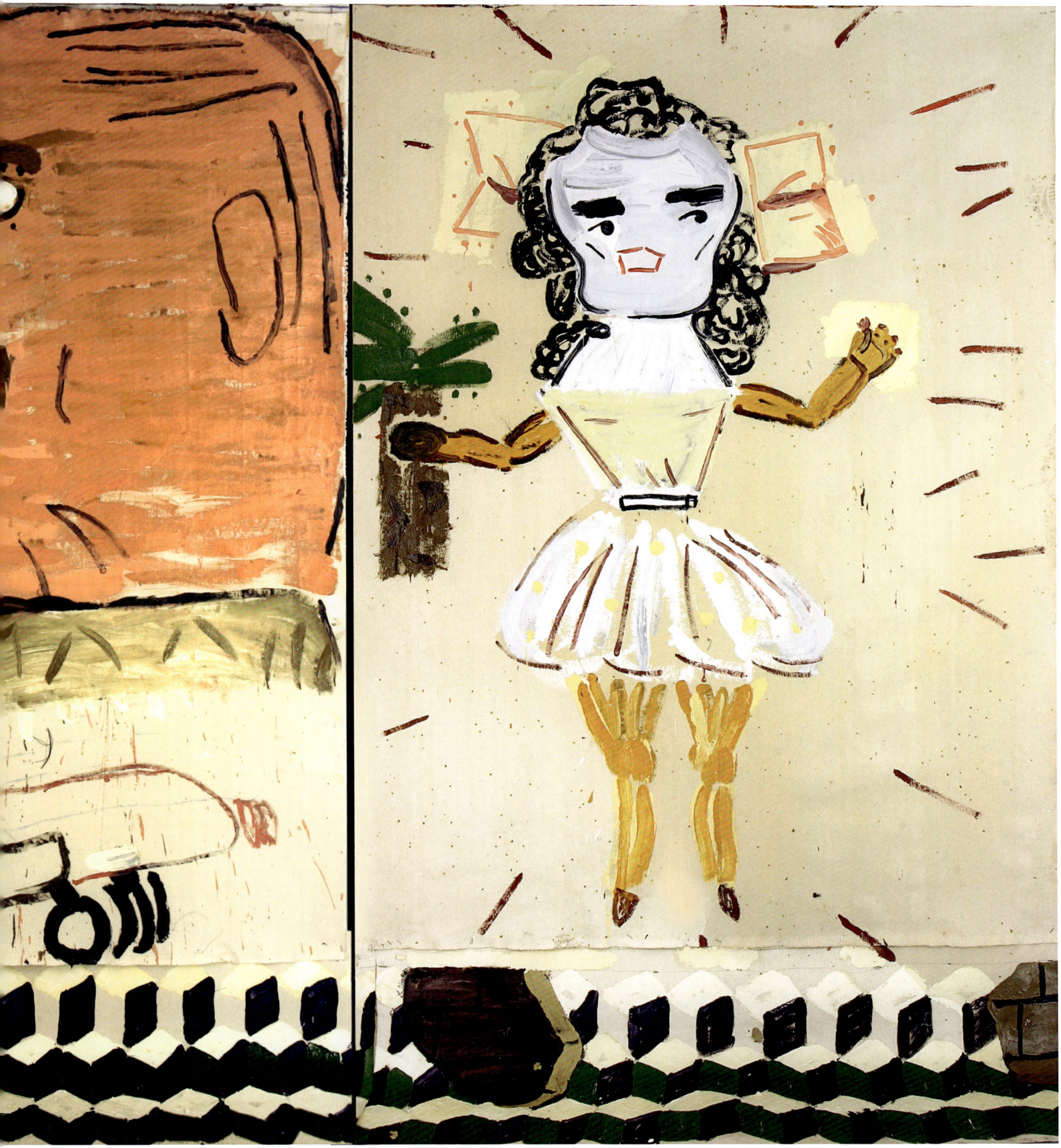

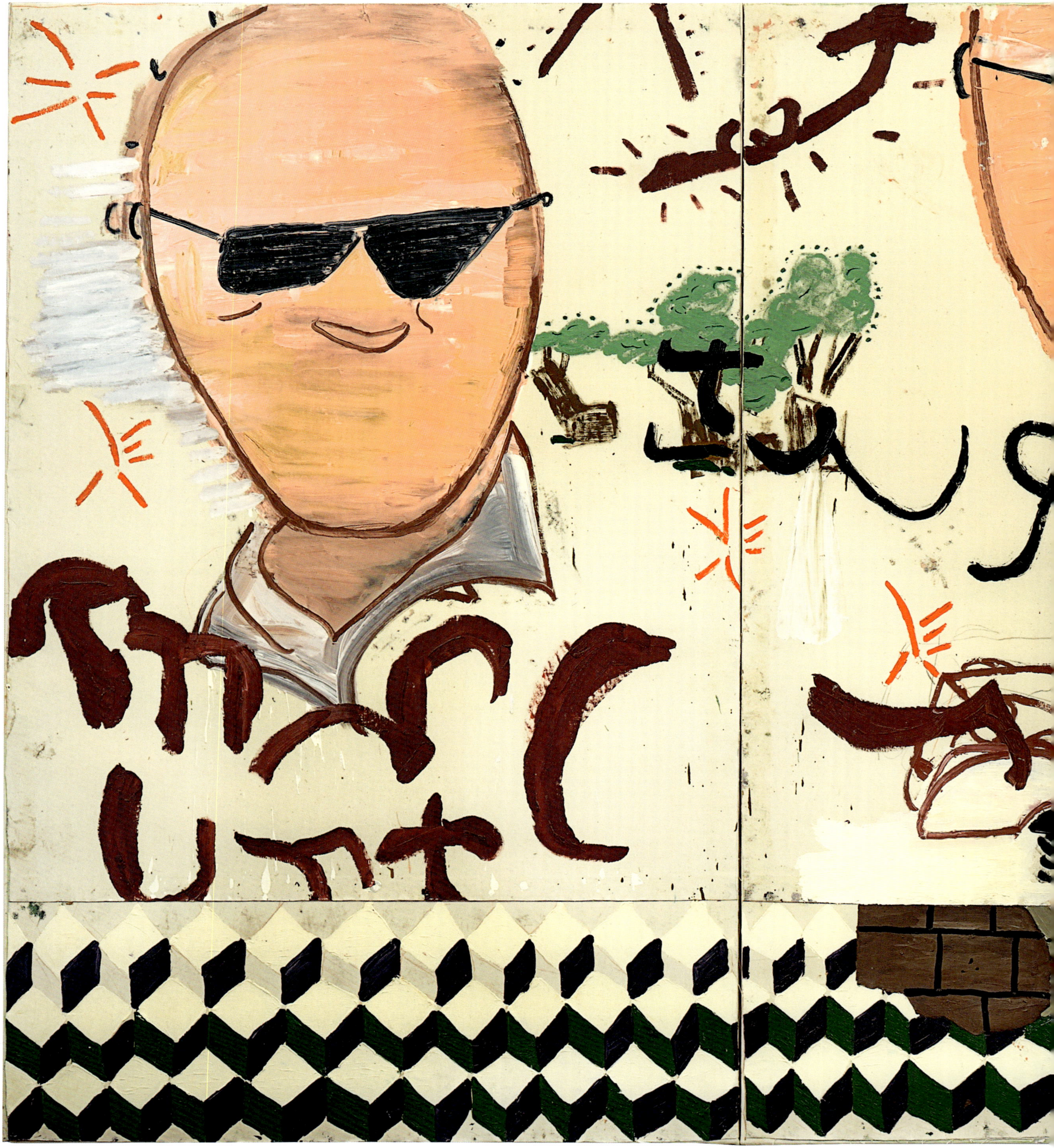

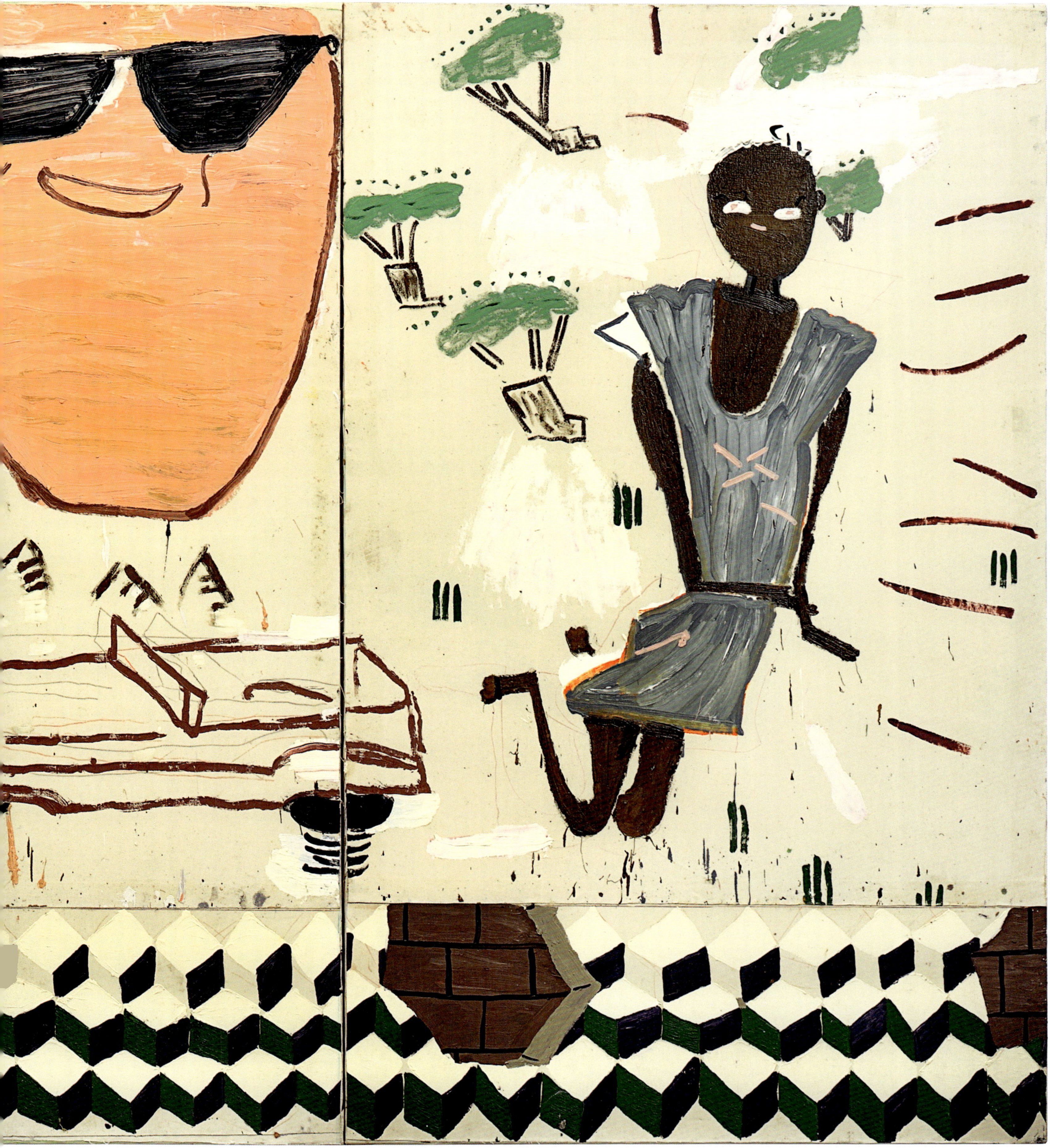

78 (pages 94–95)
Arab and Dancing Girl 2006
Oil on canvas, 231 × 435 cm (91 × 171⅜ in)
Private collection

79 (pages 96–97)
Peter Pan and Wendy 2011
Oil on canvas, 230 × 437 cm (90⅝ × 172⅛ in)
Private collection

80
House and Horse (Pink) 2007
Oil on canvas, 183 × 177 cm (72⅛ × 69¾ in)
Private collection

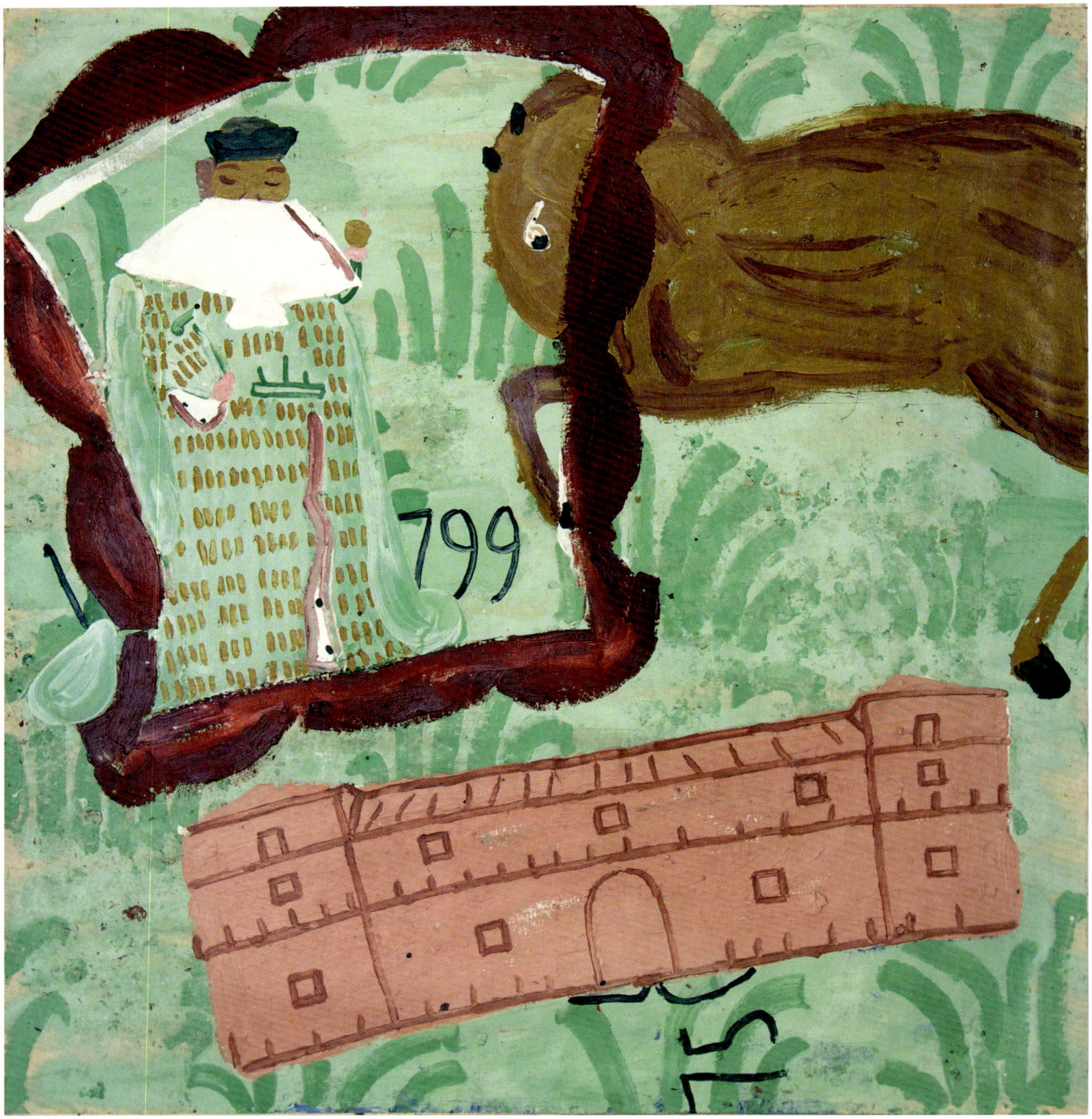

81
Willow Tree 2015
Oil on canvas, 182 × 170 cm (71¾ × 67 in)
Private collection

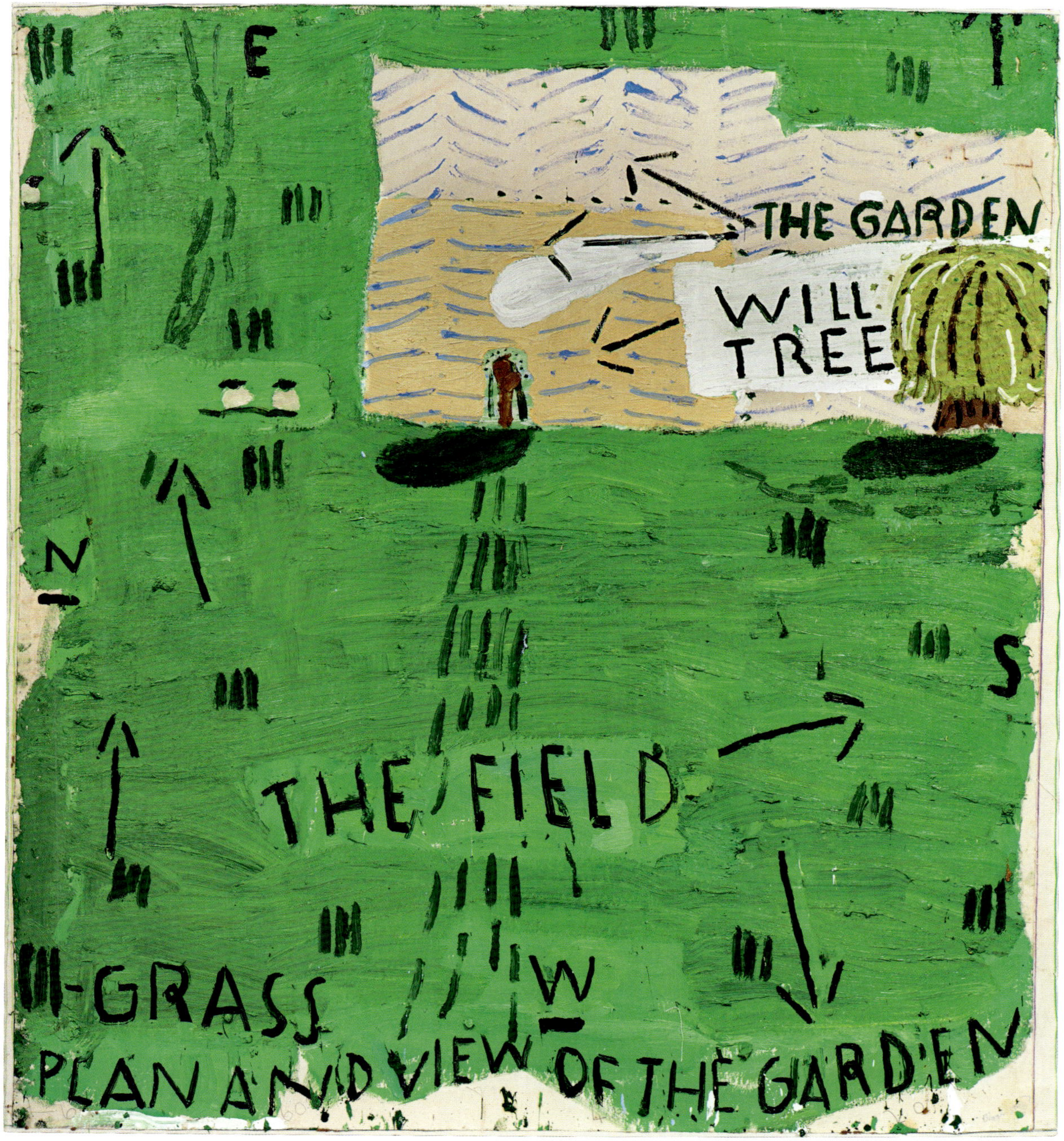

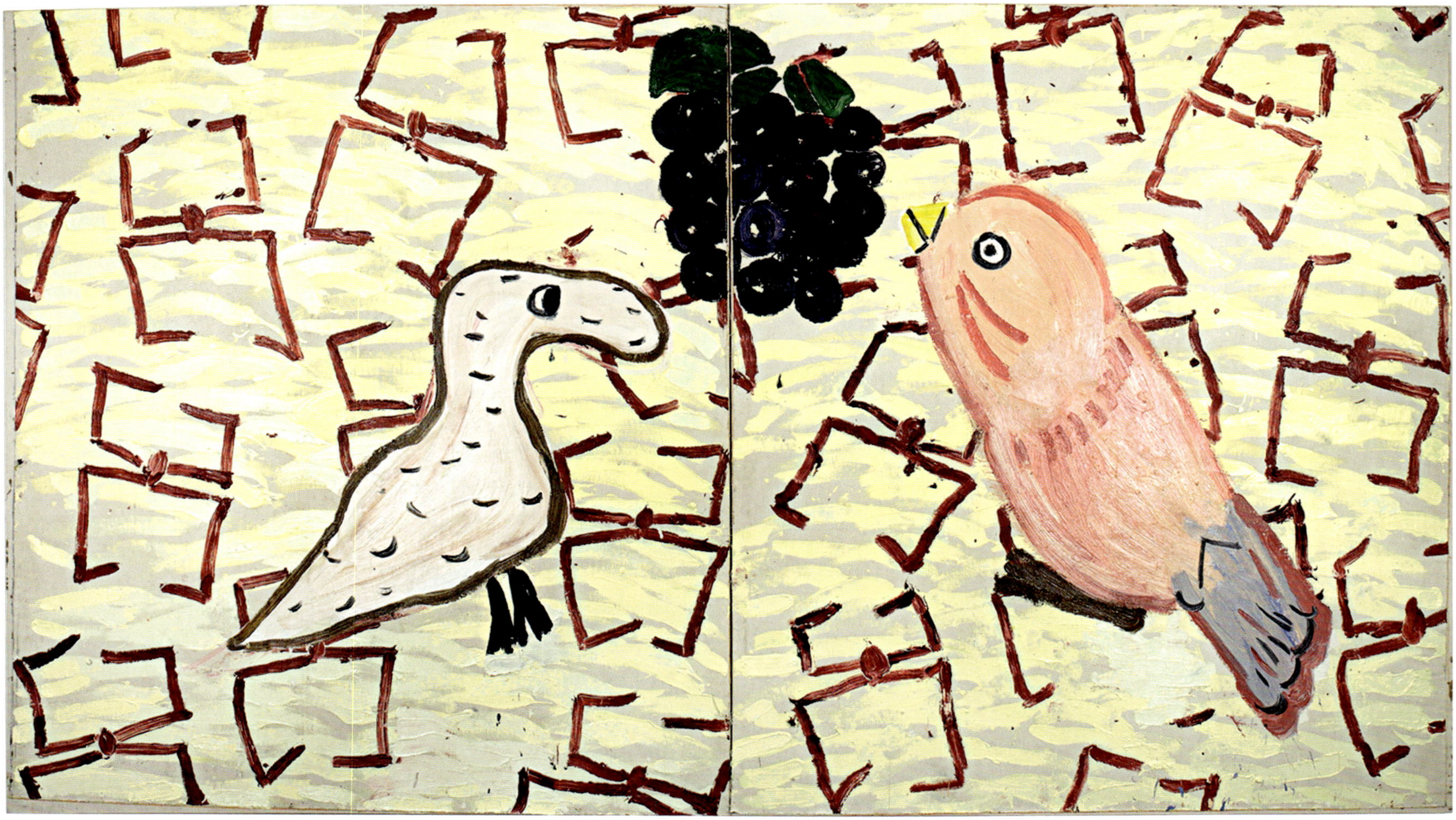

82
Toucan & Jay (Spiders & Birds) 2008
Oil on canvas, 183 × 336 cm (72⅛ × 132⅜ in)
Collection of Sarah L Elson

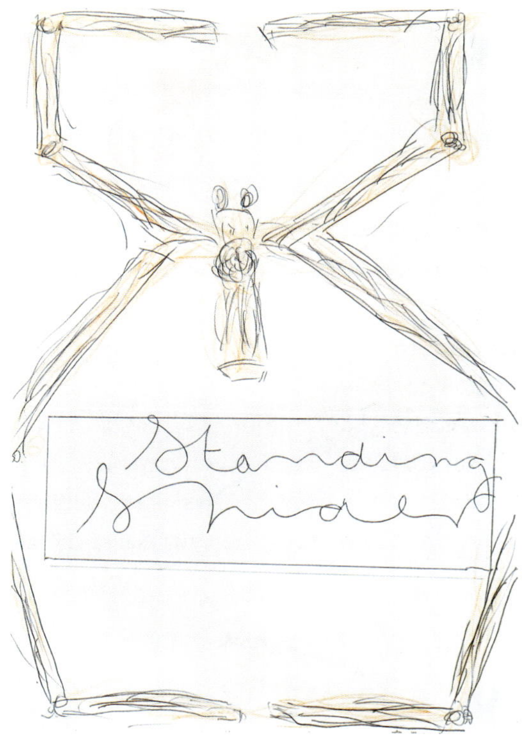

83
Standing Spider (Box) 2008
Ink on paper, 30 × 21 cm (11⅞ × 8⅜ in)
Private collection

84
Spiders (Union Jack) 2014
Ink and collage on paper
84 × 97 cm (33⅛ × 38¼ in)
Private collection

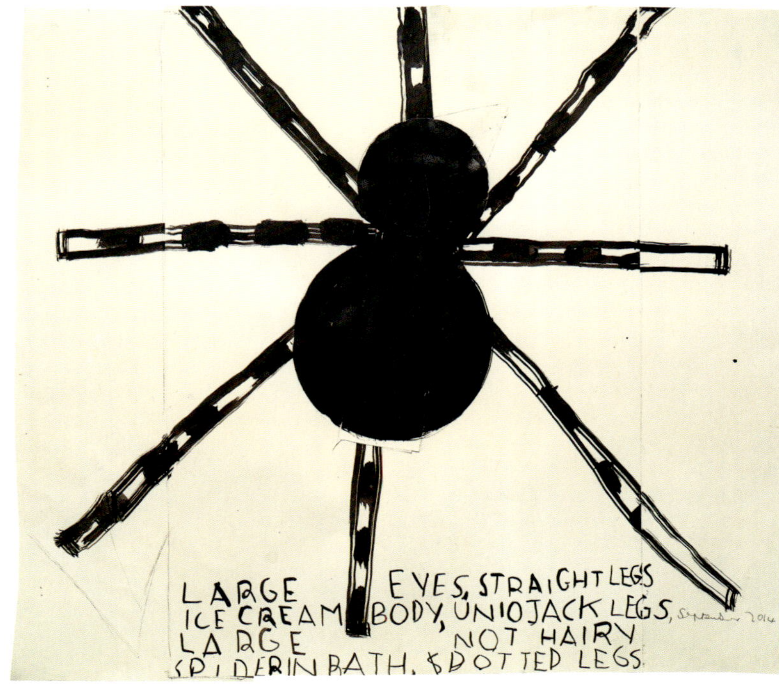

Wylie uses paint as a subversive means of expression. She prioritises 'looking' over 'reading', or 'sensing' rather than 'knowledge': the importance of pre-cognitive lived experience as opposed to conceptual thought.[67] The works are intensely felt and painted with such compulsion. They have a terrible frankness about them. Sometimes they connect the contradictory realms of the quotidian and the mysterious, but they always seem grounded in a tangible, experiential world. *Willow Tree* 2015 (fig.81), for example, maps the topology of Wylie's unweeded garden, with tufts of grass and hedgerows, whereas the oriental figure, prancing horse and fort in *House and Horse (Pink)* 2007 (fig.80) were 'copied' from wine labels found at home.

Reminiscing on a studio visit made in relation to Wylie's selection for the Washington exhibition, Sarah Elson has described how she admired *Toucan & Jay (Spiders & Birds)* 2008 (fig.82):

> a massive painting of a bird and toucan with a bunch of grapes between them, and I loved the colour and random nature of the placement and design, not to mention the large gobs of paint used to define the red spiders that form the background of the painting. Later when I used the bathroom in the house, I discovered the source material for this painting: over the toilet roll, a sticker of a bunch of grapes, and nearby, stuck on the wall, a cut-out from a tin box of biscuits – the pink bird. When I asked her about them, Rose replied, 'Oh yes, and did you find the spiders in the bath?'[68]

Wylie's work is tempered by wit and an acceptance of the world as it is; her paintings reflect how we react and reason in our struggle to make sense of it all. Perhaps unsurprisingly, given her connection with Kent, Wylie's work (like Russell Hoban's) shows parallels with Geoffrey Chaucer's *The Canterbury Tales* in its concern with the kaleidoscopic variety of human experience. Written in the late fourteenth century, *The Canterbury Tales* incorporates almost every style of medieval narrative – bawdy anecdote, allegorical fables, violence and romance – and Wylie has a similar wideness of vision, encompassing the richness and diversity of lived lives, circumscribed by the universal horizon of our embodied and

85
Princess and Mine Victim 1997
Oil on canvas, 168 × 366 cm (66¼ × 144⅛ in)
Private collection

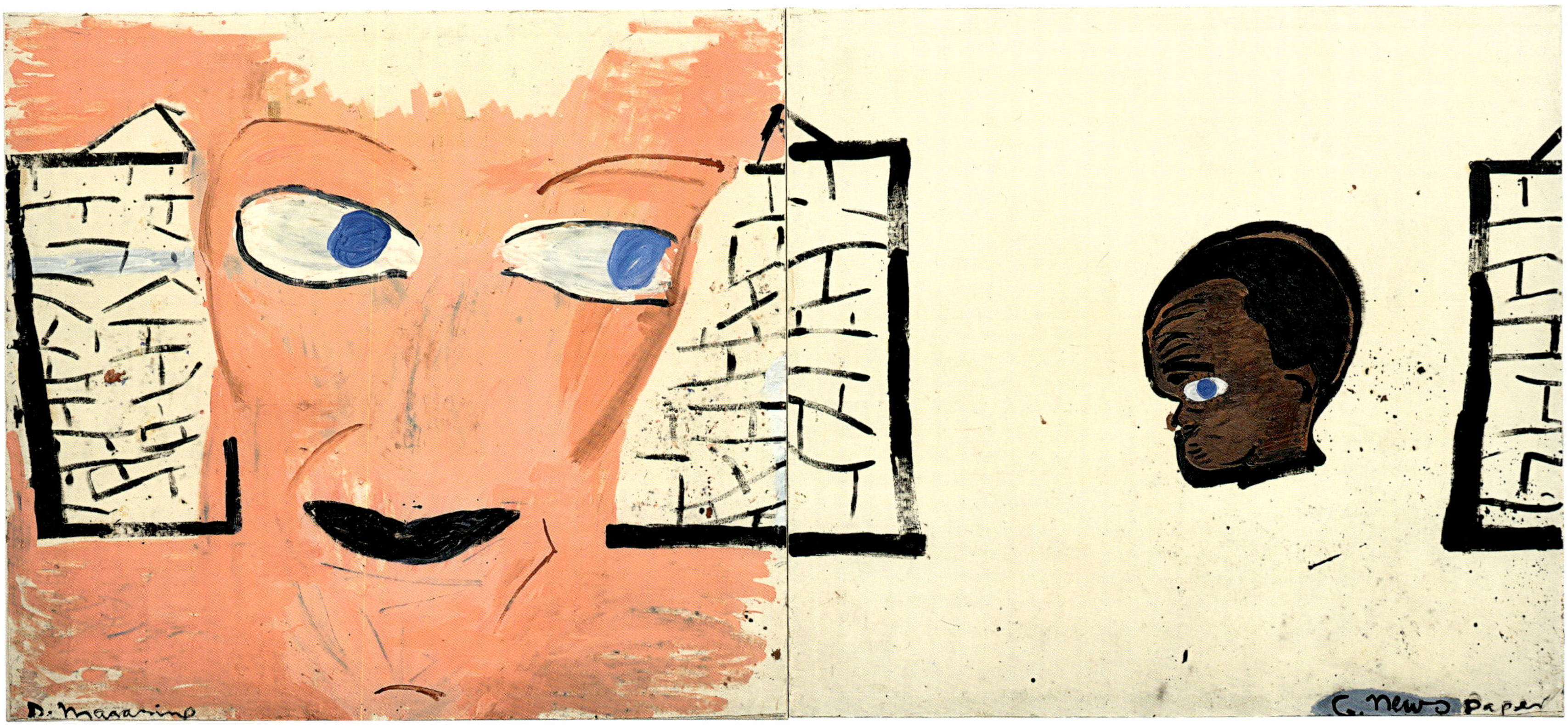

86
The Manufacturers 2008
Oil on canvas, 187 × 335 cm (73⅝ × 132 in)
Private collection

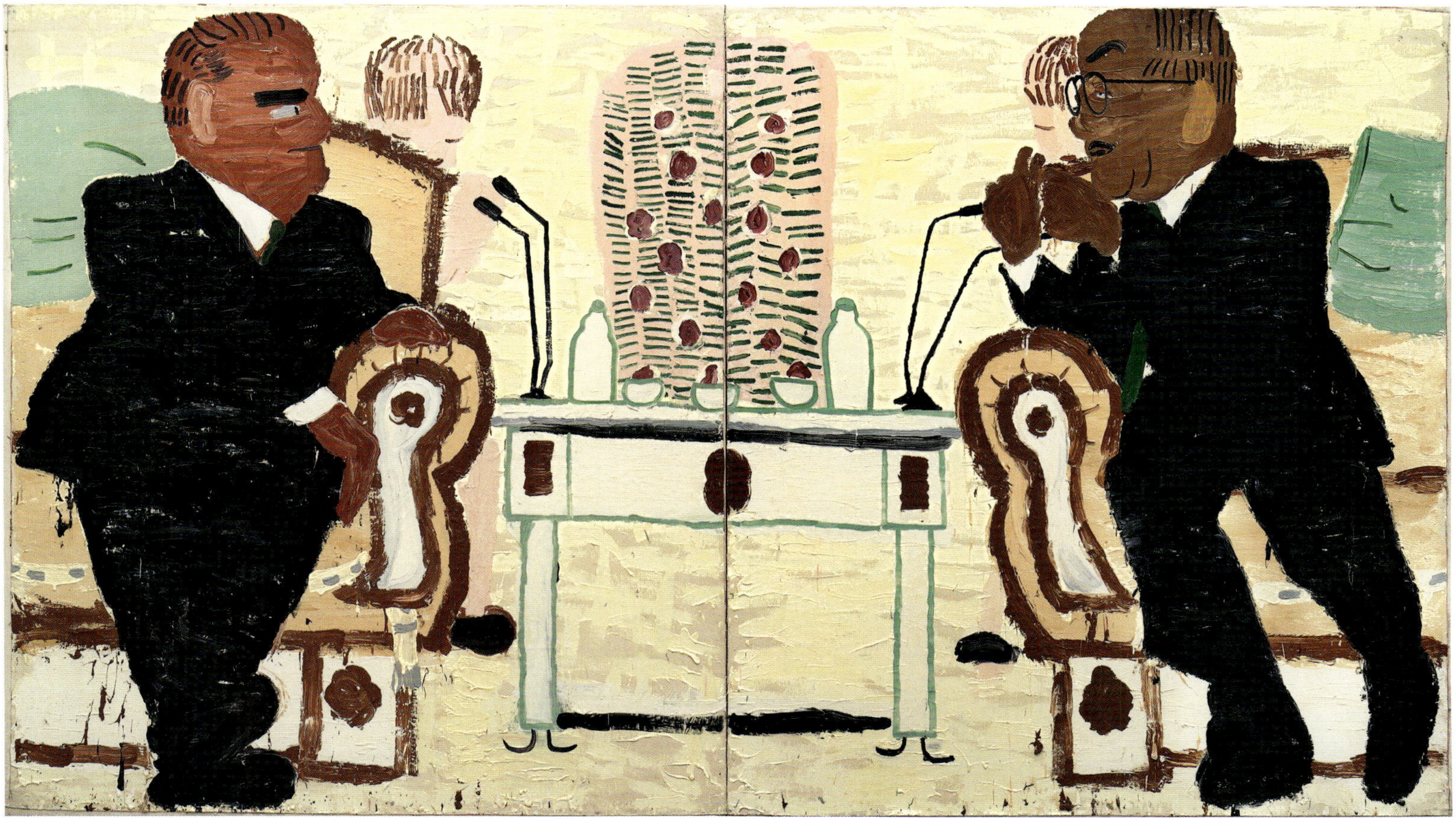

87 (overleaf)
Yasser Arafat Funeral 2004
Oil on canvas, 180 × 360 cm (70⅞ × 141¾ in)
Private collection

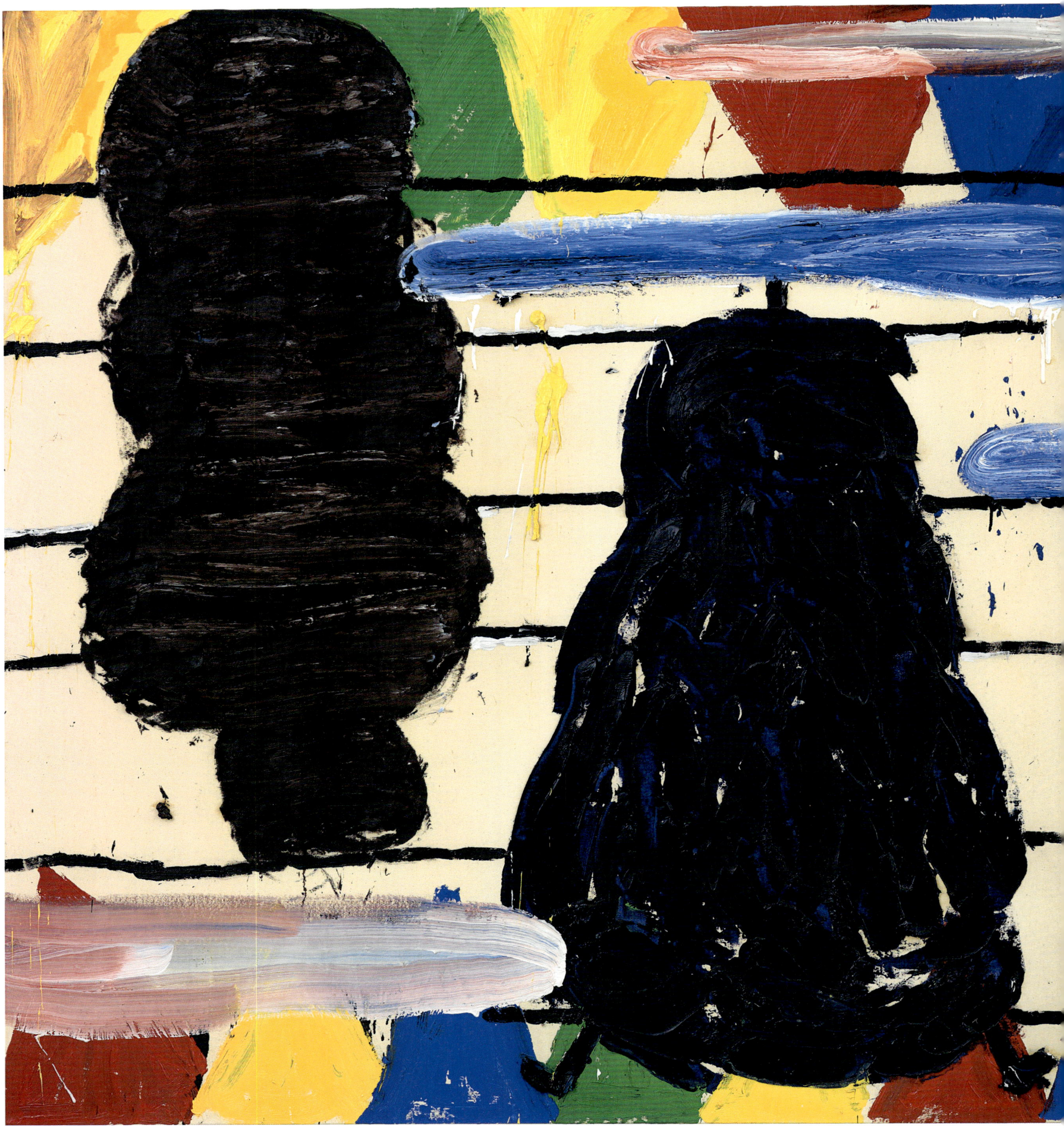

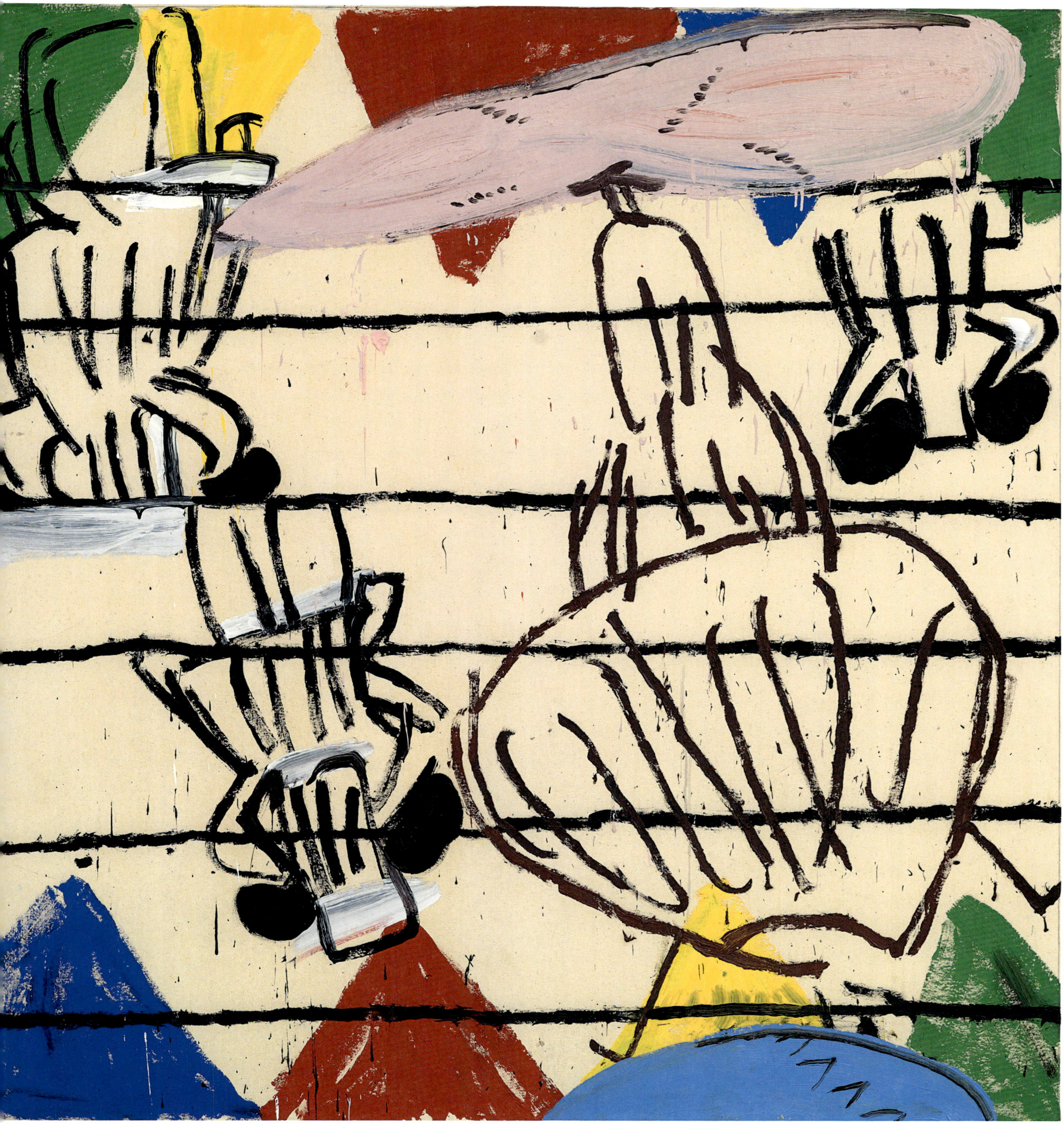

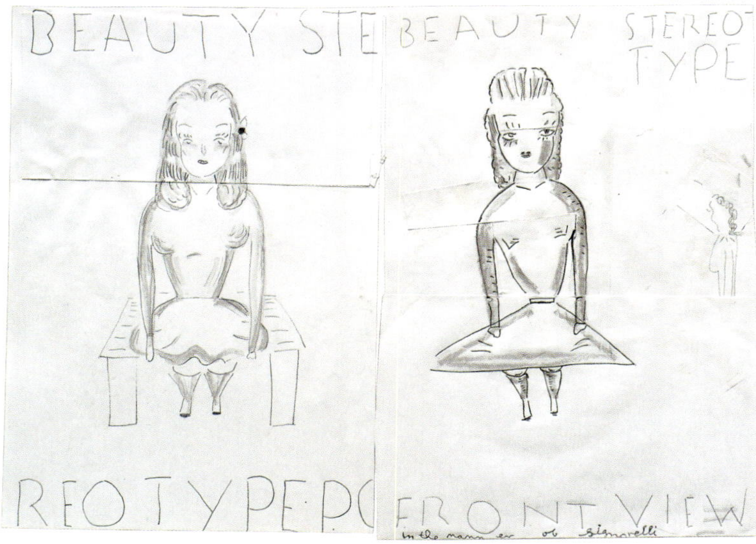

88 (above)
Beauty Stereotype (Front View) (Film Notes) 2007
Pencil and collage on paper
30 × 42 cm (11⅞ × 16⅝ in)
Private collection

89 (below)
Dr Lacra's Cherry Frock 2006
Coloured pencil, biro and collage on paper
36 × 42 cm (14¼ × 16⅝ in)
Private collection

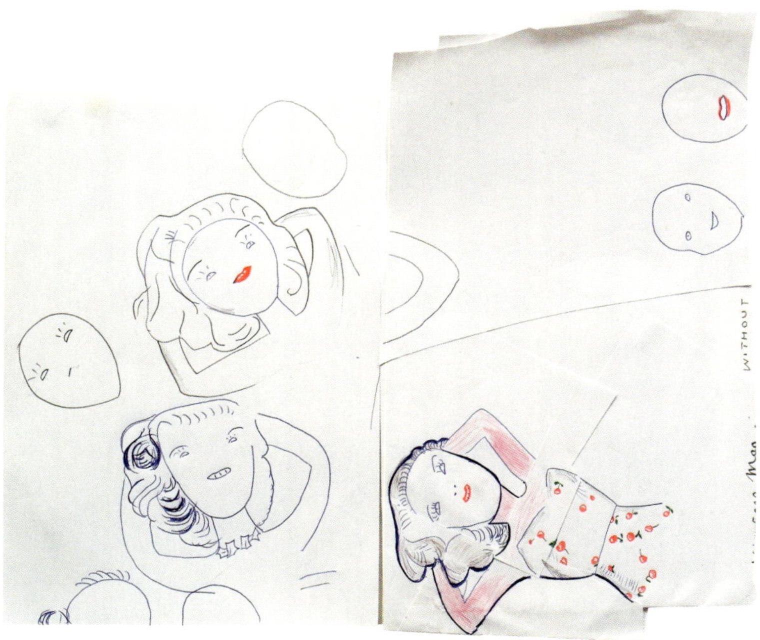

mortal nature. For Chaucer the tales unfold one after the other, each representing a different narrative style; for Wylie these different registers are present simultaneously. This simultaneity reflects the impact of new ways of experiencing the world that have developed since the time of Chaucer, including new media such as television, film and more recently the digital, that can best be described as a form of montage, essentially concerned with a condensed narrative.

Wylie is always responsive to the currents of the contemporary world around her. As seen in the painting *Yellow Girls: Säg and flop* 2017 (fig.91), her engagement with the 'real' world is in a style that is direct, honest and at times even uncomfortable. She is drawn to what she describes as 'the specific' and 'the particular'. The paintings also often offer social commentary – for example, the representation of women in the media – or touch upon pertinent issues in current affairs: Princess Diana visiting a mine victim in Angola (fig.85), Yasser Arafat's funeral (fig.87), the signing of an important international trade deal (fig.86) or the Iraq War (fig.7).

Wylie deliberately employs a straightforward style combined with a frank approach to her subject matter, and on occasion she appears herself in the painting. These spirited self-portraits have insight, integrity and humour. In *RW & Bird* 1996 (fig.12), for example, she reduces herself to a simple outline of a slim female form with a featureless lollipop head. Her body is dominated by large, triangular, pointy breasts – perhaps the result of wearing a bullet bra, one of the most iconic lingerie items of the 1950s. At the top of the painting are two studies of birds' heads with oversized beaks – suggesting a connection with the word 'bird' which tops the list of pet names British women would like banned from everyday use.[69]

Elsewhere Wylie's depiction of women is playful yet sophisticated. Her women appear at first sight as stereotypical images of femininity; her female figures are often slim with tiny hands and feet and big eyes, lashes and hair (fig.88). They are reminiscent of cartoon figures such as Betty Boop or, as Emma Dexter has noted, the drawn locker-room pin-ups of 1940s forces' sweethearts.[70] Wylie, however, transmutes these conventions through the use

90
Girl in Lights 2015
Oil on canvas, 209 × 328 cm (82⅜ × 129¼ in)
Private collection

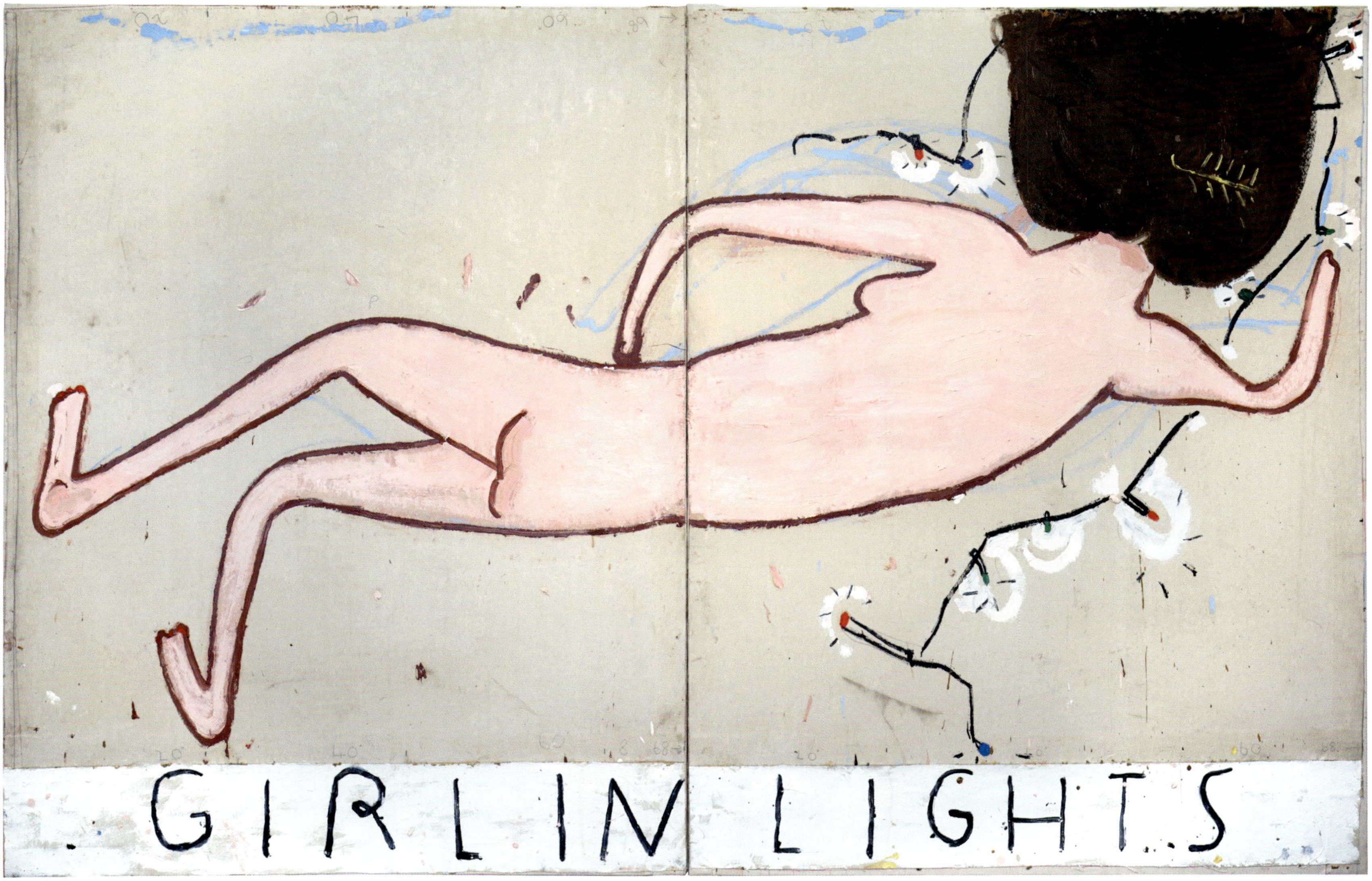

91 (overleaf)
Yellow Girls: Säg and flop 2017
Oil on canvas
183 × 334 cm (72 × 131½)
Private collection

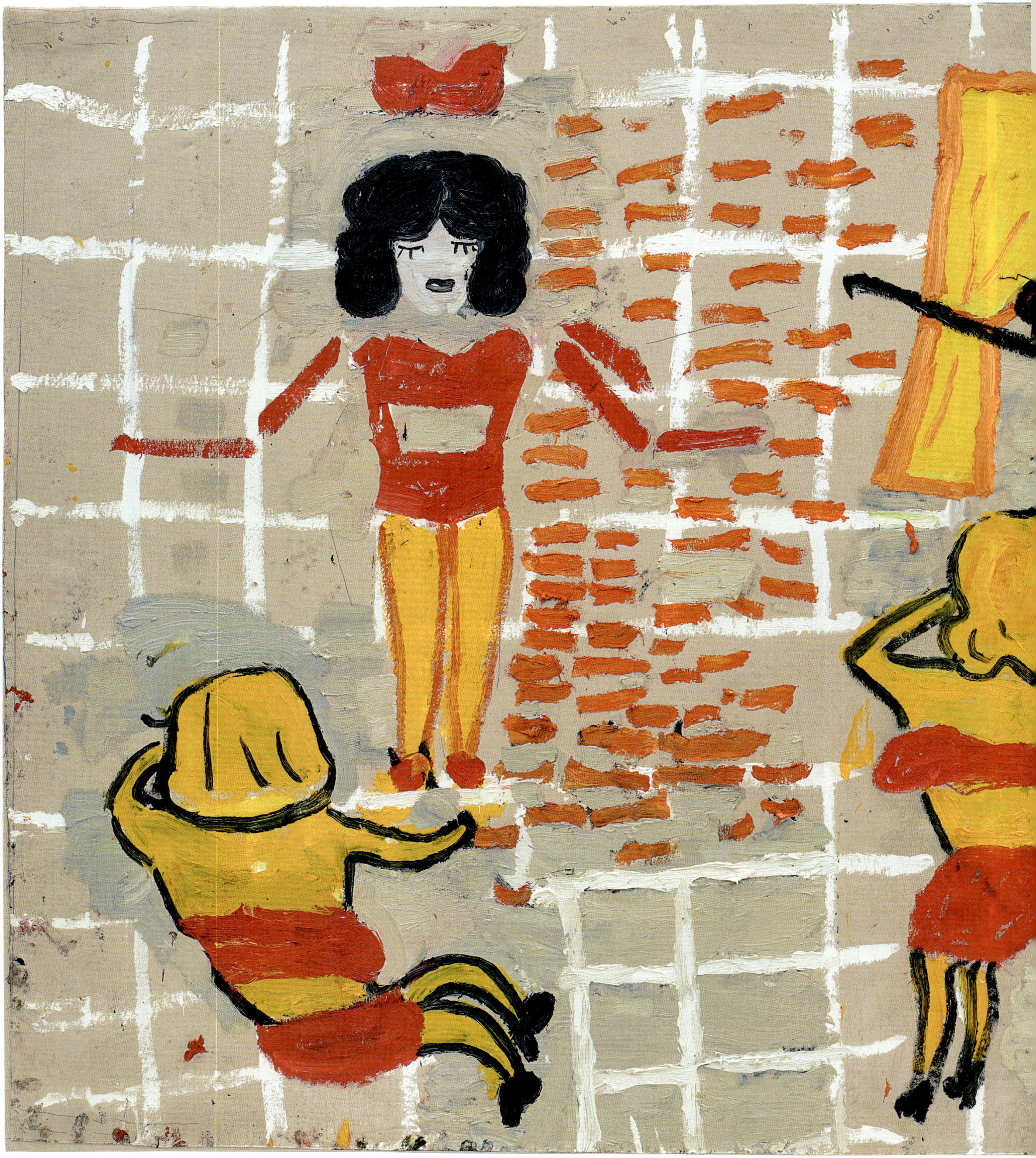

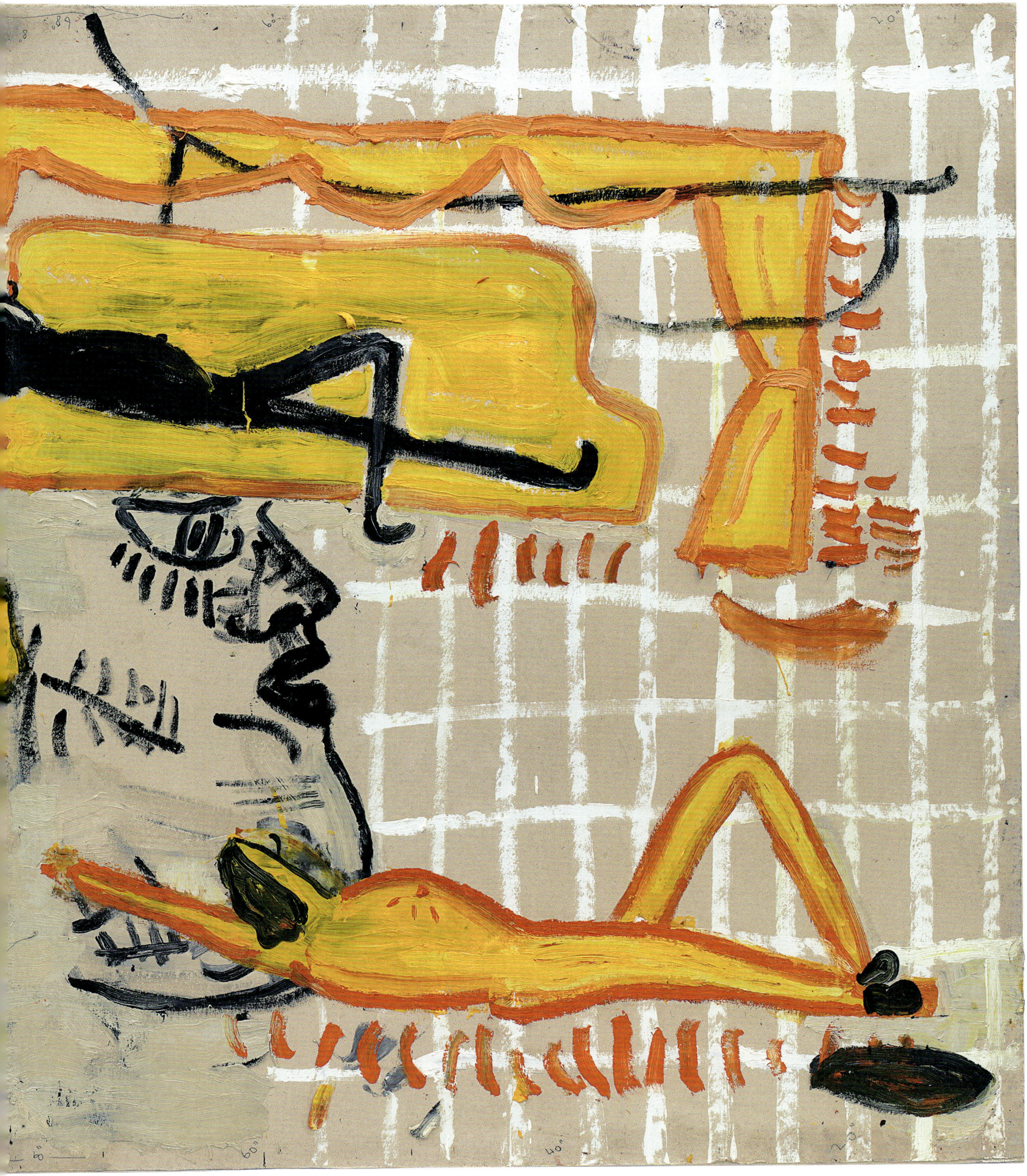

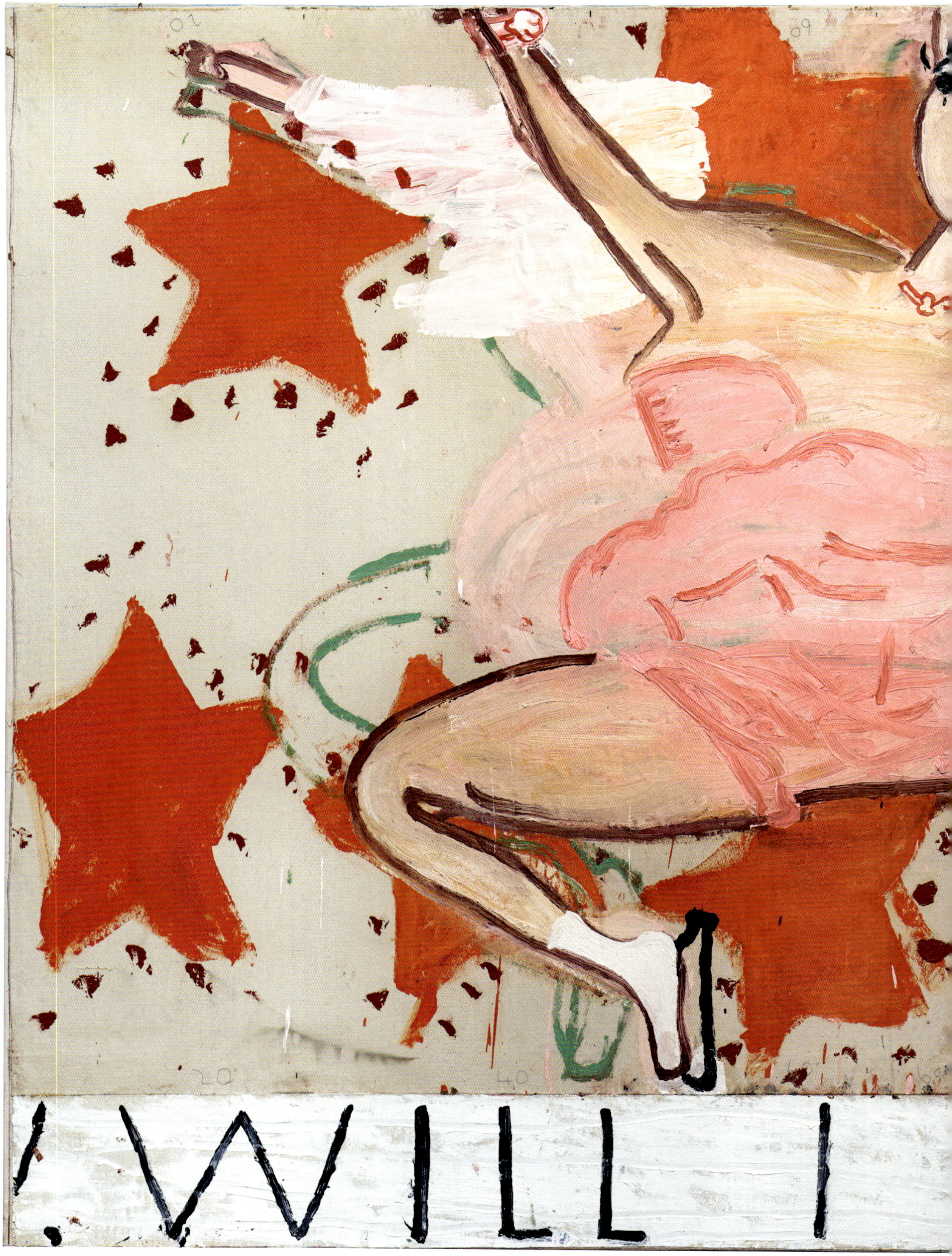
WILL I

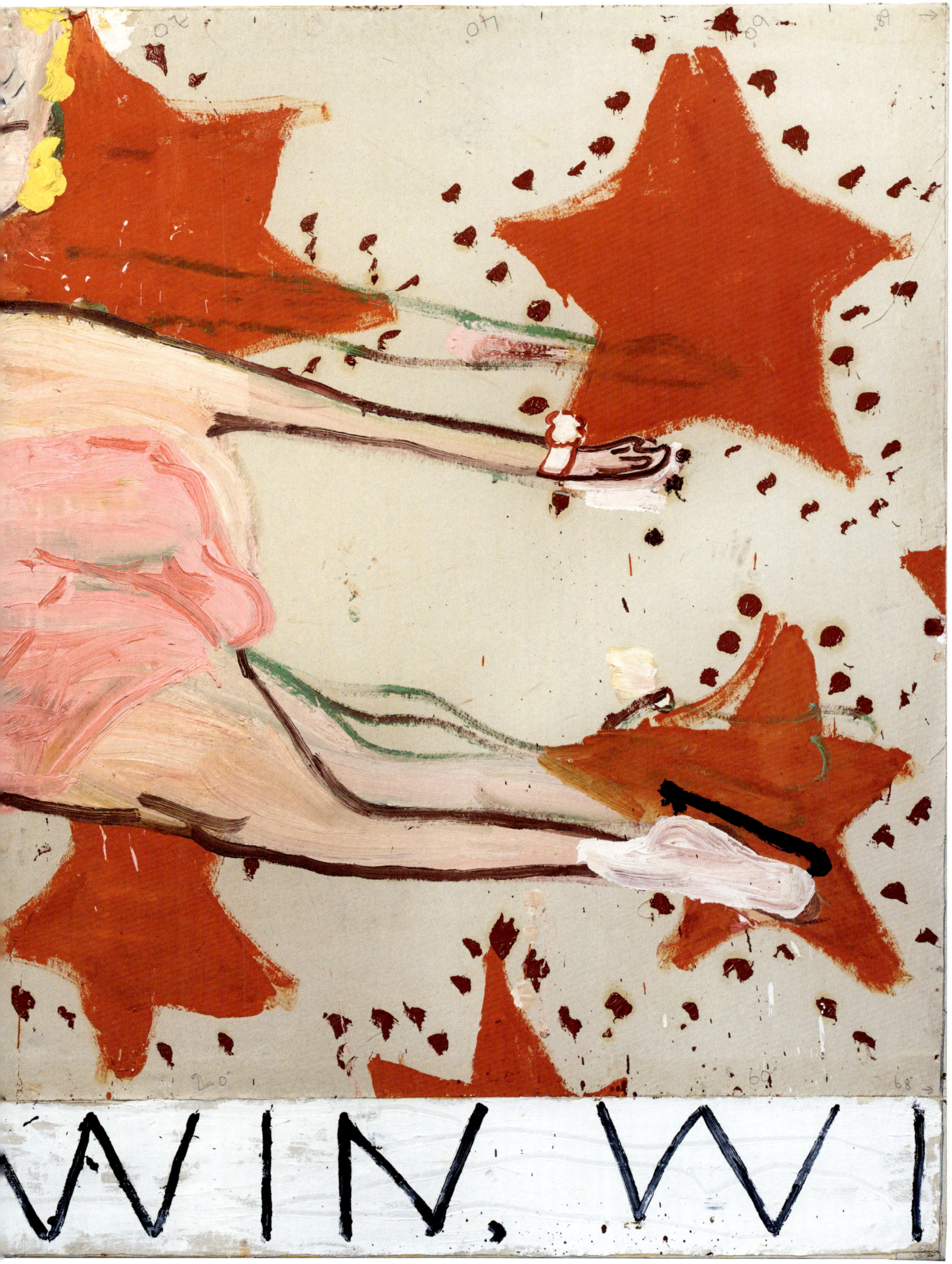
WIN, WI

92 (previous page)
Pink Skater (Will I Win, Will I Win) 2015
Oil on canvas, 208 × 329 cm (82 × 129⅝ in)
Private collection

of her own idiosyncratic style, creating icons of humorous, bold and ambitious women – for example, *Girl in Lights* 2015 (fig.90) or the jubilant *Pink Skater (Will I Win, Will I Win)* 2015 (fig.92) which presents a woman in a sugar-pink costume, orange stars bursting all around her, held in a leap so wide it straddles two canvases, while her frozen, forced smile echoes the thought bubble 'Will I Win' written below. The picture is painted with expressive fluidity, using large brushstrokes to capture personality and a sense of movement.

On one level Wylie is engaging with the feminist analysis of the nexus of representation and power, refracted through dress, deportment and conceptions of beauty. This engagement is seen through the lens of Wylie's deep knowledge and use of historical and contemporary references that span sources as diverse as Indian and Persian miniatures through to Japanese manga comics, characters from the animated sitcom *South Park* or even Angelina Jolie as Tomb Raider Lara Croft. These disparate roots are combined to create an icon which is both contemporary and ancient, reminiscent of the *korai* of archaic Greece.[71] In a similar way, Wylie embodies both a quintessential depiction of Woman and an individual, living woman. *Charlotte from the Back* 1990 (fig.93), for example, consists of the silhouette of her niece seen from behind. The body is painted in a single continuous line and effortlessly captures her tilted hips, the uneven distribution of weight down the right leg. Charlotte is seen standing in front of a series of horizontal lines, copied from preliminary drawings which were made on lined paper. Painted in the same year, the lone figure in *Girl on a Liner* 1996 was the result of a small advertisement Wylie saw in a newspaper about the glamour of sea travel. With her yellow hair, heavily defined arched eyebrows, bright red lips, long evening dress and gloves, the girl looks like a 1930s Hollywood starlet, with the Georgian house and hedge in the background derived from 'A house of a neighbour seen from the top of the hill behind the garden', acting as a substitute for the luxury liner.[72]

In *Red Twink and Ivy* 2002 (fig.94), an assortment of female figures are embellished with rectangular tabs, like paper cut-outs used by children to dress 2D figures in different outfits.

93
Charlotte from the Back 1990
Oil on paper, 84 × 60 cm (33⅛ × 23⅝ in)
Private collection

Unperturbed by these additions, they casually float across the canvas while a large cat, with a quizzical expression, stares out at the viewer. It is one from the series of *Twink and Ivy* paintings (see also figs 95 and 96) which was included in Wylie's first retrospective, *Big Boys Sit in the Front*, a nine-work show that inaugurated the Jerwood Foundation's gallery in Hastings. The title, paraphrased from a poem by the American poet Robert Creely, whom Wylie met at a party in Canada, subtly articulates a sense of women often finding themselves being loomed over.[73] The four-panel *Getting Better with Water* 2011 (fig.97) explores the healing properties of water. Based on photographs of Wylie's daughter-in-law convalescing in the Mediterranean after breast cancer, it shows three images of a woman on a sun lounger and another, with wide shoulders, in swimsuit and goggles. The name 'Rebecca Adlington', the gold-medal-winning Olympic swimmer, is scrawled across the canvas, a paragon of female strength and capability. While not an obvious likeness, the head in *PC* 2007 adopts the initials of the actress Penélope Cruz. It was originally intended for the border of a larger painting, *Sitting on a Bench with Border (Film Notes)* 2008 (fig.98), made up of several different PC heads, which when brought together appear like frames from a roll of film. The profile was made up from a list created by Wylie which detailed her 'Wolf-whistle attributes: Big hair, Eyelashes, Neck, Big Chest, Tight, pulled-to-fit top, Small waist, Skirt, Skinny legs, Long legs, Thin Ankles, Socks/High-heeled shoes.'[74] With wit, irony, pathos and stoicism, Wylie's figures continue to sit, stand, pose, as they have always done; and somehow embedded within these forms lies the memory of countless other historical representations of femininity.

Since resuming painting in the 1980s, Wylie's subject matter has drawn on iconic figures from saints to film stars, exploring how the imagery of such figures enters the everyday. These are not merely essays in representation, though, but carry a range of allusions from the personal to the social, sometimes the political. *The Fat Controller* 2006 (fig.99), for example, was painted in response to measures taken by the government to curb childhood obesity. Celebrity chef Jamie Oliver was figurehead of a campaign about poor food in schools, and it was taken up in the media before Tony

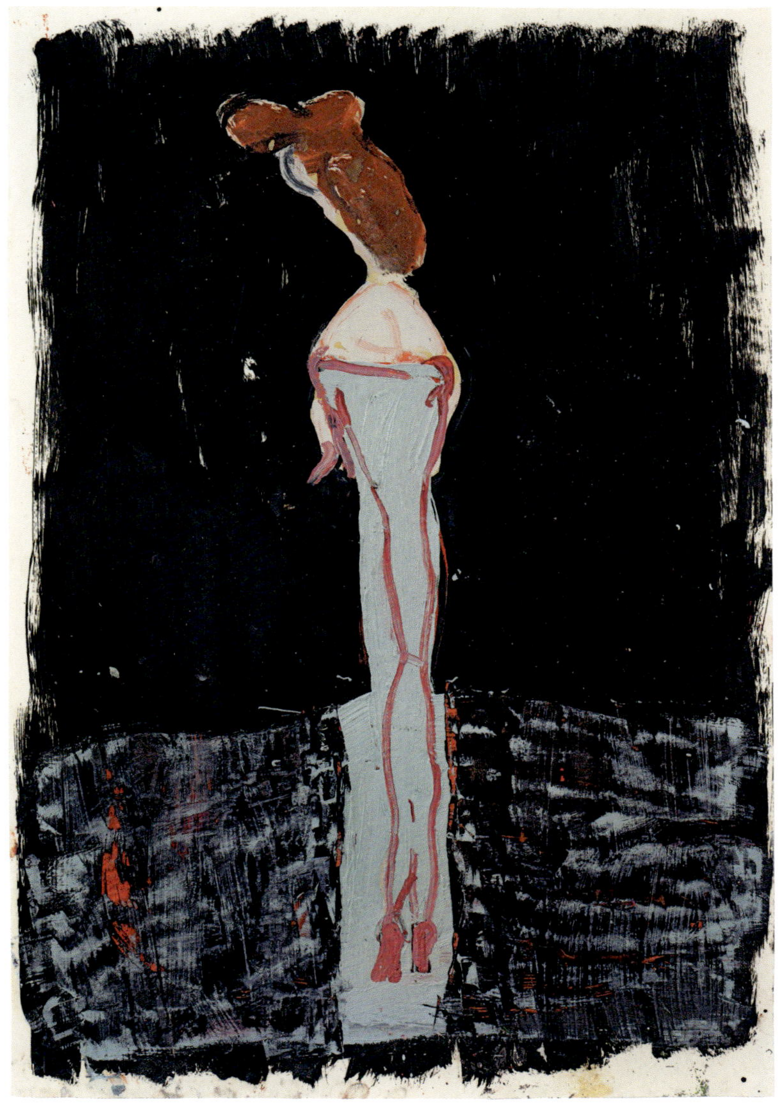

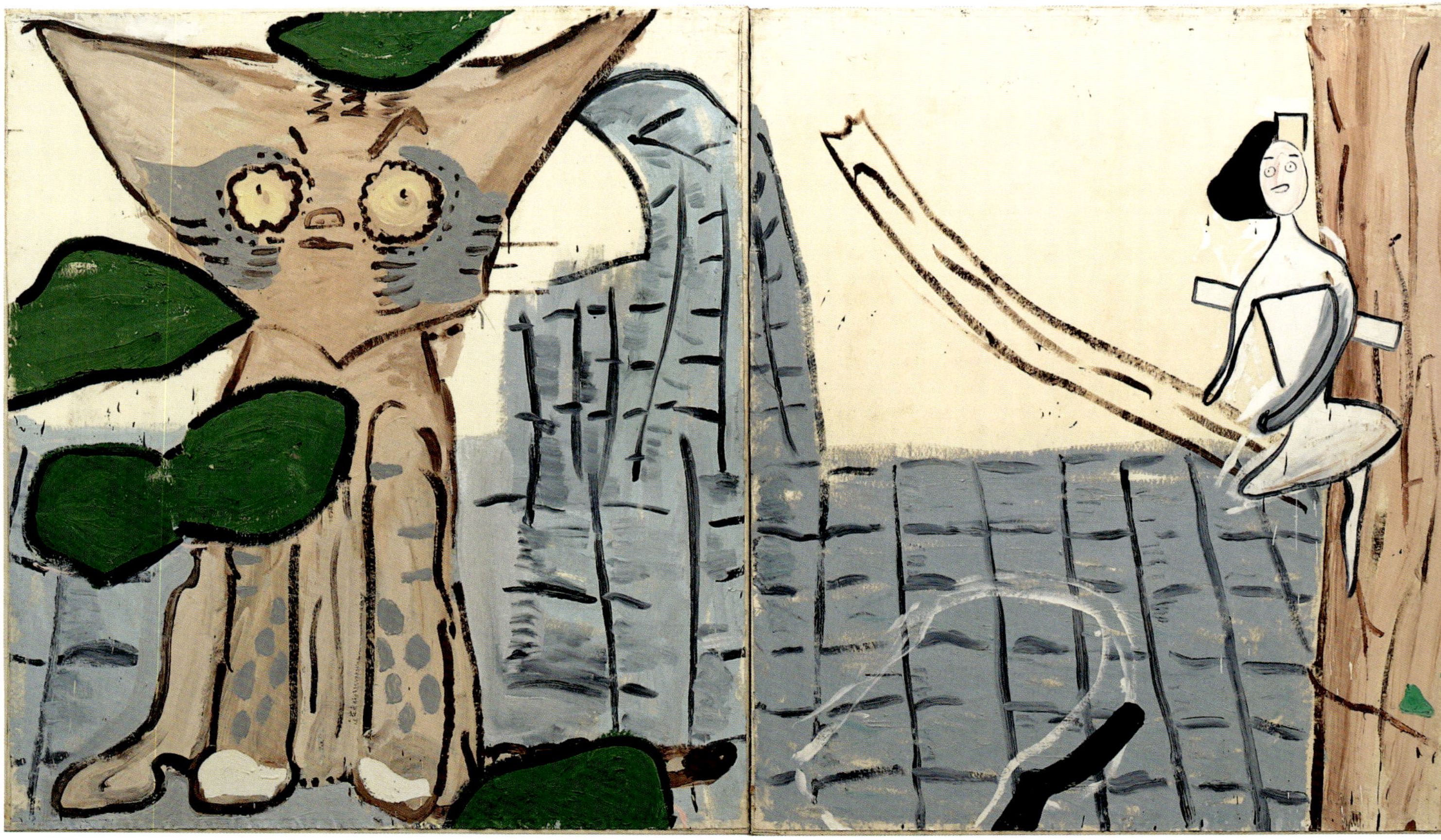

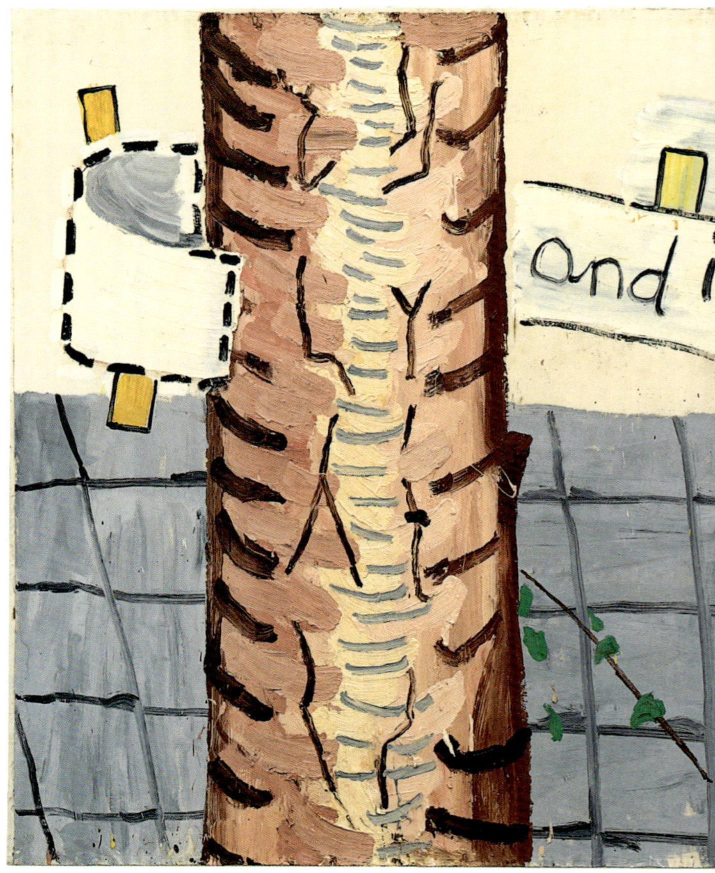
and i

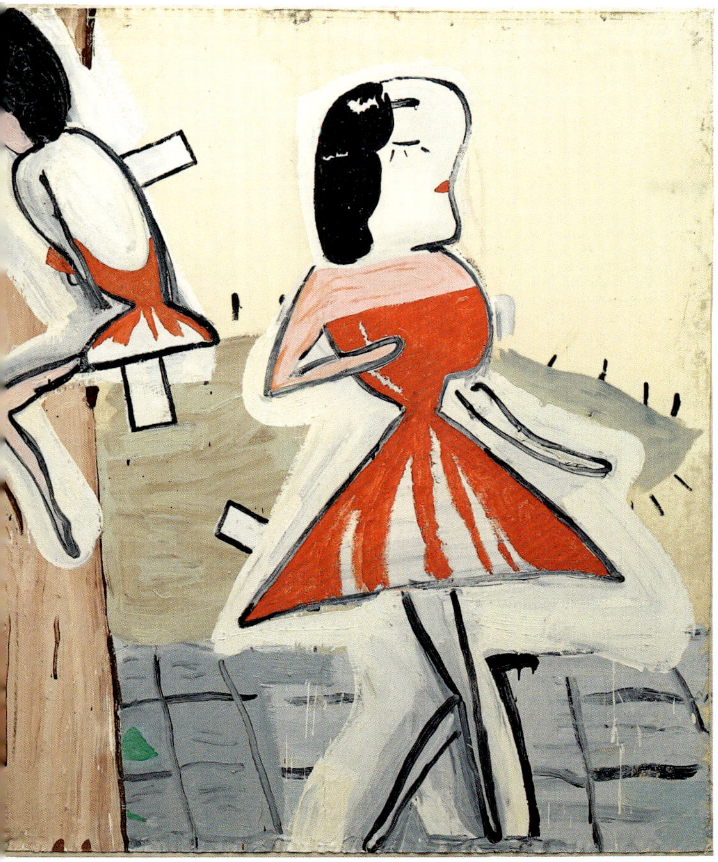

94
Red Twink and Ivy 2002
Oil on canvas, 183 × 504 cm (72⅛ × 198½ in)
Private collection

95
Green Twink and Ivy 2003
Oil on canvas, 183 × 504 cm (72⅛ × 198½ in)
Private collection

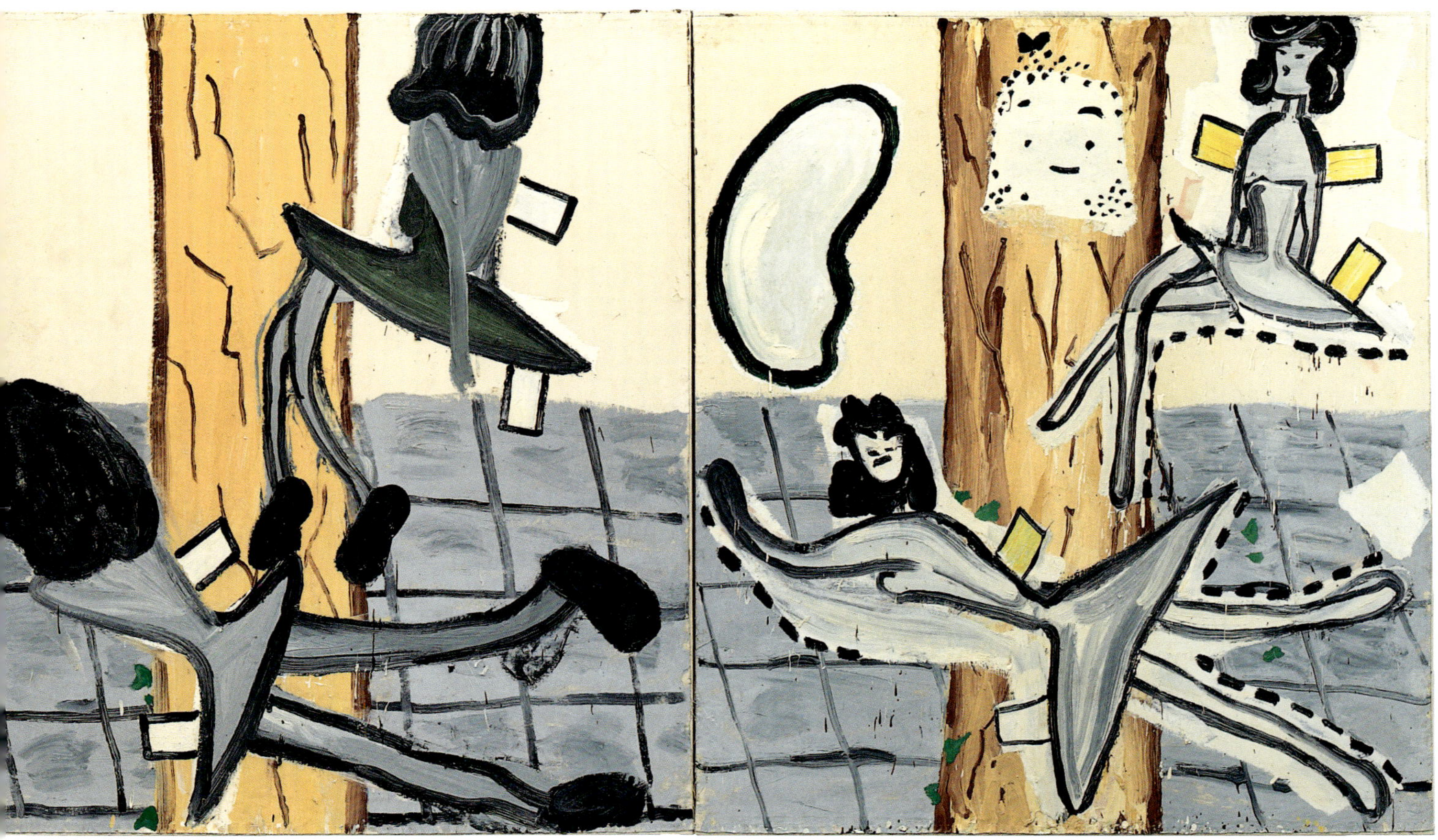

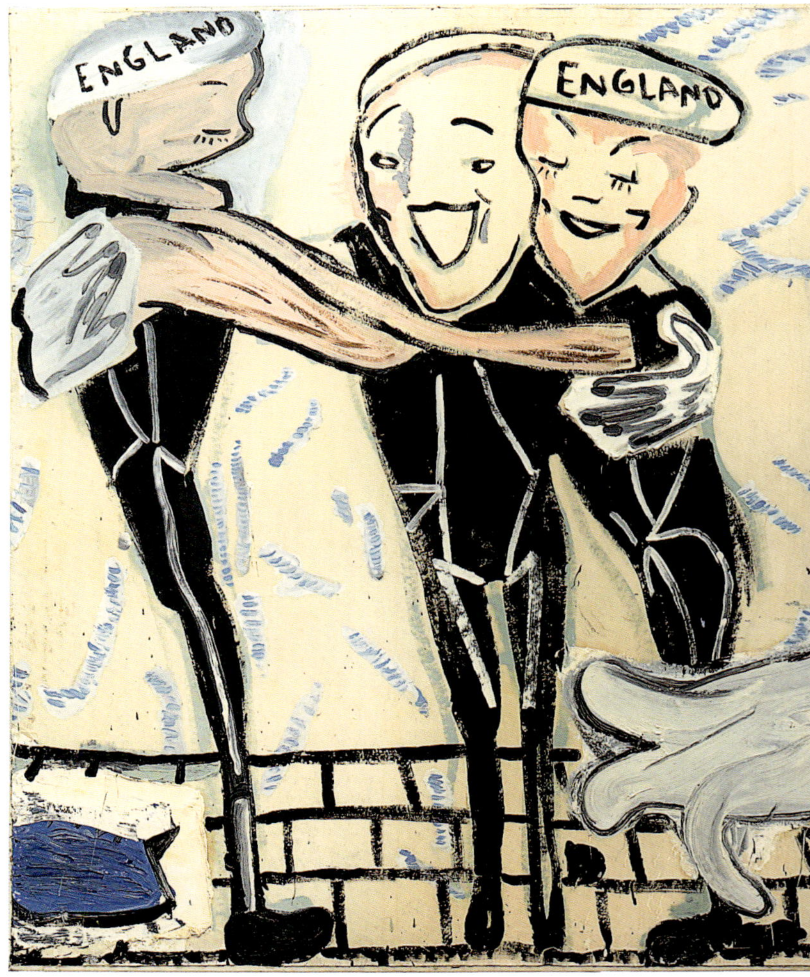

96
Swimming with Cats (Blue Twink) 2002
Oil on canvas, 183 × 498 cm (72⅛ × 196⅛ in)
Private collection

Blair announced measures in response. Wylie has said that the Fat Controller, a familiar character from the Reverend W. Awdry's Thomas the Tank Engine stories, represents Blair: a pun in which the Prime Minister tries to control fat. The four comic-like frames that make up the work all share the same yellow background. The Fat Controller appears twice: once from the back, dominating one quarter; the second time within a picture frame, as if displayed on a wall. The doubling of the image suggests the ubiquity of the character, in 'reality' and as image. It suggests an avuncular Big Brother, a paternalistic figure who is both reassuring yet slightly oppressive. The 'real' Fat Controller faces away; the viewer is not confronted by his gaze, but someone else – it is implied – is. The chocolate and biscuit are outsized compared to the sofa and framed pictures, the innocent pleasure they give rendered suspect. It is as if the muted menace that can be sensed in the metaphysical paintings of Giorgio de Chirico (1888–1978), which Wylie admires, has been introduced into a pastel-yellow domestic interior.

Her bold figurative paintings confront what she sees as society's obsession with style and self-image. Celebrity gives us a focus for our imagination, just as the gods and demigods of Ancient Greece and Rome once did. Celebrities are our myth bearers: carriers of the divine forces of good, evil, lust and redemption. Once images were a reflection of substance, a focus for faith, but the twentieth century has seen the evolution of the notion of fame. This transformation is the result of the growth of the mass media and the Internet which have served to make the images of fame more ubiquitous than they have ever been before. A series of recent paintings of Nicole Kidman (fig.101) were triggered by a photograph that Wylie saw on a website of the actress attending the Cannes premiere of her film *The Paperboy* 2012. The picture was an intriguing view from behind, showing Kidman's bare back (bar a tiny black strap) so that she appeared to be only wearing a gathered skirt and outsized shoes – something a child might do when dressing up. As with the paintings of Penélope Cruz, Wylie made a mental list from memory of all of Kidman's features: yellow hair, up, in coils/bunches, swinging earrings/bracelets. This method of working

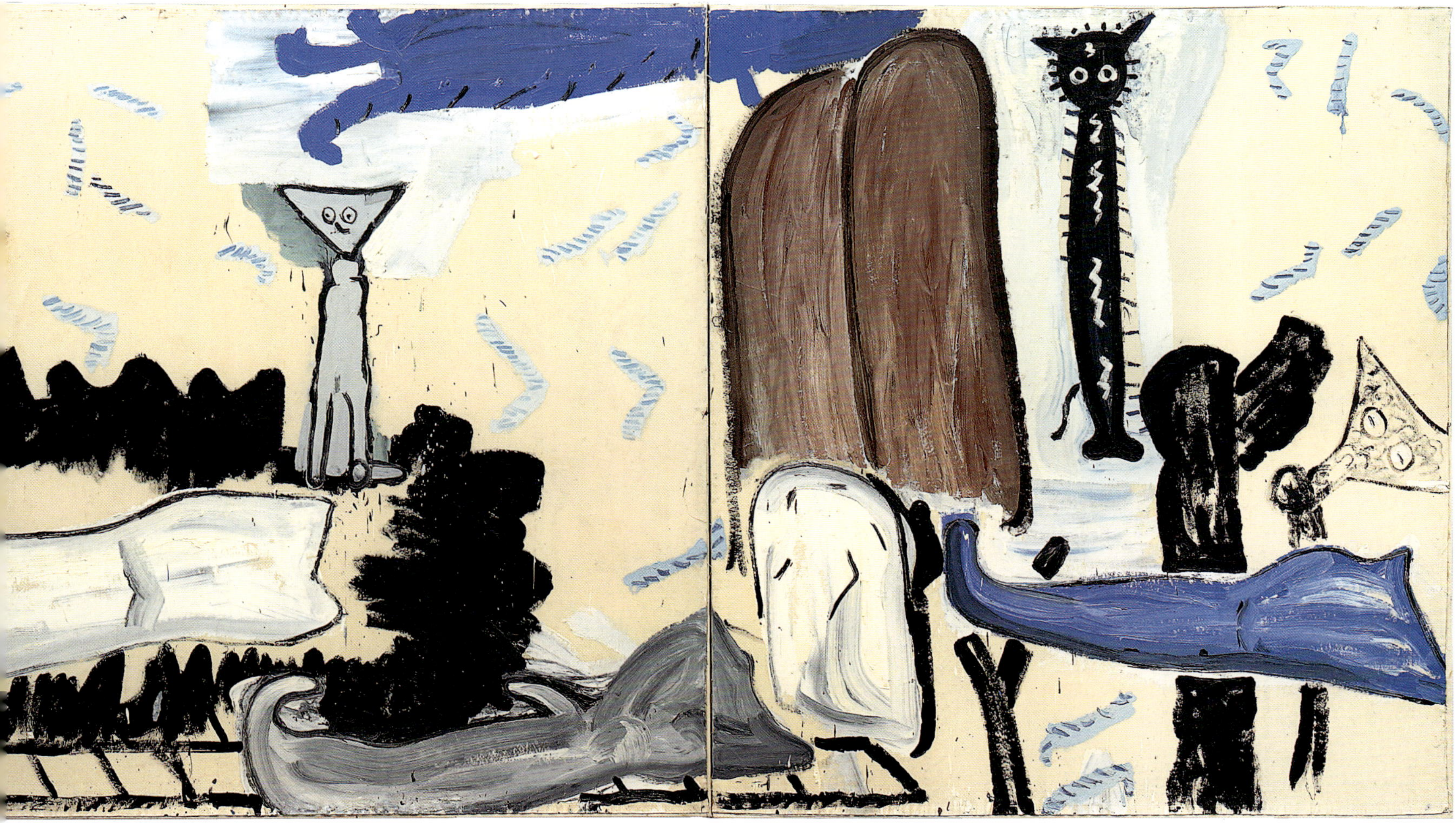

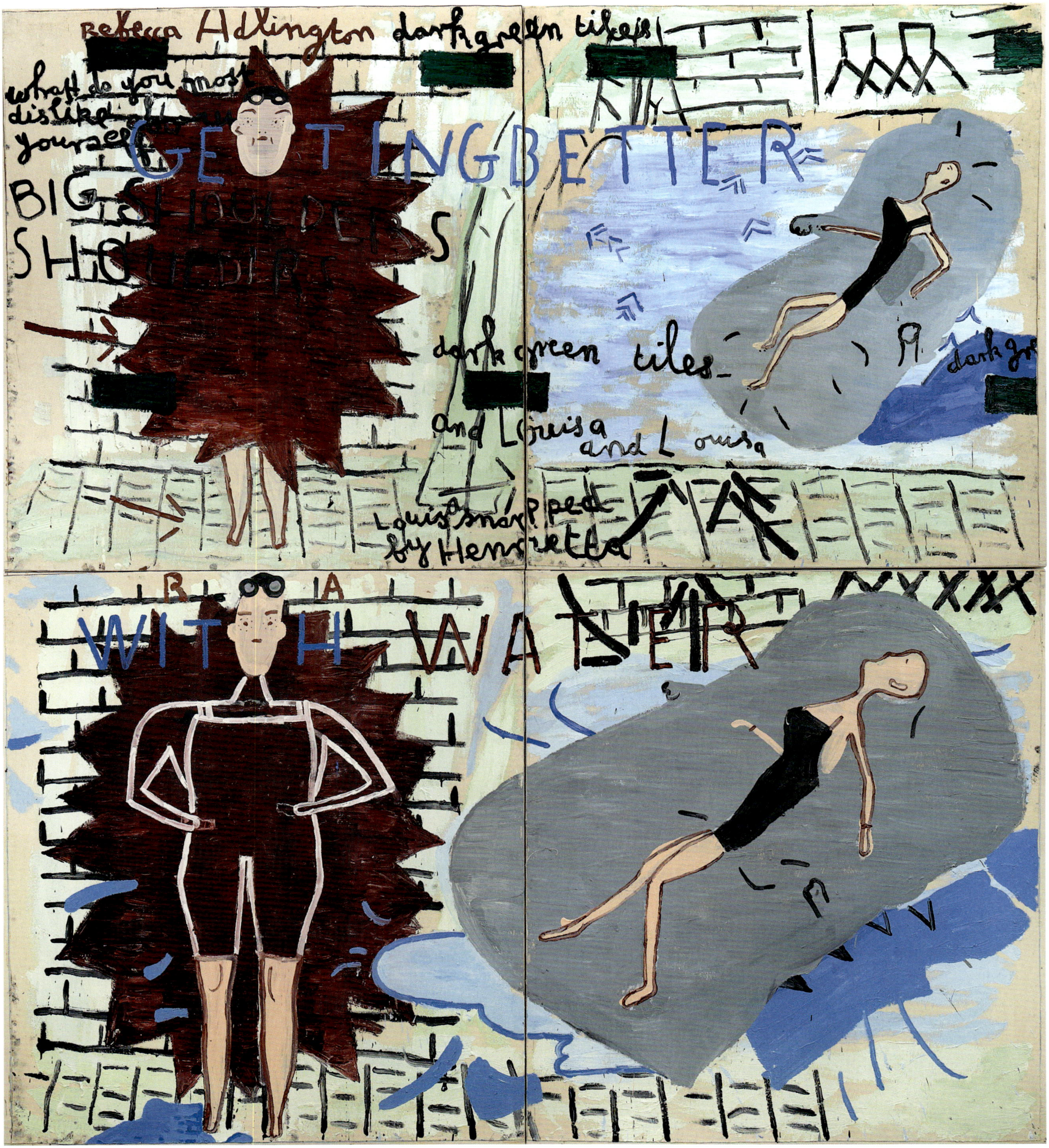
Rebecca Adlington
dark green tiles
BIG SHOULDERS
dark green tiles
dark gr
and Louisa
and Louisa
Louisa snapped by Henrietta
WITH WATER

97
Getting Better with Water 2011
Oil on canvas, 366 × 340 cm (144⅛ × 133⅞ in)
Collection of Morten Viskum

98
Sitting on a Bench with Border (Film Notes) 2008
Oil on canvas, 282 × 242 cm (111⅛ × 95⅜ in)
Private collection

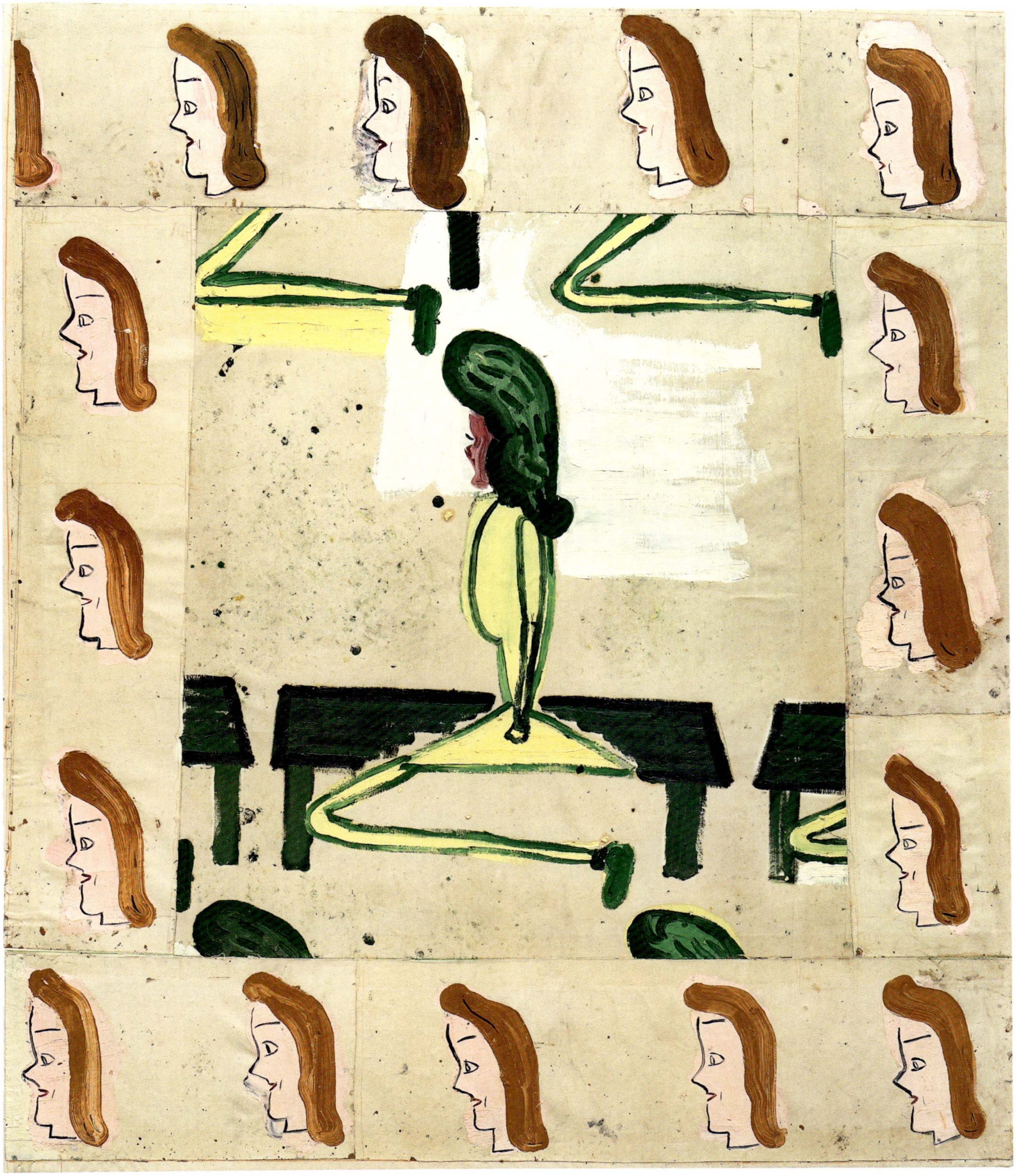

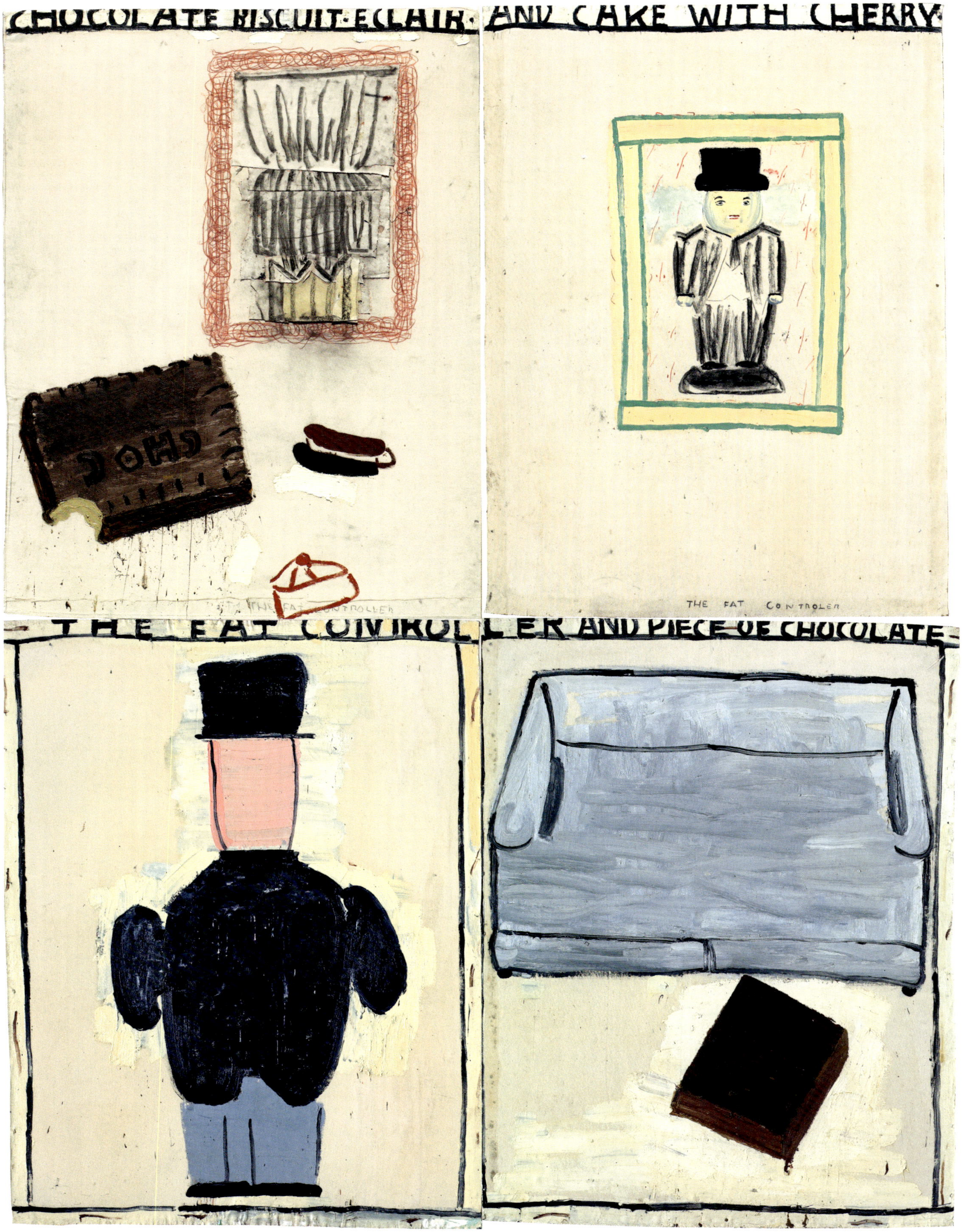
CHOCOLATE BISCUIT ECLAIR
AND CAKE WITH CHERRY
THE FAT CONTROLER
THE FAT CONTROLLER AND PIECE OF CHOCOLATE

99
The Fat Controller 2006
Oil on canvas, 366 × 248 cm (144⅛ × 97¾ in)
Private collection

100
Hong Kong Sharon 2003
Oil on canvas, 193 × 183 cm (76 × 72⅛)
Private collection

from lists (either from memory or direct observation) allows Wylie to be specific without being literal.[75] A second underlying compositional influence was a row of early 'bikini girls' the artist saw in a photograph of an ancient wall painting from Syracuse.[76] The resultant series of five paintings show a childlike Kidman, facing the crowd, in a variety of scenes. An earlier painting, *Grace Jones* 1985, was inspired by a photograph of the singer in *The Guardian* because Wylie 'liked her hair and her muscles'.[77] Wylie has also made a number of works based on a cheap, plastic doll made in Hong Kong of Sharon Osbourne (fig.100), Ozzy Osbourne's wife, as well as the film star Drew Barrymore and model Cara Delevingne (fig.103).

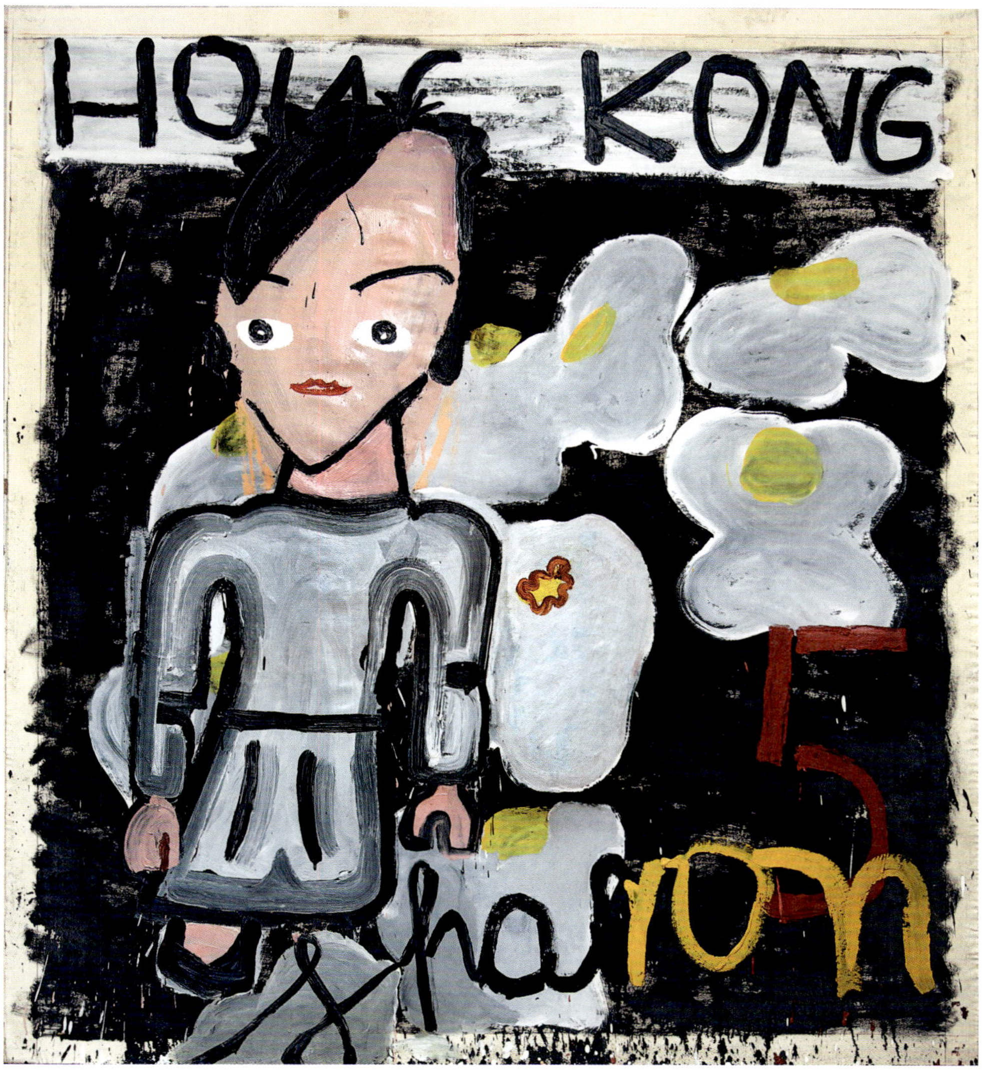

101
NK (Syracuse Line-Up) 2014
Oil on canvas, 185 × 333 cm (72⅞ × 131⅛ in)
Private collection

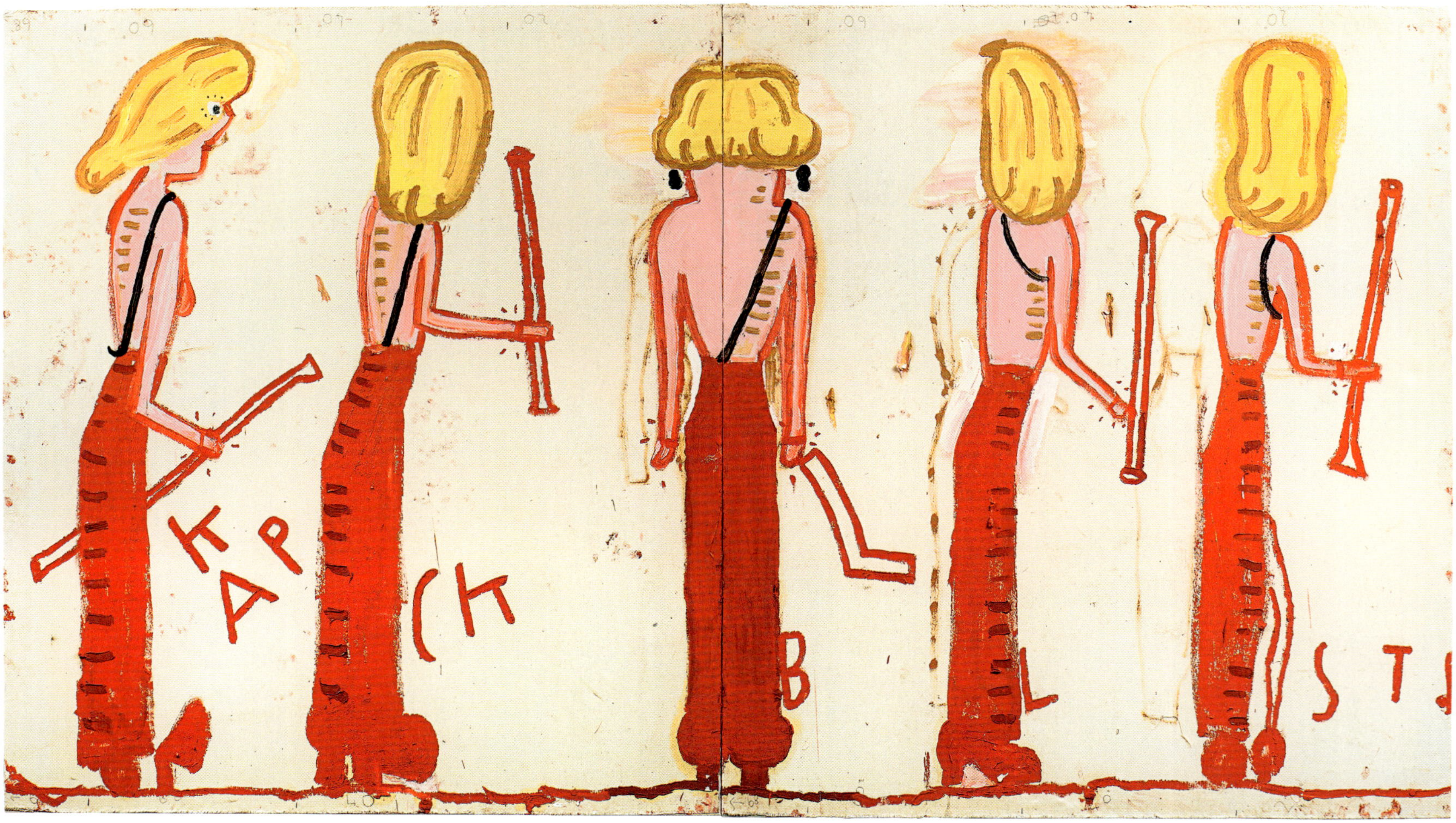

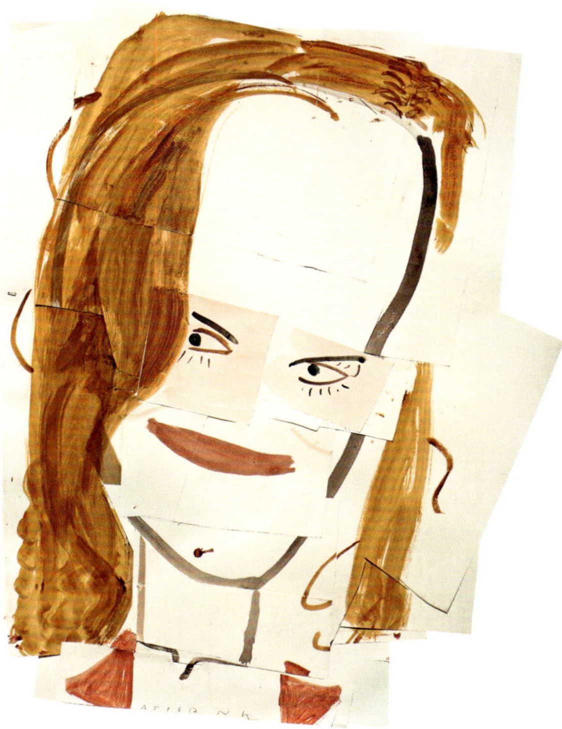

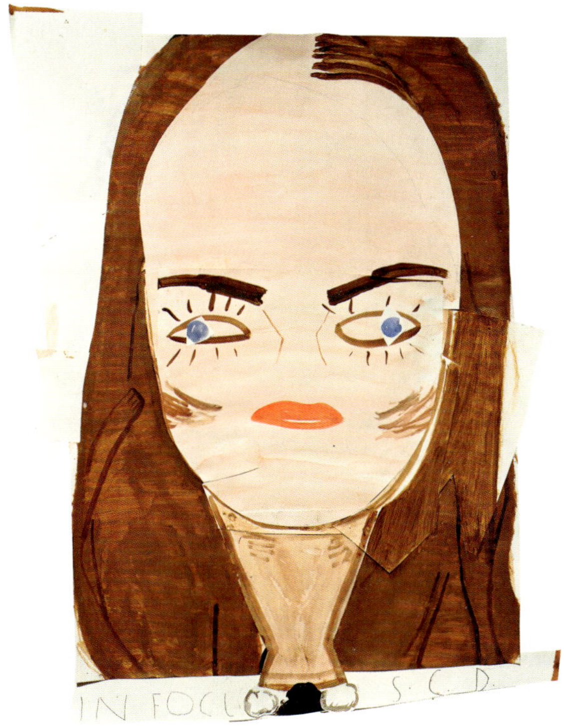

102
Cannes Film Festival (NK) 2013
Watercolour, pencil, and collage on paper
84 × 67 cm (33⅛ × 26½ in)
Collection of Henry Chow

103
Cara Delevingne (Yellow Ochre) 2013
Watercolour, pencil, and collage on paper
95.5 × 59 cm (37⅝ × 23¼ in)
Collection of Nunu Hung

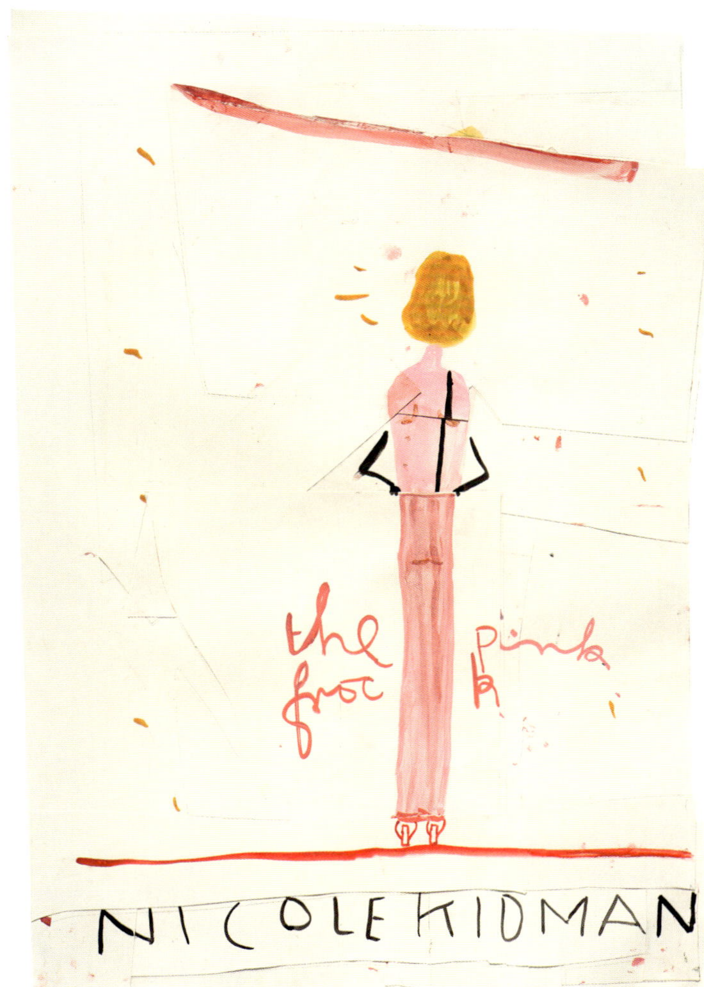

104
Nicole Kidman Pink Frock 2015
Watercolour and collage on paper
87.5 × 63 cm (34½ × 24⅞ in)
Private collection

107
Baby Jesus of Prague 1990
Oil on canvas, 224 × 219 cm (88¼ × 86¼ in)
Private collection

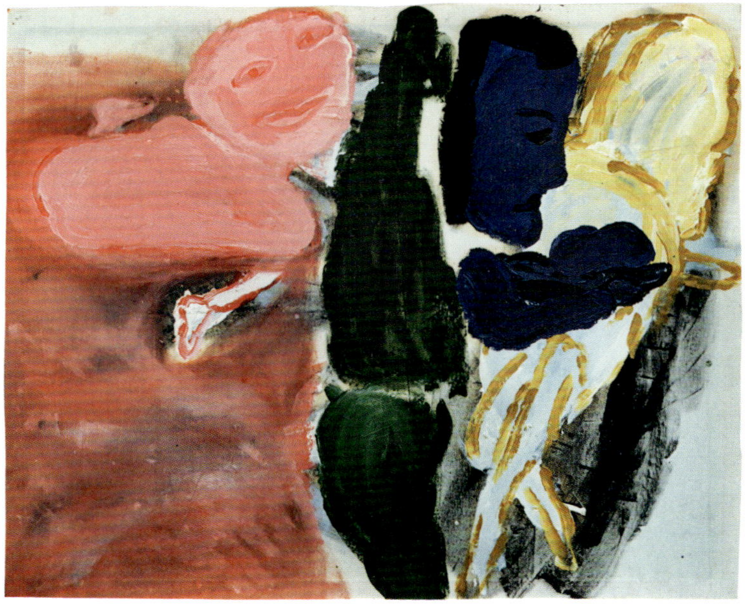

105 (above)
The Humble Disciple 1992
Oil on canvas, 142 × 183 cm (56 × 72⅛ in)
Private collection

106 (below)
Temptation of St Anthony 1987
Oil on canvas, 130 × 163cm (51¼ × 64¼ in)
Private collection

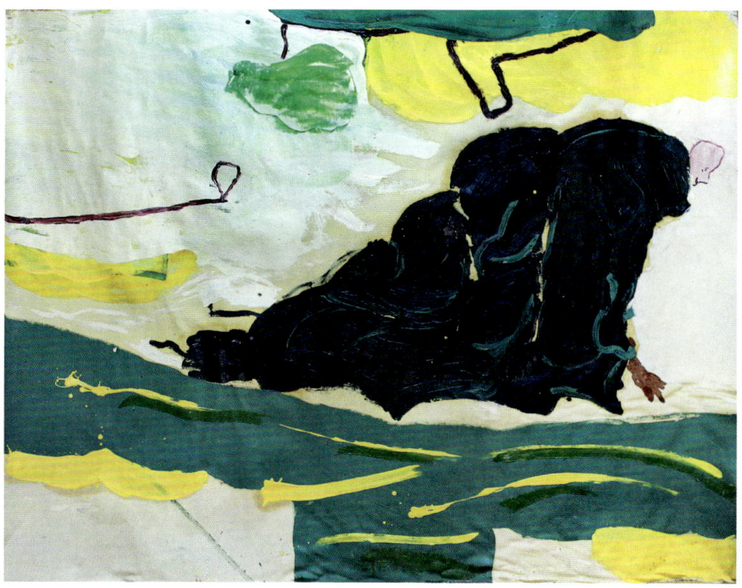

Many of Wylie's paintings indirectly address the subject of fandom, and engage with the 'hero figure' and ideas of celebrity throughout the ages. The 'hero figure' was originally tied to the sacred: from religion and myth, gods, goddesses, and mortals who were renowned themselves or linked to a sacred history. They also had an established iconography (Hermes' staff and sandals, for example, or the symbols of the saints) and possibly relics associated with them. The Bible became a resource in which all the characters could be deployed as figures of moral or allegorical interpretation. Royalty was seen as a divine office, directly ordained by God or the gods. This was often reinforced by fake genealogies that traced kings and queens back to mythic times, usually as descendants of Brutus, Aeneas or other Homeric heroes.

Wylie's imagery is full of archetypal figures found in popular culture, in medieval manuscripts and from antiquity, including *The Humble Disciple* 1992 (fig.105) and *Baby Jesus of Prague* 1990 (fig.107), depicting the sixteenth-century Roman Catholic statue of a wide-eyed wooden Christ child holding a globe in his left hand, the Greek God Zeus (*Zeus as a Rabbit* 1995) (fig.108) and the Bible story of *Salome and John the Baptist's Head* 1988 (fig.53). The title and imagery of the picture *Beggar, Cloak, Saint and Horse* 1993 refer to the traditional iconography of St Martin of Tours. Martin lived in fourth-century France and converted to Christianity at a young age; after serving as a soldier in the Roman army he subsequently became Bishop of Tours. The legend of the saint's cloak is the source of the symbols used in Wylie's picture. It tells how, while still a soldier, Martin was approaching the city gates of Amiens. Seeing a partially naked beggar, he impulsively cut his military cloak in two, giving half to the beggar. Martin was rewarded for this act of charity by a vision of Jesus. The legend has been the subject of many works of art. Wylie's most immediate influence is a depiction of it by El Greco (1541–1614): *St Martin and the Beggar* 1599. The space of El Greco's mannerist work is filled by the figures of Martin, his horse and the beggar. Wylie's work is even more extreme; the subjects are in similar poses to Greco's but in an almost claustrophobic close-up. Likewise, the use of colour is heightened: darker and more immediate than El Greco's palette,

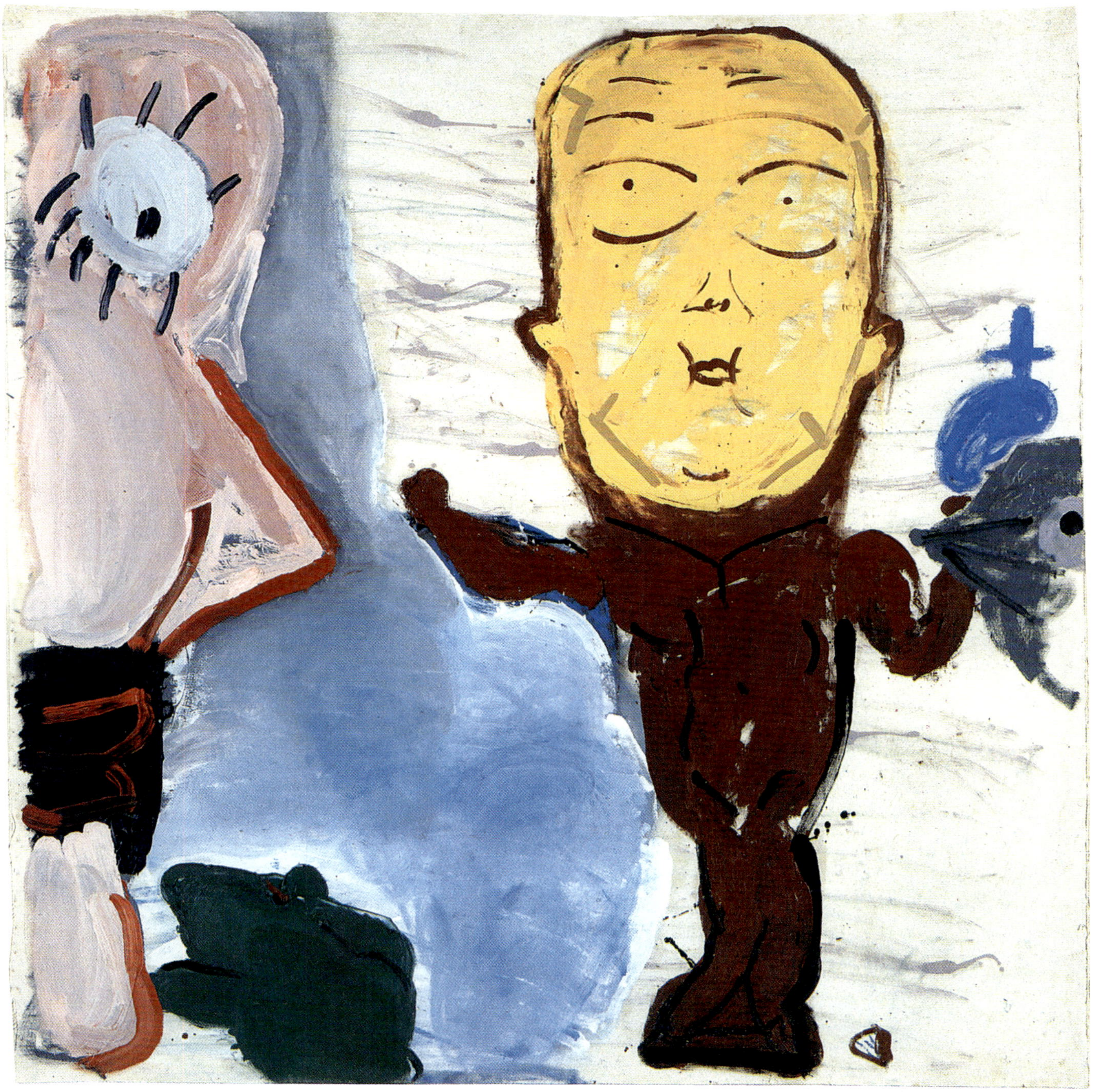

108
Zeus as a Rabbit 1995
Oil on canvas, 183 × 173 cm (72⅛ × 68⅛ in)
Private collection

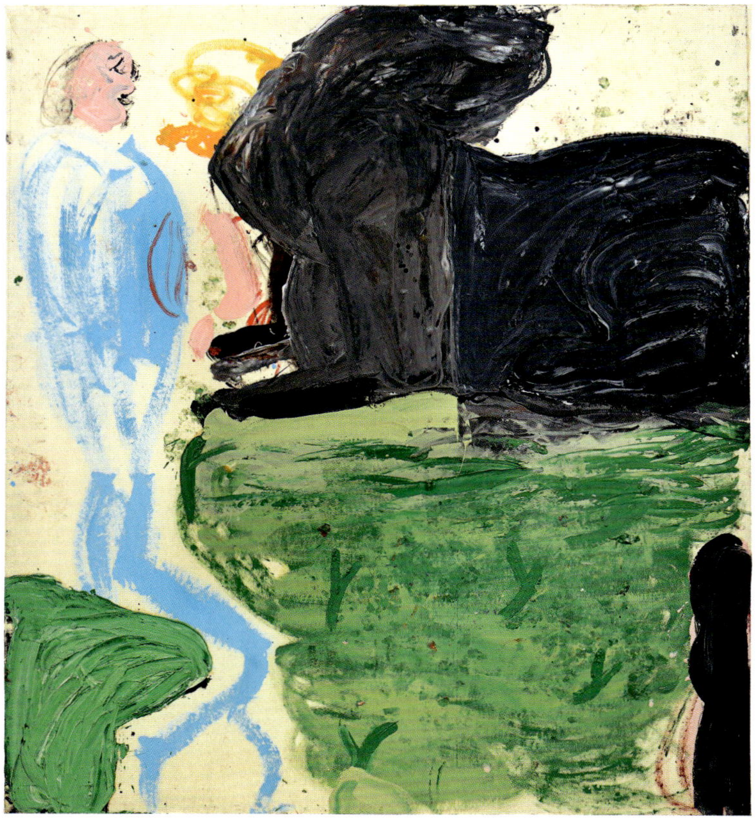

Martin's torso in dark blue merging into the background of the same colour. Wylie's picture has a vivid physicality that suggests we are close to beggar and saint, witnesses of a real act of kindness rather than distanced observers of a pious act.

Temptation of St Anthony 1987 (fig.106), like *Beggar, Cloak, Saint and Horse*, draws on hagiographic tradition and its symbolism. St Anthony the Great (*c*.251–356) was an early desert anchorite and monk, and has a long and well-established history of representation in art. The story of his temptation was first told by his near-contemporary Athanasius of Alexandria, who wrote his biography: whilst in the Egyptian desert, Anthony was beset by the Devil who tried to lure him into sin, tempting him to sloth and inciting lust with phantasms of women. The earliest extant artwork showing St Anthony being tormented by demons is from the tenth century, and the subject matter has been popular ever since. During the Middle Ages artists such as Hieronymus Bosch (*c*.1450–1516) and Matthias Grünewald (*c*.1470–1528) produced their versions of *Temptation of St Anthony*, in around 1505 and 1512–1516 respectively. More recently the Symbolists found St Anthony a compelling source of imagery (like Salome and John the Baptist, also subjects for Wylie). Gustave Flaubert gave brilliant literary treatment of the saint in his eponymous novel. For the Symbolists the interest was less in a pious religious subject and more in the opportunity it gave for florid phantasmagoria and provocative subject matter. This continued into the twentieth century, most famously with the Surrealists Max Ernst (1891–1976) and Salvador Dalí (1904–1989) who both entered a competition on the theme. Ernst won. The competition winner had his painting used in the film *The Private Affairs of Bel Ami* (1946). Wylie's take on *The Temptation* eschews the baroque luxuriousness of many past representations. Her St Anthony appears engaged in a more earthy struggle, with the saint's form stripped down to a basic figure worked in rough patches of green and blue. Background detail is absent, echoing the empty desert; and two other figures, presumably tempting demons, flank Anthony. To the left a pink figure appears to float, the body vestigial with the head alone clearly limned. Anthony faces to the right, attempting to embrace an insubstantial figure, a demon of lust maybe. The overall effect is certainly nightmarish and claustrophobic, Anthony's head a mask of pain. The painting is reminiscent of Paul Gauguin (1848–1903), or more generally of the Pont-Aven school of which Gauguin was a key player; a 'primitivism' deploying block areas of colour and carrying rough-and-ready symbolic overtones.

During the Middle Ages there arose the various bodies of myth and literature – the Matter of Britain, the Matter of France etc. – with their particular heroes, of which King Arthur is perhaps the best known and enjoyed such a vogue that the tales were told and retold, drifting from their original context. There also arose equivocal heroes such as Robin Hood, an outlaw who enjoyed massive popularity in ballads and tales which had a more secular tenor and reflected a popular discontent. Real-world figures, rulers, military and other 'celebrities' were often depicted art historically in apotheosis, following the iconography of Christian art. Modern fandom is held to have started with the fans of Sherlock Holmes (who also pioneered fan fiction). With the rise of mass media, the potential for celebrity and attendant fandoms was multiplied

109
Film Star and GM's Arm 1991
Oil on canvas, 146 × 183 cm (57½ × 72⅛ in)
Private collection

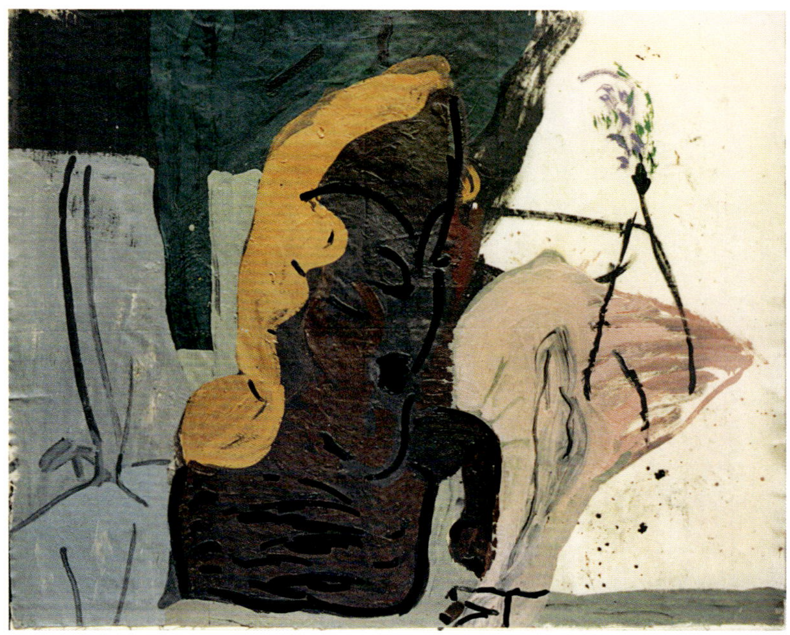

exponentially. In the earliest days of cinema the star system propelled the new medium, as it quickly became the close-up that pulled in audiences, rather than the director's name or even the storyline.

In *ER & ET* 2011 (fig.110) the figure, inspired by the Hollywood actress Elizabeth Taylor's violet eyes and voluptuous hourglass physique, is painted reclining in a bathing costume in a sea of eyes and ears, which in turn were inspired by *The Rainbow Portrait* *c.*1600–1602 of Queen Elizabeth I (fig.111), attributed to Marcus Gheeraerts the Younger (1561/2–1636). *The Rainbow Portrait* was painted towards the end of Elizabeth's reign when she was in her sixties. The monarch's cloak is decorated with eyes and ears, reminding everyone that the spies at court enabled her to see and hear all. As Wylie explains, this was the 'first time and only time I've done violet-coloured eyes. And the paparazzi eyes and ears worked for both . . . appliquéd on ER 1st's 16th C royal skirt, and hanging round ET all the time . . . happy correspondence.'[78] Wylie used another Marcus Gheeraerts portrait of Elizabeth I ('silver with orange flower motif on it, gorgeous') for her painting *Queen with Pansies (Dots)* 2016 (fig.112).

Over fifty years ago in his landmark book *The Image*, historian Daniel Boorstin defined modern fame in terms that brilliantly anticipated the rise of modern celebrity culture: 'The hero was distinguished by his achievement, the celebrity by his image. We risk being the first people in history to have been able to make their illusions so vivid, so persuasive, so realistic that we can live in them.'[79] Today celebrity exists for and by an information age. Paintings such as *Film Star and GM's Arm* 1991 (fig.109), based on a film still of Marilyn Monroe and Groucho Marx from the movie *Love Happy* (1949), communicate the enthralment of fandom and the 'pin-up' whose mass-produced pictures are disseminated widely as popular culture. They evoke the medium through which anonymous actors are projected instantly into worldwide celebrity, conjuring up apparently intimate relationships with their fans. Their portraits become ubiquitous, their smile looms over entire nations, their effigies are inescapable.

Popular enthusiasms have led to many spheres of endeavour giving rise to celebrities – actors, sportsmen, etc. Fuelled by the increasingly rapid circulation of word and image, the hunger for

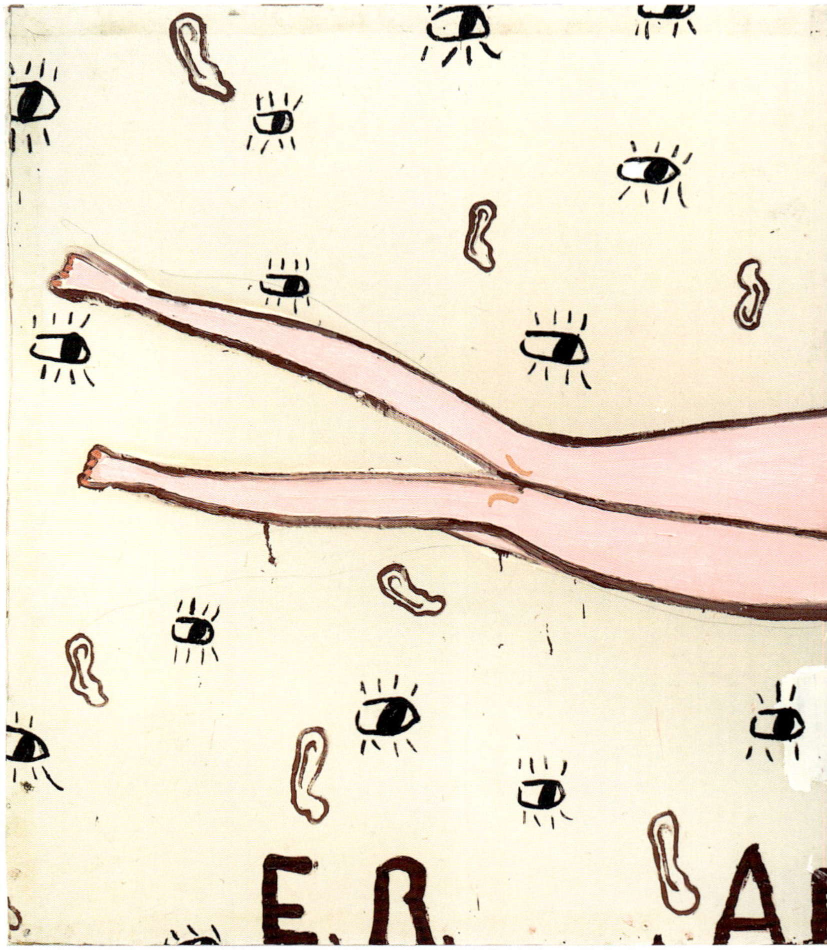

110
ER & ET 2011
Oil on canvas, 182 × 344 cm (71¾ × 135½ in)
Collection of Morten Viskum

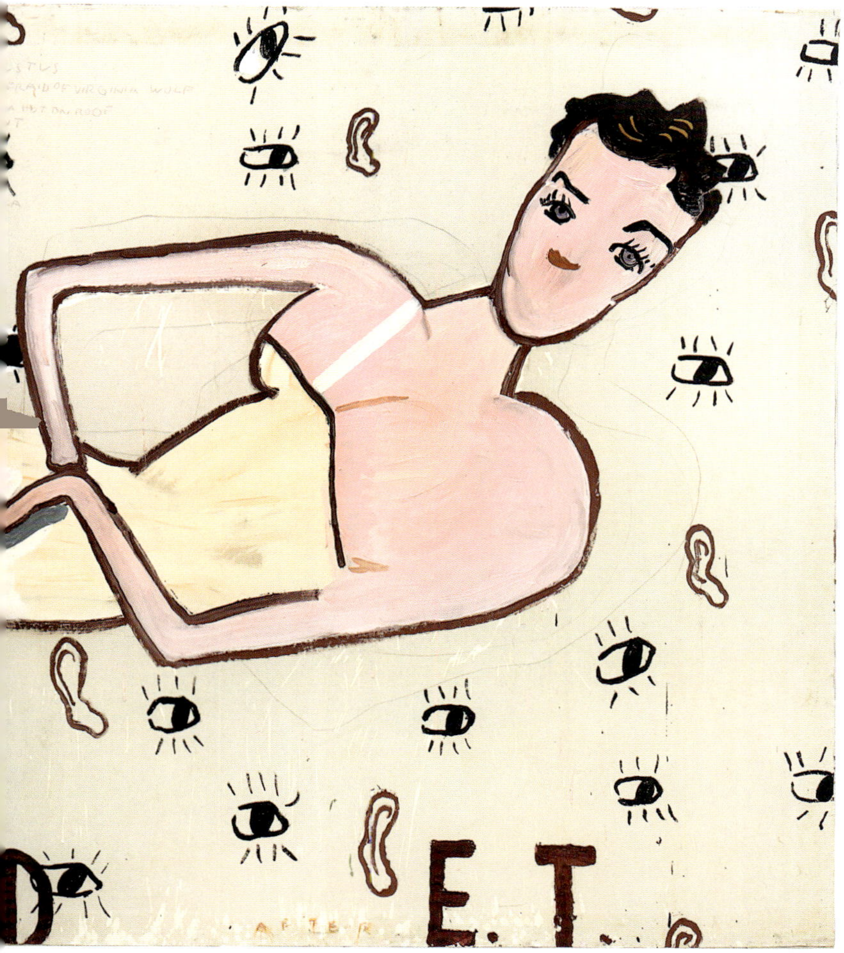

information about heroes has created a feedback that has escalated ever higher. Here again, however, there is a continuity with the past: we speak of iconic moments or images in a film; defining sporting memories such as the tennis legend John McEnroe winning Wimbledon; Gazza crying in *that* World Cup match.

If *Celebrity* 2006 (fig.4) is based on a photograph of Spice Girl-turned-fashion designer Victoria Beckham standing rather awkwardly, facing the crowd, *Pop Star with Stars* and *Pop Star with Curtains*, both 1993, depict Madonna, a musician Wylie greatly admires: 'That's why I always thought Madonna was so good, because she did something quite different and occasionally quite shocking . . . Some of the things she did were difficult for people to take, but I'm a fan. I've done loads of drawings of Madonna.'[80] Both paintings feature Madonna in the same position, with arms and legs akimbo, a stance that captures her on-stage persona with a simple economy of means. *Pop Star with Stars* has the singer set against a field of deep blue speckled with stars. The effect is ambiguous: while the figure floats magically, a star amongst the stars, suggesting a realm of enchantment, there is also a feeling that the singer is adrift and alone in the void. *Pop Star with Curtains* uses a similar dark blue for the background but the

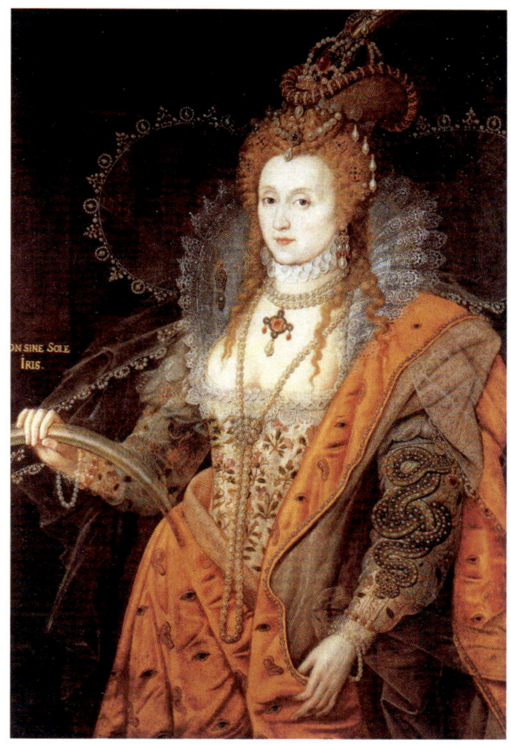

111
Marcus Gheeraerts the Younger, *The Rainbow Portrait* 1600–02
Oil on canvas, 127 × 99.1 cm (50 × 39⅛
Collection of Marquess of Salisbury, Hatfield House, Hertfordshire

112 (overleaf)
Queen with Pansies (Dots) 2016
Oil on canvas, 183 × 331 cm (72⅛ × 130⅜)
Private collection

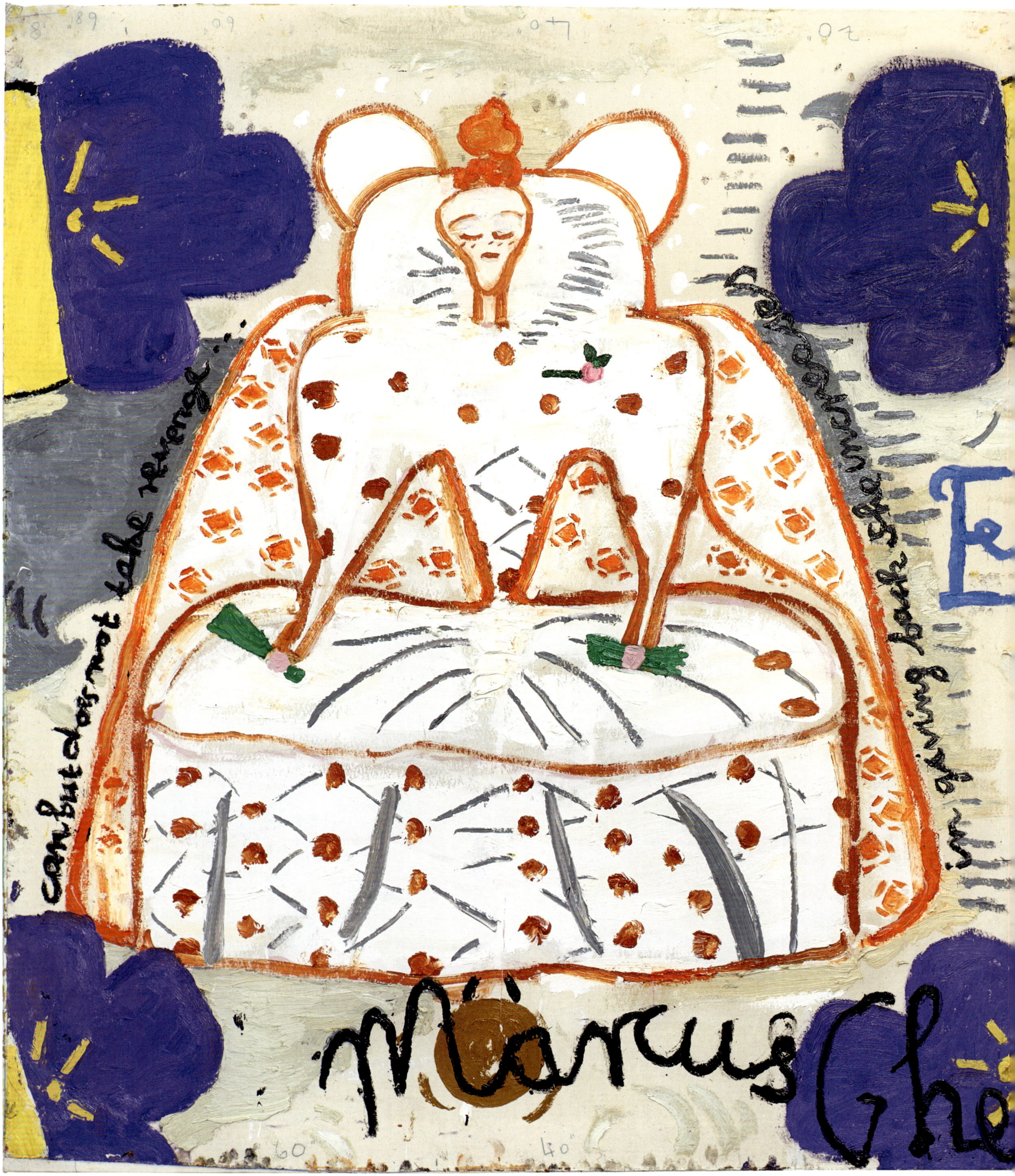

"can but does not take revenge...
in giving back the
Marcus Ghe

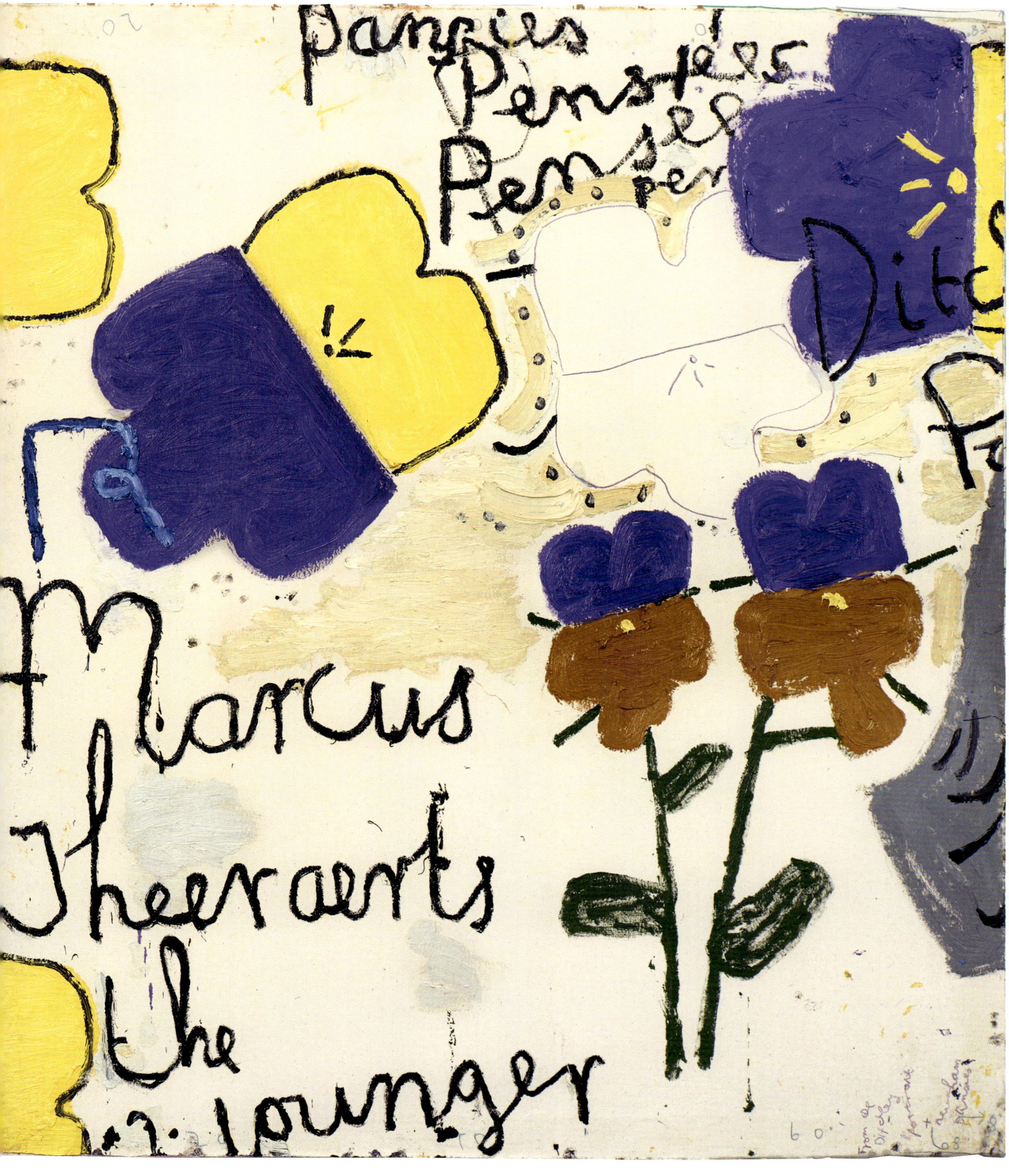
pansies
Marcus
the
younger

113
Breakfast Table (Dining Room) 2015
Coloured pencil, biro and collage on diary pages
26.4 × 20.9 cm (10½ × 8¼ in)
Private collection

114
Favourite Silk Skirt on a Hanger (Bedroom) 2015
Pencil, biro and collage on diary pages
26.1 × 21.1 cm (10⅜ × 8⅜ in)
Private collection

denser application of paint in the lower half of the picture suggests a stage. The pop star herself stands upon a rectangle of yellow light, presumably a stage spotlight: the effect is to suggest not solidity but rather a shifting surface, the spotlight a fragile boat upon the blue sea. The green curtains bunched to either side frame the figure quite closely as if they have a real physical presence; they have opened up to reveal the star but may as easily obscure her again. A patch of light behind the pop star's head serves as a secular halo and may be a reminder of Madonna's own use of religious imagery and even her name. In both pictures (and as she does in many of her other works) Wylie encompasses both the iconic and the ironic. There is an obvious and real affection for her celebrity subjects but also an awareness of the contradictions and absurdities of the mediated images we have of what are, after all, just people like us. Wylie's generosity of spirit encompasses both, avoiding cynicism or a snobbish dismissal of popular culture. In the *Pop Star* paintings the focus is perhaps Madonna's pose: is she a strong woman in control of her raunchy image or is she passively signalling her sexual availability (legs apart) as subject of a male gaze? Is she a star amongst the stars or merely lost in space? Wylie's paintings offer no simple answers and show both the strength and the fragility of her subjects, looking askance at the imagery of celebrity.

Wylie's use of the famous as figures in her paintings reminds one of *Riddley Walker*. It is as if we are survivors of catastrophe of which we are unaware; our previous history is radically foreshortened, a palimpsest in which saints rub shoulders with footballers, historical figures with film stars. The (usually) domestic settings in which these figures appear remind one of both the banality and the emotional investment of fantasies of meeting 'celebrities' – an almost dreamlike staging. In a non-judgemental, indeed generous spirit, Wylie's famous characters reflect a secular world but retain an echo of the auratic quality of the sacred.

All of Wylie's paintings are imbued with a sense of homage and reverence – whether aesthetic or personal towards her subject matter. Part of the work's appeal lies in its immediacy and her

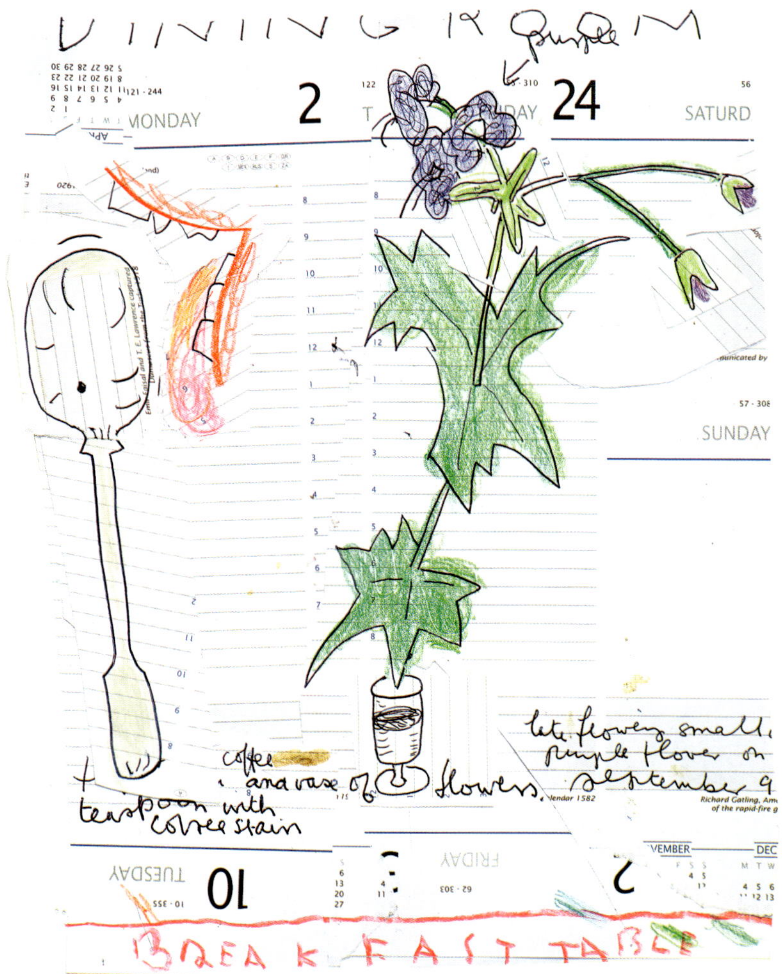

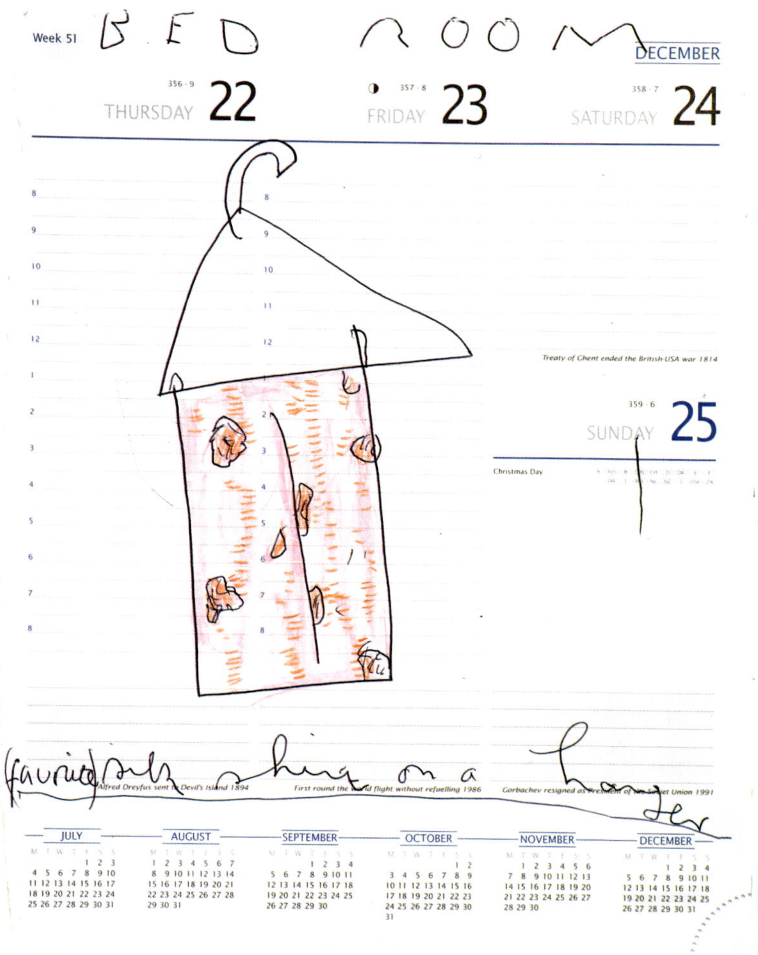

ability to find inspiration through her daily encounters with a variety of sources. As such the paintings have a diaristic quality to them, offering fresh perspectives on the world we live in and the plethora of images that make up our collective cultural memory.

Film has always been a rich source of material. Wylie remembers clearly the first time her mother took her to the Grove Cinema in Hythe to see Walt Disney's *Snow White and the Seven Dwarfs* (1937), aged three. It was the first feature-length animated movie to be produced in Technicolor, and cost nearly $1.5 million to make, an unheard-of amount in Depression-era America. The image of the wicked queen (initially conceived as a raven-haired glamour girl, and the epitome of late 1930s sophistication) who drinks an ageing potion and then shrivels, sprouting warts and claws, turning before our eyes from a sexy, voluptuous creature into a frightening old crone, left as powerful an impression on Wylie as Snow White's chirpy femininity and idealised prettiness. For all of *Snow White*'s fancifulness and charm, it retains aspects of the macabre that at the time terrified her. 'It was the scenes of the stepmother (wicked queen) running through a forest, presumably chasing Snow White, and finally falling off a cliff, again, probably screaming, that did me in . . . And I had to be taken screaming out of the cinema.'[81]

Looking back, Wylie reflects on 'The improbability of realistic outcome in the lyric "Someday my Prince will Come", and the unquestioning acceptance I received it with then'.[82] No sooner has Snow White awakened from her enchanted sleep than she allows herself to be swept away by the handsome prince to his castle. If some of the film's messages seem troublesome – that Snow White will always make scrubbing and scouring seem the nicest of chores, and that marriage is a girl's dream come true – Wylie has always enjoyed fairy tales and recognises that few forms of literature have greater power to enchant us, while their history is entangled with folklore and myth.

In hindsight Wylie has commented: 'without knowing it then, I must've responded to the drama of big close-ups, strongly

115
Plastic Bride Profile & Cat 1998
Oil on canvas, 183 × 336 cm (72⅛ × 132¼ in)
Private collection

116
Cat and Skull 2010
Oil on canvas, 183 × 343 cm (72⅛ × 135⅛ in)
Private collection

contrasting colour and cropped images; something different from real life . . . and these "likes" have stayed with me.' She also remembers how much she liked Disney's line drawings she saw published in a book while teaching on the Foundation course in Wales and has always enjoyed the graphic quality of the early films.[83] Walt Disney's early style, in common with other early animators – such as Max Fleischer (1883–1972), the creator of Betty Boop – had a close relation to the highly individual drawn style of Wylie; this approach, idiosyncratic and personal, gradually disappeared as teams of animators were taken on to complete cartoons, working to a more unified 'house style'. Early animation made up its own rules as it went along, immediately translating the drawn imagination of a single creator; and Wylie's work likewise has the feel of an unpremeditated creation following the drawing hand, untrammelled by convention. *Blackbird, Butterfly and Tulips* 1994 shows the outline of a bird's eye and beak pecking at rough spontaneous brushstrokes of a (doomed) turquoise butterfly, with the silhouette of a red tulip on the right. The two-part painting *Plastic Bride Profile & Cat* 1998 (fig.115) pitches a close-up of the simplified, exaggerated form of the bride's head, eyes wide open,

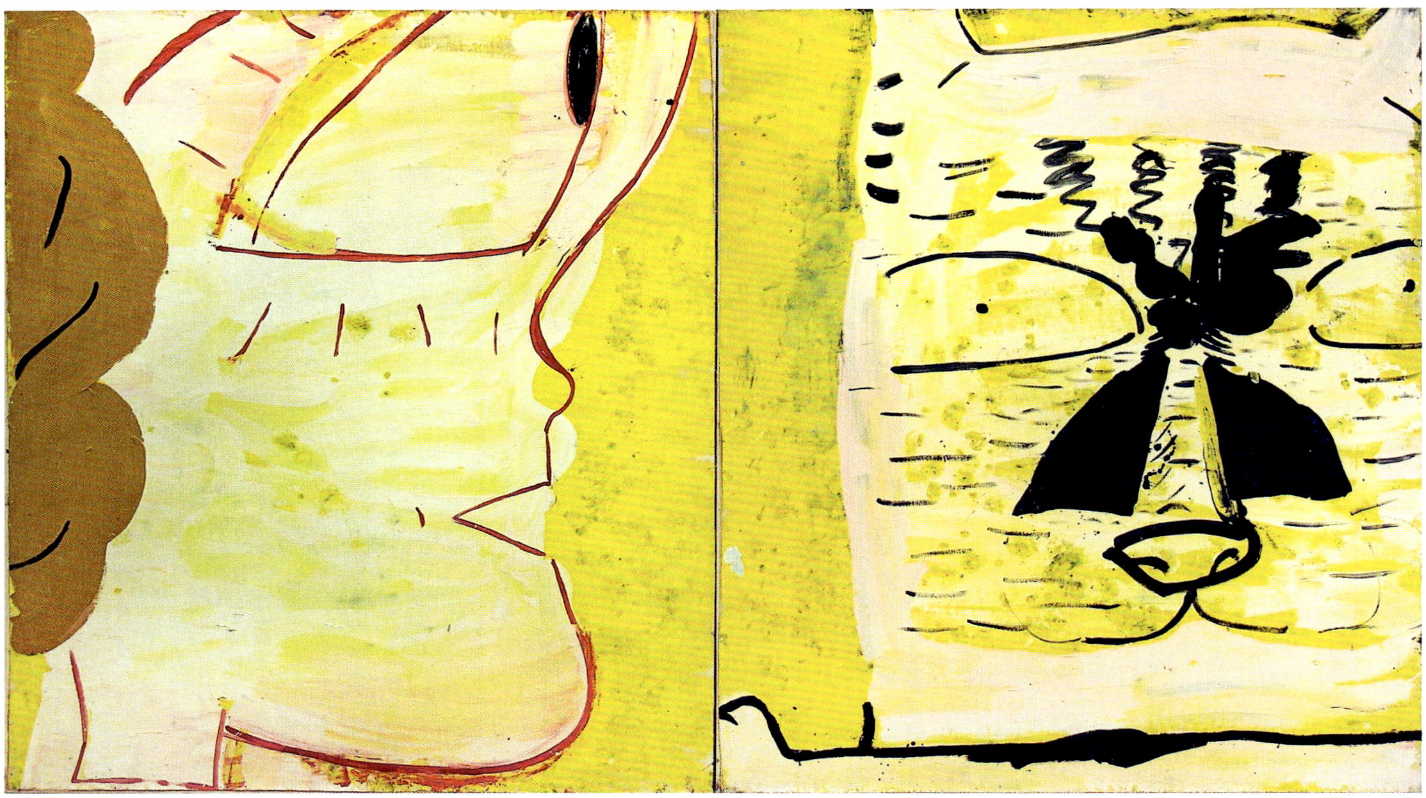

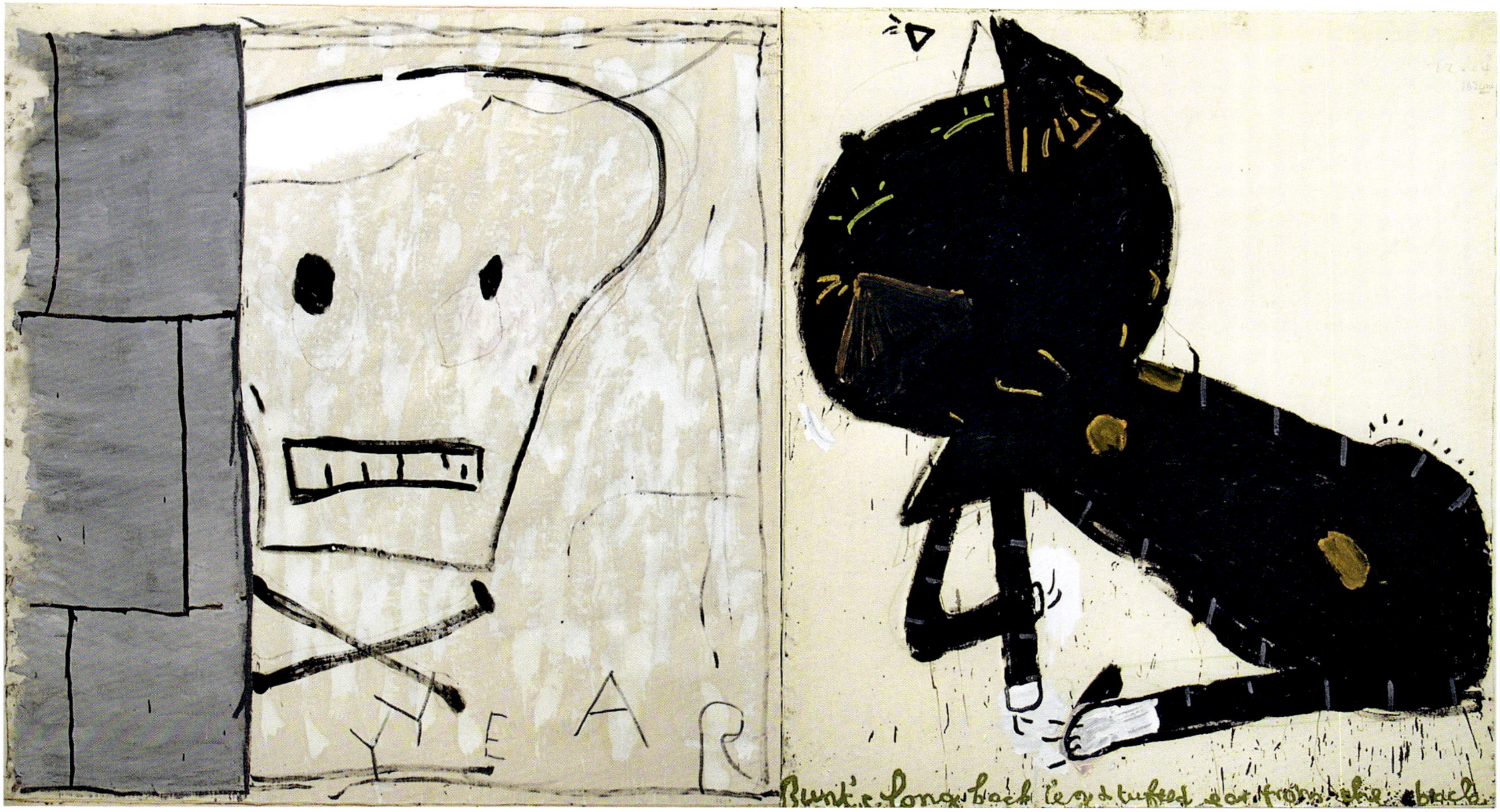

next to a large cat's head. Once again in *Cat and Skull* 2010 (fig.116), each of the key motifs fills half of the bifurcated composition. On the left-hand side, the human skull, poking out from behind a grey breeze-block wall, is simply delineated with two different-sized dots for eyes and a long thin rectangle for a mouth. On the right, a black cat is poised, its triangular ears pointing towards the top of the canvas.

Esther Leslie's book *Hollywood Flatlands: Animation, Critical Theory and the Avant-Garde* (2002) explores the positive reception of Disney by high modernist artists and thinkers.[84] Leslie shows that the fascination animated cartoons held for these thinkers was to be found in their anarchic creativity and refusal of representational realism. The violence and frenetic madness of cartoons reflected the contemporary world but also held the utopian promise of an endless and fertile inventiveness. The world depicted in cartoons was one in which objects could suddenly come to life and bodies could behave like objects. This fecund comic creativity is also found in Wylie's large canvases. Her cartoon-like use of film imagery is

117
Face and Skull 2011
Oil on canvas, 182 × 351 cm (71¾ × 138¼ in)
Private collection

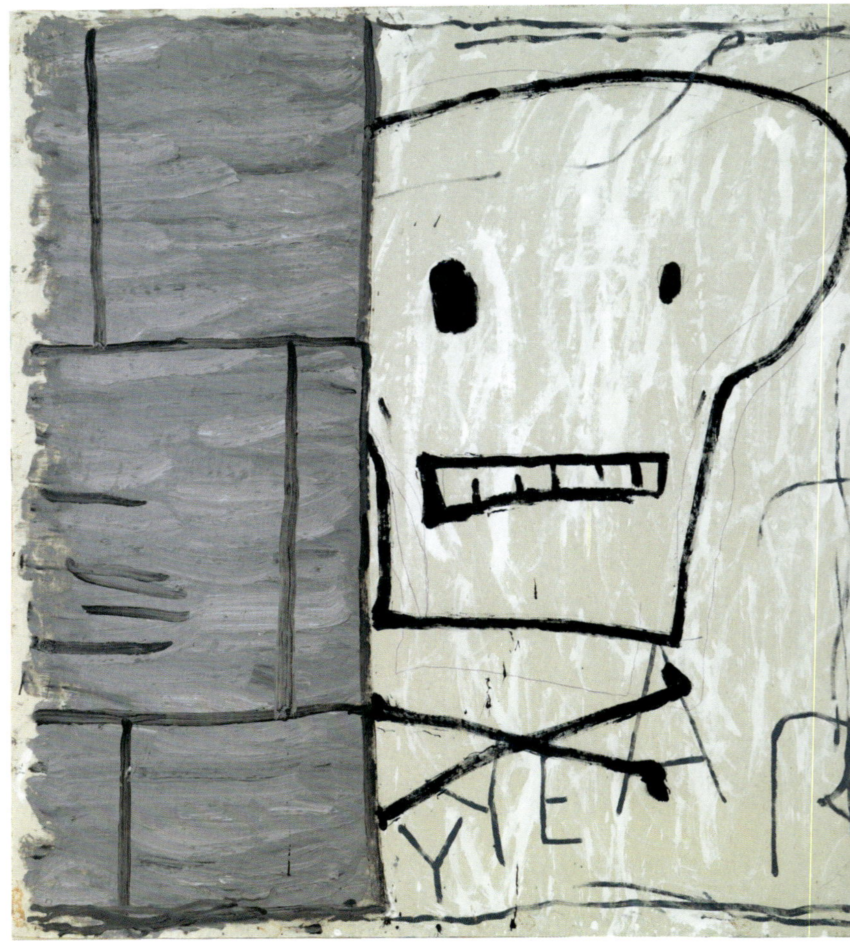

playful, deploying forms across the blank canvas and democratically refusing to prioritise any element of the picture. For example, in the *Twink and Ivy* paintings 2002–2003 (figs 94 and 95), the *Boy Meets Girl* series 2015 (figs 44, 45 and 48) (its title suggestive of a hackneyed romantic situation) or *Swimming with Cats (Blue Twink)* 2002 (fig.96), figures and object are combined in disconcerting ways, and elements float in space with differences in scale. These elements exist in suggestive juxtaposition and are also subject to the exuberant deformations of a Disney film.

Over the years Wylie's interest in film has found its way into a number of paintings including *Sweetie* 1996, whose title references the film by Jane Campion, and *Pin Up and Porn Queen Jigsaw* 2005 (fig.43), where the pin-up on the left is based on the actress Marilyn Monroe. Wylie's works are knowing about film in the sense of having a fan's love of the medium, and she is also a champion of it as a much-maligned art form. A series of paintings based on the Spanish actress Penélope Cruz herald the beginning of her ongoing *Film Notes* series, which she embarked upon in 2006. *Sitting on a Bench with Border (Film Notes)* 2008 (fig.98) is one of five paintings based on Cruz's character in Pedro Almodóvar's film *Volver* (2006). It depicts a young women sitting in profile framed by multiple headshots that all appear very slightly different from one another, like the frames in 16 mm film.

The *Film Notes* series pays respect to film directors the artist admires, including Almodóvar, Werner Herzog, Quentin Tarantino and Béla Tarr. These works can be understood as a homage to the source material; not merely as a formal exercise or a critical interrogation but more as a real fan's reaction to well-loved films. They are always depictions of the scenes Wylie can remember. This echoes the literary theorist Roland Barthes's distinction between '*studium*' and '*punctum*'.[85] While he developed the distinction in regard to photography, it is equally applicable to any work involving images. The *studium* is the culturally normative way of reading an image – we look over it and attempt to read the creator's intended meaning. The *punctum*, in contrast, is the detail in an image that

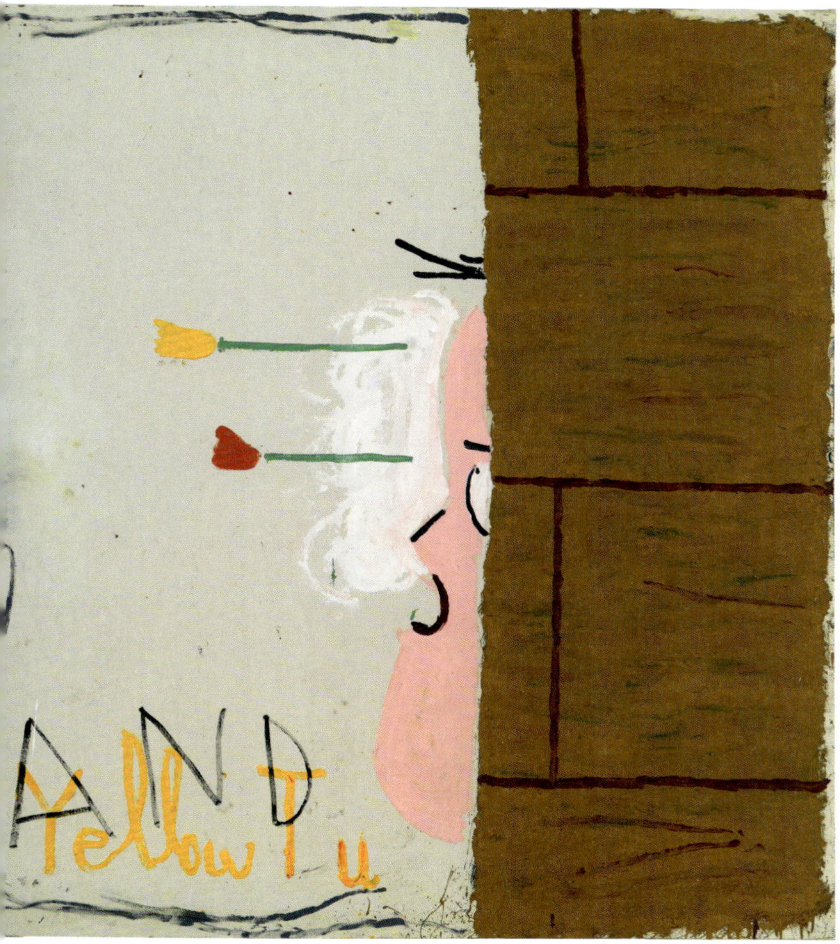

disrupts the culturally sanctioned reading and surprises and involves us intensely: this may be something that triggers a personal memory or feeling, a recognition that is exclusive to ourselves. Wylie's work seems to privilege the *punctum*, the moment when she responds with an (emotional) investment to what otherwise could be another mediated idea. In this respect the *Film Notes* can be understood as a record of the moments of the films she has seen and responded to – of her own affective engagement with film. Here again Wylie finds working from memory a useful way of filtering essential characteristics and avoiding too literal a translation so that 'memory filters and condenses' and that she paints the memory, not the film.[86] In so doing, she hopes to make an equivalent image with a measure of the same excitement she felt when seeing the original.

Subjects such as *Natural Born Killers* 1994, an American satirical black comedy crime film directed by Oliver Stone (figs 118a–c), and Quentin Tarantino's film *Inglourious Basterds* 2009 are distilled into succinct observations where the use of text gives additional emphasis to her recollections. *Inglourious Basterds (Film Notes)* 2010 (fig.119) was chosen as a subject out of respect for Tarantino's intense theatricality and extraordinarily good photography. The painting depicts three figures set on a white background with a few faint horizontal lines that economically lend depth to the picture field. There are also a few yellow stars, suggestive of the badges that Jews were forced to wear in Nazi Germany, scattered on the background along with orange flames. The figures themselves are in uniform. The figure to the right has only the most schematic representation of a head and the outline of a military hat while the figure to the left has no head at all, as if they are nothing but their uniforms. The central figure is better defined with a swastika armband and a more dynamic pose. This is Colonel Hans Landa, one of the film's principal protagonists. Landa is named twice in the writing on the canvas along with his epithet 'The Jew Hunter' and the name of the actor, Christoph Waltz, who played him. The film's title and Quentin Tarantino's name are in the largest lettering, clearly indicating the subject of this 'homage'. In the

118a
Natural Born Killers, Long-shot (Film Notes) 2018
Oil on canvas, 183 × 165 cm (72 × 64⅞ in)
Private collection

118b
Natural Born Killers, Head lights (Film Notes) 2018
Oil on canvas, 183 × 164 cm (72 × 64⅝ in)
Private collection

118c
Natural Born Killers, Close-up (Film Notes) 2018
Oil on canvas, 183 × 164 cm (72 × 64⅝ in)
Collection of Elisabeth and Alex Tynberg

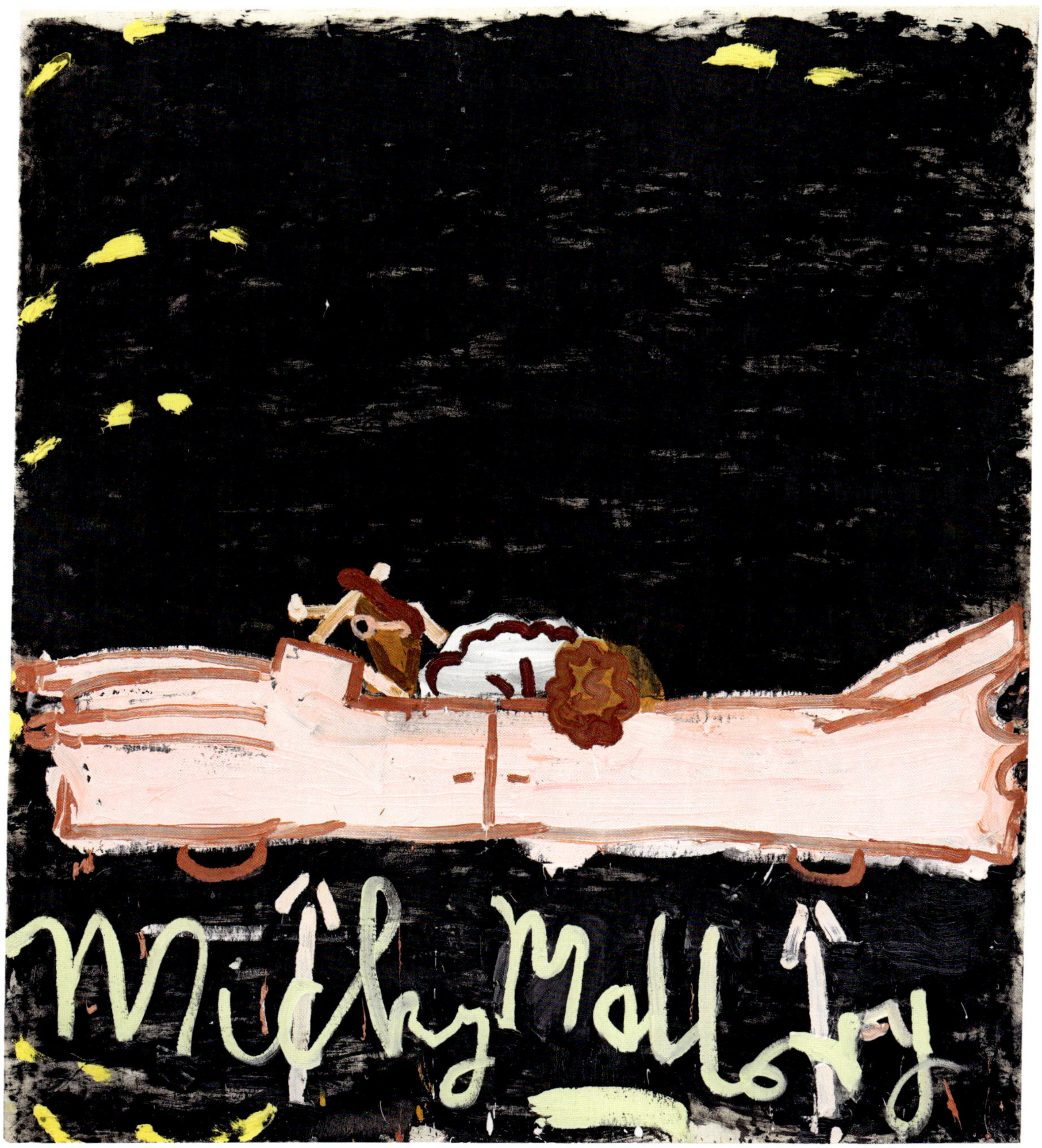

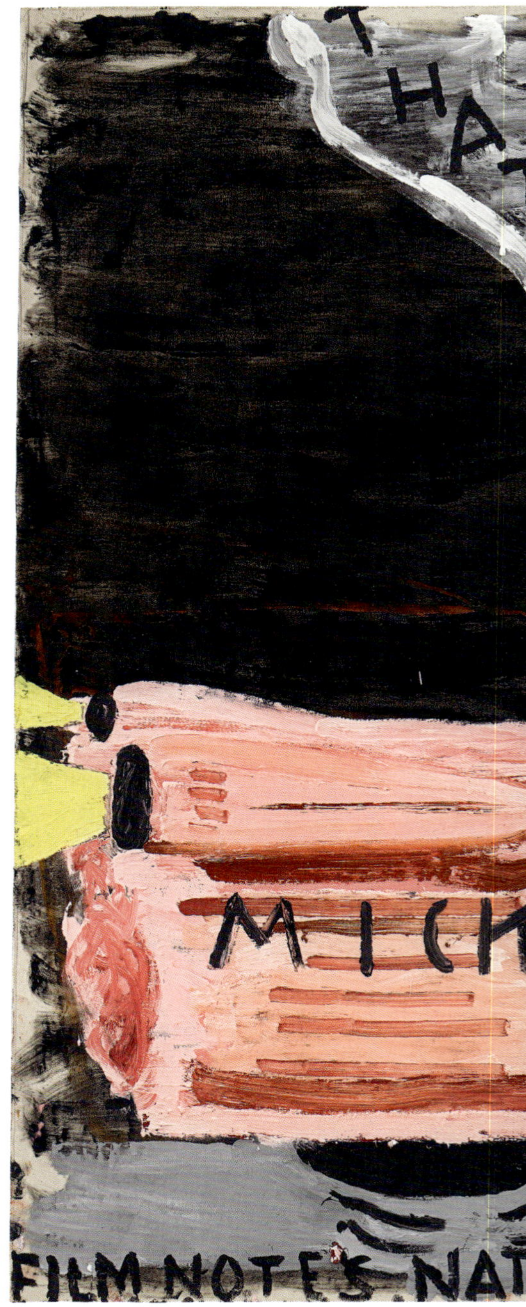

119 (overleaf)
Inglourious Basterds (Film Notes) 2010
Oil on canvas, 181 × 338 cm (71⅜ × 133⅛ in)
Private collection

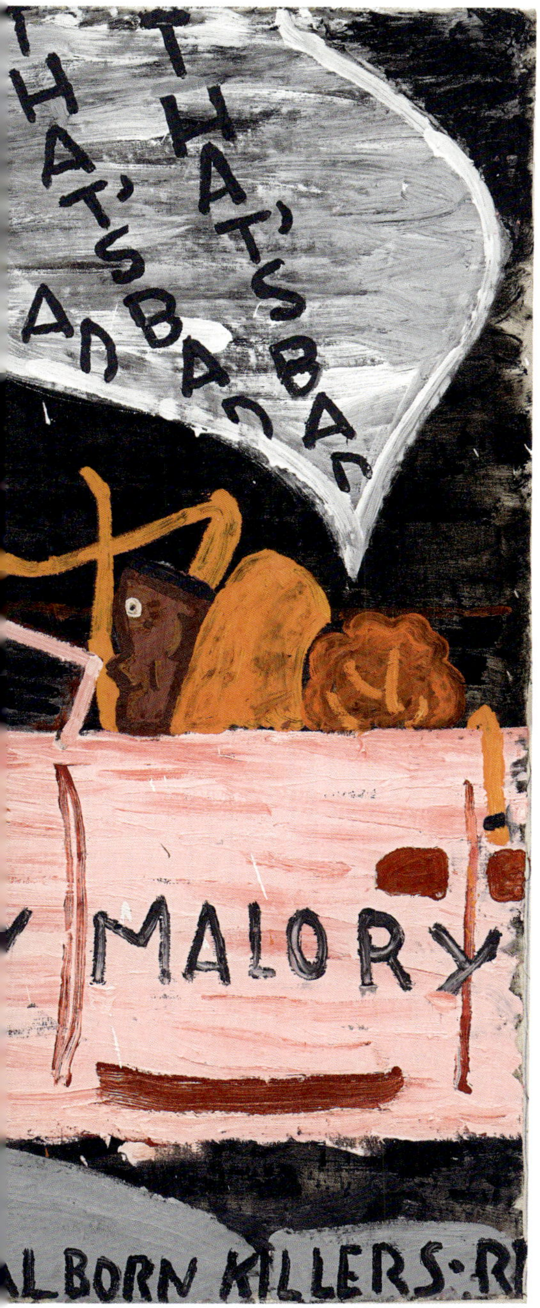

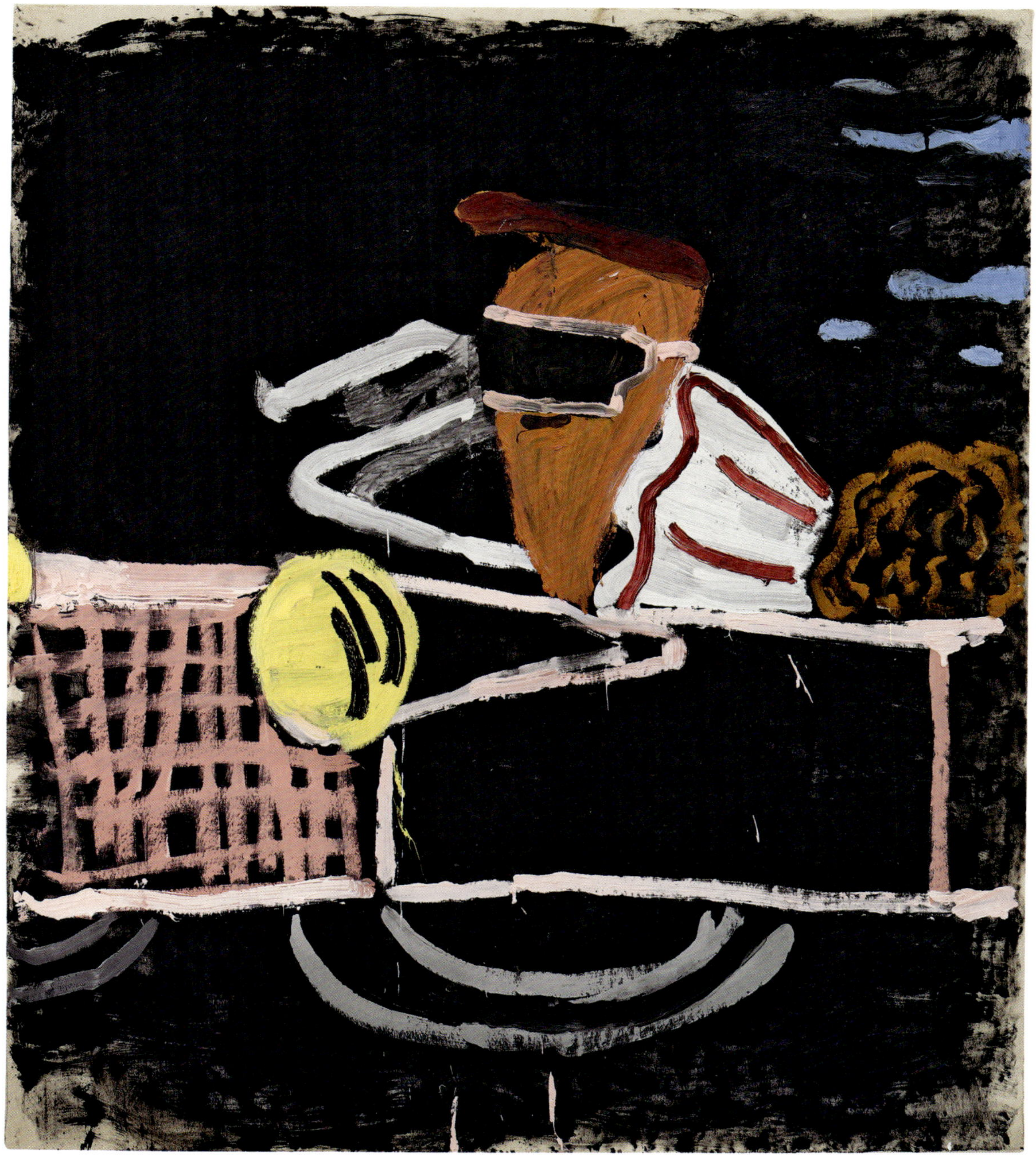

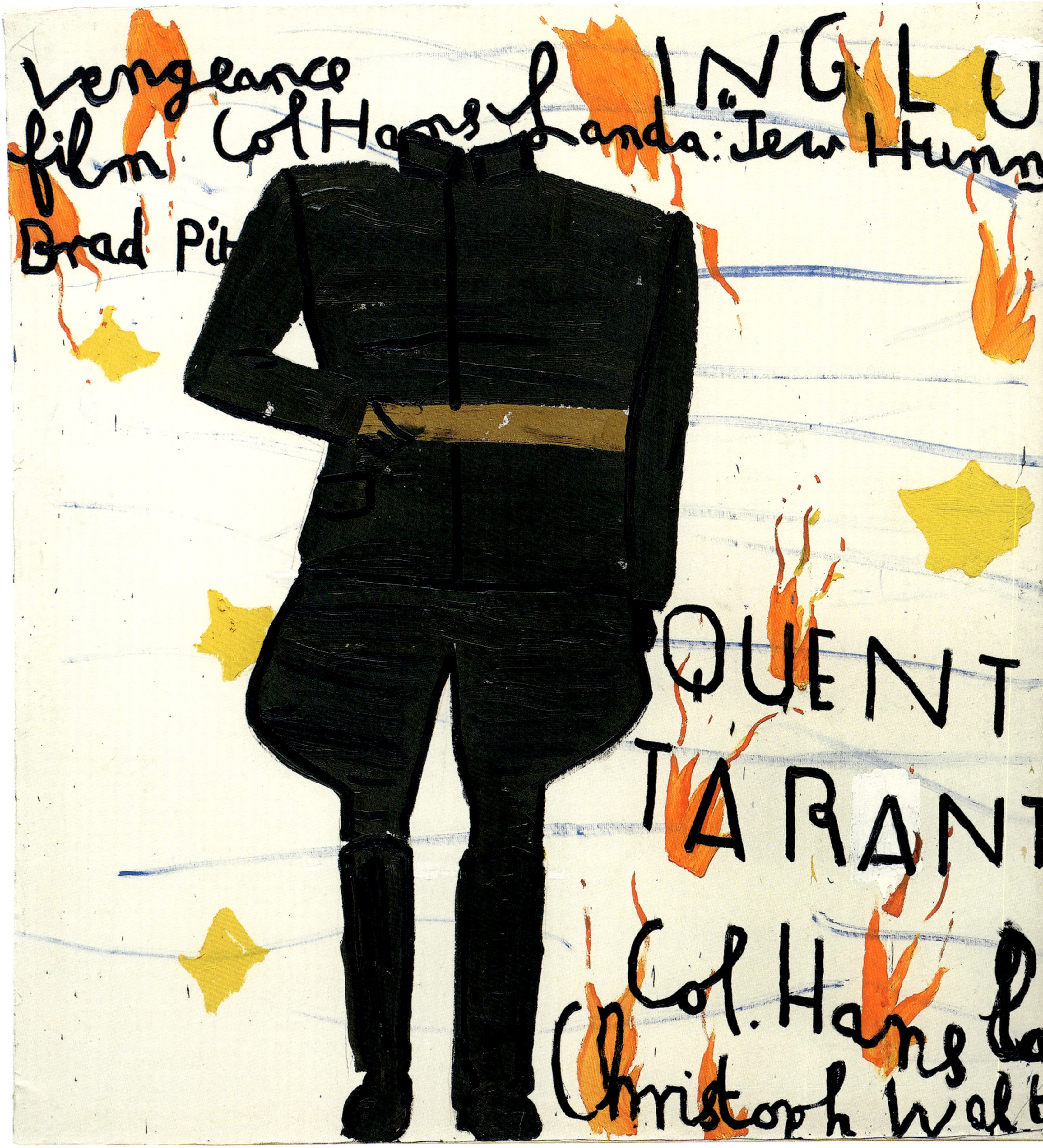
vengeance
film Col Hans Landa: Jew Hunn
Brad Pit
INGLU
QUENT
TARANT
Col. Hans La
Christoph Walt

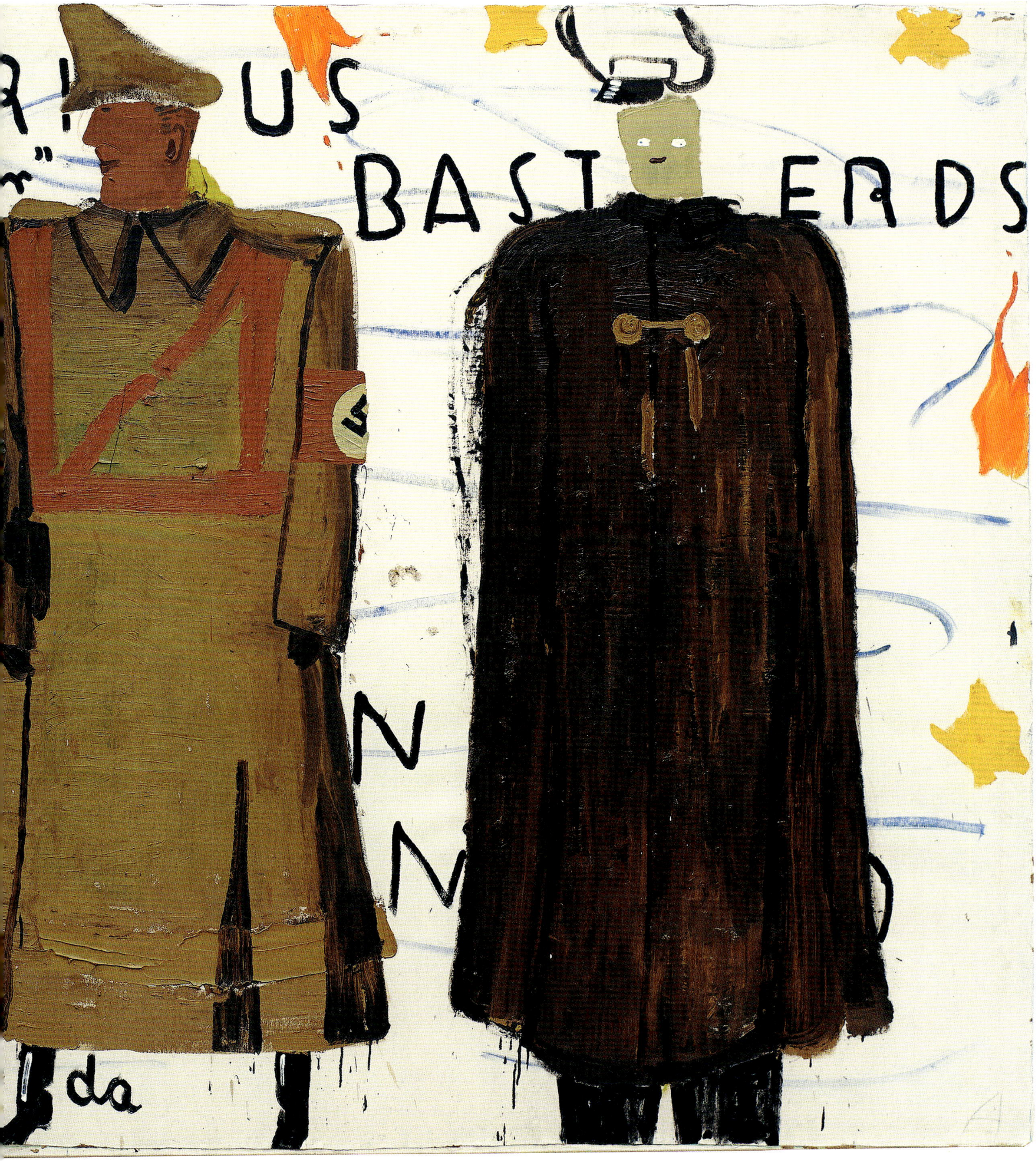
R! US
BAST ERDS
da

topmost left corner are the words 'vengeance film' which may offer ironic comment on the vicarious emotion we experience at the revenge visited on the Nazi elite in the film. The monumental centrality of the figures suggests the dark allure of the film's narrative and the power the fascist figures wield. Wylie has said that the picture was augmented by reference to a book on Nazi regalia and that the flames referenced the work of Giovanni di Paolo, but the picture as a whole was an act of memory, built from her response to the film which she describes as 'visual shots'.[87]

Wylie's work can also be read in terms of film technique – framing shots that are transmuted from a film narrative into still images, her style suggesting the individual cells of an animated film. Wylie's way of revising the image by splicing or cutting is reminiscent of the montage present in cinema. This gives rise to an intriguing paradox; still images that are abstracted from another medium that gives the illusion of movement. The larger works could therefore be seen as opening shots which are usually long, wide ones that set the scene for the narrative that is to unfold. Her more intimate canvases are an analogue of the close-up. Perhaps

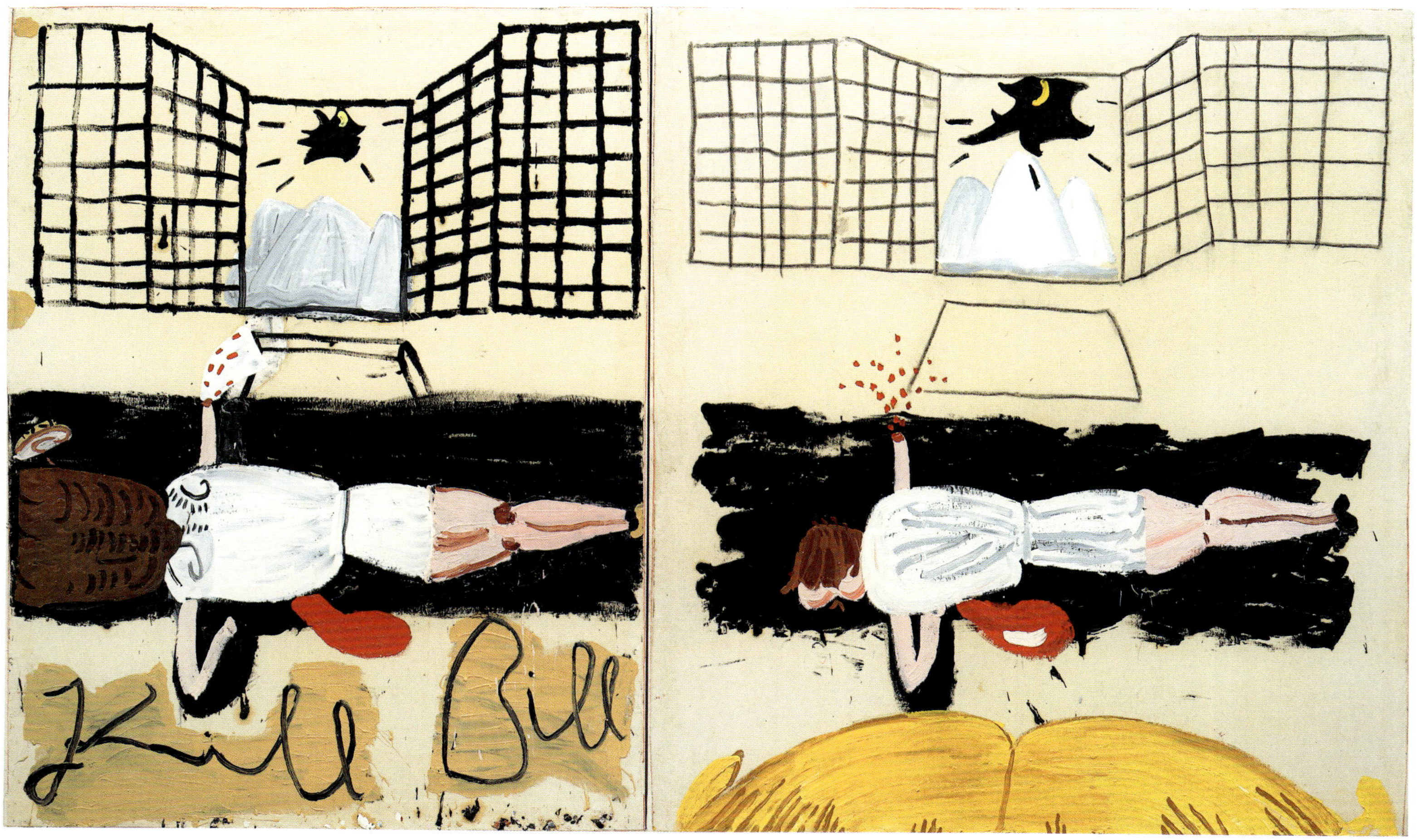

120
Kill Bill (Film Notes) 2007
Oil on canvas, 180 × 308 cm (70⅞ × 121⅜ in)
Private collection

121
Battle in Heaven (Film Notes) 2008
Oil on canvas, 183 × 336 cm (72⅛ × 132⅜ in)
Private collection

the most suggestive comparison would be between Wylie's work and B-rolls in film. B-rolls are shots that supplement opening or narrative shots; they do not further the story but add 'colour' or background. Wylie's works have a similar oblique relation to narrative – they suggest a slightly askance view.

Wylie herself has compared her practice to film-making, and has described in a conversation with the artist and experimental film-maker Ben Rivers how she envies the convenience of the film edit to shift point of view and emphasise dramatic effect. 'In film you have movement from the close-up to the distant shot in a click. If you paint them it's not "click" into close-up at all. A camera shot is so much more economical.'[88]

Kill Bill (Film Notes) 2007 (fig.120) duplicates a scene from Tarantino's film from two slightly different perspectives – the panel on the right includes the top of Uma Thurman's blond crown as she gloats over a brutally vanquished body lying in a bright pool of blood. Similarly, two paintings from the 2005 film *Syriana* – *Pink Table Cloth (Long Shot) (Film Notes)* 2013 (fig.122) and *Pink Table Cloth (Close-up) (Film Notes)* 2013 (fig.123) – describe a panoramic

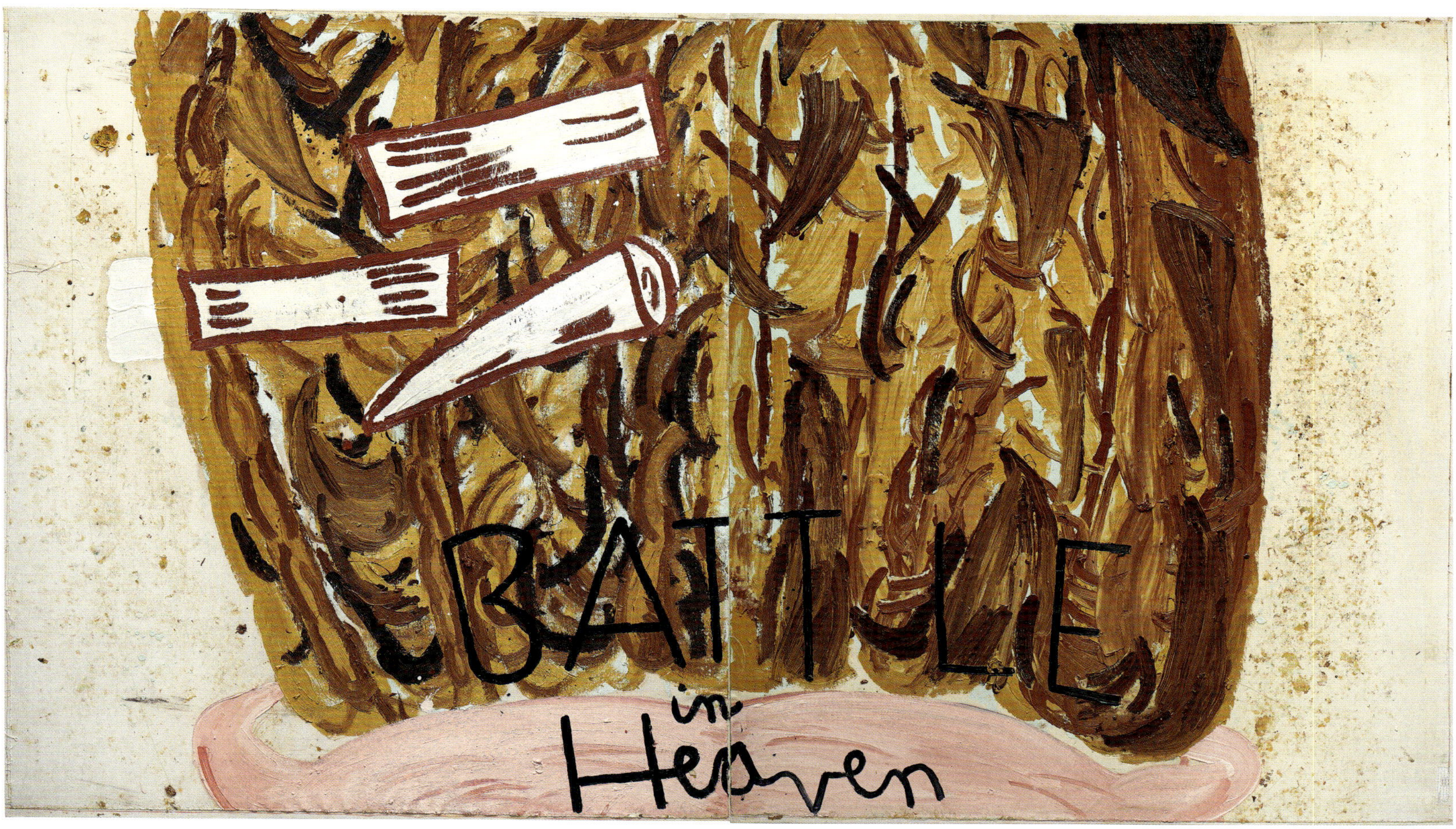

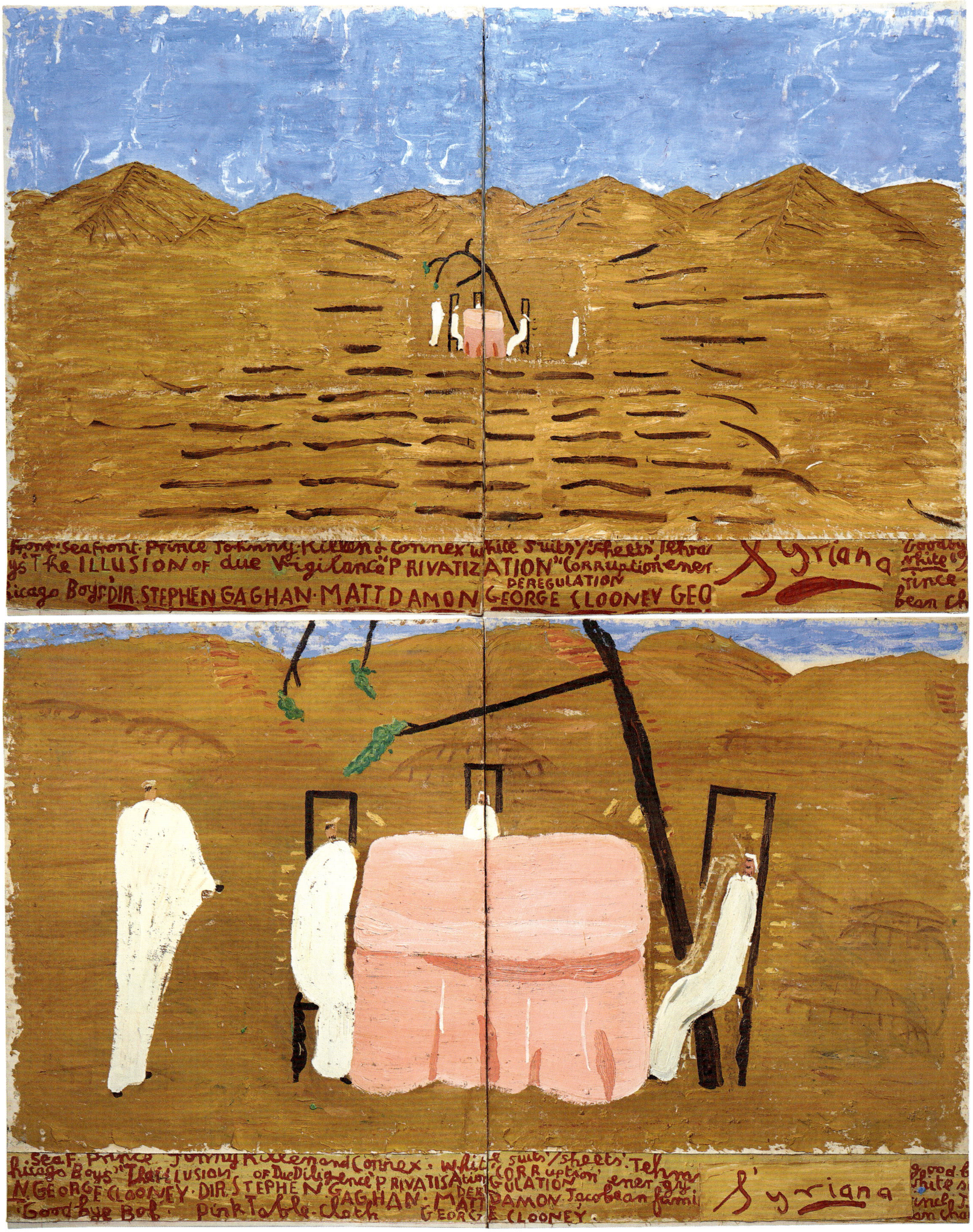
front · Seafront · Prince Johnny · Killen & Connex white suits/sheets' Tehra
The ILLUSION of due Vigilance "PRIVATIZATION" Corruption ener
DEREGULATION
icago Boys DIR. STEPHEN GAGHAN · MATT DAMON GEORGE CLOONEY GEO
Syriana
Goodby
white
rince
bean ch
Seaf. Prince Johnny Killen and Connex · white suits/sheets' Tehr
hicago Boys "The ILLUSION of Due Diligence" PRIVATISATION "CORRuption" energy
N GEORGE CLOONEY · DIR. STEPHEN GAGHAN · MATT DAMON · Jacobean fami
DEREGULATION
Goodbye Bob · Pink Table-cloth
GEORGE CLOONEY
Syriana

122
Pink Table Cloth (Long Shot) (Film Notes) 2013
Oil on canvas
208 × 330 cm (82 × 130 in)
Private collection

123
Pink Table Cloth (Close-up) (Film Notes) 2013
Oil on canvas
207 × 330 cm (81½ × 130 in)
Collection of Jeremy Levison

124
Japón Driving (Film Notes) 2008
Coloured pencil and collage on paper
22 × 30 cm (8¾ × 11⅞ in)
Private collection

125
Japón Driving (Film Notes) 2009
Oil on canvas
183 × 336 cm (72⅛ × 132⅜ in)
Private collection

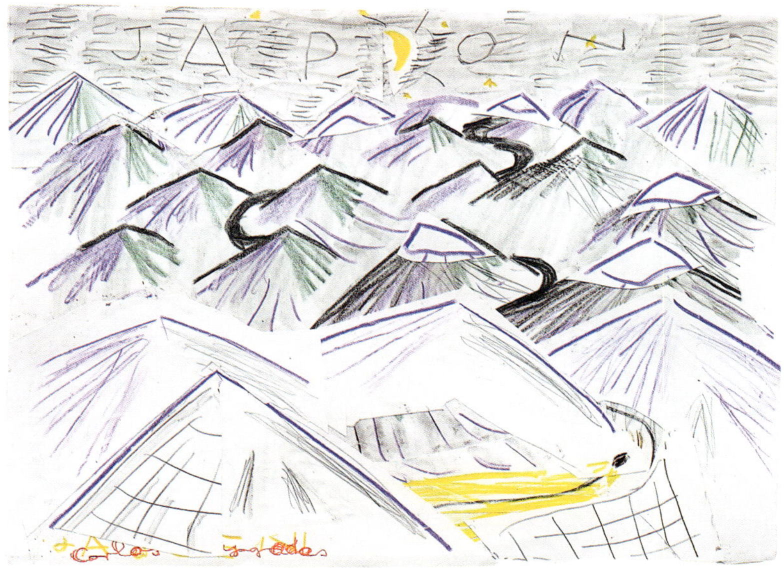

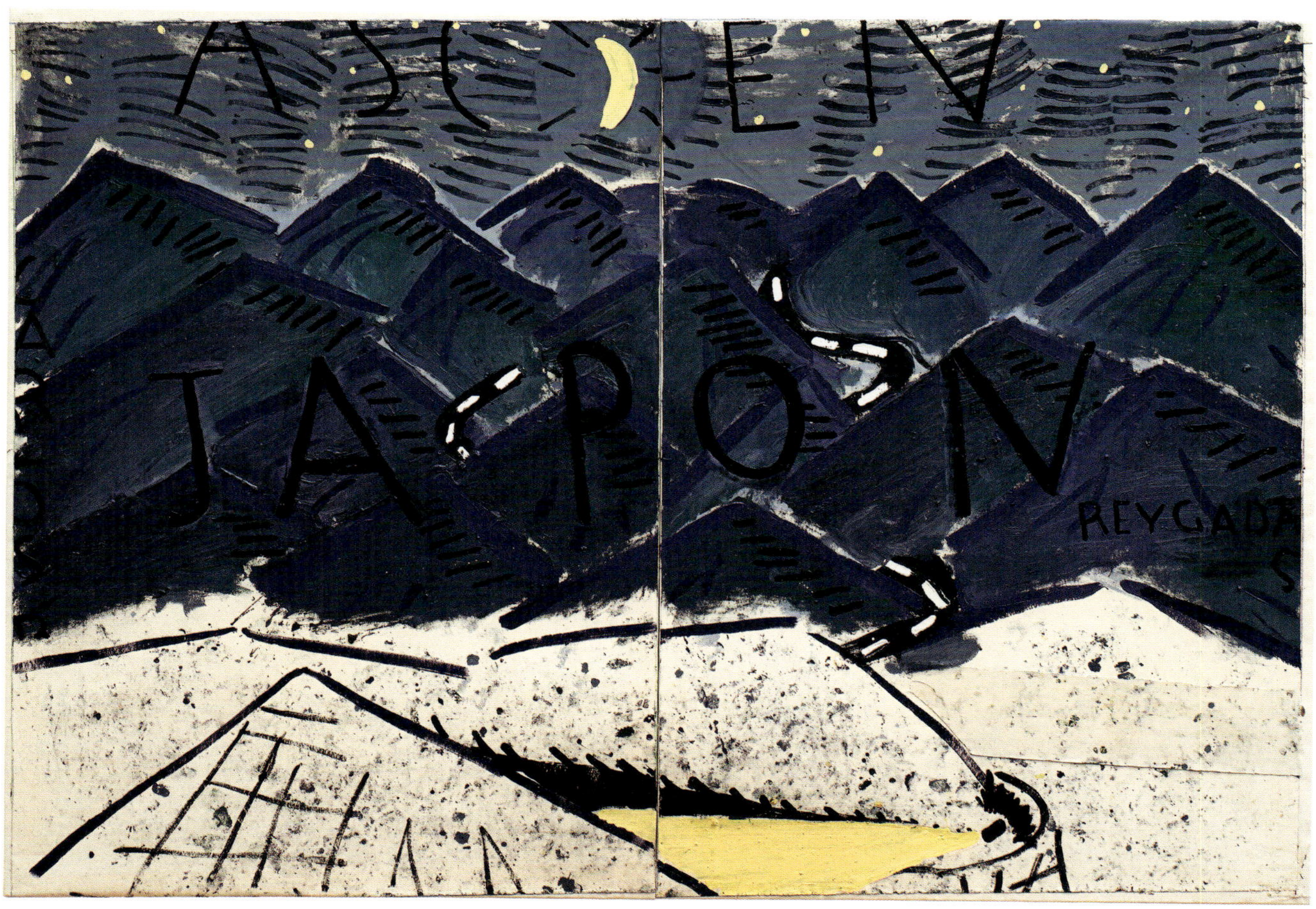

126
Savarin Trifle (Film Notes) 2010
Watercolour and collage on paper
84 × 59 cm (33⅛ × 23¼ in)
Private collection

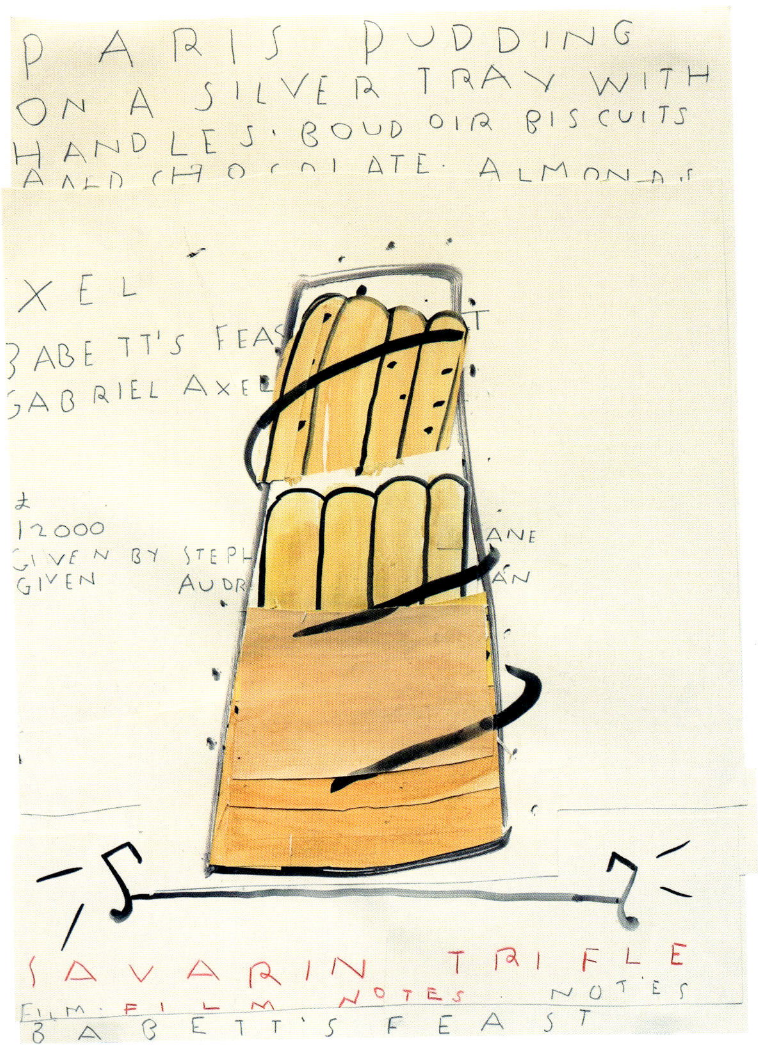

127
Jack Goes Swimming (Jack) 2013
Oil on canvas, 207 × 167 cm (81½ × 65¾ in)
Private collection

long shot and close-up image of a meeting in the desert at a table with a pink table cloth. *Battle in Heaven (Film Notes)* 2008 (fig.121) is directly taken from a full-frontal sex scene in the film of the same name, by Carlos Reygadas – a director who, Wylie notes, 'deals with huge subjects; salvation and guilt'.[89] *Japón Driving (Film Notes)* 2009 (fig.125) is based on another of Reygadas's films, *Japón*. Offering a bridge to Wylie's interest in Japanese manga, it draws on the film's imagery of a landscape that overwhelms humans and that represents a raw existential duality of sex and death, carnality and cruelty. The foreground of the painting is light and speckled, suggesting a road passing through a valley: it is wholly dominated by the looming dark mountains and night sky that seem oppressive and forbidding. The film's title and director's name are lettered boldly across the canvas, suggesting a title shot from a film's opening.

Elsewhere the drawing *Savarin Trifle (Film Notes)* 2010 (fig.126) comes from the multi-course banquet in Gabriel Axel's 1987 film *Babette's Feast*, while *The Hunt (Thomas)* 2013 pays homage to the fellow Danish director Thomas Vinterberg and his 2012 film *The Hunt*. In the foreground is the outline of a figure in swimming trunks, taken from a film still Wylie saw in *The Observer*. The image of the swimmer is juxtaposed against text from Lars von Trier and Thomas Vinterberg's *Dogme 95 Manifesto*. These were rules to create films which excluded the use of elaborate special effects or technology in an attempt to return power to the director as artist, as opposed to the film studio. *Jack Goes Swimming (Jack)* 2013 (fig.127) also features a bather. It references the late Philip Seymour Hoffman's romantic comedy *Jack Goes Boating* (2010) and recalls a scene where the central protagonist visualises himself in a swimming pool.

Wylie also describes other types of work as 'homage' paintings, beyond those prompted by her response to films. *City Road* 1999 (fig.130), for example, was inspired by a picture of Little Bo-Peep that Wylie saw painted onto a cafe window in City Road, London; and *Brown Berlin Bear's Head* 2008 (fig.128), which features the front of a man's head wearing a bear costume, was the result of the exposure given in newspapers to *Sleeper*, a 2005 film by Mark Wallinger (b.1959) of himself wandering around a deserted German gallery disguised as a bear, which was shown during the 2007 Turner Prize exhibition.[90] The girls on the left-hand side of

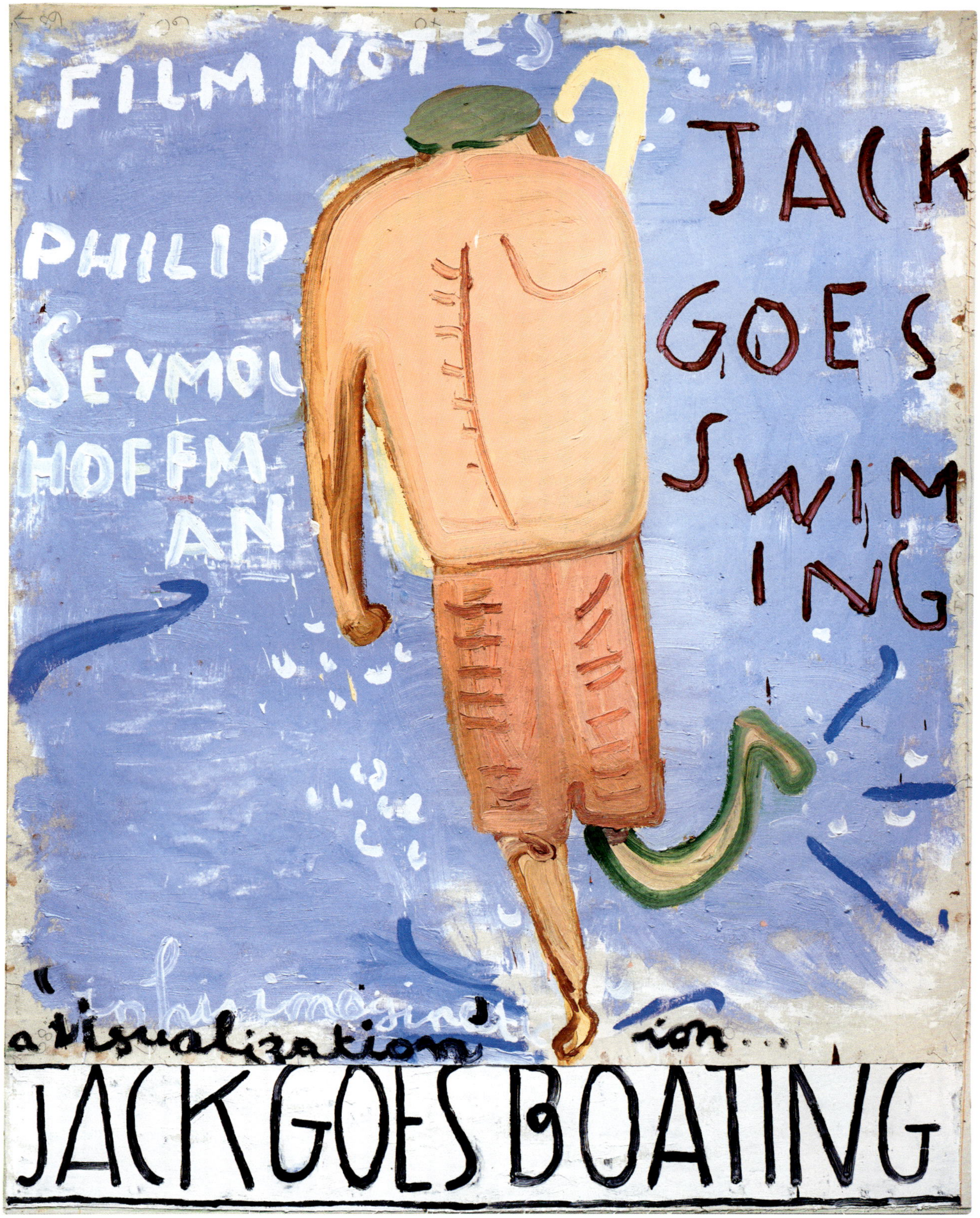
FILM NOTES
PHILIP SEYMOU HOFFM AN
JACK GOES SWIM ING
a visualization
ion...
JACK GOES BOATING

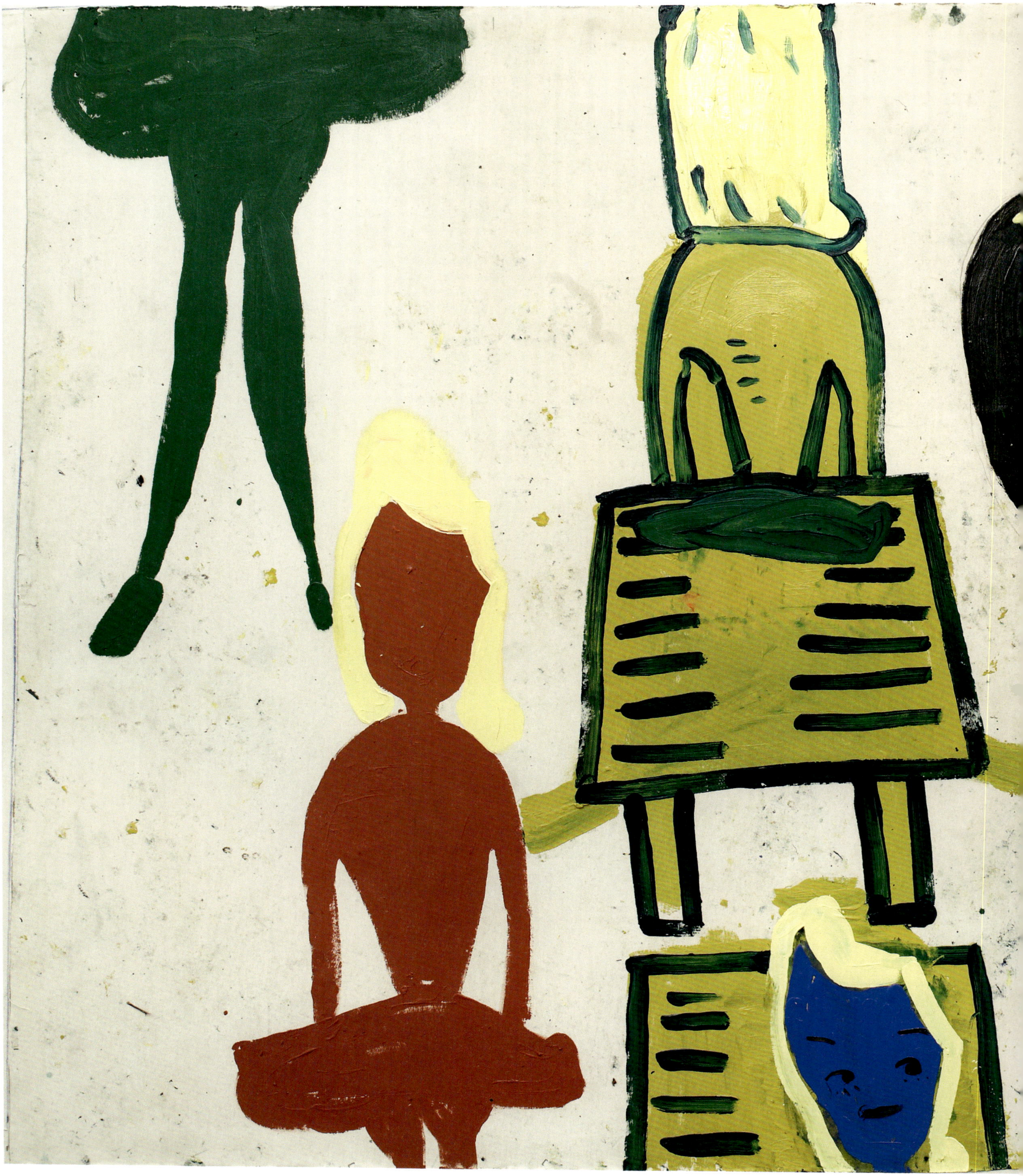

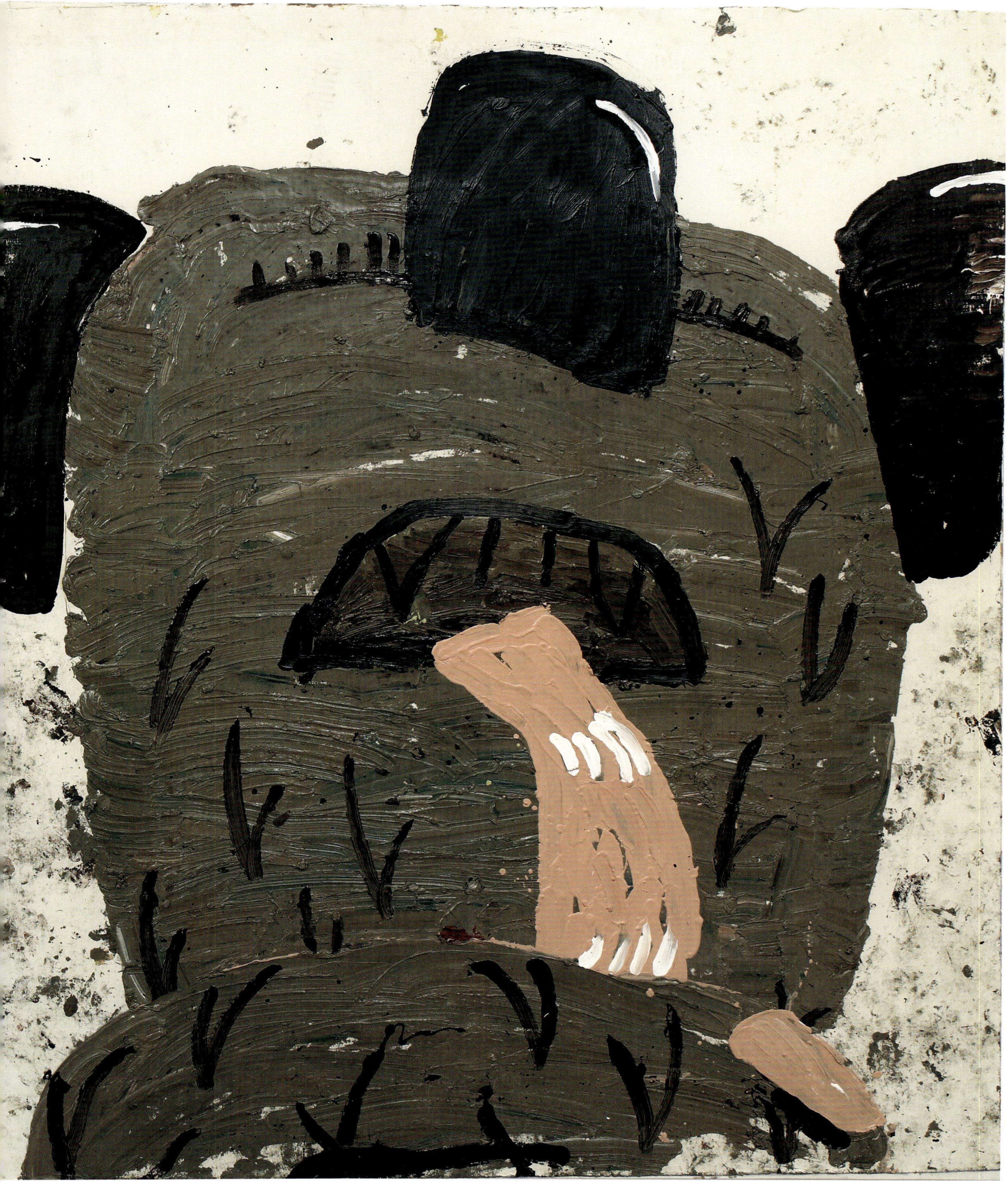

128 (previous pages)
Brown Berlin Bear's Head 2008
Oil on canvas, 183 × 336 cm (72⅛ × 132⅜ in)
Private collection

129
Listening to Miss S. 1993
Oil on canvas, 168 × 183 cm (66¼ × 72⅛ in)
Private collection

130
City Road 1999
Oil on canvas, 183 × 183 cm (72⅛ × 72⅛ in)
Collection of Tiziana Castelluzzo

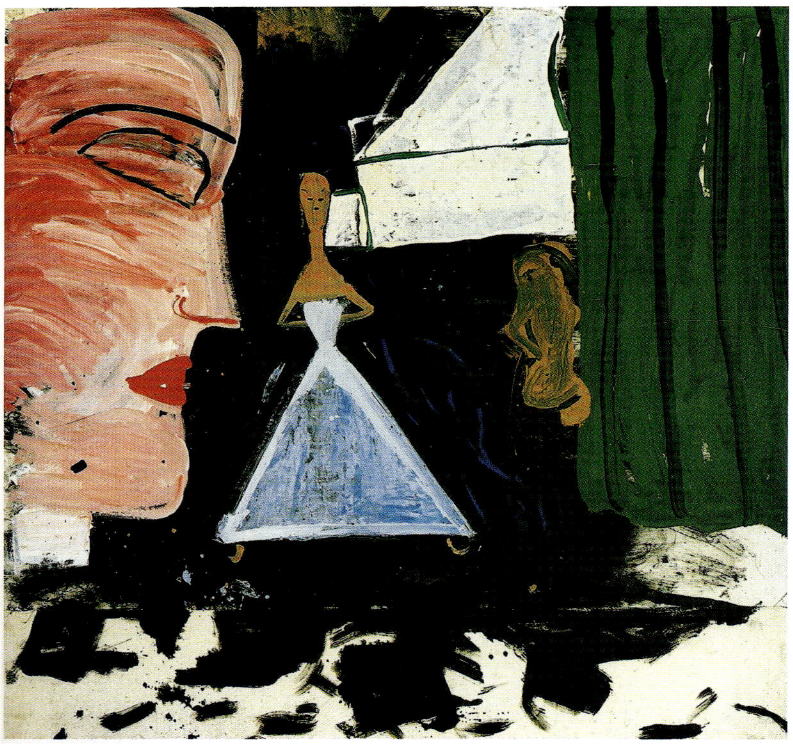

the latter picture were based on another series of drawings Wylie made of Penélope Cruz in Almodóvar's film *Volver*.[91] Wylie's work has a generosity of spirit, an openness to the totality of life's experience. Her subject matter is approached not in a spirit of aloofness but rather engages with it fully, with respect for and often in homage to those things that have especially affected her. It is playful and ironic, a working journal of a lived life.

Her presence as a looming head at the side of the canvas in paintings such as *Baby Jesus of Prague* 1990 (fig.107) or *Listening to Miss S.* 1993 (fig.129) serves to remind the viewer that she is also an imagining spectator and that looking is not simply a process of passive observation but an active and deliberate thing; a thing that not only produces the world, but alters and disrupts it. Wylie confronts her subject matter both directly, as she sees it before her, and also as it is remembered. In both cases she does so without preconceptions, and embraces the selective and partial nature of memory that operates as a filter. The act of painting for Wylie is an event about time, emotional connection and response – between herself, the material of paint, the motif and what results.

At the beginning of *Riddley Walker*, the story's protagonist explains in phonetic English, 'That's why I finely come to writing this all down. Thinking on what the idear of us myt be. Thinking on that thing whats in us lorn and loan and oansome.'[92] Wylie has developed a unique and distinctive style that, like Hoban's *Riddley Walker*, is articulated in an allusive and strange idiolect. The pictures are acts of memory, at once personal and social. Her responses are gently questioning – renderings of a wonder and perplexity when faced with the range of our experience as inheritors of a fragmented history and tradition whose imagery is multiplied through newer modern media such as film and digital technology. Wylie, however, is not a cultural conservative who despairs at the loss of a common culture, and nor does she draw narrowly on art historical tradition: the entirety of lived experience is considered and transmuted in her art. Wylie's paintings convene disparate elements onto the field of the canvas, altering and adding to arrive at a distillation of a wide diversity of sources in a way that is immediate and concrete. She operates in a variety of registers that are present simultaneously: narrative, homage, social comment, and religious and mythic resonance are fused into a celebration (and sometimes critique) of life as it is lived today.

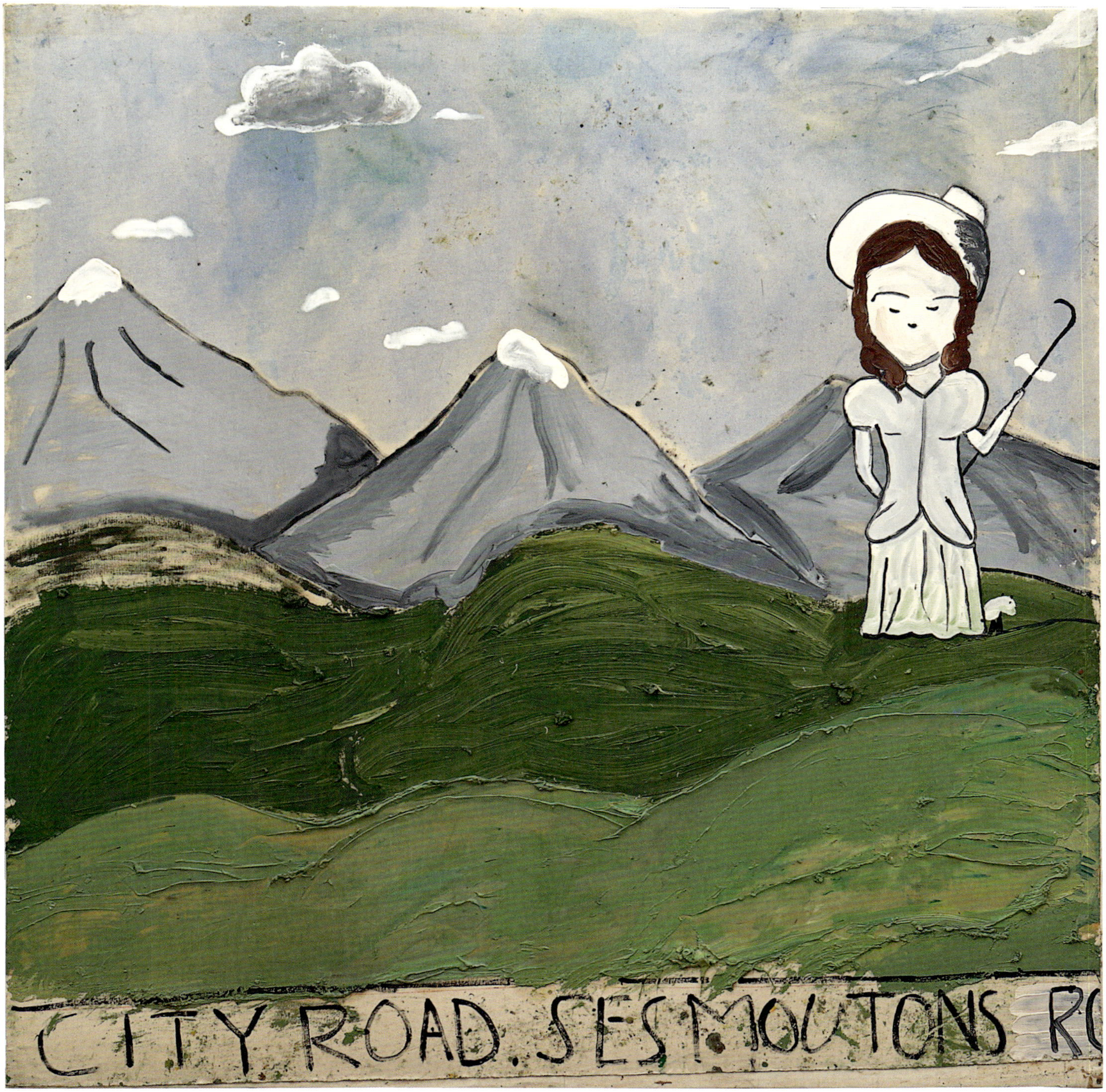
CITY ROAD. SES MOUTONS RO

Notes

1 Russell Hoban, *Riddley Walker*, Picador, London, 1980.
2 Mel Gooding, 'Rose Wylie: likeness in the unlikeness', *Rose Wylie*, exh.cat., Reed's Wharf Gallery, London, 1995.
3 Artist in conversation with author, 11 August 2017.
4 ibid.
5 ibid.
6 'Fonetic drawing: Giovanni di Paolo asks Rose Wylie four questions', *Rose Wylie, Twink and Ivy, and Other Paintings and Small Drawings: 1999–2003*, exh.cat., published to coincide with *Rose Wylie: Room Project – Twink and Ivy*, Trinity Theatre, Tunbridge Wells, 2004, p.12.
7 Artist in conversation with author, 8 February 2018.
8 Artist in conversation with author, 11 August 2017.
9 'Jeff McMillian interviews Rose Wylie', *Turps Banana*, no.10, 2011, p.2.
10 ibid.
11 Artist in conversation with author, 9 November 2017.
12 Artist in conversation with Hans Ulrich Obrist, Goethe-Institut, London, 12 December 2017.
13 'Fonetic drawing: Giovanni di Paolo asks Rose Wylie four questions', *Rose Wylie, Twink and Ivy, and Other Paintings and Small Drawings: 1999–2003*, exh.cat., published to coincide with *Rose Wylie: Room Project – Twink and Ivy*, Trinity Theatre, Tunbridge Wells, 2004, p.12.
14 Artist in conversation with author, 9 February 2018.
15 See Clive Ashwin, *Art Education: Documents and Policies 1768–1975*, Society for Research in Higher Education, London, 1975, pp 83–4.
16 'it was the context I loved . . . I wanted to paint.' Artist in conversation with author, 11 August 2017.
17 ibid.
18 ibid.
19 Artist in conversation with author, 7 August 2017.
20 Email from artist to author, 1 September 2017.
21 Rose Wylie, 'Girl on a Liner', in *One Day, Something Happens: Paintings of People*, exh.cat., Towner Art Gallery, Eastbourne, 2015, p.98.
22 Artist in conversation with author, 11 August 2017. The Group of Seven was a group of self-proclaimed modern artists in the 1920s, originally consisting of Franklin Carmichael, Lawren Harris, A.Y. Jackson, Frank Johnston, Arthur Lismer, J.E.H. MacDonald and Frederick Varley.
23 ibid.
24 Fiona Maddocks, 'In the studio with Rose Wylie RA', *Royal Academy Magazine*, Winter 2016, www.royalacademy.org.uk/article/in-the-studio-with-rose-wylie-ra.
25 Rose Wylie, 'An enquiry into some attitudes to teaching drawing in the Fine Art Departments of English art schools', Department of Cultural History, Royal College of Art, May 1981. Wylie's choice of topic was in part informed by her own experience of running the painting course at Sittingbourne.
26 ibid., Preface, p.6.
27 ibid., Preface, p.1 and p.66.
28 ibid., Preface, p.6.
29 Marcus Reichert, 'Rose Wylie: transcending memory,' www.state-media.com/state/index.php?q=profile.
30 *Rose Wylie: Lined Paper Paintings*, exh.cat., Stephen Lacey Gallery, London, 1999, unpaginated.
31 Artist in conversation with author, 11 August 2017.
32 Wylie has commented that she 'did a lot of what I called "domestic sculpture" drawings. Still doing it with the Halloween Choc ptgs (ghosts and chopped-finger) now in Seoul. Domestic Sculpture also included scent-bottles (Ralph Lauren, with a woman's figure inside'. Email from artist to author, 4 September 2017.
33 Email from artist to author, 30 January 2013.
34 Wylie first read Gertrude Stein when she was in Vancouver.
35 Gertrude Stein, *What Are Masterpieces*, Pitman Publishing, New York, 1940.
36 John Cogan, 'The phenomenological reduction', Internet Encyclopedia of Philosophy, www.iep.utm.edu/phen-red/.
37 André Lhote, *Traité du paysage*, in Jean-Louis Ferrier *et al.*, *Art of Our Century, The Chronicle of Western Art, 1900 to the Present*, Prentice Hall, New York, 1988, p. 383.
38 Rose Wylie in '8 painters on painting', *Frieze*, no.160, January/February 2014, p.98.
39 'Jeff McMillian interviews Rose Wylie', *Turps Banana*, no.10, 2011, p.2.
40 Rose Wylie quoted in Jennifer Higgie, '8 painters on painting', *Frieze*, 11 January 2013, https://frieze.com/article/8-painters-painting.
41 ibid.
42 Cherry Smyth, 'Coming unstuck', in *Rose Wylie: Tilt the Horizontal into a Slant*, exh.cat., Chapter Gallery, Cardiff, 2016, p.11.
43 Email from artist to author, 12 February 2018.
44 ibid.
45 Cherry Smith, 'Coming unstuck', in *Rose Wylie: Tilt the Horizontal into a Slant*, exh.cat., Chapter Gallery, Cardiff, 2016, p.12.
46 Email from artist to author, 30 January 2013.
47 Artist in conversation with author, 7 December 2017.
48 Email from artist to author, 30 January 2013.
49 Rose Wylie, 'Notes: process and series', sent to author, 8 July 2014.
50 Christos M. Joachimides (ed.), *A New Spirit in Painting*, Royal Academy of Arts, London,

15 January–18 March 1981. Artists: Frank Auerbach, Francis Bacon, Balthus, Georg Baselitz, Pier Paolo Calzolari, Alan Charlton, Sandro Chia, Rainer Fetting, Lucian Freud, Gotthard Graubner, Philip Guston, Dieter Hacker, Jean Hélion, David Hockney, Howard Hodgkin, K.H. Hödicke, Anselm Kiefer, Per Kirkeby, R.B. Kitaj, Bernd Koberling, Willem de Kooning, Jannis Kounellis, Markus Lüpertz, Brice Marden, Roberto Matta, Bruce McLean, Mario Merz, Malcolm Morley, Mimmo Paladino, A.R. Penck, Pablo Picasso, Sigmar Polke, Gerhard Richter, Robert Ryman, Julian Schnabel, Frank Stella, Cy Twombly and Andy Warhol.

51 Email from Sarah Elson to author, 1 January 2018.

52 Wylie was first selected for EAST*international* in 1994 and again in 2004 and 2007.

53 Greer visited after three separate but connected events: a solo show at Union Gallery, London; a second solo show with Thomas Erben, New York; and, importantly, being selected as the only UK artist for the National Museum of Women in the Arts *Women to Watch* show in Washington, D.C.

54 Germaine Greer, *The Guardian*, 9 July 2010, www.theguardian.com/artanddesign/2010/jul/09/germaine-greer-rose-wylie-artist.

55 Roberta Smith, 'Rose Wylie: "What With What"', *New York Times*, 12 November 2010. www.nytimes.com/2010/11/12/arts/design/12galleries-002.html.

56 Artist in conversation with author, 9 December 2017.

57 Email from artist to author, 23 July 2014: 'A New Spirit in Painting was a terrific show . . . v exciting. Guston, too for the 1st time, as well as Sch. Then Schnabel (a bit later) was shown at the Tate and later again at the Whitechapel.'

58 Email from artist to author, 30 January 2013. Marina Warner, *From the Beast to the Blonde: On Fairy Tales and Their Tellers*, Chatto & Windus, London, 1994.

59 John Manning, *The Emblem*, Reaktion Books, London, 2002, p.29.

60 In discussing Rousseau's work, Wylie has cited many paintings as influential: 'Flamingos; Peace Delegates coming to Salute. . . ; Seine & the Eiffel Tower in the. . .; Landscape with milkmaids; Landscape with Bridge; Banks of the Oise; Happy Birthday; The Fisherman and the Biplane; View of the Chair Shop; Excise Office; Liberty Inviting artists to celebrate. . .;The Storm Tossed Vessel; Beauty and the Beast (a favourite title).' Email exchange between artist and author, 23 July 2014.

61 Artist in conversation with author, 7 December 2017.

62 Email from artist to author, 27 September 2017.

63 Press release from *Rose Wylie: Henry, Thomas, Keith & Jack*, Union Gallery, London, May 2013.

64 At £25,000, it is one of the most significant art prizes awarded in Britain.

65 Email from artist to author, 30 January 2013.

66 ibid.

67 ibid.

68 Email from Sarah Elson to author, 1 January 2018.

69 Hattie Garlick, 'Being called a bird is infantilising: such terms hold women back', *The Guardian*, 30 September 2016, www.theguardian.com/commentisfree/2016/sep/30/bird-infantilising-hold-women-back.

70 Emma Dexter, 'Wear What You Like', in *Rose Wylie: Wear What You Like*', exhibition leaflet, Transition Gallery, London, 2008, unpaginated.

71 *Korai* (singular: *kore*) were statues that depicted a woman, usually with one leg forward and holding her dress away from her feet. The clothing was important; unlike the male statues (*kouroi*), which were naked, *korai* were always robed, the drapes of the cloth both concealing and revealing the bodily form beneath. It is as if Woman is always mediated by the cultural forms of adornment. The face was likewise conventionally represented, serene but somewhat unreadable. Even though heavily stylised, it is important to note that later *korai* also depicted an individual, indicative of a culture that begins to value the solitary human being as a distinct entity.

72 Email from artist to author, 17 February 2018.

73 Email from artist to author, 22 October 2017.

74 Email from artist to author, 26 May 2014.

75 Artist in conversation with author, 8 February 2018.

76 Artist in conversation with author, 7 August 2014.

77 Email from artist to author, 14 September 2017.

78 Email from artist to author, 7 September 2017 (abbreviations by artist).

79 Daniel Boorstin, *The Image: A Guide to Pseudo-Events in America*, Vintage Books, New York, 1962.

80 See Art4theSpirit blog, 19 August 2013, http://art4thespirit.blogspot.co.uk/2013/08/rose-wiley_19.html.

81 Email from artist to author, 25 November 2017.

82 'The improbability of realistic outcome in the lyric "Someday my Prince will Come", and the unquestioning acceptance I received it with then, is still a fun gap-area to consider now . . . a stereotypical handout for children, and why not . . . I like a fairy story, and elements of truth are always worth sifting around and embedding.' Artist in email exchange with author, 25 November 2017.

83 Email from artist to author, 25 November 2017.

84 Esther Leslie, *Hollywood Flatlands: Animation, Critical Theory and the Avant-Garde*, Verso, London and New York, 2002.

85 Roland Barthes, *Camera Lucida*, Hill and Wang, New York, 1981.

86 Artist in conversation with author, 7 December 2017.

87 Email from artist to author, 10 July 2014.

88 *An Evening with Ben Rivers and Rose Wylie*, Tate Britain, 21 September 2017. In 2015 Ben Rivers created the film *What Means Something*, an intimate portrait of Rose Wylie. See also 'Interview between Ben Rivers and Rose Wylie', in *Rose Wylie: Tilt the Horizontal into a Slant*, exh.cat., Chapter, Cardiff, 2016, pp 59–67.

89 Email from artist to author, 12 July 2014.

90 Wylie has commented: 'Respect and homage: City Road is another "homage" painting (as is Arab & Dancing Girl). The Bo-Peep scene was originally painted onto a cafe-window in the City Road by an unknown artist. The kind of thing I like . . . and as with Brad's Art the painting is very like, but more like, the original (which has since been vandalized, and so no longer is in existence). There are many drawings which extend the painting; but I did in fact stay close to the original by using a photograph I'd taken. If there is something you wish to "respect" there seems to be little point in losing the connection in a promotion of authorship and subjectivity.' Email from artist to author, 30 January 2013.

91 ibid.

92 Russell Hoban, *Riddley Walker*, Picador, London, 1980, p.7.

131

Blackbird and Spring Flowers 2015

Oil on canvas

183 × 328 cm (72 × 129⅛ in)

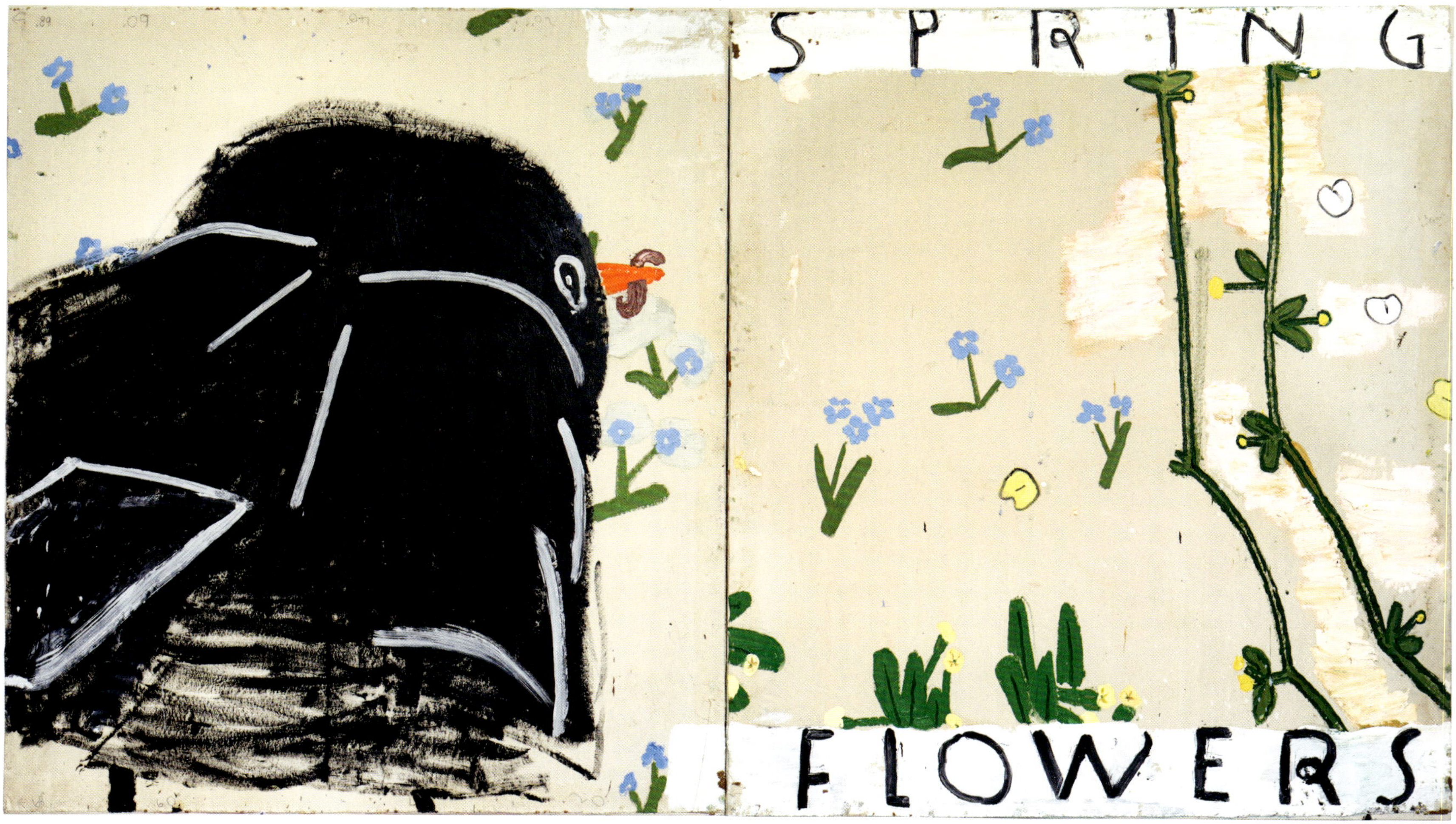

Chronology

1934 Born in Hythe, Kent, the youngest of seven children. Wylie spends the first few years of her life in India before returning to England shortly before the outbreak of the Second World War.

1939 The family live in Bayswater, London, before moving to Farnborough, Hampshire.

1945 After the end of the war the family move back to Hythe.

1948 Accompanied by her mother, Wylie makes her first trip to Europe and visits the Prado and the Louvre.

1951 Wylie visits the National Gallery in London and becomes acquainted with the paintings of Giovanni di Paolo (1398–1482), an artist she very much admires.

1952 On the basis of her portfolio of drawings and paintings, Wylie is admitted as a student on the Fine Art course at the Folkestone and Dover School of Art.

Mid-1950s Wylie regularly models for the artist John Stanton Ward CBE (1917–2007).

1955 Wylie is painted by Anthony Devas (1911–1958) for one of a series of portraits commissioned by Rowntree's to advertise its Aero chocolate bar.

1956 Wylie graduates from the Folkestone and Dover School of Art with a National Diploma in Design (NDD).

1956–7 Wylie studies on the teacher training course at Goldsmiths College, London. Here she meets fellow student, the painter Roy Oxlade (1929–2014) and marries him the following year.

1958 Luke John, the first of three children, is born. The family moves to Vancouver.

1960 Elizabeth, their second child, is born.

1962 The family returns to England. Oxlade accepts a job as Senior Lecturer in Art at Cartrefle College of Further Education in Wales and so the family moved to Bryniau Bach in Llangollen and later to Bank Cottage in Rhostyllen, a mining village, south-west of Wrexham.

1964–8 Wylie is a full-time Lecturer on the Art Foundation course Denbighshire Technical College teaching painting, drawing and textiles.

1966 Their third child, Henrietta, is born.

1968 Oxlade is appointed Head of the Art Department at Sittingbourne College of Further Education and the family move to Newnham, Kent.

1970s Wylie is Senior Lecturer at Sittingbourne College of Further Education.

Late 1970s Wylie becomes Head of Painting at Sittingbourne College of Further Education.

1979–81 Wylie returns to study as a mature student in the Department of Cultural History at the Royal College of Art, London. Her MA dissertation is titled 'An enquiry into some attitudes to teaching drawing in the Fine Art departments of English art schools'.

1982 Wylie exhibits a pencil drawing *Boy Meets Girl* in the *Hayward Annual: British Drawing*, Hayward Gallery, London, selected by Kenneth Armitage, Gillian Ayres, Frances Carey, Mark Francis and Euan Uglow.

1985 First exhibition of paintings is held at the Trinity Arts Centre, Royal Tunbridge Wells, Kent.

1991 Wylie exhibits the painting *Artist in Studio, with Stove, Sofa, Plan Chest and Drapes* 1991 in the *John Moores 17*, Walker Art Gallery, Liverpool.

1992 Wylie exhibits a painting *Derain's Cat and Our Cat* 1992 in the *Royal Academy Summer Exhibition*, Royal Academy of Art, London.

1993 Wylie wins Joint First Prize for the open exhibition *Interiors*, Towner Art Gallery, Eastbourne.

1994 Wylie is invited by Rudi Fuchs and Jan Dibbets to exhibit for the first time in **EAST***international 1994*, Norwich Gallery, Norwich.

1995 The exhibition *Rose Wylie: Likeness in the Unlikeness* takes place at Reed's Wharf Gallery / Stephen Lacey, London.

1996 The drawing *Supermodel* 1996 is included in the Cheltenham Open Drawing Exhibition by selectors Peter de Francia, Deanna Petherbridge and Anita Taylor.

1997 Three paintings are shortlisted for Jerwood Painting Prize: *Size 8 Orange* 1996, *Tree Canterbury* 1997 and *AFW* 1997.
The drawing *Erotic Lily Bud* 1997 is included in the Cheltenham Open Drawing Exhibition by selectors Timothy Hyman, Felicity Lunn and Nick Tite.

1998 The exhibition *Rose Wylie: Red Legs and Other Paintings* takes place at Abbotsbury Studios, Abbotsbury, Dorset.

1999 Wylie's exhibition *Lined Paper Paintings* at the Stephen Lacey Gallery is accompanied by a catalogue for which she contributes a text, 'How I would like my paintings to be and what I do'.
Wylie wins the Sunny Dupree Family Award for a Woman Artist, Royal Academy of Arts, London.

2000 The ballpoint and pen drawing, *Popstar Plays Tennis* 2000, is included in the Cheltenham Open Drawing Exhibition, selected by Andrew Brighton, Mel Gooding, Isobel Johnstone and Doris Lockhart Saatchi.

2002 Wylie is shortlisted for the Jerwood Drawing Prize with two works, *Pink Japanese Purse* 2002 and *Wearing a Check Skirt with Small Head: Consequences* 2002, selectors Marco Livingstone, Cornelia Parker and Marina Warner.

2004 Wylie exhibits the *Twink and Ivy* series in *Room Project* at Trinity Theatre, Tunbridge Wells, Kent. The catalogue includes an imagined interview between the artist and Giovanni di Paolo.
Wylie participates in EAST*international 2004*, Norwich, selected by Neo Rauch and Gerd Harry Lybke.
Wylie is awarded £1000 prize to produce a print for the EAST*international* Print Commission.
Wylie also has a joint exhibition with her husband, Roy Oxlade, at Rutherford College, University of Kent, Canterbury.

2006 Wylie has her first exhibition with Union Gallery, London. The show is called *Paintings* and the selection includes *H & O Tennis* 1999, *St Francis and with Patches* 2000, *Faversham Hedge Dog* 2000, *Mexican Floosie* 2002 and *Pin Up and Porn Queen Jigsaw* 2005. To coincide with this she self-publishes a small book with Oxlade called *Rose Wylie: Some Drawings 1987–2005*.

2007 Wylie's work is selected by Matthew Higgs and Marc Camille Chaimowicz for EAST*international 2007*.

2008 Wylie has exhibition *Rose Wylie: Wear What You Like* at the Transition Gallery, London.

2009 The painting *The Manufacturers* 2008 is shortlisted for the Threadneedle Prize.

2010 Wylie exhibits a group of *Film Notes* paintings, including *Japón Driving (Film Notes)* 2009, *Battle in Heaven (Film Notes)* 2009 and *Sitting on a Bench with Border (Film Notes)* 2008 at the Union Gallery, London.
The painting *Lords and Ladies* 2009 is selected by Sarah Elson and Sheena Wagstaff for inclusion in *Women to Watch – Body of Work: New Perspectives on Figure Painting*, National Museum of Women in the Arts, Washington, D.C.
Sisters Savannah and Sienna Miller of the fashion label Twenty8Twelve invite Rose to collaborate with them on a tee-shirt design and, on the occasion of the *Women to Watch* exhibition, a conversation between Wylie and Savannah Miller is held in Westbourne Grove Church, London.
In the autumn Wylie has her first exhibition at the Thomas Erben Gallery, New York.

2011 Wylie is awarded a Paul Hamlyn Prize for Visual Arts by the Paul Hamlyn Foundation, London.
Wylie has her first exhibition at the Galerie Michael Janssen, Berlin.

2012 Wylie has her first exhibition at the Regina Gallery, Moscow.
In the spring Wylie has her first major monographic exhibition *Big Boys Sit in the Front* which is the inaugural show at the Jerwood Gallery, Hastings.
In the autumn the exhibition *Rose Wylie: After Daphne* takes place at the Rosenwald-Wolf Gallery, Philadelphia University of the Arts, Philadelphia.

2013 The exhibition *Woof-Woof* takes place at the Haugar Vestfold Kunstmuseum, Tønsberg, Norway.
On the occasion of the relaunch of London's Tate Britain, Wylie is honoured with a *BP Spotlight: Rose Wylie* which showcases recent works including *Inglourious Basterds (Film Notes)* 2010 and *The Queen of Sheba and JT* 2012. To coincide with this, Tateshots make a short film *Rose Wylie on Storytelling and Painting Big*.
Frieze also make a film *At Home with Rose Wylie* which explores how living in the Kent countryside for four decades has influenced her paintings.

2014 Roy Oxlade dies after a long battle with cancer.
Wylie wins the John Moores Painting Prize and is elected a Senior Royal Academician, Royal Academy of Arts, London.
She also has a solo exhibition at the Städtische Galerie Wolfsburg, Germany, as well as her first exhibition at CHOI&LAGER, Cologne.
Wylie produces *Pink Girls, Yellow Curls 1*, a series of nine etchings and *Pink Girls, Yellow Curls 2*, a series of 26 unique works.

2015 Wylie has a solo exhibition at the Douglas Hyde Gallery, Dublin, and exhibits a painting – *Red Cardinals Are Protected* 2015 – in *Venice Biennale: Vita Vitale*, Azerbaijan Pavilion, Venice.
Rose & Roy, a documentary film by Adolfo Doring that follows Wylie and Oxlade during preparation for Wylie's monographic show in Hastings in 2012, is released.
Wylie's painting *Herr Rehlinger in White Armour* 2014 wins the Charles Wollaston Award for the 'most distinguished work' at the *Royal Academy Summer Exhibition*.
Ben Rivers makes the 16 mm film *What Means Something*, a portrait of Wylie. This is presented in his exhibition at Camden Arts Centre, London.
Wylie produces *CFF Nicole Kidman*, a portfolio of seven etchings and *CFF NKK*, a series of seven unique works.
In November the exhibition *Rose Wylie* takes place at VW (VeneKlasen/Werner), Berlin.

2016 Wylie has solo exhibitions at Turner Contemporary, Margate, Kent, and the Chapter Gallery, Cardiff, Wales.
She also has an exhibition at Space K, Seoul, South Korea.
For Polígrafa Obra Gràfica she produces a portfolio of 66 lithographs, *Things Around the House*.
In the winter she has her first exhibition at David Zwirner, London.

2017 Wylie has her second exhibition, at CHOI&LAGER, Cologne.
To coincide with the annual *Royal Academy Summer Exhibition* she designs a tee-shirt, pair of socks and cap.
In the late autumn she has a solo exhibition, *Quack Quack*, at the Serpentine Sackler Gallery, London, for which she produces two limited-edition lithographs *Gingery Brown* and *Self Portrait with Shut Mouth*.

2018 Wylie exhibits in the Tate Members Room, Tate Modern. Handmade glass sculptures produced by Berengo Studio, Venice, are displayed alongside vinyl cut-outs which derive from four *Scissor Girls* paintings, each 3.7 metres (12 feet) long, all from 2017.
For the Hepworth Wakefield, and in collaboration with the Curwen Studio, Wylie produces the lithograph *King John, Frog*.
In the spring she has her second exhibition at David Zwirner, London.
She also has a solo exhibition, *History Painting*, at Plymouth Arts Centre, Plymouth and at CAC (Centro de Arte Contemporáneo de Málaga) and at the Newlyn Art Gallery & The Exchange, Penzance.
To mark the occasion of the Royal Academy's 250th anniversary and annual Summer Exhibition, Wylie is invited along with Royal Academicians Grayson Perry, Cornelia Parker and Joe Tilson to design flags for the streets of Mayfair and St James's. Wylie decides to use details of her recent *Lolita's House* series for the flags of Bond Street. The title references a house across the street from Wylie's Kent home in the 1970s, where the neighbour's teenage daughter would often wash their car in the driveway.
Wylie wins the South Bank Sky Arts Award for her exhibition *Quack Quack* at the Serpentine Sackler Gallery and is honoured with an OBE in the Queen's birthday list.

Exhibitions, publications, awards and collections

SOLO EXHIBITIONS

2018 *Rose Wylie: Hullo, Hullo*, CAC Malaga (Centro de Arte Contemporáneo de Malaga), Malaga, Spain (4 May – 9 September)
Rose Wylie: Lolita's House, David Zwirner, London (19 April – 26 May)
Rose Wylie: History Painting, Plymouth Arts Centre, Plymouth, England (29 March – 30 May) [itinerary: Newlyn Art Gallery & The Exchange, Cornwall, England (9 June – 15 September)]
Rose Wylie, Tate Members Room, Tate Modern, London (27 March – spring 2018)

2017 *Rose Wylie: Quack Quack*, Serpentine Sackler Gallery, London (30 November 2017 – 11 February 2018)
Rose Wylie: The Curator is Present, WILLAS Contemporary, Oslo (24 August – 8 October)
Rose Wylie: Yellow Sax, Brand New Gallery, Milan (31 May – 9 September)
Rose Wylie: Use What You've Got, Neue Galerie Gladbeck, Germany (5 May – 23 June)
Rose Wylie: Drawings, Christian Larsen, Stockholm (6 April – 13 May)
Rose Wylie: Cupid & Fur Coat, CHOI&LAGER, Cologne, Germany (10 March –7 May)

2016 *Rose Wylie: Horse, Bird, Cat*, David Zwirner, London (24 November 2016 – 7 January 2017)
Rose Wylie: Queens & Chocs, Space K, Seoul (26 September – 30 November)
Rose Wylie: Tilt the Horizontal into a Slant, Chapter Gallery, Cardiff (13 February – 29 May)
Rose Wylie, Turner Contemporary, Margate, England (12 January – 13 March)

2015 *Rose Wylie: Dressed to Kill*, VW (VeneKlasen/Werner), Berlin (14 November 2015 – 16 January 2016)
Rose Wylie: Yellow Bird and Leaves, Nunu Fine Art, Zhongzheng, Taipei (31 October – 6 December)
Rose Wylie: Yellow Desert Paintings, Union Gallery, London (3 April – 12 June)
Rose Wylie: Girl and Spiders, Thomas Erben Gallery, New York (2 April – 9 May)
Rose Wylie, Douglas Hyde Gallery, Dublin (6 March – 13 May)
Galleri Star: Rose Wylie, Vestfossen Kunstlaboratorium, Vestfossen, Norway (dates unknown)

2014 *Rose Wylie: Pink Girls, Yellow Curls*, Städtische Galerie Wolfsburg, Germany (14 October 2014 – 1 February 2015)
Rose Wylie: Pink Girls, Yellow Curls, Nansensgade 62, Copenhagen (12 October – 13 November)
Rose Wylie: What Means Something, Vous Etes Ici, Amsterdam (17 May – 14 June)
Rose Wylie: What Means Something, CHOI&LAGER, Cologne, Germany (8 February – 29 March)

2013 *BP Spotlight: Rose Wylie*, Tate Britain, London (14 May – 29 September)
Rose Wylie: Henry, Thomas, Keith & Jack, Union Gallery, London (11 May – 13 July)
Rose Wylie – Works on Paper, Galerie Michael Janssen, Berlin (27 April – 1 June)
Rose Wylie, Woof-Woof, Haugar Vestfold Kunstmuseum, Tønsberg, Norway (19 January – 10 March)

2012 *Rose Wylie: After Daphne*, Rosenwald-Wolf Gallery, Philadelphia University of the Arts (2 October – 20 November)
Rose Wylie, Big Boys Sit in the Front, Jerwood Gallery, Hastings, England (17 March – 1 July)
Rose Wylie: Rosemount, Regina Gallery, Moscow [catalogue] (3 February – 14 March)

2011 *Rose Wylie: Six Works on Paper and One Painting*, Vous Etes Ici, Amsterdam (15 October – 27 November)
Rose Wylie: Picture on the wall . . . , Galerie Michael Janssen, Berlin (9 September – 15 October)

2010 *Rose Wylie: What with What*, Thomas Erben Gallery, New York [catalogue] (14 October – 13 November)
Rose Wylie: Film Notes, Union Gallery, London (30 January – 19 March)

2008 *Rose Wylie: Wear What You Like*, Transition Gallery, London (11 October – 9 November)

2006 *Rose Wylie: Paintings*, Union Gallery, London (25 January – 25 March)

2004 *Rose Wylie: Room Project – Twink and Ivy*, Trinity Theatre, Tunbridge Wells, Kent, England (7 February – 11 March)

1999 *Rose Wylie: Lined Paper Paintings*, Stephen Lacey Gallery, London (4 March – 10 April)

1998 *Rose Wylie: Red Legs and Other Paintings*, Abbotsbury Studios, Abbotsbury, Dorset, England (20 September – 17 December)

1995 *Rose Wylie: Likeness in the Unlikeness*, Reed's Wharf Gallery / Stephen Lacey, London (3 February – 4 March)

1985 *Rose Wylie*, Trinity Arts Centre, Royal Tunbridge Wells, Kent, England (dates unknown)

SELECTED GROUP EXHIBITIONS

2018 *250th Summer Exhibition*, Royal Academy of Arts, London (12 June – 19 August)
Rose and Torey on Paper, The Journal Gallery, New York (31 May – 26 June)

2017 *and per se and, Part XVI: Rose Wylie and Frank Walter*, Ingleby Gallery, Edinburgh (11–21 October)
and per se and, Part XV: Louise Bourgeois and Rose Wylie, Ingleby Gallery, Edinburgh (20–30 September)
Artist First | paper only | The Exhibition, Francis Boeske Projects, Amsterdam (10 September – 4 November)
Collateral Drawing 5, BEASTON Projects, Folkestone, England (2 September – 5 November)
Royal Academy Summer Exhibition, Royal Academy of Arts, London (13 June – 20 August)
31 Women, Breese Little, London (2 June – 31 July)
Figure.Out: Charlie Billingham, Dale Lewis and Rose Wylie, Union Gallery, London [curated by William Gustafsson] (3 March – 15 April)
A New Subjectivity: Figurative Paintings after 2000, Pratt Manhattan Gallery, New York (24 February – 12 April) [itinerary: Fine Arts Center, University of Arkansas, Fayetteville, Arkansas (16 August – 22 September); Reece Museum, East Tennessee State University, Johnson City, Tennessee (16 October – 15 December)]
Drawing Island, The Journal Gallery, New York (16 February – 26 March)

2016 *Morten Viskum – Self Portraits*, Haugar Vestfold Kunstmuseum, Tønsberg, Norway (1 October – 30 December)
Towards Night, Towner Art Gallery, Eastbourne, England (24 September 2016 – 22 January 2017)
Beyond the Cartoon: Cartoons in Contemporary Art, ARTUNER, New York (15 September – 29 October)
Mixed Signals, Christian Larsen Gallery, Stockholm [curated by Shane Bradford] (25 August – 7 October)
Royal Academy Summer Exhibition, Royal Academy of Arts, London (13 June – 21 August)
FOUND, Foundling Museum, London [curated by Cornelia Parker] (27 May – 4 September)
Aviary, Transition Gallery, London (23 April – 21 May)
Paper in Practice, Moran Bondaroff, Los Angeles (9 April – 7 May)
RCA Secret, Royal College of Art, London (8–15 April)
Imagine, Brand New Gallery, Milan (2 March – 2 April)
The Conformist, Belmacz Gallery, London (23 February – 16 April)

2015 *Contemporary Drawings from Britain*, Museum of Xi'an Academy of Fine Arts, China (1–6 December)
One Day Something Happens: Paintings of People, Towner Art Gallery, Eastbourne, England (15 October – 8 January)
GIN3, 6Gins, Liverpool, England (25 September)
Boy Meets Girl: Zachary Armstrong & Rose Wylie, GNYP Artspace, Berlin (12 September – 1 November)
Wet With Wet, The Observer Building, Hastings, England (19 July – 2 August)
Painting 1, 2, 3: Katherine Bernhardt, Rebecca Morris, Rose Wylie, Kate MacGarry, London (12 June – 18 July)
Royal Academy Summer Exhibition, Royal Academy of Arts, London (8 June – 16 August)
Venice Biennale: Vita Vitale, Azerbaijan Pavilion, Venice (13 May – 26 November)
Demolition Derby, Fold Gallery, London (14 March – 18 April)
Drawing Biennial 2015, The Drawing Room, London (5 March – 30 April)
Chantal Joffe Beside the Seaside, Jerwood Gallery, London (31 January – 12 April)
Rose Wylie, Tom Anholt, Billy Childish and Ryan Mosley: The Islanders, Galerie Mikael Andersen, Copenhagen (9 January – 21 February)

2014 *Show-Off*, LeandaKateLouise, London (8–9 November)
Collages by Modern British and Contemporary Artists, Wilson Stephens & Jones, London (15 October – 8 November)
Art Everywhere, UK (21 July – 31 August)
John Moores Painting Prize 2014, Walker Art Gallery, Liverpool, England (5 July – 30 November)
Save Yourself!, Hannah Barry Gallery, London (26 June – 27 July)
30×2, 40×2 - Holy and Profane, Nunu Fine Art, Zhongzheng, Taipei (1 June – 17 August)
All A Tremulous Heart Requires, ZieherSmith, New York (26 January – 15 August)
Old Tin Cutlery Before the Invention of the Fork, Breese Little, London (21 January – 22 February)

2013 *Characters: Portraits and People from the Arts Council Collection*, Roper Gallery, The Holburne Museum, Bath, England (12 October 2013 – 7 January 2014)
2Q13 Women Artists, Lloyds Club, London (18 September – 5 December)

2012 *Recent British Painting*, Grimm Gallery, Amsterdam (18 October – 24 November)
Jonathan Meese, Peter Strauss, Rose Wylie, Ritter/Zamet Gallery, London (20 June – 4 August)

2011 *Evan Holloway, Rose Wylie*, The Approach, London (2 September – 2 October)
15 Years Thomas Erben Gallery, Thomas Erben Gallery, New York (6 May – 4 June)
Drawing Biennial 2011, The Drawing Room, London (7 April – 18 May)

2010 *In Dreams*, Timothy Taylor Gallery, London (8 September – 2 October)
Women to Watch – Body of Work: New Perspectives on Figure Painting, National Museum of Women in the Arts, Washington, D.C. (2 July–12 September)
Royal Academy Summer Exhibition, Royal Academy of Arts, London (14 June – 22 August)
Animated Matter, Thomas Erben Gallery, New York (25 February – 3 April)

2009 *Turner Contemporary Open*, Turner Contemporary, Margate, England (27 June – 6 September)
Royal Academy Summer Exhibition, Royal Academy of Arts, London (8 June – 16 August)
Drawing Biennial 2009, The Drawing Room, London (30 April – 20 May)

2008 *Swans Reflecting Elephants*, Kate MacGarry, London (5 July – 3 August)
Royal Academy Summer Exhibition, Royal Academy of Arts, London (9 June – 17 August)

2007 *Multiple Discipline*, Union Gallery, London (18 July – 8 September)
EAST*international 2007*, Norwich Gallery, Norwich, England (14 July – 18 August)
Project 4: Painted Ladies, The Surgery, London (10 March – 1 April)
Drawing as Vital Practice: Drawings by Ten International Artists, Pitshanger Manor Gallery & House, London (19 January – 3 March)

2006 *One Love: The Football Art Prize*, The Lowry, Manchester, England (2 December 2006 – 25 March 2007)
Royal Academy Summer Exhibition, Royal Academy of Arts, London (12 June – 20 August)

2005 *Royal Academy Summer Exhibition*, Royal Academy of Arts, London (7 June – 15 August)

2004 Roy Oxlade and Rose Wylie: Paintings, Rutherford College, University of Kent, Canterbury, England (closed 17 December)
EAST*international 2004*, Norwich Gallery, Norwich, England (3 July – 21 August)
Royal Academy Summer Exhibition, Royal Academy of Arts, London (8 June – 16 August)

2003 *Royal Academy Summer Exhibition*, Royal Academy of Arts, London (2 June – 10 August)

2002 *Reverse Engineering*, Pearl, London (22 November – 15 December)
Jerwood Drawing Prize 2002, University of Gloucester, Cheltenham, England (2 – 26 September) [itinerary: Jerwood Space, London (20 October – 10 November); MAC Birmingham, Birmingham, England (23 November 2002 – 5 January 2003); Glasgow School of Art, Glasgow, Scotland (14 January – 22 February 2003); EICH Gallery, Hull, England (3 March – 4 April 2003); Promenade Gallery, Salford Quays, England (12 April – 22 June 2003)]
As it Seems, Cheltenham Art Gallery & Museum, Cheltenham, England (31 August – 13 October)
Royal Academy Summer Exhibition, Royal Academy of Arts, London (11 June – 19 August)
The Pizza Express Prospects, Essor Gallery Project Space, London (22 May – 1 June)

2001 *Royal Academy Summer Exhibition*, Royal Academy of Arts, London (5 June – 13 August)

2000 *Not enough*, VELAN CENTER for Contemporary Art, Turin, Italy (opened November 2000)
Cheltenham Open Drawing Exhibition, East Wing Painting Studios, Pittville, Cheltenham, England (4 – 21 September) [itinerary: EICH Gallery, Hull, England (dates unknown); Künstlerwerkstaff Bahnhof Westend, Berlin (February – March 2001); Kunsthalle, Sierre, Switzerland (24 March – 13 April 2001)
Royal Academy Summer Exhibition, Royal Academy of Arts, London (29 May – 7 August)
Give and Take, Harris Museum & Art Gallery, Preston, England (15 April – 3 June) [itinerary: Jerwood Gallery, London (17 June – 30 July) and The Economist Plaza, London (7 July – 20 August)]

1999 *Royal Academy Summer Exhibition*, Royal Academy of Arts, London (June 7 – 15 August)

1998 *Royal Academy Summer Exhibition*, Royal Academy of Arts, London (2 June – 16 August)
Hullo Lawrence, Hullo Leo, Wrexham Arts Centre, Wrexham, Wales (dates unknown) [itinerary: Aberystwyth Arts Centre, Wales (dates unknown)]

1997 *Jerwood Painting Prize*, Lethaby Galleries, Central Saint Martins College of Art & Design, London (30 September – 18 October)
Cheltenham Open Drawing Exhibition, East Wing Painting Studios, Pittville, Cheltenham, England (8 – 22 September [itinerary: EICH Gallery, Hull, England (dates unknown)]
Royal Academy Summer Exhibition, Royal Academy of Arts, London (1 June – 17 August)

1996 *Cheltenham Open Drawing Exhibition*, Cheltenham, England (9 – 23 September [itinerary: EICH Gallery, Hull (dates unknown)]

1994 EAST*international 1994*, Norwich Gallery, Norwich, England (9 July – 3 September)

1993 *Royal Academy Summer Exhibition*, Royal Academy of Arts, London (6 June – 15 August)

1992 *Royal Academy Summer Exhibition*, Royal Academy of Arts, London (7 June – 16 August)

1991 *John Moores 17*, Walker Art Gallery, Liverpool, England (18 October 1991 – 19 January 1992)
Royal Academy Summer Exhibition, Royal Academy of Arts, London (9 June – 18 August)

1990 *Royal Academy Summer Exhibition*, Royal Academy of Arts, London (16 June – 19 August)

1988 *Women & Water*, Odette Gilbert Gallery, London (2 November – 28 November)

1982 *Hayward Annual: British Drawing*, Hayward Gallery, London (17 July – 30 August)

MONOGRAPHS AND SOLO EXHIBITION CATALOGUES

2018 *Rose Wylie: Hullo, Hullo...* Texts by Fernando Francés and Alison Gingeras. CAC Malaga (Centro de Arte Contemporáneo de Malaga), Malaga, Spain (exh. cat.).
Rose Wylie: Lolita's House. David Zwirner Books, New York [limited edition zine]

2017 *Rose Wylie: Quack Quack*. Edited by Melissa Blanchflower and Agnes Gryczkowska. Texts by Melissa Blanchflower, Barry Schawbsky, Tal R and Lynette Yiadom-Boakye. Serpentine Sackler Gallery, London (exh.cat.).
Rose Wylie: Cupid & Fur Coat. Text by Karl H. Lötzer. CHOI&LAGER Gallery, Cologne, Germany (exh.cat.)
Rose Wylie and Fraser Taylor: 'Collisions', Steidl-Werk No.24. Curated by Alison Harley. Texts by Rose Wylie on Fraser Taylor, Fraser Taylor on Rose Wylie, Oona Brown on Rose and Fraser, Jo Melvin and Jeff Gibbons, Liam Scully on Rose Wylie, and Jimmy Cosgrove on Fraser Taylor. Printed by Steidl, Germany.

2016 *Rose Wylie: Dressed to Kill*. VW (VeneKlasen/Werner), Berlin (exh.cat.).
Rose Wylie: Tilt the Horizontal into a Slant. Text by Cherry Smyth. Interview between Ben Rivers and Rose Wylie. Chapter Gallery, Cardiff (exh.cat.).
Rose Wylie: Queens & Chocs. Text by Liam Scully. Space K / Kolon Industries, Seoul (exh.cat.).

2015 *Rose Wylie*. Texts by John Hutchinson and Sara Baume. The Douglas Hyde Gallery, Dublin (exh.cat.).

2013 *Rose Wylie: Woof-Woof*. Texts by Jennifer Higgie and Tone Lyngstad Nyaas. Interview with Rose Wylie by Jeff McMillan. Haugar Vestfold Kunstmuseum, Tønsberg, Norway (exh.cat.).

2012 *Rose Wylie: Big Boys Sit in the Front*. Texts by Katie Kitamura, Phoebe Hoban and Rose Wylie. Jerwood Gallery, Hastings, England (exh.cat.).
Rose Wylie: Rosemount. Text by Tom Morton. Regina Gallery, Moscow (exh.cat.).

2011 *Rose Wylie: Picture on the Wall* .... Text by Katie Kitamura. Galerie Michael Janssen, Berlin (exh.cat.).

2010 *Rose Wylie: Film Notes and Other Paintings, 2006–2009*. Text by Martin Herbert. Union Gallery, London (exh.cat.).
Rose Wylie: What with What, Paintings 1993 to 2010. Text by Luke Gottelier. Thomas Erben Gallery, New York (exh.cat.).

2008 *Rose Wylie: Wear What You Like*. Text by Emma Dexter. Transition Gallery, London (exh.cat.).

2005 *Rose Wylie: Some Drawings, 1987–2005*. Self-published by Rose Wylie to coincide with exhibition at Union Gallery, London the following year.

2004 *Rose Wylie: Twink and Ivy, and Other Paintings and Small Drawings: 1999–2003*. Text by Roy Exley. Imagined interview between the artist and Giovanni di Paolo. Trinity Theatre (Gallery), Tunbridge Wells, Kent, England (exh.cat.).

1999 *Rose Wylie: Lined Paper Paintings*, text by Jill Lloyd, Stephen Lacey Gallery, London (exh.cat.).

1995 *Rose Wylie: Likeness in the Unlikeness*, text by Mel Gooding, Reed's Wharf Gallery / Stephen Lacey, London (exh.cat.).

ARTIST'S TALKS AND SPECIAL PROJECTS

2017 'Rose Wylie in conversation with Hans Ulrich Obrist', Goethe-Institut, London
'An evening with Ben Rivers and Rose Wylie', Tate Britain, London
'Only artists: Rose Wylie and Stewart Lee', BBC Radio 4

2016 'Rose Wylie, Ben Rivers and Skye Sherwin in conversation', The Horsebridge Centre, Whitstable, England
'Rose Wylie in conversation with Alastair Sooke', Turner Contemporary, Margate, England
'Art in the City Talks – Rose Wylie', Arnolfini Centre for Contemporary Arts, Bristol, England
'Contemporary Art Talks: Rose Wylie', Goldsmiths University of London, London

2015 'Stanley Picker Lectures: Rose Wylie', Institute of Contemporary Arts, London

2014 'Culture Now: Rose Wylie in conversation with Clarrie Wallis', Institute of Contemporary Arts, London
'John Moores Painting Prize: Talk Tuesdays with Rose Wylie', Liverpool Biennial, Liverpool, England

2013 'Artist Talk: Rose Wylie', Tate Britain, London

2010 'Rose Wylie and Savannah Miller in conversation', Westbourne Grove Church, London [organised on the occasion of *Women to Watch – Body of Work: New Perspectives on Figure Painting* by National Museum of Women in the Arts, Washington, D.C., in association with Twenty8Twelve and Union Gallery, London]

AWARDS

2018 The South Bank Sky Arts Award for Visual Arts

2015 Charles Wollaston Award

2014 Senior Royal Academician, Royal Academy of Arts, London
John Moores Painting Prize, Walker Art Gallery, Liverpool, England

2011 Paul Hamlyn Prize for Visual Arts, Paul Hamlyn Foundation, London

2004 **EAST***international* Print Commission

1999 The Sunny Dupree Family Award for a Woman Artist, Royal Academy of Arts, London

1993 Interiors, Towner Art Gallery, Eastbourne, Joint First Prize

SELECTED PUBLIC COLLECTIONS

Arario Museum, Seoul
Arts Council of England, London
British Council
Contemporary Art Society, London
David Roberts Art Foundation, London
Depart Foundation, Los Angeles
Government Art Collection, UK
Hammer Museum, Los Angeles
Jerwood Foundation, London
Monsoon Collection, London
National Museum of Women in the Arts, Washington, D.C.
New Hall Collection, Cambridge, England
Norwich Gallery, Norwich, England
Railtrack, London
Royal Academy of Arts, London
Royal College of Art, London
Space K, Seoul
Städtische Galerie Wolfsburg, Germany
Tate, London
University College, University of Oxford, England
Walker Art Gallery, Liverpool, England
York City Art Gallery, York, England
Zabludowicz Collection, London

Index

NOTE Page numbers for illustrations appear in *italics*.

ACKNOWLEDGEMENTS

This book is for Rose in the hope that I have opened up some avenues of conversation around her work.

In the course of writing this book many people have helped me and deserve thanks but I am particularly indebted to Rose and her children Luke John and Henrietta for their continual encouragement and support. I would also like to convey my gratitude to Jari Lager of CHOI&LAGER and William Gustafsson at Rose's studio and the designer Philip Lewis. I would also like to acknowledge the help of Emma Lilley who suggested to Lucy Clark at Lund Humphries that they commission this monograph and the Paul Mellon Centre for Studies in British Art who provided me with a research grant.

I have benefited enormously from conversations with colleagues and friends and I would like to mention in particular Melissa Blanchflower, Martin Jenkins, Honey Luard and Andrew Wilson. Thanks also to Iwona Blazwick, Livia Cerasi, Penelope Curtis, Sarah den Dikken, Emma Dexter, Sarah Elson, Lucie Ewin, Tom Furness, Ann Gallagher, Lisa Garrison, Liz Gilmore, Doro Globus, Abigail Grater, McClain Groff, Mark Hallett, Andy Holden, Martin Jenkins, Celia Jennison, Simon Ling, Jeff McMillan, Lynda Morris, Hans Ulrich Obrist, Cornelia Parker, Deanna Petherbridge, James Piper, Kate MacGarry, Ben Rivers, Tate Library & Archive, Anita Taylor, Sarah Thorowgood, Rodolphe von Hofmannsthal and David Zwirner.

Special thanks to my family.

First published in 2018 by Lund Humphries

Lund Humphries
Office 3, Book House
261A City Road
London EC1V 1JX
UK

www.lundhumphries.com

Rose Wylie © Clarrie Wallis, 2018
All rights reserved
Unless otherwise stated illustrations are courtesy of Rose Wylie and Private Collections

ISBN 978-1-84822-225-0

A Cataloguing-in-Publication record for this book is available from the British Library

All rights reserved. No part of this publication may be reproduced, stored in a retrieval system or transmitted in any form or by any means, electrical, mechanical or otherwise, without first seeking the permission of the copyright owners and publishers. Every effort has been made to seek permission to reproduce the images in this book. Any omissions are entirely unintentional, and details should be addressed to the publishers.

Clarrie Wallis has asserted her right under the Copyright, Designs and Patent Act, 1988, to be identified as the Author of this Work.

Copy edited by Abigail Grater
Designed by Philip Lewis
Set in Rosart and Aspen
Printed in Slovenia

FRONT COVER Detail of *Yellow Girls: Säg and flop* 2017, detail of fig.91, pp.106–107
BACK COVER Detail of *Charlotte from the Back* 1990, detail of fig.93, p.111
FRONTISPIECE Detail of *Cuban Scene, Smoke* 2016, fig.75, pp.88–89
PAGES 4–5 Detail of *Natural Born Killers, Head lights (Film Notes)* 2018, fig.118b, p.137

IMAGE CREDITS
Archivart / Alamy Stock Photo: 13; Courtesy the artist and Pace Gallery / © Julian Schnabel / ARS, New York / DACS 2018: 58; Borthwick Institute for Archives / by permission of Nestlé UK and Ireland: 15a–b; © The Estate of Philip Guston, courtesy Hauser & Wirth: 60; Heritage Image Partnership Ltd / Alamy Stock Photo: 10; Joe McGorty, 2017: endpapers; Rose Wylie: (Photo: Soon-Hak Kwon) 1, 4, 5, 6, 7, 8, 11, 12, 14, 20, 22, 23, 24, 25, 26, 27, 29, 31, 32, 33, 34, 35, 36, 37, 38, 39, 40, 41, 42, 43, 44, 45, 46, 47, 48, 49, 50, 51, 54, 55, 56, 57, 59, 61, 62, 64, 66, 68, 69, 70, 71, 73, 74, 75, 76, 78, 79, 80, 81, 83, 85, 86, 87, 88, 89, 92, 94, 95, 96, 97, 98, 99, 101, 102, 103, 104, 108, 110, 112, 114, 116, 117, 119, 120, 121, 122, 123, 124, 125, 126, 127, 128, 130, 131; Rose Wylie and David Zwirner: (Photo: Soon-Hak Kwon) 9, (Photo: Anna Arca) 91, (Photo: Jack Hems) 118a–c; Wikimedia Commons: The Yorck Project: 67; World History Archive / Alamy Stock Photo: 111

Supported by the Paul Mellon Centre for Studies in British Art

PAUL MELLON CENTRE
for Studies in British Art

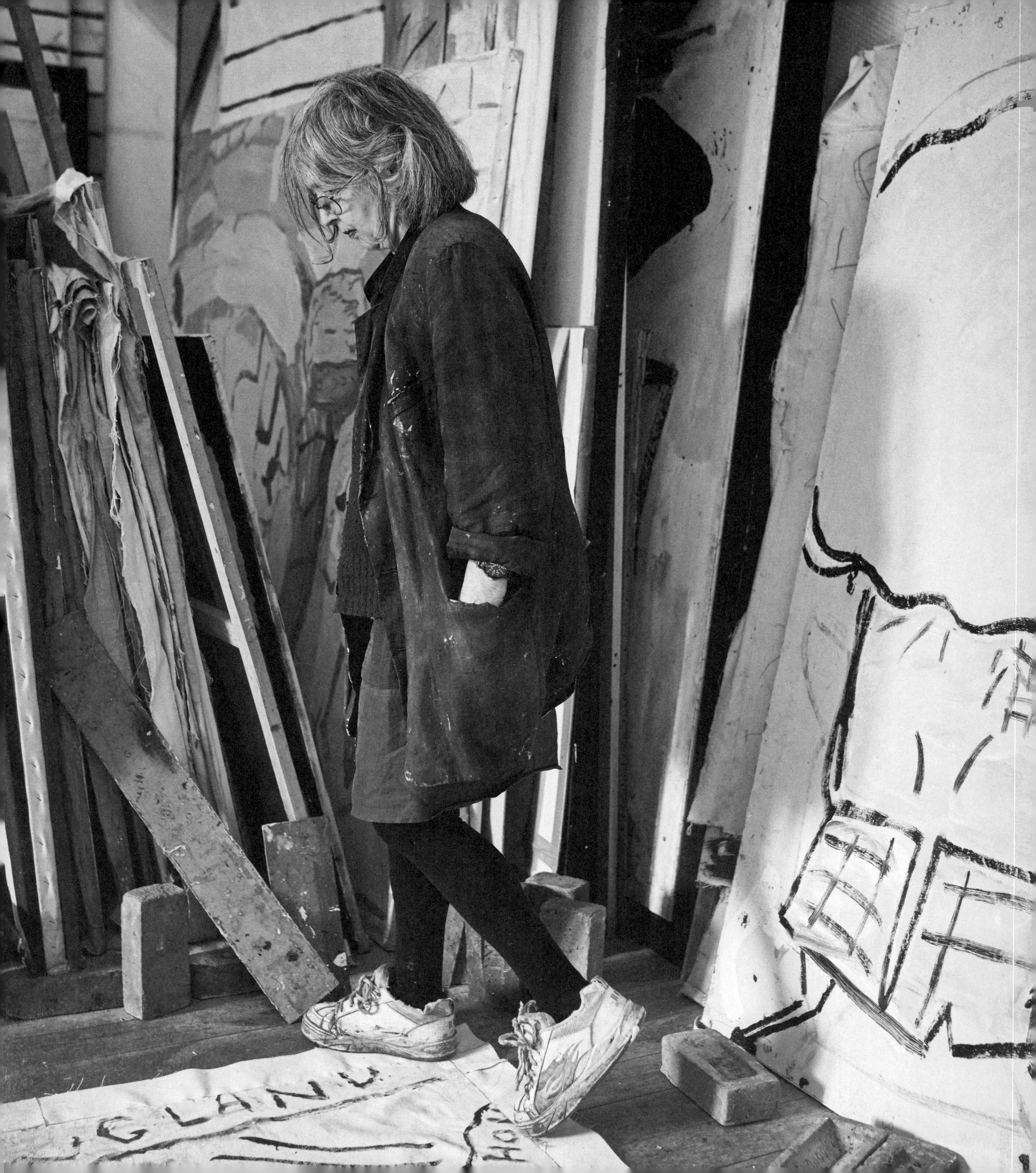